Critical Issues
in Juvenile
Delinquency

Critical Issues in Juvenile Delinquency

Edited by
David Shichor
California State College
San Bernardino

Delos H. Kelly
California State University
Los Angeles

LexingtonBooks
D.C.Heath and Company
Lexington, Massachusetts
Toronto

Library of Congress Cataloging in Publication Data

Main entry under title:
  Critical issues in juvenile delinquency.

  Bibliography: p.
    1. Juvenile delinquency—United States—Addresses, essays, lectures.
  2. Juvenile delinquency—United States—Prevention—Addresses, essays, lec-
  tures. 3. Juvenile corrections—United States—Addresses, essays, lectures.
  I. Shichor, David. II. Kelly, Delos H.
  HV9104.C74   364.36'0973   77-18579
  ISBN 0-669-02103-2

Copyright © 1980 by D.C. Heath and Company

Published simultaneously in Canada.

Printed in the United States of America.

International Standard Book Number: 0-669-02103-2

Library of Congress Catalog Card Number: 77-18579

Contents

Acknowledgments

We would like to thank each of the authors for the contribution they have made to this volume. We also would like to acknowledge the efforts of our editor, Margaret Zusky, at Lexington Books. The secretarial help of Jane Rowland and Mary Schmidt is also greatly appreciated.

Critical Issues in Juvenile Delinquency

Introduction

Juvenile delinquency is considered to be a major social problem in both developed and developing societies. Many social scientists attribute increased delinquent activity to the rapid industrial development, technological change and urbanization, and to the rising level of affluence. The increase in the volume of delinquency following World War II triggered a rising concern with the etiology and prevention of juvenile delinquency and the treatment of juvenile lawbreakers. In spite of the rapid, voluminous, and diffused efforts devoted to these social issues, few works offered an overall comprehensive review of these problems by social scientists specializing in specific aspects of these critical issues.

This volume attempts to undertake this by no means easy task by providng original contributions addressed to the analysis of major problem areas of juvenile delinquency that have captured the attention of academicians, researchers, practitioners and policymakers. Some of the major controversial issues of the 1970s in juvenile delinquency are: the increased awareness of political aspects of theoretical perspectives, the impact of rapidly changing family styles, the growing decline in the confidence concerning the effectiveness of traditional rehabilitation models, the changes in the nature and extent of female delinquency and the societal reaction to it, greater sophistication in the analysis of gang structure and behavior, the emerging interest in international aspects of delinquency with special focus on the similarities and differences between developing and developed societies, problems involved in developing, implementing, and evaluating public policy regarding the prevention of delinquency and the treatment of delinquents, and renewed interest in the potential biosocial factors of juvenile misconduct.

The various chapters which follow explore these topics and others in depth and also offer policy-related suggestions. In "Explaining Juvenile Delinquency: Changing Theoretical Perspectives," Don C. Gibbons gives a review of theoretical developments in the field of juvenile delinquency. He reviews briefly the biological and the psychological approaches, then he deals in more detail with the "mainstream sociological perspectives." He focuses especially on the social disorganization approach, the subcultural explanations, the labeling or social reaction perspective, and finally on the various control theories. Gibbons goes on to provide an analysis into the theoretical sources, assumptions and interrelations of these various approaches. He also evaluates their major contributions for the understanding of juvenile delinquency. Finally, he devotes his attention to the emerging radical criminology and its perspective on juvenile delinquency, by providing an analysis of its major tenets, contributions, and the criticisms that

1

have been leveled against this approach. Gibbons concludes his chapter with a strong criticism of sociological criminology, which according to him resembles an art form rather than hard science, and discusses its failure to provide clear and reliable advice to the question, "What shall we do about juvenile delinquency?"

In "Juvenile Justice Legislation: A Framework for Evaluation," Katherine S. Teilmann and Malcolm W. Klein offer a model that can be used to assess the reception and impact of new legislations. They develop their framework from the experience with the new California's Assembly Bill 3121. They preface their statements by identifying three major trends that have occurred recently: the children's rights movement, the "war on crime," and legalization, particularly with respect to due process. Teilmann and Klein, with these three trends in mind, begin developing a framework that can be used for prediction and assessment. The framework is composed of three major components: signals, reflections, and control. Each of these, in turn, contains various subparts. Once developed, the researchers select four major provisions of AB 3121 (that is, provisions relating to "secure detention of status offenders," "development of alternative resources," "remand," and "district attorney in court") and then proceed to systematically apply their framework. For example, their model would predict that deinstitutionalization would be met with a good deal of resistance, and Teilmann and Klein's analysis suggests that it did. They conclude their chapter by speculating that of the eight framework subparts, "the three of legislative mandate, fiscal implications, and philosophic resonance will prove to be the most predictive of levels of implementation."

"Delinquency in Nonmetropolitan Areas," by Christine Alder, Gordon Bazemore, and Kenneth Polk, addresses a problem of rising concern to many: the increase in rural or nonmetropolitan delinquency. The researchers argue initially that even though there remain some differentials in the character or nature of rural crime, similarities in the incidence and pattern of change in nonmetropolitan and urban crime are becoming evident; this phenomenon appears to hold for both males and females. In trying to account specifically for changing patterns of rural delinquency, the investigators focus on such factors as social class and the nature of the school experience. It is noted, for example, that although much of the theorizing about urban delinquency stresses the importance of class it appears that such perspectives are unable to explain the rise of rural misconduct. Factors, however, that do stand out in the backgrounds of both rural and urban delinquents are linked to the structure and process of schooling. In this regard, the evidence reviewed offers a very clear and recurring pattern: "failures" who are not a part of the general success flow of the school frequently become involved in a pattern of peer rebellion; this pattern seems to obtain for urban settings, as well as for some other cultures. Not only this, but poor performance in school invariably limits opportunity in the employment sphere. In fact, one's work role appears to be the most essential component in building a "legitimate identity." And if practitioners are to make any inroads in terms of reducing the incidence of rural delinquency, they must be cognizant of this fact. They must also be aware of the rather unique problems and resources that characterize rural settings. The actual strategies employed must be centered on a "fundamental realignment of educational and employment policy priorities."

Rose Giallombardo, in "Female Delinquency," points out initially that most theories of delinquency have been focused on males and, as a result, female crime and delinquency have been virtually overlooked. Moreover, those theories that have specifically addressed the issue of female delinquency have tended to emphasize the importance of biological and psychological factors. Giallombardo contends that such approaches are not only pseudo-scientific but most unproductive, at least as far as trying to enhance our understanding of female delinquency. In a manner of speaking, then, the issue of female crime needs to be systematically reexamined from a solid theoretical and empirical base. Giallombardo attempts such an analysis. Initially she reviews the existing literature on female crime and delinquency. Thereafter, she offers recent data on patterns of female crime; she also compares data on males and females. Giallombardo concludes her analysis by examining the relationship between sexism and the administration of justice. She points out, for example, that existing "delinquency laws clearly discriminate against females"; these, in turn, frequently give rise to differential treatment and processing of females. Quite clearly, Giallombardo argues that we need to seriously examine the content of our laws.

John W.C. Johnstone, "Delinquency and the Changing American Family," analyzes the role of the family in the etiology of juvenile delinquency. He points out that although the literature in this area is voluminous, it is also most inconclusive. Some argue that the family is the most important determinant of delinquent activity, while others contend that there is no basis on which to postulate a direct causal connection between the two factors. This confusion and ambiguity, Johnstone contends can be attributed to several factors such as family structure and dynamics, which are chosen for analysis, the type of research design employed, the actual conceptualization and measurement of delinquency utilized, and the way relationships are assessed. Johnstone provides substance to his claims by outlining some of the important changes that have occurred with respect to the structure of the American family, most notably the sharp rise of single-parent female-headed families. Changes such as these obviously have certain ramifications for the way in which family structure is assessed and measured. In this respect, Johnstone points out that "the literature simply has ignored the fact that there are different types of broken families." Not only this but different family arrangements may have different effects on the children involved. Johnstone then discusses some research design problems, as well as some issues concerning the nature of family functioning.

Delos H. Kelly's chapter, "The Educational Experience and Evolving Delinquent Careers: A Neglected Institutional Link," after reviewing traditional works in the area of delinquency, provides an in-depth analysis of how organizational components and processes articulate with individual attributes to produce the career of the delinquent. Kelly's focus is placed upon a critical domain: the American educational system. Throughout his analysis, the argument is advanced to the effect that by virtue of our rather exclusive professional concern with such factors as social class and race, we have generally neglected to consider how institutions use such factors in the initiation and perpetuation of delinquent and deviant careers. Kelly offers recent data in support of this position. He concludes his analysis by not only delineating various institutional components and processes that require systematic study but also by describing several concrete steps that could be taken to reduce the number of deviants, delinquents, and so-called misfits manufactured by the educational system.

In "Gangs, Groups, and Serious Youth Crime," Walter B. Miller contends initially that very little systematic attention has been given to collective youth crime. Not only this but "no satisfactory unit of analysis has ever been developed for this area." The only concept that has been used to analyze this phenomenon has been the notion of the "gang." This unit of analysis, however, is fraught with many limitations and shortcomings. Miller argues that this concept needs to be refined, and he then proposes a new unit of analysis that can be used for examining collective youth crime, namely, the law-violating youth group. Thereafter, Miller offers an outline of types and subtypes of law-violating youth groups. He then proceeds to apply his unit of analysis to an examination of the delinquency problem as it is perceived in several major U.S. cities. Some interesting and important findings emerge, especially when distinctions are made between problems with gangs and problems with groups. The results clearly indicate that Miller's needed refinement and upgrading of the gang concept appears to hold great promise. The author concludes his chapter by offering several policy statements. For example, in terms of gathering "collective offender" type of data, efforts should also be made to delineate "the numbers, locations, and particularly the types of law-violating youth groups in given jurisdictions."

Simon Dinitz and John P. Conrad, in "The Dangerous Two Percent," look into some of the proposals which were suggested to deal with juvenile delinquents after the widespread belief in rehabilitation had declined. The basic questions addressed are "How real is the problem of dangerous and violent juveniles?" "Is there anything to the idea that the judicious incapacitation of a small proportion of the youth population will alleviate both the fear and the actuality of significant juvenile involvement in personal injury and other types of crime?" The authors review the existing literature on the subject, and then summarize their own large-scale study of five birth cohorts in Columbus, Ohio. One of their major findings indicates that only 1.6 percent of all age-eligible youth in the community were arrested for one or more violent crimes. One of the conclusions offered by Dinitz and Conrad is to the effect that the juvenile crime problem is only minimally a problem of violence. Although generalizations about violence tend to be drawn on data collected in large urban areas, the authors suggest that it is a much lesser problem in mid-size cities.

LaMar T. Empey, in "Revolution and Counterrevolution: Current Trends in Juvenile Justice," indicates that the past two decades have been associated with noticeable changes in the American concepts of delinquency and juvenile justice. He then proceeds to describe such phenomena as the invention of the notion of juvenile justice and the traditional functions of the juvenile court (for example, the functions of enforcing the modern concept of childhood, and serving as a surrogate for family and community). After delineating specific functions of the juvenile court, Empey goes on to describe how the underlying philosophy and functions have become rather radically altered. For example, a national fad exists whereby nonserious offenders are diverted to agencies other than the court. He also examines the factors and processes by which the idea that the court "should be society's superparent has been discredited and is being discarded." Empey continues his analysis by describing how other presumed and traditional functions of the court have also become altered (for example, changed notions of delinquency prevention, discriminalization, and rehabilitation). Empey concludes his chapter by questioning whether the changes he has noted can really be viewed as steps forward.

Maynard L. Erickson and Jack P. Gibbs, in "Punishment, Deterrence, and Juvenile Justice," note initially that although juvenile justice policy has been traditionally guided by the notion of rehabilitation, it has, in recent years, come under serious attack. "The apparent failure of the rehabilitative approach" has, moreover, given rise to two alternative approaches or models: (1) the "hands-off" approach and (2) the return to classical penal policy. This latter strategy is characterized by three major reforms: lowering the age of accountability for crime, abolition of the juvenile court, and punishing or incapacitating the offender. Erickson and Gibbs then address the question: "What might be the outcome of attempts to reduce the volume of delinquency by implementing a policy that emphasizes punishment or incapacitation?" The researchers attempt to shed some light on this important question through use of a series of distinct student and adult surveys conducted from 1974 to 1976. The authors generally conclude that their findings "cast doubt on any attempt to further deterrence in the juvenile justice system." Thereafter, they offer certain suggestions that have a direct relevance for policy formulation.

Solomon Kobrin, Frank R. Hellum, and John W. Peterson, in "Offense Patterns of Status Offenders," analyze and interpret data from a large-scale national study of deinstitutionalization of status offenders. They point out that there are two major assumptions connected with the deinstitutionalization movement. The supporters of the movement contend that status offenders constitute a distinctive and identifiable category of juvenile delinquents, largely free of involvement in criminal activities. It follows from this that the use of secure detention and commitment to correctional institutions has neither legal nor ethical justification. A second assumption holds that, by virtue of being accorded standard police and court treatment, status offenders tend increasingly to commit the more serious criminal offenses. Hence, the removal of status offenders from the jurisdiction of the juvenile justice system is expected over time to prevent delinquency. After an empirical analysis of the offense patterns of status offenders and the assessment of the validity of these assumptions, the authors present their conclusions regarding the status offender deinstitutionalization movement. Although their findings are tentative, they believe that this movement has merits especially "for that category of status offenders which shows little inclination to engage in more serious forms of delinquency."

In "Recurring Issues in the Evaluation of Delinquency Prevention and Treatment Programs," Delbert S. Elliott recounts some of the conceptual and methodological issues he has encountered during his evaluations of delinquency prevention and treatment programs. Many of these issues are not only recurring but they have a direct bearing on the general validity and utility of the evaluations conducted. The major problem, according to Elliott, is the observation that very few programs are founded on a solid theoretical framework or paradigm. Elliott provides ample evidence and illustrations to support such a claim. He notes, for example, that even though some funding agencies underscore the need for the application of theoretical models, the actual programs funded "were developed without reference to the theoretical orientation" espoused by the granting agencies. He notes, further, that not only are applications frequently "dressed-up" to give the appearance of compliance but the "new" strategies implemented are often nothing more than some variation of the individual casework or counseling method. Elliott goes on to specifically delineate the ways in which the lack of any clear theoretical rationale undermines the evaluation of most delinquency prevention and treatment programs. The author offers some possible ways to deal with these problems. For example, a joint effort can be made to develop a theoretical rationale or model prior to implementing the evaluations. Overall, Elliott provides a valuable and practical account of the many theoretical and methodological problems and issues that the evaluator is likely to encounter.

Sarnoff A. Mednick, in "Primary Prevention of Juvenile Delinquency," begins by noting that, similar to the approach of medicine, attempts "to control crime start with the individual already delinquent or criminal." The efforts to control crime, moreover, are concentrated on techniques of control (for example, building nicer jails and developing faster court systems). Unfortunately, less effort has been placed on what Mednick terms "the primary prevention of crime." Primary prevention is concerned with methods of early intervention—methods that should prevent the individual from engaging in deviant behavior. Three major avenues exist: (1) ecological alterations, (2) systematic societal change, and (3) individual intervention. Mednick concentrates his analysis on possible individual psychological and biological predispositions to crime. Of major focus is the way in which a biological factor might interact with social variables to produce motivations for crime. And in an attempt to specify important biological variables, Mednick reviews evidence relating to the potential "heritability of antisocial behavior," particularly data generated by twin and adoption studies. Mednick concludes by outlining how biological factors may interact with social factors. Mednick's approach, it should be noted, has received renewed attention in recent years.

Theodore N. Ferdinand, in "Delinquency in Developing and Developed Societies," tries to assess the impact of change from traditional to modern societies, particularly as it relates to delinquent behavior. He notes that developing societies have two similarities with developed societies: "urban based commercialism is the dominant form of social organization, and in both this pattern contrasts sharply with the village-based communalism of the hinterland." In developing societies there is a large-scale migration of rural people to urban areas, and the government often cannot adequately solve the problems created by this migration. Most of the rural immigrants occupy the lowest social class in the urban areas. The author then describes how separate adult and young male subcultures develop in the slums, and how family ties become weaker. The young male culture is characterized by delinquent gang formations. Developed societies are distinguished by bureaucratic organization and by relatively high standards of living. Many of them are characterized by the emergence of a hedonistic youth culture. Delinquent behavior in these societies is often the expression of the identification with the adolescent culture and not alienation from it.

James F. Short, Jr., in "Political Implications of Juvenile Delinquency: A Comparative Perspective," reviews the relationships between politics and youth crime in the United States and in several other countries. According to him, in the United States traditionally there was an alliance between politicians and gang members. These ties were weakened during the Depression and World War II. After the war the population composition of the big cities and the composition of gangs changed. There was also an increase in the rate of crime and delinquency. During the sixties a renewed interest occured in gangs and politics. Some of the program funds of the war on poverty were channeled through gangs, a practice which was motivated, at least partially, by political considerations. The hopes regarding the abilities of these gangs to provide the needed assistance to the slums were unrealistic, and the political interest in them subsided quite rapidly. Following his brief review of the scene in the United States, Short explores differences and similarities in various societies in the relations among youth, delinquency, and politics.

David Shichor, in "Some Issues of Social Policy in the Field of Juvenile Delinquency," briefly analyzes various views concerning the role of the social scientist in public policymaking and also examines the interrelations between policymaking and political ideology. From there he proceeds to review the three major political approaches to criminal and juvenile justice policies—the radical, the liberal-mainstream, and the conservative. He describes how the liberal-mainstream approach, which was prevalent during most of the twentieth century, has come under severe attack by both radical and conservative quarters in the last ten to fifteen years. Shichor then analyzes the claims of the various positions and their impact on social policy formulation in the field of juvenile delinquency in its prevention and treatment.

Explaining Juvenile Delinquency: Changing Theoretical Perspectives

Don C. Gibbons

Introduction

If a group of citizens were asked to identify some of the major inventions of the past hundred years, they would probably nominate television, jet airplanes, space satellites, and other technological developments. Few would declare that juvenile delinquency was a major social invention. Nonetheless, the first juvenile court and the legal category of juvenile delinquency were initiated in 1899. This new social apparatus quickly spread throughout the nation, as did the new social category of deviant, the juvenile delinquent.

The child-saving movement that led to the creation of the juvenile court and juvenile delinquency was part of a larger sweep of events in nineteenth century American society, often designated by historians as the Progressive Era. The progressive movement centered about reformist concerns regarding the harsh concomitants of rapid industrialization and urbanization overtaking the country. American sociology and the criminological enterprise within it also arose in considerable part as a response to the social dislocations generated by nineteenth century industrialization and urbanization (Gibbons 1979).

Over this developmental period from the turn of the century to the present, a great many specific explanations of perspectives on delinquency have grown up. Youthful offenders were originally viewed as victims of social disorganization produced by rapid social change and later as driven to lawbreaking because of social strains arising from their disadvantaged position in the social order. More recently, official delinquents have been seen as capriciously selected by the juvenile justice system from among the ranks of American juveniles, most of whom are thought to be involved in misbehavior. Other theorists have pointed to the breakdown in the social bonds linking youths to conformity. Finally, radical criminologists have located the sources of modern delinquency in the structural flaws of the political economy of corporate capitalism.

This chapter provides a brief, kaleidescopic view of the major twists and turns that have been taken by criminological theorists in their efforts to explain delinquency.[1] This short chapter must of necessity oversimplify and even vulgarize a rich, variegated, and discordant body of theorizing. Also, this overview implies that those who have studied delinquency come neatly packaged as control theorists, labeling theorists, or as exponents of one or another explanatory framework. Actually, many criminologists show allegiance to eclectic combinations of these major perspectives, hence real-life students of delinquency are not so neatly categorized. Many who probe into the etiology of juvenile misconduct find elements of value in a number of the causal formulations that are described briefly in this chapter

The great mass of theorizing and empirical research on juvenile delin-quency in the United States has been produced by sociologists who have examined a large variety of sociogenic arguments which assert that delin-quency is the product of social processes and social factors. Some have been particularly attentive to social-structural influences that are related to delin-quency rates and patterns, and others have exhibited more of a social-psychological bent, zeroing in on interactional patterns among gang members, self-concept patterns among offenders, and the like. But all of them have proceeded on the assumption that juvenile offenders are psychologically normal youngsters whose deviance is a response to deleterious social circumstances and kindred influences.

Although sociologists have produced much of the existing theory and research evidence, alternative formulations have been put forth by psychiatrists and psychologists, contending that delinquency is carried on by youths who are psychologically troubled or disturbed and that their lawbreaking is a response to these pressures emanating from "within the skin," so to speak. Additionally, there has been a relatively long tradition of speculation and research by biological scientists, in which delinquency has been attributed to various biological imperatives that impel some youngsters along deviant pathways.[2] Let us begin with biogenic and psychogenic competitors to the sociogenic orientation toward delinquency before examining variants of the latter in more detail.

Biological and Psychogenic Perspectives

Biogenic hypotheses holding that criminality is a response to biological forces of one kind of another have existed since the time of Cesare Lombroso (1836-1909), an Italian physician who argued that many crim-inals are atavists or biological throwbacks to an earlier type of human than *Homo sapiens*. That now-discredited work was followed by efforts to show that criminals and delinquents are biologically inferior, feebleminded, and most recently, that delinquents are differentially selected from among per-sons of mesomorphic or muscular somatotype or bodily build (Sheldon, Hartl, and McDermott 1949; Glueck and Glueck 1956; Cortes and Gatti 1972).

However, the search for biological correlates of criminality has been flawed throughout by low-level theorizing in which claims have been made that are inconsistent with modern knowledge in biology and genetics. Then, too, nearly all of the biological research to date has been plagued with methodological deficiencies of such seriousness as to render invalid the findings of these studies. For reasons of this kind, and equally because biogenic hypotheses run counter to the theoretical preferences of sociological criminologists, biological hypotheses are out of popularity with those persons.

Although the deficiencies of biological work to the present cannot be gainsaid, it would be a grievous non sequitur to conclude, as some have done, that biological hypotheses can safely be ignored and bypassed in the search for etiological understanding. A careful reading of the evidence suggests, instead, that the last word may not have been heard on biological forces in human behavior and that this question remains open for further examination and study (Shah and Roth 1974; Hippchen 1977).

Indeed, recent admonitions by sociologists regarding the need to "bring beasts back in" (Van den Berghe 1974) have been followed by new efforts to uncover biosocial processes in human behavior (Wilson 1975). In particular, Hirschi and Hindelang (1977) have recently contributed to this renewed dialogue on biologically related factors in lawbreaking through their detailed review of the research evidence on delinquency and intelligence. They show that intelligence is strongly related to delinquency, probably because of its effects on school performance. Youths with lower IQs who do poorly in school become engaged in juvenile misconduct. The facts seem clear that intelligence is an extremely important variable that differentiates juvenile offenders from nondelinquents, in spite of much sociological wisdom to the contrary.

Turning to psychogenic or psychodynamic arguments about causation, it would be well to acknowledge the immense popularity of this line of explanation for social deviance of various kinds. As expressed by laymen, this view takes the form of conclusions that "there must be something wrong with a person who would do that." This interpretation is offered for homosexuality, criminality, political radicalism, drug addiction, and a host of other forms of socially disapproved behavior. Concerning delinquency, many laymen would doubtless agree with August Aichhorn (1955), a pioneering figure in the development of psychiatric theories of delinquency, who asserted that "there must be something in the child himself which the environment brings out in the form of delinquency" (p. 30). In other words, delinquents are thought to behave as they do because they are in some way "sick," "maladjusted," or "emotionally disturbed."

Contentions about the psychologically aberrant character of deviants of various kinds have been advanced with much enthusiasm by psychiatrists and psychologists. A large quantity of theorizing and research evidence of a psychogenic form has been accumulated, so much so that it is extremely difficult to provide an adequate, brief summary of it. However, the largest share of this work centers around arguments that various emotional and psychological problems that have grown out of disturbed or unsatisfactory parent-child interactional patterns lead troubled youths into delinquency or other forms of maladjustment. These psychogenic hypotheses are virtually silent regarding the possible impact of social-structural influences on offenders. Thus they echo Aichhorn's assumption that social and environmental factors are of only peripheral importance in delinquency.

The yield from psychogenic explorations has not been impressive or convincing, at least in the opinion of sociologically oriented students of delinquency. Many of the research studies of psychological problems among delinquents have been methodologically deficient, and thus any results in them favorable to the emotional problems argument are suspect (Gibbons 1976: 74-89). In many other cases of psychogenic research, relatively slight differences in psychological adjustment between delinquents and nondelinquents have turned up (Glueck and Glueck 1950; Conger and Miller 1966).

One of the most recent cases of psychogenic theorizing to capture the allegiance of many persons is the I-levels (interpersonal maturity levels) theory, developed in California and utilized in the juvenile corrections system in that state (Warren 1976). The I-levels argument asserts that most juvenile delinquents show poorly developed interpersonal skills, and are thus socially immature, whereas nondelinquents are thought to be interpersonally or socially competent. Although proponents of this perspective have been vigorous in urging its adoption as a basis for treatment of delinquents, critics have pointed out a number of deficiencies (Gibbons 1970; Beker and Heyman 1972). Even more important, research studies have failed to find evidence to bear out the claims of the theory concerning maturity levels among offenders (Butler and Adams 1966; Austin 1975).

Although convincing support for the thesis that delinquency is a response to psychological problems and pressures has not been provided by those who favor that view, it would be premature to conclude that this is a dead issue. For one thing, as we shall see later in this chapter, the hypothesis that many youngsters become engaged in delinquency because they lack positive self-concepts to insulate them from criminogenic influences in their social environment has been put forth by some sociologists and is enjoying a measure of popularity among a number of other sociological criminologists. Also, delinquency analysts would do well to heed the more fundamental point that has been made convincingly by Inkeles (1970), namely, that sociological accounts of human behavior will continue to be incomplete and inadequate until they provide some place for individual differences and psychological variations among human actors.

Mainstream Sociological Perspectives
on Delinquency

The plethora of viewpoints on causes of delinquency advanced by sociologists has already been noted, along with the fact that sociological perspectives on etiology have not remained constant over the period of twentieth century American sociology. The fads and fashions in criminological theorizing and the twists and turns in arguments about delinquency have been noted by a number of observers (Gibbons 1979; Hirschi and Rudisill 1976; Sykes 1972). In particular, Finestone (1976) has written at length about the social disorganization perspective that grew up in Chicago in the 1950s and 1960s, and about social reaction or labeling arguments, which gained many adherents in the 1970s. In this chapter, sociological perspectives are sorted out in a parallel, chronological fashion. Our examination begins with the views of Clifford Shaw and Henry D. McKay concerning the role of social change and social disorganization in delinquency, followed by commentary on more recent subcultural formulations which also locate the sources of juvenile lawbreaking in cultural pressures. Then, attention turns to the labeling or social reaction perspective and to some recent versions of social control theory. All of these formulations fall within the parameters of mainstream criminology that has dominated American sociology until recently.

Mainstream criminology refers to a host of theories regarding the causes of crime and delinquency in American society, all of which direct attention to criminogenic conditions or defects in the American social order, but which also refrain from wholesale condemnation of the prevailing social system. This chapter also touches upon radical or Marxist analyses which have been urged upon us by those who claim that mainstream criminology is theoretically bankrupt.

Social Change, Ecological Patterns, and
Social Processes in Delinquency

It would be difficult to overestimate the significance of the studies carried on by Clifford Shaw and Henry D. McKay (1931) in Chicago and certain other American cities during the 1920s and 1930s. These investigations represented the first major foray into the study of delinquency by sociologists. Moreover, the results of their inquiries provided much of the intellectual capital upon which criminologists have continued to draw, even to the present time.

In their ecological studies, Shaw and McKay found that rates of delinquency as measured by juvenile court referrals varied widely in areas of Chicago and that rates were highest in neighborhoods of rapid population change, poor housing, and poverty, and where high rates of tuberculosis, adult crime, and mental disorders existed. Also, delinquency followed a gradient pattern, with higher rates near the city center and lower rates near the periphery of the community. Shaw and McKay also noted the existence of "delinquency areas," that is, deteriorated neighborhoods around the city center in which particularly high rates of delinquency existed. Even more important, they observed that delinquency rates had remained stable or consistently high in these neighborhods over a thirty-year period, even though the population composition of the areas had changed markedly. It was this observation that led them to conclude that delinquency and criminality represented a cultural tradition in some urban neighborhoods.

Shaw and McKay also examined the processes through which youths become enmeshed in lawbreaking in delinquency areas. They concluded that delinquents were psychologically normal youngsters whose involvement in misconduct occurred within a network of interpersonal relationships including family, gang, and neighborhood influences. In short, youngsters were seen as being drawn into adolescent misbehavior as they came under the influence of criminogenic conditions in their neighborhoods, that is, the delinquency traditions existing there.

The explanation offered by Shaw and McKay for these findings drew heavily upon the theorizing of W.I. Thomas regarding the cyclical processes of social change involving social organization, disorganization, and reorganization. They saw delinquency as a part of the natural history of the settlement process experienced by newly arrived groups in the urban community. In their view, it occurred against a backdrop of social disorganization experienced by immigrants as they and their children encountered the influences of the new culture into which they had moved. This disorganization was manifested in the form of lessened social bonds in immigrant neighborhoods which led to alienation of children from their parents and community institutions. These detached and alienated juveniles then drifted into association with other like-minded youngsters who collectively became involved in delinquent acts.

Although the social disorganization view initially seemed to make a good deal of sense out of many aspects of delinquency, Shaw and McKay ultimately drew back from it, in favor of an interpretation which sought to explain adult and youthful lawbreaking in delinquency areas in terms of the economic pressures encountered by citizens there. However, as Finestone (1976) has indicated, they did not venture beyond a tentative formulation along these lines, so that it remained for a subsequent generation of criminologists to explore the argument in detail.

Subcultural Theories of Delinquencies

Relatively little theoretical work was carried on concerning delinquency in inner-city, working-class neighborhoods from the 1930s to 1955, when

Albert Cohen's *Delinquent Boys* (1955) appeared. The central thesis of that slim volume was that subcultural or gang delinquency is endemic in working-class community areas because it offers a solution to problems of low status experienced by boys who are socially disadvantaged as a result of their placement in the social order. Many working-class boys become the target of invidious social ranking by school teachers and other middle-class citizens because of their inability to perform well in school or to measure up to other middle-class standards. According to Cohen, the delinquent gang provides those boys with a protective social setting which insulates them against assaults upon their self-esteem.

Cohen's book touched off a flurry of reactions. It was initially greeted with enthusiasm but later came under attack by a number of critics who claimed to have detected flaws in the argument. Additionally, a full-scale alternative perspective was presented by Richard Cloward and Lloyd Ohlin (1960) who contended that delinquent subcultures serve to reduce the shared problems of working-class boys that center around their perceptions of economic injustice rather than low social status.[3] According to these authors, gang delinquency is most common among boys who perceive that their life chances are considerably less favorable than the economic positions to which they aspire.

Still another argument in the subcultural genre was represented by Walter Miller's view (1958) that gang delinquency is a response to the values or focal concerns of lower-class culture, which in turn arise out of the economic disadvantages as well as the general precariousness of the life circumstances of those who are at the bottom of the economic heap.

Two points can be made about these causal perspectives. First, these are basically similar arguments, constituting what some have termed "strain" theories. They all contend that delinquents are driven to lawbreaking by subculturally acquired motivational patterns. These shared norms, values, and motives have been generated by perceptions of social or economic discrimination held by gang members. Second, the research evidence that has accumulated from studies designed to test these formulations has provided only partial support, at best, for any of them (Gibbons 1976: 125-140).

Labeling or Social Reaction Views of Delinquency

The interpretations of delinquency offered by Shaw and McKay were predicated on an implicit assumption that police arrest figures and juvenile court referrals provide a relatively accurate measure of the social and spatial distribution of total delinquency within a community. In contrast, subcultural theorists often conceded that some juvenile misconduct escapes the attention of the authorities, but they also assumed that hard-core, serious gang delinquency is concentrated in lower-class areas in the community, and it was this form of juvenile lawbreaking which they endeavored to explain.

A major challenge to these assumptions about the nature and social distribution of delinquency appeared in the 1950s, in the form of studies of hidden delinquency, that is, self-reported and undetected offenses. A host of investigators carried out inquiries of this kind which amply demonstrated that most American youngsters engage in at least a few relatively minor acts of misbehavior during adolescence (Gibbons 1976:23-31; Nettler 1977:97-117). These research findings were less clear on the issue of whether serious, repetitive delinquency is equally common at all social class levels and on certain other questions, but they did demolish the assumption that most youngsters move through the adolescent period without engaging in misconduct.

The investigations of hidden delinquency contributed to the development of the labeling or social reaction perspective on deviance which captured the interest of large numbers of sociologists in the 1960s (Gibbons and Jones 1975; Goode 1978). The labeling or social reaction view centers around the proposition that among persons who engage in acts of nonconformity, only a small share of them get singled out by police, mental health workers, juvenile court personnel, or other social control agents and labeled as "deviants." Moreover, becoming tagged as a "delinquent," an "alcoholic," or as "mentally disturbed" or escaping that fate is often most heavily influenced by one's biography rather than by the behavior in which the individual is engaged. Indeed, questions about the etiology of deviant acts tend to evaporate in labeling formulations. Applied to delinquency, the labeling view holds that it is blacks, lower-class members, and other socially disadvantaged persons who most often are capriciously selected by control agents and processed as offenders. Finally, social reaction notions claim that actions taken against identified deviants and undertaken in the name of treatment or social reintegration often have quite the opposite effect, stigmatizing the labeled deviants, foreclosing on their opportunities to withdraw from deviance, and driving them further into nonconformity.

One consequence of the development of the social reaction perspectives on deviance and criminality has been that justice system and correctional organizations have come under greater sociological scrutiny. A considerable quantity of evidence has now accumulated, indicating that important variations exist in the structure, major goals, and other features of these organizations. In turn, those differing organizational patterns play a major role in the social drama that produces the delinquency problem. On this point, studies have indicated that the level of recognized or official delinquency in different communities is heavily influenced by the organizational structure of police departments (Wilson 1968), while other investigators

have drawn attention to organizational features of juvenile courts or probation departments that affect the life chances of youths who are processed
through this social machinery (Emerson 1969; Circourel 1968). Finally,
juvenile correctional programs across the nation have been shown to vary
markedly in terms of goal emphasis, staff attitudes, and the like, with cor-
related effects on the youthful charges dealt with by these programs (Vinter,
Newcomb, and Kish 1976).

The social reaction perspective on deviance has enjoyed considerable
popularity during the past decade or so, even though it has also been the
target of a good deal of criticism. For example, the research evidence at
hand dealing with the alleged deleterious effects of social reaction and intervention experiences upon deviants of one kind or another has generally
failed to confirm that contention (Gibbons and Jones 1975; Gove 1975).

Labeling arguments have been applied in detail by some students of
criminality and delinquency (Schur 1973). Among other things, social reaction notions have been employed by those who have argued for a lessened
role for juvenile courts, adoption of diversion policies, and the like.
According to this line of argument, delinquency is usually transitory,
episodic, and relatively inconsequential in character, thus the best strategy
is often one of benign neglect or of nonintervention by official social control agencies. Although when applied to delinquency many of these themes
have a ring of plausibility, it also must be acknowledged that firm empirical
support for them is lacking. In particular, the evidence at hand does not
provide much confirmation for arguments about the harmful effects of control agency intervention upon delinquents (Wellford 1975; Mahoney 1974).

Control Theories and Delinquency

A markedly different view of offenders and delinquency is contained in the
work of social control theorists, for these persons argue that delinquents do
differ from nonoffenders, particularly in the strength of inner control
(psychological) factors of one kind or another.

Walter C. Reckless has been a major figure in the articulation of the
social control perspective. He and his associates became involved in a series
of studies in the 1950s, in which they studied samples of youngsters who had
been nominated by schoolteachers as "good boys," likely to stay out of
trouble, or "bad boys," probably destined for difficulties with the law
(Reckless, Dinitz, and Murray 1956; Reckless and Dinitz 1967). According
to Reckless et al., the youngsters selected by teachers as good boys showed
positive self-concepts and were on good terms with their parents, whereas
the bad boys were on poorer terms with their parents and had less positive
self-images. And, a much higher proportion of bad boys subsequently

acquired official records with the police or juvenile court than did the good boys. Reckless concluded that a positive self-concept insulates boys from involvement in lawbreaking, protecting them from the harmful influence of delinquent companions and delinquent subcultures.

Reckless ultimately expanded these notions about insulating factors into a broader argument which he termed "containment theory," the thrust of which is that a variety of internal and social environmental influences work to draw individuals into delinquency or criminality or to impel them away from lawbreaking. Although the broad argument appears reasonable, a number of critics have remained unimpressed by this thesis and have drawn attention to a variety of serious flaws in the self-concept research which undergirds containment theory, as well as to a host of ambiguous claims and logical errors in the general argument (Schrag 1971; Schwartz and Tangri 1965; Tangri and Schwartz 1967; Orcutt 1970).

Another version of social control theory has been offered by Travis Hirschi (1969). The central thesis of his argument is that juveniles become free to commit delinquent acts when their ties to the conventional social order are severed. Unlike strain theorists, Hirschi found no reason to posit some special learned or acquired motivation toward delinquency on the part of youthful lawbreakers.

Hirschi identified several dimensions along which the bond of the individual to society varies: attachment, commitment, involvement, and belief. Attachment has to do with the ties to others such as parents or peers, whereas commitment designates the devotion of the person to conventional lines of conduct. Individuals also vary in involvement in activities that restrict the time they have available for deviant endeavors. Finally, belief refers to the strength of one's attitudes toward conformity.

This argument about social control and delinquency formed the basis for a large-scale study by Hirschi (1969) in a California city, in which he uncovered substantial support for this formulation. Some other research studies have also turned up findings that lend confirmation to the Hirschi argument (Hindelang 1973; Hepburn 1976).

Mainstream Perspectives: An Evaluation

This cursory review has done no more than to limn the bare outlines of a number of mainstream sociological theories of delinquency. It is not possible in a few pages to capture the rich details of many of these formulations. In addition, this survey of criminological perspectives has slurred over some lines of work that have engaged a number of criminologists. For example, a number of investigators have explored the role of family processes and parent-child relationships in delinquency (Rodman and Grams 1967), while other researchers have devoted a good deal of attention to probing the ways in which negative experiences in schools may contribute to involvement of youngsters in lawbreaking (Polk and Schafer 1972).

The dominant imagery that runs throughout many of the theoretical perspectives considered to this point is one in which delinquents are seen as pushed or driven into lawbreaking through deleterious social circumstances. For example, the tracking programs of urban high schools, along with other negative features of these places, have been identified as critical experiences that create adjustment problems for many youths, with delinquency being one response to those institutional pressures (Polk and Schafer 1972). Then, too, juvenile offenders are assumed to differ from nondelinquents in terms of attitudes and motivational patterns. Juvenile delinquents are seen as lacking in inner controls as a result of their faulty socialization or as positively motivated to engage in deviant acts. This portrayal of delinquency is quite probably accurate for many offenders. But at the same time, some mention ought to be made of another view which some have put forth, pointing to the possibility that youngsters may sometimes drift into misconduct and that their commitment to delinquency may be more attenuated than suggested in some lines of theorizing (Matza 1964). A closely related point has been made by those who have argued that criminality and delinquency may be importantly influenced by situational pressures and inducements to deviance, rather than by long-term criminogenic learning experiences (Briar and Piliavin 1965; Gibbons 1971).

It should be clear from this brief overview that the mainstream sociological position on juvenile delinquency is a multicausal one, in which not one or two but a large number of factors are seen as playing some part in youthful lawbreaking. Then, too, many of the research findings relative to particular mainstream formulations regarding delinquency have provided only partial rather than complete support for these specific arguments, which implied that if delinquency is to be explained, some kind of complex argument that blends elements of a number of the views examined here will be required.[4]

Radical-Marxist Theories and Delinquency

American sociological criminology has been in existence for about three-quarters of a century. During most of that time, mainstream causal arguments of the kind examined to this point have dominated. Most of these etiological formulations have directed attention to flaws in the social order which are thought to be implicated in lawbreaking, but none of them have mounted full-scale critical attacks on the dominant social structure. However, a number of voices have been heard in recent years, declaring that

mainstream criminology is theoretically tarnished and that it must be replaced by a new paradigm variously identified as radical, Marxist, or critical
criminology (Gibbons 1979). Radical or Marxist criminology frontally attacks the political-economic structure of corporate capitalism.

A pivotal proposition of radical criminology is that criminal laws reflect
the interests of a monolithic ruling class and are created by legislatures serving as an instrument of that ruling class. According to this argument, the
owners and managers of the resources of society, in particular the powerful
heads of corporate enterprises, utilize the criminal law as an instrument
through which to maintain and perpetuate the existing social and economic
order. And contrary to the perceptions of the masses of powerless citizens in
modern corporate capitalist societies, the criminal law is employed in order
to oppress them and maintain them in their disadvantaged economic positions, not to protect them.

The critics have not been kind to radical or Marxist criminologists, for
many of them have scored these theorists for the gross exaggerations of the
real world that are said to characterize this new brand of theorizing. According to the critics, criminal lawmaking is a markedly more complex matter than described in radical formulations, being responsive to many more
interests than solely those of a ruling class. Indeed, a number of persons
have argued that political power is much more diffuse and complex than
captured in radical contentions about a national ruling class, and thus the
ruling class hypothesis itself is rejected by those critics.

The radical-Marxist argument is relatively new and is still relatively in-
choate in form. For one thing, radical theorists have had little to say about
the different arguments that may be required in order to provide a full explanation of all of the forms of lawbreaking in modern societies. Property
crimes, homicides, sex offenses, and other forms of criminality may not all
be accounted for by some single, overarching explanation. On this point,
the radical-Marxist formulations that have been advanced to date have been
virtually silent on the question of juvenile delinquency.

One attempt to provide a Marxist interpretation of juvenile delinquency
in capitalist societies has been provided by David Greenberg (1977) in which
he drew together a large collection of research evidence on youthful misconduct. His general thesis was that the disproportionate involvement of
juveniles in major crimes is a product of the historically changing position
of youths in industrial societies.

Greenberg's starting point was with the available evidence concerning
age relationships in delinquency. He argued that subcultural theories cannot
account for the fact that involvement in serious lawbreaking reaches a peak
at about age fifteen or sixteen and then declines in magnitude. The thrust of
subcultural arguments is that delinquent activities are valued positively by
juveniles, and if so, subcultural members ought to continue in those
endeavors beyond age sixteen.

The formulation proposed by Greenberg emphasized the strains experienced by many youngsters in the transition period from childhood to adolescence. During this period, attachments to parents weaken at the same time that youths become highly sensitive to peer judgments and peer standards. This peer group culture places pressures on adolescents to engage in a hedonistic life style, but increasing numbers of these youths are incapable of financing those activities because of the decline of teenage employment opportunities in capitalist societies. However, as these adolescents get older, they become less vulnerable to peer evaluations at the same time that legitimate opportunities to earn money increase, with the consequence that adolescent theft declines among older youths.

The status problems of many juveniles in modern societies are exacerbated by negative school experiences. Greenberg emphasized the restraints imposed upon the autonomy of youngsters by modern high schools, along with the stigmatizing and degrading experiences to which many adolescents are exposed while in school. Those who have a reduced stake in conformity rebel against these negative experiences by engaging in hostile acts directed at the schools and school personnel.

A third, related source of delinquent motivation identified by Greenberg results from the lack of employment for adolescents, which creates anxiety about one's prospects for attaining masculine status in American society. In Greenberg's opinion, these three pressures upon juveniles account for most of the delinquency in capitalist societies.

Greenberg was not the first sociologist to point to exclusion of juveniles from the labor market as a major factor in youthful misconduct. But, contrary to most interpretations that regard this situation as a recent and short-range one, created by invasion of women into the labor market, teenager preferences for part-time work, and the like, Greenberg argued that it represents a fundamental failing of the capitalist system to general sufficient demand for labor. Greenberg's argument comes down to the thesis that juvenile delinquency in industrialized societies rests on the disadvantaged structural position of adolescents in advanced capitalist economies. If so, it follows that it is not likely to be reduced markedly by the kinds of remedies that have been proposed in the United States, such as job training for youths. Job training in a situation in which jobs for teenagers are limited or nonexistent is likely to be of little value.

Conclusion: Paradigms, Perspectives, and Policies

During the 1970s, a number of sociologists have appropriated Thomas Kuhn's notion (1962) of scientific paradigms and applied it to sociology. But, there is reason to question this practice, for it surely is not the case that sociology is characterized by a single, dominant theoretical perspective which informs the day-to-day activities of sociologists. As this chapter has indicated, the subarea of criminology within sociology shows a number of separate theoretical orientations to which groups of scholars hold allegiance. In short, the study of juvenile delinquency involves a welter of causal arguments rather than a single, dominant perspective.

It would be naive to suppose that this situation will soon be overcome once the results of more empirical studies of delinquency become available. For one thing, a plethora of research evidence is already at hand; thus, the existence of discordant perspectives is not attributable simply to a lack of hard facts. Additionally, empirical investigations are never perfect, containing as they do various methodological deficiencies, sampling problems, and so on. As a result, research studies lend equivocal support, at best, to broad theoretical formulations. Then, too, specific studies themselves usually report equivocal findings, in the form of significant but relatively low correlations among factors and other qualified results.

The other side of the coin is that many of the theoretical arguments that have been pursued by criminologists contain poorly defined concepts, ambiguous propositions, and other defects. As a consequence, it is often difficult to persuade a skeptical criminologist that a particular theoretical contention and some specific body of evidence relate to each other.

The result of all these problems of theory and research methods is that sociology is to some extent an art form rather than a hard science (Nisbet 1976). Sociological theories often show more literary elegance than logical rigor. Sociologists sometimes pick and choose among research findings, selecting those which conform to the theoretical perspective that they favor and dismissing the others. Finally, this situation provides little encouragement for those who would look to sociologists and criminologists for clear and convincing advice regarding the question, "What shall we do about juvenile delinquency?"

Notes

1. A fuller treatment of delinquency theory and research can be found in Gibbons (1976), Empey (1978).

2. Relatively few attempts have been made to articulate theoretical views on delinquency which provide a place for biological and psychological elements in etiology, along with sociological factors. For some efforts in that direction, see Cortés and Gattie (1972); Martin and Fitzpatrick (1964).

3. For an extension of the Cloward and Ohlin formulation, see Elliott and Voss (1974).

4. For one effort in this direction, see Elliott, Ageton, and Carter (1978).

References

Aichhorn, August (1955). *Wayward Youth*. New York: Meridian Books.

Austin, Roy L. (1975). "Construct validity of I-level classification." *Criminal Justice and Behavior* 2:113-129.

Beker, Jerome, and Heyman, Doris S. (1972). "A critical appraisal of the California differential treatment typology of adolescent offenders." *Criminology* 10:3-59.

Briar, Scott, and Piliavin, Irving (1965). "Delinquency, situational inducements, and commitment to conformity." *Social Problems* 13:35-45.

Butler, Edgar W., and Adams, Stuart N. (1966). "Typologies of delinquent girls: some alternative approaches." *Social Forces* 44:401-407.

Circourel, Aaron V. (1968). *The Social Organization of Juvenile Justice*. New York: Wiley.

Cloward, Richard A., and Ohlin, Lloyd E. (1960). *Delinquency and Opportunity*. New York: Free Press.

Cohen, Albert K. (1955). *Delinquent Boys*. New York: Free Press.

Conger, John Janeway, and Miller, Wilbur C. (1966). *Personality, Social Class, and Delinquency*. New York: Wiley.

Cortés, Juan B., and Gattie, Florence M. (1972). *Delinquency and Crime: A Biopsychosocial Approach*. New York: Seminar Press.

Elliott, Delbert S., and Voss, Harwin (1974). *Delinquency and Dropout*. Lexington, Mass.: Lexington Books, D.C. Heath.

Elliott, Delbert S., Ageton, Suzanne S., and Carter, Rachelle J. (1978). *An Integrated Theoretical Perspective on Delinquent Behavior*. Boulder: Behavioral Research Institute, University of Colorado.

Emerson, Robert M. (1969). *Judging Delinquents*. Chicago: Aldine.

Empey, LaMar T. (1978). *American Delinquency*. Homewood, Ill.: Dorsey.

Finestone, Harold (1976). *Victims of Change*. Westport, Conn.: Greenwood.

Gibbons, Don C. (1970). "Differential treatment of delinquents and interpersonal maturity levels theory: a critique." *Social Service Review* 44:22-33.

———— (1971). "Some observations on the study of crime causation." *American Journal of Sociology* 77:262-278.

———— (1976). *Delinquent Behavior*. 2d ed. Englewood Cliffs, N.J.: Prentice-Hall.

———— (1979). *The Criminological Enterprise*. Englewood Cliffs, N.J.: Prentice-Hall.

Gibbons, Don C., and Jones, Joseph F. (1975). *The Study of Deviance*. Englewood Cliffs, N.J.: Prentice-Hall.

Glueck, Sheldon, and Glueck, Eleanor (1950). *Unraveling Juvenile Delinquency*. Cambridge: Harvard University Press.

_____ (1956). *Physique and Delinquency*. New York: Harper and Row.

Goode, Erich (1978). *Deviant Behavior*. Englewood Cliffs, N.J.: Prentice-Hall.

Gove, Walter R. (ed.) (1975). *The Labeling of Deviance*. New York: Halsted Press.

Greenberg, David F. (1977). "Delinquency and the age structure of society." *Contemporary Crises* 1:189-223.

Hepburn, John R. (1976). "Testing alternative models of delinquency causation." *Journal of Criminal Law and Criminology* 67:450-460.

Hindelang, Michael J. (1973). "Causes of delinquency: a partial replication and extension." *Social Problems* 20:471-487.

Hippchen, Leonard J. (1977). "Biochemical research: its contributions to criminological theory." In Robert F. Meier (ed.) *Theory in Criminology: Contemporary Views*, pp. 57-67, Beverly Hills: Sage.

Hirschi, Travis (1969). *Causes of Delinquency*. Berkeley: University of California Press, p. 31.

Hirschi, Travis, and Hindelang, Michael J. (1977). "Intelligence and delinquency: a revisionist review." *American Sociological Review* 42:571-587.

Hirschi, Travis, and Rudisill, David (1976). "The great American search: causes of crime, 1976-1976." *Annals of the American Academy of Political and Social Science* 423:14-22.

Inkeles, Alex (1970). "Sociological theory in relation to social psychological variables." In John C. McKinney and Edward A. Tiryakian (eds.) *Theoretical Sociology*, pp. 403-431. New York: Appleton-Century-Crofts.

Kuhn, Thomas (1962). *Structure of Scientific Revolutions*. Chicago: University of Chicago Press.

Mahoney, Ann Rankin (1974). "The effect of labeling upon youths in the juvenile justice system: a review of the evidence." *Law and Society Review* 8:583-614.

Martin, John M., and Fitzpatrick, Joseph P. (1964). *Delinquent Behavior*. New York: Random House.

Matza, David (1964). *Delinquency and Draft*. New York: Wiley.

Miller, Walter B. (1958). "Lower class culture as a generating milieu of gang delinquency." *Journal of Social Issues* 14:5-19.

Nettler, Gwynn (1977). *Explaining Crime*. 2d ed. New York: McGraw-Hill.

Nisbet, Robert (1976). *Sociology as an Art Form*. New York: Oxford University Press.

Orcutt, James D. (1970). "Self-concept and insulation against delinquency: some critical notes." *Sociological Quarterly* 2:381-390.

Polk, Kenneth, and Schafer, Walter E. (eds.) (1972). *Schools and Delinquency*. Englewood Cliffs, N.J.: Prentice-Hall.

Reckless, Walter C., and Dinitz, Simon (1967). "Pioneering with self-concept as a vulnerability factor in delinquency." *Journal of Criminal Law, Criminology and Police Science* 58:515-523.

Reckless, Walter C., Dinitz, Simon, and Murray, Ellen (1956). "Self-concept as an insulator against delinquency." *American Sociological Review* 21:744-756.

Rodman, Hyman, and Grams, Paul (1967). "Juvenile delinquency and the family: a review and discussion." In *The President's Commission on Law Enforcement and Administration of Justice, Task Force Report: Juvenile Delinquency and Youth Crime*, pp. 188-221. Washington, D.C.: U.S. Government Printing Office.

Schrag, Clarence (1971). *Crime and Justice: American Style*. Rockville, Md.: National Institute of Mental Health.

Schur, Edwin M. (1973). *Radical Non-Intervention: Rethinking the Delinquency Problem*. Englewood Cliffs, N.J.: Prentice-Hall.

Schwartz, Michael, and Tangri, Sandra S. (1965). "A note on self-concept as an insulator against delinquency." *American Sociological Review* 30:922-926.

Shah, Saleem, and Roth, Loren H. (1974). "Biological and psycho-physiological factors in criminality." In Daniel Glaser (ed.) *Handbook of Criminology*, pp. 101-173. Chicago: Rand McNally.

Shaw, Clifford, and McKay Henry D. (1931). *Social Factors in Juvenile Delinquency*. Vol. 2. National Commission on Law Observance and Enforcement, Report on the Causes of Crime. Washington, D.C.: U.S. Government Printing Office.

Sheldon, William H., Hartl, Emil M., and McDermott, Eugene (1949). *Varieties of Delinquent Youth*. New York: Harper and Row.

Sykes, Gresham M. (1972). "The future of criminality." *American Behavioral Scientist* 15:409-419.

Tangri, Sandra S., and Schwartz, Michael (1967). "Delinquency research and the self-concept variable." *Journal of Criminal Law, Criminology and Police Science* 58:182-190.

Van den Berghe, Pierre L. (1974). "Bringing beasts back in: toward a bio-social theory of aggression." *Amrican Sociological Review* 39:777-788.

Vinter, Robert D., Newcomb, Theodore M., and Kish, Rhea (eds.) (1976). *Time Out: A National Study of Juvenile Correctional Programs*. Ann Arbor: National Assessment of Juvenile Corrections, University of Michigan.

Warren, Marguerite Q. (1976). "Intervention with juvenile delinquents." In Margaret K. Rosenheim (ed.), *Pursuing Justice for the Child*, pp. 176-204. Chicago: University of Chicago Press.

Wellford, Charles (1975). "Labeling theory and criminology: an assessment." *Social Problems* 22:322-345.

Wilson, Edward C. (1975). *Sociobiology: The New Synthesis*. Cambridge: Harvard University Press.

Wilson, James Q. (1968). "The police and the delinquent in two cities." In Stanton Wheeler (ed.), *Controlling Delinquents*, pp. 9-30. New York: Wiley.

2

Juvenile Justice Legislation: A Framework for Evaluation

Katherine S. Teilmann and *Malcolm W. Klein*

Introduction: The Current Legislative Ferment

The legislative and judicial structure of juvenile justice in America is undergoing rapid change and, as so often happens, social science is beginning to recognize the change in its later stages, too late for ideal assessment of its impact, if not its meaning. As assessors of the impact of recent legislative changes in California, we are painfully aware of the need for a conceptual framework that might guide such impact assessment and enhance predictions of the acceptance of new legislative endeavors.

This chapter introduces such a framework. It derives inductively from our work in California and thus may be limited in its utility elsewhere. However, familiarity with new legislation in other states, both enacted and proposed, suggests to us that there are common contexts and procedures which can be abstracted in different jurisdictions and that the basic framework presented herein can be applied rather broadly. The framework is presented and illustrated with preliminary observations from the California situation in order that others may undertake to test its applicability elsewhere.

The authors of the Deinstitutionalization of Status Offenders final report (Kobrin and Klein 1979) have noted a significant change in the federal government's posture toward the crime and delinquency problem; they refer to this as the transition from traditional federalism to active federalism. Initiated in part by the development of policy-relevant theories of causation and control (opportunity structure, labeling, and the Youth Development and Delinquency Prevention Administration national strategy) and exemplified in a series of major legislative initiatives, the nature of active federalism is perhaps best exemplified by report of the President's Commission on Law Enforcement and the Administration of

Prepared under Grant Number 77-JN-99-0012 from the National Institute for Juvenile Justice and Delinquency Prevention, Office of Juvenile Justice and Delinquency Prevention, Law Enforcement Assistance Administration, U.S. Department of Justice. Points of view or opinions in this document are those of the authors and do not necessarily represent the official position or policies of the U.S. Department of Justice.

Justice (1967) and the mandates in the 1974 Juvenile Justice and Delinquency Prevention Act.

The commission's report succinctly documented the frustrations and failures of the current justice system and recommended specific remedial steps to be sanctioned by the federal establishment. The 1974 act specifically prescribed desired changes in state practices concerning status offenders and provided a fiscal carrot to achieve such changes. In both instances, these federal involvements both mirrored and accelerated changes already under way.

In the illustrative cases of status offender deinstitutionalization, Hellum's summary of state legislation (Klein 1979) indicates that twelve states had initiated change prior to the federal act, and that by the end of 1977 an additional thirty-two states had undertaken some form of legislation to limit status offender detention or incarceration. Similarly, diversion has been legislatively sanctified for application to minor offenders.[1] And at the same time, more severe sanctions for serious offenders, along with the lowering of age levels for treatment as adults, is appearing more commonly in proposed state legislation.

One can identify in all this legislative ferment three major trends that seem to coexist somewhat peacefully, but that are not logically bound to do so. These trends provide an impetus for current legislative changes. The last-minute development of assembly bill 3121 in California was an explicit acknowledgement of this conflicting context.

First, there is the children's rights movement. As the "last oppressed minority" (Sarri and Vinter 1976: 165), children are reaping the benefits of the rights movements associated with racial minorities, women, the elderly, the gays, and others who have found routes to organized advocacy. The difference in the case of the young is that advocacy on their behalf is stronger than it has been—or perhaps can be—among the young themselves. This advocacy, however, has not altered the thrust of the movement.

The second major trend is the well-advertised war on crime. Fed by frustrations with the seemingly endless increases in serious delinquency rates and by the polemics of election year politics, the general thrust of this concern has been with the handling of (1) juveniles with long records of delinquency involvement and (2) perpetrators of serious predatory crimes. The crackdown on serious offenders is manifested in lowering of age limits, facilitating remands to adult court, increasing the role of police and prosecution in case handling, increasing penalties for serious delinquencies, and allowing sentencing to adult institutions.

The fact that both trends can coexist, one favoring a hands-off treatment policy for minor offenders and the other a more severe handling of serious offenders, is in itself evidence for the implicit philosophical coexistence between the two sets of adherents we mentioned earlier. Tying them together even more effectively is the third trend, that of legalization. Interestingly (and if a bit of sterotypy may be allowed), the liberal and conservative adherents have employed legalization differently to bolster their different positions. For those concerned principally with minor offenders, legalization has taken the form of a concern for due process. Due process, in turn, has meant keeping youngsters away from juvenile court because that institution often sacrifices due process to achieve its paternalistic goals. The clearest case is that of status offenders who have committed no crime but are nonetheless subject to the court's jurisdiction.

The conservative adherents, by way of contrast, use legalization as a means of assuring adultlike handling of serious juvenile offenders through a focus on the offense, rather than on the offender. Since such major case law as that occurring in the Gault, Kent, and Winship cases assigns to juveniles some of the rights previously accorded only to adults, the rationale is that if juveniles are no longer to be treated in the traditional fashion, let them be treated fully as adults. The way to do this is to adjudicate them in the adult system: adult treatment for adults crimes.

Obviously, this brief overview cannot do full justice to any of the three trends, but it is sufficient to suggest their general thrusts. To understand the spate of forthcoming state legislation, it is important to recognize these three trends. As we see it, the new legislation is in many ways a reflection, a codified embodiment, of them. The conceptual framework to be presented in this chapter has in fact been developed in the context of one major piece of legislation, California's AB3121, which embodied all three trends at once.

Framework for Prediction and Assessment

To the extent that legislation developing across the country reflects or rejects our three trends, such development can be seen as a generalized phenomenon. We anticipate more legislation to be passed as part of these three trends. We need a general framework to predict and assess the acceptance of the new legislation. We have developed a framework with three major foci and find it to be quite promising. The framework was developed to assess legislation reflecting the three trends discussed above but may well have more general applicability. The three foci of the framework are called signals, reflections, and control, each having several subparts. We turn to these in order.

Signals

Each new piece of legislation mandates certain changes and activities; it usually suggests others; it intiates new procedures, or propogates new standards for existing procedures. It does all these with varying levels of clarity.

One way of looking at these legislative thrusts is to think of them as signals to the anticipated audiences. In our case, the audiences are usually the practitioners of the juvenile justice system: the judges, prosecutors, defenders, probation and parole officers, police, social workers, school and other officials whose activities constitute what is done about delinquents. Among these signals to the practitioners, one can discern several important facets.

Clarity. Leaving aside the writing style of most legislation, it is nonetheless true that much legislation comprises a rather ambiguous stimulus, amenable to alternative selection and interpretation. Therefore we often speak of "legislative intent," the stated or assumed purposes of new laws. This intent presents signals which transcend the explicit provisions of a particular bill. In the case of omnibus bills containing a multiplicity of provisions, legislative intent becomes a crucial issue since many provisions seem often to suggest intents not intrinsically related to each other.

Some examples using AB3121 are pertinent. This bill, passed late in 1976 and effective on January 1, 1977, contained over twenty provisions. Some of these dealt with mandating the end of secure detention[2] of status offenders and providing more social services for minor offenders. Others increased the likelihood of more severe sanctions for serious offenders. Still others provided more due process guarantees for both minor and serious offenders. But if one asks practitioners about the content of AB3121, many of the provisions prove to be forgotten or at best imperfectly recalled; only a very few provisions are remembered, emphasized, and correctly stated.

With respect to legislative intent, an interesting example emerged recently when one of the authors of AB3121 reported to an audience that had been the intent all along that some reinstitution of limited secure detention for status offenders would be forthcoming. Given its prohibition in the bill, his own earlier public pronouncements about giving the bill a year's chance to prove itself, and the federal guidelines severely limiting such secure detention, this statement of intent is astounding. Such intent was never made clear, even in the face of statewide denouncement of the detention provision by public and private officials—especially the police. The controversy over corrective legislation (AB958) to reinstitute secure detention never reflected this original intent. Indeed it took a year and a half for AB958 to pass. In any case, this seeming contradiction provides a good case in point about the ambiguity of legislative signals.

Other examples abound. For instance, there has been a controversy over the question of whether violation of probation, when probation is for a status offense, constitutes a delinquent act. If so—it is delinquent to disobey a court order—then secure detention is a viable disposition. A runaway who leaves a court-assigned, nonsecure placement has violated a court order and can be securely detained because this violation constitutes a delinquent act. Almost immediately upon enactment of AB3121, this disposition was employed by a juvenile court judge, appealed by the defense, and decided by the appellate court in favor of the offender; it was judged that secure detention for violation of probation resulting from a status offense was not consonant with legislative intent. The intent was to remove all status offenders from secure places of detention. Signals often require authoritative (or arbitrary) interpretation.

We also have the example of the appeal to the attorney general of the state of California, from the director of the California Youth Authority, for legal interpretations of various provisions of AB3121. This document effectively illustrates the ambiguity of the legislative signals which threatened to hamstring correctional officials in the absence of clarity in the legislation itself:

> Chapter 1071, Statutes of 1976, substantially amended the Juvenile Court law, Welfare & Institutions Code Section 507 was mended by adding subsection (b) thereto, to require, in substance, that Welfare & Institutions Code Section 601 wards (all statutory references are to the Welfare & Institutions Code, unless otherwise indicated), or persons taken into custody on grounds that they are persons described by Section 601, may not be detained in any jail, lockup, juvenile hall, or other secure facility. Instead, if such persons must be detained, the detention alternatives presented by Section 507 (b) are a sheltered-care facility or crisis resolution home as provided for in Section 654, or a non-secure facility as provided for in Section 727 (a), (b), (c), or (d).

> Several county officials have and are raising questions regarding the proper interpretation of the newly enacted statutes in regard to appropriate places of detention for persons alleged or found to be described by Section 601. The questions are as follows:

> 1. May a portion of a juvenile hall be declared to be an appropriate place for detention of persons alleged or found to be described by Section 601? If so, under what circumstances (example, unlocked doors)?
> 2. May persons placed in shelter care facilities or crisis resolution homes pursuant to Section 507 (b) be allowed to commingle under certain circumstances with persons alleged or found to be described by Section 602 who are detained in a secure facility? For example, during recreation periods, in schools operated under the auspices of the probation department, or during meals. In the alternative, must such facilities be maintained entirely independent and/or physically separated from the juvenile hall?

3. Sections 628.1 and 636.2 authorize the placement in secure detention of a minor who violates a specific condition of home supervision release (Section 628.1) or who leaves a nonsecure detention facility without permission (Section 636.2). Should these sections be read as exceptions to the provision of Section 507 (b), or should they be read as applying only to persons alleged or found to be described by Section 602 who are so placed?
4. May a minor who is alleged or found to be a person described by Section 601 legitimately be alleged or found to be a person described by Section 602 if he or she leaves a non secure placement in violation of an order of the juvenile court so placing the minor? Under what circumstances?

Chapter 1071 is effective January 1, 1977. The counties require answers to these questions as soon as is possible so appropriate plans may be made. I would, therefore appreciate an early response that we might share with the counties.

Finally, we might mention the terribly perplexing problem of what, in fact, constitutes a status offender. Since published data document that the "pure" status offender is a rare phenomenon (Erickson 1979; Klein 1971; Rojek 1978; Thomas 1976; Wolfgang et al. 1972) and since different states define status offenders differently, if at all (Kobrin and Klein 1979), and since there are multiple routes to the designation of a status offender (White 1976), any legislation bearing on status offenders starts out in trouble. For the serious reader who is skeptical about this problem, we recommend a perusal of the references noted above.

Legislative Mandate. Legislation varies in the degree to which it requires its will to be carried out. The dimension moves from mere authorization, to encouragement, to incentives, to mandates with room for interpretation, to unequivocal mandates. Among those provisions of AB3121 we have been studying more carefully, there are examples of most of these points on the continuum. The county probation officer was authorized to develop and use more disposition alternatives, but there was a clear mandate that status offenders were no longer to be securely detained. New criteria for remands to adult court were set in the form of a mandate but a significant number of "escapes" from the mandate were provided; it is still quite possible for the district attorney and the judge involved to exercise considerable discretion. Finally, the court is encouraged to use restitution, uncompensated work programs, and so forth, as dispositions for wards of the court.

If new legislation is abundantly clear about what it permits, authorizes, encourages, and mandates, then the failure of its interpreters will often account for failures to comply properly. But if this clarity is not there, if the legislation provides mixed signals, then compliance will cross the boundary between proper discretion and probable chaos. Compliance, in the context of ambiguity, may constitute an unfair standard, although it certainly provides grist for the researcher evaluator's mill.

Fiscal Implications. Legislation will vary with respect to the appropriations made available to carry it out. The presence of adequate appropriations strongly signals the intent of the legislature and provides the wherewithal to satisfy that intent. Costly mandates in the absence of adequate appropriations certainly offer signals of a different sort than mandates with adequate appropriations. The mixed signals situation is not at all unusual, however, especially in legislative structure which place responsibilities for legal content and appropriations in different committees of the legislature.

With respect to AB3121, it was suggested that the bill would be a "wash"; that is, the expenses necessitated at the local (county) level would be balanced by savings in personnel, bed space, and similar costs. Therefore no state funds were allotted for the bill's enactment. There were several immediate consequences.

1. Counties began specific cost-accounting procedures to document their losses, with a view to suing for recovery from the state.
2. Private agencies, sensing lack of financial resources in the county coffers (along with other problems) failed to come forth as advertised to provide nonsecure placements for status offenders.
3. County officials began the process of lobbying for new state legislation which would reimburse them for the costs of AB3121. This effort, combined with others, finally led to yet another major piece of legislation, AB90, enacted over a year and a half later.

To what extent the fiscal matters associated with AB3121 are typical is not clear to us. What is clear from this experience is that the signals provided by the fiscal implications of new legislation are pivotal concerns to the evaluation of the reception and success of that legislation. Most social scientists tend to "leave it to the economists": Clearly, it must not be left to anyone. The fiscal implications, whether appropriations are provided or not, are part and parcel of the legislative substance to be assessed.

Reflections

New legislation obviously does not come out of the blue. It results from perceived needs and pressures. It indicates what has gone before, and thus may often be more a reflection of movement in the field than an initiator of such movement to predict and assess the impact of legislation, it is important to know what it reflects. We can cite two particular facets of this reflection that illustrate this component of the framework.

Codification of Trends. A classic error committed by many a newcomer to evaluation is to portray a trend line during and after an experimental program and assume that the trend is attributable to the program. But if there is a strong prior trend, it is hard to demonstrate incremental change. It is, of course, equally true that a lesser trend already initiated describes a momentum on which one can capitalize either to predict or to claim success.

Applying this logic to new legislation allows one to assess the degree to which that legislation postdates trends already under way, and thus codifies practices already initiated or well established. Data from the AB3121 assessment illustrate the point.

1. In the first half of 1977—the period immediately following the effective date of the legislation—status offense arrests statewide dropped 45 percent from the number in the first half of 1976. But a trend line illustrates that the 1976 numbers are a decline of 9 percent from 1975 and of 23 percent from 1974. Thus the most appropriate conclusion about AB3121 might be that it legitimated and accelerated a decline that already had a three-year history.

2. Similarly, as one would expect, law enforcement referrals of status offenders to probation dropped by 54 percent in 1977, but had already dropped by 15 percent in the prior two years.

3. Statewide arrests for delinquent offenses rose slightly in the first half of 1977—by just 1.3 percent. One might well miss the significance of this tiny difference in the absence of a prior trend line which shows a rather steady decline of up to 12 percent in the preceding two years. Here, perhaps because of the AB3121 provisions' increasing the adultlike handling of delinquent cases, one might assume the cessation of an earlier trend. However, a closer look at the trend reveals that it had in fact bottomed out in the second half of 1975. Thus enactment of the legislation cannot, on the basis of these data above, be credited with any increase or decrease in delinquency referrals.

Data from another source also illustrate the point that new legislation reflects what has already been initiated in practice on a national level and therefore complicates assessments of impact. When the Office of Juvenile Justice and Delinquency Prevention of the Law Enforcement Assistance Administration (LEAA) sponsored a number of large status offender deinstitutionalization programs around the country in 1976, it funded a number of those programs in jurisdictions which had already gone so far toward total deinstitutionalization that the funded demonstrations could not, in fact, have produced evidence of change (Klein 1979).

Philosophic Resonance. Although the points about legislation as codification of trends related most directly to assessment, the notion of philosophic resonance relates to implementation through the medium of acceptance. The intent of a piece of legislation may be more or less in agreement with the underlying philosophy of those who are meant to carry out the legislation. To the extent that there is such agreement, there is philosophic resonance. For instance, the deinstitutionalization element of AB3121 is quite at odds with the juvenile justice philosophy of many of the people who must carry it out. On the other hand, the delinquency prosecution provision and the adult court remand procedures are very much in tune with the philosophic perspectives of the district attorney who is primarily responsible for implementing these provisions.

These examples allow one to predict receptiveness (or resistance) to the various provisions of the legislation and consequently any unintended consequences. For instance, the deinstitutionalization provision, being anathema to the police, led to predictions that police would find various ways to circumvent the intent of the provision. Our preliminary data analyses reveal a dramatic decrease in status offender arrests in the face of police inability to detain these offenders, a tendency to charge mixed offenders with delinquent or dependent behavior (both allowing detention), and the suggestion of a slight increase in temporary mental health detention of youngsters previously handled as status offenders.

On the other side, where philosophic resonance is high, as in provisions which facilitate remanding older, serious offenders to adult court, there is obvious occasion to predict an increase in remands. Both the police, who carry out the relevant investigations, and the district attorney's staff, whose prosecution on behalf of the police is facilitated by AB3121, are strongly in favor of the remand provisions. In Los Angeles County, where we have collected data, the result has been a very marked increase in placement of juveniles in adult court. In many other counties, no increases have occurred.

Thus the degree to which legislation reflects the practicing philosophies of the practitioners (philosophic resonance) bears directly on levels of implementation of the legislation. In the case of AB3121, where the resultant legislation was an amalgam of provisions more acceptable to the politicians than the practitioners, resistance and low levels of implementation have been more common than the framers of the legislation themselves might have predicted.

Control

The third major component of our framework is concerned with control. However this is interpreted—power, autonomy, self-determination, influence, accountability—it has to do with the accommodations between the major actors in the system to which the legislation refers. In our case, in the juvenile justice system, these actors include judges, prosecutors, defense lawyers, probation officers, police, community agency personnel, and the clients themselves. Three aspects of control can be specified.

Discretion. Under this heading we are concerned primarily with the clients or subjects of the system, the juvenile offenders (or suspects). Agency staffs, police officers, probation officers, prosecutors, and judges have enormous amounts of discretion available in deciding on actions to be taken in each juvenile case. The legislative and judicial trends of the 1960s and 1970s have served more to decrease than to increase this discretion, but it remains very considerable. Analysis of shifts in discretion implicit or explicit in new legislation will inform the analyst of likely reception and impact.

Some provisions of AB3121 increased the discretion available to those affected, and others decreased the decision-making power of those affected. Clearly, the deinstitutionalization component of the law vastly decreased the discretionary power of police, probation, and courts over status offenders. In our framework, this would predict resistance to the legislation. On the other end of this dimension, again, are the delinquency prosecution and the remand provisions which gave to the district attorney far more discretionary power than was previously available. Naturally, this would predict prosecutorial pleasure with the legislation and therefore success in implementation. The alternative disposition and service provisions neither increased nor decreased discretion over clients available to the probation officer; the suggested alternatives were available before AB3121, and the new law merely encouraged the increased use of them.

The next two aspects of control relate to one additional facet in the justice system that is almost unique; the justice system is an adversarial system and the actors come to think of themselves as opponents. Far more than is the case in the educational, social welfare, or health systems, the conflicting values of actors in the justice system breed sometimes mild and sometimes serious conflicts. Offensive and defensive postures are common: it's the police *against* probation, prosecution *against* defense, private counselors *against* police, and so on.

The level of antagonism varies widely from location to location and from time to time, but it does exist and will be impacted by major new pieces of legislation. Legislation allots discretionary power, assigns monitoring functions, and distributes resources. To do so, and to effect changes in these, is to shift and fix relative levels of control. Understanding the control mandates and implications of the legislation improves one's chances of predicting its acceptance and assessing its likely impact.

Interorganizational Power. One of the dimensions along which legislation can vary is the degree to which it apportions power among the actors and their organizations. Four illustrations of the reapportioning of power can be offered.

1. Under AB3121, the transfer of the prosecutorial function from the Probation Department to the District Attorney's Office was, in essence a transfer of power. The district attorney now sets the rules by which law enforcement and the Probation Department will operate with respect to the court handling of delinquent cases. No other element of AB3121 carried with it the interorganizational power implications that this provision does.

2. The procedure in adult court remands calls for the district attorney to determine who will and will not have fitness hearings, but this is counter-balanced to some extent by the fact that the court can nevertheless declare juveniles fit for juvenile court at the fitness hearing; further, the probation officer has a strong voice in the judge's determination of fitness.

3. The deinstitutionalization provision decreased the probation officer's interorganizational power and did not give it to anyone else.

4. The development of social service facilities for handling juveniles pre and postadjudication would, other things being equal, constitute an opportunity for the exercise of interorganizational power. The other organizations involved, however, were service agencies on the periphery of the system, thus decreasing somewhat the amount of power involved.

Although there are many ways in which these shifts of power might affect the reception and impact of the new bill, we are becoming particularly interested in one which we hope to investigate. This is the matter of "corrective legislation," such as AB958, which reinstituted temporary detention of status offenders, and AB90, which included appropriations for past expenses incurred under AB3121. It seems reasonable to expect that the type and degree of effort, including lobbying, to enact corrective legislation will depend in part on who lost significant levels of control in the initial bill.[3]

Diffusion of Control. One question to be asked is whether control is lodged centrally or in a diffused setting. For example, control lodged in the court is quite diffused. The criminal court system in a large jurisdiction includes many judges, and each judge functions independently for the most part—court decision making is centralized in each individual judge. To a greater extent, control is centralized in the District Attorney's Office in a large jurisdiction because each deputy district attorney is accountable to the same elected official even though each must, in the practice of his job, exercise considerable autonomy. The level of centralization or diffusion provides useful clues to the degree to which provisions of legislation will be uniformly implemented. In observing changes in Los Angeles County following AB3121, we noticed a highly coordinated exercise of new controls by the prosecution (the Office of the District Attorney). At the same time, the diffused nature of the juvenile court yielded no such coordination; indeed, we were hard put to it to discover any consistent pattern of change in the court.

To summarize this section, then, we have suggested a way to facilitate predictions of the acceptance of new legislation and its consequent impact on the system to which it refers. Presumably, acceptance and system impact, in turn, will have demonstrable effects on the system's clients in ways that may also be predicted and assessed. Our suggestion takes the form of a general framework with three major components, and we have attempted to illustrate each of these by reference to recent changes in juvenile justice legislation in California.

The first component we have referred to as *signals*, the implicit and explicit messages to the practitioners about what they must do, can do, are encouraged to do or not do. We have suggested that these legislative signals can be quite clear or quite ambiguous, that they speak to the degree of mandated action on the part of the system's practitioners, and that in particular the fiscal signals may become paramount in predicting reactions to the legislation.

The second component we called *reflections*. Under this heading, we noted two issues. First there is the question of the degree to which the new legislation mirrors and codifies practices already extant. Second is the question of the degree to which individual provisions of the bill are philosophically resonant with the practitioners who are expected to carry out these provisions. These factors, too, predict legislative impact.

The third component we labeled *control*. Concerns listed under this heading were, (1) the discretion given or removed over decisions about the system's clients, (2) the distribution of power among the organizations in the affected system, and (3) diffusion of control within the system component in which it is lodged.

Now, even though we have provided illustrations of these three components with their eight subparts, the question still remains as to how usefully this framework can be applied to a given piece of legislation. We cannot provide an independent test; that must be left to the future or to other investigators. And because our work on the assessment of changes following AB3121 is only at the halfway point, we are short of data with which to apply the framework back to the experience from which it was induced. Nor, of course, could such a reapplication constitute a fair independent test. Nonetheless for purposes of illustration only, we will attempt such a reapplication in the final section of this chapter.

AB3121: Predicting Its Reception and Assessing Its Impact

The framework consists of eight subparts arranged under three major headings. These are:

Signals
Clarity
Legislative mandate
Fiscal implications

Reflections
Codification of trends
Philosophic resonance

Control
Discretion
Interorganizational power
Diffusion of control

We will use the framework to review the situation of four major provisions of AB3121. These four provisions are used because, of over twenty provisions in the bill, these have stood out as the major ones in the minds of most practitioners while most of the others have receded in importance and visibility.

Secure Detention of Status Offenders

AB3121 provided that no status offender could be placed in secure detention. Not surprisingly, this provision came into very clear focus. However, the meaning of "secure" detention was not delineated in the bill with the result that ambiguity and flexibility in both interpretation and practice results.

Nonetheless, the level of the mandate was clear; nonsecure forms of detention were still permitted, but there could be no secure detention. The fiscal implications were not spelled out, nor any funds provided. Of course, funds may be needed to avoid some actions, but if alternative action is implied, then this alternative could be costly. No funds were provided for nonsecure placement as an alternative to secure detention.

In summary, the signals were relatively clear but occasionally contradictory. Secure detention could not be employed, the use of nonsecure alternatives was implied, but no fiscal support for the latter was provided. One might already predict some practitioner resistance. Looking next at the reflections component of the framework, we find it likely (data are not immediately available) that the deinstitutionalization provision did indeed codify a trend already under way. California reports mirror those from other states over the past few years, that fewer status offenders are being securely institutionalized. California data available from the state's Bureau of Criminal Statistics reveal a steady decrease in status offender arrests, in referrals to probation, and in petitions filed. There is every reason to expect detention rates to evidence the same trend.

Although this codification of an existing trend would lead one to predict ready acceptance of the provision, the issue of philosophic resonance would not. The intent of the provision is at odds with the working philosophy of many practitioners. The police in particular tend to see detention as a deterrent and as a means of facilitating their investigative functions. Many treaters as well, both public and private, see secure detention both as a necessary precurser to the provision of treatment and even as a form of treatment (Lerman 1975). From these two quarters alone—police and treaters—one would predict considerable resistance.

With respect to control issues, the secure detention provision clearly was likely to result in negative responses. By removing police and probation discretion over one significant aspect of client activity, the provision gave more control over their own lives to the clients. Status offenders could simply walk away from police stations and even from the court; they could run away from nonsecure placement without fear of secure placement sanctions; they could, in effect, flaunt their own power and control, and obviously not to the liking of practitioners who were used to having more control. Under these circumstances, practitioner resistance is predictable.

Development of Alternative Resources

With the foregoing example as an extended illustration, we can move more rapidly through the remaining example. A second major provision of AB3121 authorized and encouraged probation to develop alternative resources for offender services. As a treatment provision, this resulted in a reasonably clear focus but was authorized rather than mandated and was accompanied by no financial support.

It did constitute a codification of ongoing trends (that is, diversion trends), although such codification was already in existence. Philosophic resonance was generally high.

With respect to control, some centralization through the probation officer was achieved, along with the assignment of a little more power to the Probation Department relative to private agencies. No change in discretion was attendant to this provision since these disposition options were already present. In fact, additional rights assigned to the clients (through agreement on conditions of probation) would tend to decrease overall discretionary control over clients.

The general expectation from this brief review could be that probation departments would be pleased with the alternative resources provision and attempt to implement them within constraints resulting from the absence of monetary support and the provision of countervailing client rights. The net effect, then, would be negligible.

The Remand Provision

For a specified set of serious offenses (homicide, arson, armed robbery) AB3121 made it easier to give jurisdiction over sixteen and seventeen year olds to the adult criminal court. This provision, given the current public concern with violent offenders, emerged with great clarity very quickly. The remand process was authorized, rather than mandated, however, and again no financial support was provided.

So far as we can determine with presently available data, there was no statewide trend in the direction of increased use of adult remands. The provision represents an increase in discretion and some interorganizational power opportunities. The idea of the provision is clearly philosophically resonant with the distrct attorney's perspective, but less certainly so at the court level.

Because the initial decision is given to the prosecutor, diffusion of control was reduced, interorganizational power was increased, and discretion over the client's options was also increased. But because later decisions are lodged with the court, this control increase was limited by a later control diffusion and by the interorganizational power of the court. From all of this we would anticipate considerable potential impact on the juvenile justice system. However, because it is not unequivocally mandated, there is room for a good deal of variation in the level of implementation depending on the enthusiasm of the district attorney for the provision and on the district attorney's prior relationship with the court and the Probation Department.

The District Attorney in Juvenile Court

In concert with the national trend toward a more adultlike, adversarial approach to the juvenile court, AB3121 prvided that the district attorney must appear in all delinquency hearings and that he must decide whether or not the juvenile goes to court. In prior years, this was not necessary, and the interest of "the people" were only inconsistently represented by the judge, the probation officer, the police, or the occasional appearance of the district attorney.

The clarity of this provision's focus was relatively high, especially because it proposed a change that had long been discussed. Now it was mandated, although once again no financial support was provided.

This provision did codify an ongoing trend, and philosophical resonance was high; in fact a large county's district attorney worked hard to get this provision into the bill.

Centralization of control was increased by virtue of the centralization normally associated with the District Attorney's Office. The district attorney's interorganizational power was increased, primarily at the expense of the probation officer, and the former's discretion was also increased as it became his view of the evidence which would determine progress of a case.

Generally, then, we would predict rather high compliance with this provision. The framework spells out a series of contingencies, most of which end up on the positive (implementation) side in this instance. In fact, of the four provisions reviewed here, this is the only one for which the framework would predict high compliance along with low resistance.

Conclusion

We have presented a framework for the prediction of reactions to new juvenile legislation. The framework arose from a particular experience, but one which is being repeated in variations across the nation. Rather than conclude this presentation with yet another repetition of the framework, we offer instead a few very preliminary findings from our assessment of reactions to AB3121, findings which reflect directly on the four provisions of the bill which were used to illustrate the framework.

The deinstitutionalization provision, judging from the framework, should have run into a good deal of resistance. It did. While the mandate made secure detention and placement all but impossible, variations were high because no practical definition of secure detention was provided. Thus some police felt they could not transport a youngster to the station, or hold him pending the parents' arrival. Some probation departments altered their juvenile halls; one took the locks off the doors of one wing but kept the surrounding fence locked; another turned a wing of the hall into a veritable open-door crash pad for runaways. Other trends include the following:

1. A decrease of up to 50 percent in status offense arrests
2. Relabeling of status offenders as delinquents or dependent/neglected in order to achieve secure detention
3. Relabeling of status offenders as requiring mental health commitments
4. Organizing political and community support for corrective legislation to reinstitute temporary detention for status offenders (successful, with the passage of AG958)
5. Organizing political support for the provision of state funds to the costs of alternative, nonsecure placements (successful, with the passage of AB90), as well as for the costs of other AB3121 provisions

The alternative resources provision has not led to high levels of activation. Los Angeles County had already set up its system prior to enactment of the bill and is thus mistakenly seen by some as a success story. We have encountered few examples of the bill's intent being realized; perhaps the funds made available through AB90 will correct this situation.

With respect to remands of sixteen- and seventeen-year-old serious offenders, reaction was highly varied. Two counties showed dramatic upturns in adult-court remands, although most counties remained at pre-AB3121 levels, and many are too small to make assessments of reaction.

Finally, the provision which places the district attorney in delinquency hearings has, of all four, been the most readily implemented provision, as far as our current information suggests. In Los Angeles County, this change was already well under way (Los Angeles contributes up to 40 percent of all cases in the state). In other counties, only the question of costs has provided any significant difficulty in the implementation of this provision.

On the basis of our very preliminary data and observations we would hazard the guess that of the eight framework subparts, the three of legislative mandate, fiscal implications, and philosophic resonance will prove to be the most predictive of levels of implementation. The other five are of equal interest to the understanding of legislative enactment and compliance but may have less value for prediction. We would expect, however, that future applications of the framework in other settings will provide modifications both of the framework and of our suggestions for its predictive utility.

Notes

1. Examples include the 1976 legislation in California and the 1977 legislation in Washington.

2. Secure detention refers here to both temporary detention and long-term institutionalization.

3. One might entertain the possibility, therefore, that there is no such thing as an "initial bill": each is part of discernible trends and each, to some extent is corrective of its predecessors.

References

Erickson, Maynard, L. (1979). "Some empirical questions concerning the current revolution in juvenile justice." In LaMar T. Empey (ed.), *The Future of Childhood and Juvenile Justice*. Charlottesville: University of Virginia Press.

Klein, Malcolm W. (1971). *Street Gangs and Street Workers*. Englewood Cliffs, N.J.: Prentice-Hall.

———— 1979. "Deinstitutionalization and Diversion of Juvenile offenders: a litany of impediments." In Norval Morris and Michael Tonry (ed.), *Crime and Justice, 1978*. Chicago: University of Chicago Press.

Kobrin, Solomon, and Klein, Malcolm W. (1979). Final Report: National Evaluation of the Program for the Deinstitutionalization of Status Offenders. Los Angeles: Social Science Research Institute, University of Southern California, unpublished.

Lerman, Paul (1975). *Community Treatment and Social Control: A Critical Analysis of Juvenile Correctional Policy*. Chicago: University of Chicago Press.

President's Commission on Law Enforcement and Administration of Justice (1967). *The Challenge of Crime in a Free Society*. Washington, D.C.: U.S. Government Printing Office.

Rojek, Dean G. (1978). Evaluation of Status Offender Project, Pima County, Arizona: Quarterly Progress Report. Tucson: University of Arizona, unpublished.

Sarri, Rosemary C., and Vinter, Robert D. (1976). "Justice for whom? Varieties of juvenile correctional approaches." In Malcolm W. Klein (ed.), *The Juvenile Justice System*, pp. 161-200. Beverly Hills: Sage.

Thomas, Charles W. (1976). "Are status offenders really so different?" *Crime and Delinquency* 22:438-455.

White, Joseph L. (1976). "Status offenders: Which side of the road?" *Criminal Justice Review* 1:23-43.

Wolfgang, Marvin E., Figlio, Robert M., and Sellin, Thorsten (1972). *Delinquency in a Birth Cohort*. Chicago: University of Chicago Press.

Delinquency in Nonmetropolitan Areas

Christine Alder,
Gordon Bazemore, and
Kenneth Polk

Introduction: The Small Community in Metropolitan Society

In a nation that is overwhelmingly metropolitan both in population and outlook, it can be difficult to draw attention to issues involving nonmetropolitan areas. It is certainly no easy task to obtain an accurate and detailed analysis of problems found in such contexts. A review of criminology and delinquency literature over the past decade serves to illustrate this point. Although crime rates are higher in metropolitan areas, still well over two million crimes were reported by the police of rural areas and small cities in 1975 (Uniform Crime Reports 1975:154). Yet few writers have addressed the problem of crime and delinquency in nonmetropolitan areas.

This paper will deal with delinquency in the rural areas and smaller cities of the United States. In so doing, it covers a wide range of people and communities. In 1970 a total of 63 million persons resided in non-metropolitan areas, this being just under one-third (31 percent) of the total population (U.S. Department of Commerce, Bureau of the Census 1975:3). These individuals are spread over a number of different kinds of communities and regions. There are the rural farm areas, although these vary from widely scattered wheat farms to the quite different and more compact array found among citrus and avocado groves. There are the small towns organized around such extractive activity as fishing, mining, or logging (each with distinctive cultural and social elements). There are the small cities that serve as business, communication, transport, and in many instances, governmental centers, in the outlying counties and states of the country.

The problems faced by young persons throughout these nonmetropolitan communities will be in some part similar to those problems faced by all youths. Since the early 1960s, for example, jobs for young people have been vanishing both in and out of cities. Yet, the form that these problems take, and especially the solutions that might be considered, are affected dramatically by the particular setting.

The Nonmetropolitan Setting

An analysis of the problems of nonmetropolitan youth requires some understanding of the economic backdrop. There is a general pattern of slight economic disadvantage among nonmetropolitan populations. One of the more notable indicators is income, and in this arena we obtain sharp differences. The 1973 median family income for persons residing in nonmetropolitan areas in 1974 was $10,327, a figure somewhat lower than the median $11,343 reported for residents of central cities, and well below the $14,007 reported for persons residing in the suburban rings (U.S. Department of Commerce, Bureau of the Census 1975:15).

Closely related is the finding that poverty is somewhat more common in nonmetropolitan, in contrast to urban areas. While nonmetropolitan areas comprised less than 30 percent of the total population in 1973, in that same year 40.1 percent of all persons falling below the poverty line were residents of such areas (U.S. Department of Commerce, Bureau of the Census 1975:16).

Putting it another way, although in 1973 the average proportion of individuals for the nation as a whole below the poverty line was 13.7 percent, for nonmetropolitan areas, close to one individual in every five (19.1 percent) fell below this line (U.S. Department of Commerce, Bureau of the Census 1975:16).

One factor which has had a dramatic effect on the economic structure of rural areas has been the tremendous increase in productivity of such areas, without a corresponding increase in demand, which would call for a simultaneous increase in employment. As one economist observes:

> Gross factor productivity, i.e., output in ratio to all inputs, has risen sharply and continuously since 1920. Even more spectacularly, the charted indexes of total labor input and of output per man-hour have diverged at almost right angles since 1940. If agricultural output had faced an indefinitely expansible market, total productivity could have been more greatly increased and thereby enabled the retention of a greater proportion of the earlier farm labor force. [Fuller 1970:20]

One consequence of this structural change has been the low rate of growth in employment in the more rural areas, a rate far below the U.S. average. The nonmetropolitan area as a whole also had a low rate of growth in employment; over 84.1 percent of the employment growth in the 1960s occurred in the metropolitan areas. Employment growth in metropolitan areas (22.7 percent) was almost twice that of nonmetropolitan counties (Hines et al. 1975).

It is well known that the problem of youth unemployment has increased in magnitude in both metropolitan and nonmetropolitan settings since the

1960s. The Organization for Economic Cooperation and Development (OECD) at its recent conference on youth unemployment, recognizing the urgency of this issue, concluded that youth unemployment is the result of a combination of slower rates of economic growth, demographic trends, and structural factors affecting the demand for and supply of labor. With this in mind and given the economic situation in nonmetropolitan areas outlined above, it would seem that the youth in these areas are faced with a chronic problem of unemployment.

Education is another arena in which sharp differences obtain between nonmetropolitan and metropolitan populations. In 1974, in the nation as a whole, 53.9 percent of nonmetropolitan individuals over age twenty-five had completed a high school education, contrasted with 59.8 percent in central cities and 68.5 percent in the suburban rings. Within this nonmetropolitan group, more exacting breakdowns stretch out the differentials. In counties with no place larger than 2,500, only 42.5 percent of the adults have completed high school, compared with 52.8 percent in counties with a place between 2,500 to 24,999 and 62.0 percent in those designated nonmetropolitan that have a place of 25,000 or more (U.S. Department of Commerce, Bureau of the Census 1975:54).

It should be noted, as Irwin Sanders (1977:103) observes, that even these figures are a bit deceptive, since currently at age sixteen or seventeen, just as high a proportion of rural young persons are enrolled in school as is the case for urban youth of the same age, so that the dropoff occurs rapidly after that period, resulting in significantly lower proportions enrolled in higher education.

This is consistent with a great number of studies that have shown significantly lower levels of educational aspiration among rural and farm adolescents (Nelson 1973; Mueller 1974; Schwarzweller 1976; Slocum 1967; Haller and Sewell 1967; Bender, Hobbs, and Golden 1967).

Data drawn from the Marion County Youth Study, an ongoing longitudinal investigation of youth in a medium-sized county in the Pacific northwest, provides further confirmation of the educational disadvantage of rural youth.[1] The findings indicate that there is a persistent pattern of lower educational commitment and attainment among the rural population than the urban (small-city) population.[2] The rural population was more likely to have low grades (33 percent having grade point averages below 2.00), in contrast to the urban group (14 percent). Furthermore, not only was the rural group the least likely to plan on going to college while in high school (44 percent expected to go contrasted with 76 percent of the urban population), they were over the years the least likely to have completed a four-year college degree (21 percent compared with 43 percent of the urban group).

The educational disadvantage, poverty, and unemployment confronting youth are crucial factors for an understanding of delinquency in nonmetropolitan areas. Before theoretically linking these structural aspects of the nonmetropolitan setting to delinquency, an overview of the nature and extent of the problem of delinquency in these areas is required.

Delinquency and Crime in Nonmetropolitan
Areas: A Description

Delinquency and crime are not evenly distributed throughout the United States. Rural areas typically report a lower incident of both juvenile and adult deviance. Figures on delinquency released by the U.S. Children's Bureau, for example, show that in 1974 the rate of delinquency (per 1,000 child population) was 26.6 percent in rural areas, compared with 41.9 percent in semiurban and 38.1 percent in urban areas (Juvenile Court Statistics 1974:14). Analysis of rates for adult criminality yield similar results. Highest rates are obtained in cities of over 50,000 population, with lower rates in cities under 50,000, and the lowest rates in rural areas.

Even though the rates of deviance are lower in nonmetropolitan areas, they still reflect the presence of a problem of public concern. In 1976 over two million offenses were known to the police agencies in rural and small-city communities. In rural areas over one million persons under the age of eighteen years were arrested by police in 1976 (Uniform Crime Reports 1976). The lower rates, in other words, should not blind us to the fact that large numbers of individuals do engage in delinquent activities outside megalopolis.

There is also some evidence that there has been a recent increase in criminality in smaller communities. Between the years 1971 and 1976 the average yearly increase in offenses known to police was greatest in rural areas and cities under 10,000. The lowest yearly mean increase was in the largest cities (table 3-1).[3]

Available statistics suggest that the extent of the problem of criminality in nonmetropolitan areas is paralleled by the problem of delinquency. Although commitment rates may be a measure of official response, a possible indication of the extent of delinquency in small communities is provided by figures recently collected by the Governor's Task Force on Juvenile Corrections in Oregon. These findings show that, for the last ten years, urban communities have maintained a lower commitment rate to state institutions (per 100 risk population) and a lower proportion of state commitments (compared to resident risk population) than have the other nonurban counties.

Rates of delinquency released by the U.S. Children's Bureau indicate that there is a closing gap between the rates in rural areas and those in urban

Table 3-1

Mean Yearly Increase in Offenses Known to Police, 1971-1976, by Community Size

Size of Community	Mean Yearly Increase (Percent)
Over 1,000,000	1.3
500,000 to 1,000,000	3.0
250,000 to 500,000	3.7
100,000 to 250,000	4.1
50,000 to 100,000	5.6
25,000 to 50,000	6.9
10,000 to 25,000	8.3
Under 10,000	8.9
Rural areas	8.3

Source: Uniform Crime Reports from 1971 to 1976.

areas. In 1963 the rate in rural areas was 10.3 percent compared to 31.8 percent in urban areas (Juvenile Court Statistics 1963:11). By 1976, the rate in rural areas had more than doubled to 26.6 percent, while the rate in urban areas had risen to 38.1 percent. While more data is necessary to clarify the differences in the extent and rate of delinquency in urban and nonmetropolitan areas, these summary statistics suggest that the problem of delinquency in nonmetropolitan areas is perhaps increasing disproportionately to the problem in urban areas and warrants further investigation.

Since the mid-1960s there has been a scarcity of research dealing with the problems of rural youth and their delinquency. Earlier studies of delinquency have suggested that rural youth in general commit offenses of a less serious nature than their urban counterparts. In his study of youth in a state institution in Wisconsin, Lentz (1956) reports that rural boys more often than urban boys were institutionalized for offenses such as nominal burglary and general misconduct, but less often for the more serious offenses such as auto theft and serious burglary. There were no substantial differences between the groups in their commission of sex offenses, theft, and truancy.

Similar findings emerge from the self-report study of public school youth in Illinois conducted by Clark and Wenninger (1962). In comparing youth from different kinds of community environments, they found that rural youth differ very little from urban youth in the extent to which they confess to minor theft, the telling of lies, loitering, beating up other youngsters without specific reason, the use of narcotics (rare in all groups), and arson (also rare). In contrast, rural farm youth engage less, according to Clark and Wenninger, in such activities as major theft, consumption of alcohol, taking money on the pretence that it would be repaid, and skipping school.

More recent statistics support these earlier findings that rural youth seem to be involved in less serious offenses than their urban counterparts, although the differences are not large. In 1976 a higher percentage of rural than urban adolescent arrests were for minor misconduct offenses (table 3-2).

Not only are their acts less serious, but, as we might expect, one uniform finding of the earlier studies was that delinquent youth from nonmetropolitan areas were much less sophisticated in their delinquencies than were the urban boys. Clinard (1944), for example, found that rural offenders do not exhibit the characteristics of a definite criminal social type as defined by (1) an early start in criminal behavior, (2) progressive knowledge of criminal techniques and crime in general, (3) resort to crime as the sole means of livelihood, and (4) a self-concept of being criminal. Partial support for these findings is contained in the work of Lentz (1956) who reports that rural offenders were less likely to be repeat offenders and that they displayed much less knowledge of criminal practices in the commission of their offenses.

Among rural youth, the existence of a distinct criminal or delinquent subculture was reported only rarely. In his early study of rural criminal offenders, Clinard (1942) noted a comparative absence of gangs in the life histories of his subjects; even where companions were noted, usually only two or three persons rather than a gang were involved. Lentz reported that

Table 3-2
Percentage of Arrests of Persons under Eighteen Years by Type of Crime and Community Area, 1976

Variable	City (N = 1,455,734)	Rural (N = 100,324)
Index crimes[a]	38	32
Minor misconduct[b]	42	50
Other[c]	20	18

Source: *Uniform Crime Reports*, 1976 (Washington, D.C.: U.S. Government Printing Office), tables 36 and 48.

[a]Index crimes are criminal homicide, forcible rape, robbery, aggravated assault, burglary, larceny, and motor vehicle theft.

[b]Minor misconduct offenses are liquor laws, drunkenness, disorderly conduct, vagrancy, all other except traffic, suspicion (not included in totals), curfew and loitering law violations, and runaways.

[c]Other offenses are other assaults, arson, forgery and counterfeiting, fraud, embezzlement, buying, receiving, possessing stolen property, vandalism, carrying, possessing weapons, prostitution and commercialized vice, sex offenses (except forcible rape and prostitution), narcotic drug laws, gambling, offenses against family and children, and driving under the influence.

52 percent of the rural boys compared with only 1.6 percent of urban boys in Wisconsin were lone offenders. Further, 22 percent of rural boys compared with 87 percent of urban boys were members of gangs known to be composed of delinquent boys.

More recent studies provide evidence that nonmetropolitan delinquent youth are more likely than nondelinquents to be involved in peer-originated activities with other adolescents and to more readily accept peer over adult pressures (Polk and Halferty 1966; Galvin 1975). From the Marion County Youth Study, Polk concludes:

> The most deviant categories (of adolescents) are much more peer-oriented than the least deviant ones, and the major difference holds through time. Compared to the least deviant and nondeviant types, approximately twice as many of the most deviant spend substantial amounts of time with friends, enjoy "cruising around to see what is going on," have "friends who could get in trouble with police," and perceive themselves as troublemakers. [1974:6]

Although such findings do not support the existence of gangs as described in studies of urban delinquency, they do suggest the involvement of rural delinquents in a protective subculture or youth collectivity.

There appear to be then some differences in the character of the misbehavior of rural and urban youth. Similarities, however, in the incidence and pattern of change in nonmetropolitan and urban crime have recently been noted. Polk (1974) comments on the "remarkable similarities" between the findings of the Marion County Youth Study, a study of delinquency in rural areas and small cities, and those of a study of deviance among Philadelphia high school boys. Contrary to earlier studies that suggested differences in the incidence of delinquency, Polk concludes that nonmetropolitan youths have just about as many official contacts with the law. In the Oregon study, 25 percent of the juveniles had some record of delinquency as did 29 percent of the white youths in the Philadelphia sample. Looking at the amount of repeated delinquencies, Polk found that almost half of the Oregon teenage offenders (45 percent) and only slightly more than half of those in Philadelphia (54 percent) had committed offenses that entangled them with the law more than once (Polk 1974:1-2).

Similarities have also been found in the patterns of female crime in rural and urban areas. Recent studies of the changing patterns of female crime have indicated that over the period of the 1960s to the mid-1970s the rate of increase in arrests was higher for women than for men and that this difference is accounted for by an increase in the rate of property crime for women (Simon 1975; Noblit and Burcart 1976). In their examination of trends in female crime in the rural United States since 1962, Steffensmeier and Jordan conclude that the "trends in patterns of rural female crime parallel those of urban women, except that female levels of larceny theft are rising faster among urban women" (1978:87).

This pattern of change may be somewhat different for adolescents. Noblit and Burcart (1976) found that, in contrast to adult women, increases in violent and property arrests among adolescent women have been about the same. Attention has not yet been directed to exploring whether this pattern is equally true for rural as urban female adolescents. However, a summary glance at the 1976 Uniform Crime Reports suggests that the increase in arrests for violent crime was higher for rural than urban adolescent females. In rural areas the percentage change from 1975 to 1976 was $+0.4$ while in city areas this figure was -10.0 (Uniform Crime Reports 1976, table 40).[4]

Speculation about the possible causes of change in the nature and frequency of female crime and delinquency has centered around such factors as the changing nature of peer involvement (Giordano 1978), changing sex roles (Adler 1975), expanding opportunities to commit property crime (Simon 1975) and changes in the official reaction to female deviance (Smart 1976; Levanthal 1977). According to Steffensmeier (1978:88), recent research has generally shown comparable changes in behavior and attitudes between rural and urban women during the 1970s. Rural-urban differences exist throughout this period with respect to female unemployment and educational attainment, but differential change itself is not observed. Such a situation suggests that the possible explanations for changes in female crime and delinquency noted above are probably as applicable to rural females as they are to urban females.

Accounting for Rural Delinquency

What are the factors that appear to help account for the patterns of delinquency that exist in rural areas? At the onset, there appears to be one important difference between metropolitan and nonmetropolitan delinquency. The general weight of theoretical thinking about urban delinquency has stressed, overwhelmingly, the role of social class (Cohen 1955; Miller 1958; Cloward and Ohlin 1960). Over the years, evidence has been building in nonmetropolitan contexts which suggests that such delinquency is much less likely to be a function of class position. Uniformly, self-report studies in rural areas show little difference in delinquency by social class (Short and Nye 1957; Dentler and Monroe 1961; Clark and Wenninger 1962). Even the official data, however, are distinctive in that what is suggested is that small or minimal differences exist between lower- and middle-class young persons in terms of their levels of delinquency (Polk and Halferty 1966; Kelly and Balch 1971). In rural areas, at least, some alteration of extension of much of classical sociological thinking will be necessary if we are to account for the phenomenon of youthful misbehavior.

One such potentially useful line of inquiry focuses on the importance of the school. Persistently, the more recent analysts have found delinquency to be tied closely to low levels of performance and related processes of the school. In one of the first intensive studies of the impact of school behavior on deviance in a nonmetropolitan area, Stinchcombe (1964) argued that the experience of being channeled into the noncollege track of the high school contributes directly to the development of patterns of adolescent alienation and rebellion. In another analysis, Kelly and Balch (1971) found that those young persons integrated into the successful life of the school, regardless of social class position, were less likely to become delinquent. In supporting these findings, Polk (1975) has argued for the importance of the school in contemporary industrialized and industrializing (especially important in rural areas) society, where education comes to serve as the gatekeeper for adult occupational attainment.

Once the adolescent is a failure in school and is directed into a flow leading to a low status future, the compelling logic of the substance of education no longer resonates. For such youth the future begins to take on a different meaning since they see fairly clearly that for them there *is* little future. Pearl suggests that such youth "develop a basic pessimism because they have a fair fix on reality. They rely on fate because no rational transition by system is open to them. They react against schools because schools are characteristically hostile to them" (1965:89).

This hostility and rejection can take a number of forms. In their research, for example, Vinter and Scarri found that students who were seen as doing poorly in school were, as a consequence, denied

> a wide variety of privileges and opportunities within the school. They lost esteem among their classmates, they were seldom chosen for minor but prestigeful classroom or school assignments, and they were excluded from participation in certain extra-curricular activities. This process, in turn, often subjected such students to negative parental responses, representing a third penalty. [1965:9][5]

Polk and Halferty (1966) suggest that such a pattern of rejection of commitment to school success, once it accumulates, is accompanied by a concomitant involvement in a pattern of peer rebellion against adults. Pearl expresses the role such processes play in enabling youngsters to cope with the locking out process, arguing that when limited gratification exists in striving for the impossible, youth, as a consequences, "create styles, coping mechanisms, and groups in relation to the systems which they can and cannot negotiate. Group values and identifications emerge in relation to the forces opposing them" (1965:90).

The point of this discussion is that these youth are not passive receptors of the stigma that develops within the school setting. When locked out they respond by seeking an interactional setting where they can function comfortably. Consequently, these adolescents, according to Polk (1975) become involved in the antischool rebellious peer culture which then provides the social buffer important for delinquency, since school failure is connected with delinquency only when it is accompanied by such supports, for when these peer supports are absent the level of delinquency is about the same as for those who are doing well in school.

While the evidence from such studies can be woven together to suggest the significance of the school experience for rural delinquency, it can also be suggested that this pattern is generalizable to other settings as well. Certainly, considerable evidence exists to suggest that in metropolitan as well as in rural areas, there is a strong connection between how a person does in school and the level of delinquency. In the Philadelphia cohort study, for example, those with lower levels of achievement in school were considerably more likely to have accumulated a record for delinquency than is the case for those with higher levels of achievement (Wolfgang et al. 1972:63). Other investigators have also found important connections between a number of different school behaviors and delinquency (for example, Elliott and Voss 1974; Hirschi 1969; Rhodes and Reiss 1969). In fact, there is some data to suggest that this finding holds across some cultures as well. Hargreaves (1967), for one, in his study of a secondary school in England reports a close connection between the streaming system and behavior such as delinquency. And, central to the present argument, the work of Vaz (1967) in Canada, and Sugarman in England (1967) can be shown to indicate the important interconnection between doing poorly at school, the mediating influence of supportive peer culture influences, and then delinquent behavior (see Polk and Pink 1971; Polk 1971).

It is essential in reviewing these studies that the issue be seen not only in the limited context of education, but also in the connection between school and work. Schooling is important for youthful alienation in at least two ways, according to the view advanced by Pearl (1972). First, schools alienate particular groups of students (those defined as nonacademic) by denying them equal opportunities for decent employment (which is the consequence of being defined as noncollege material). Second, by separating the world of the school from the everyday world of work, politics, and culture, the young are rendered temporarily superfluous, without any way of significantly participating or contributing to the world around them. In both, employment is central. Others have observed one or another of these problems. For example, Greenberg (1978:69-70) notes:

> Among the structural sources of adolescent crime identified here, the exclusion of juveniles from the world of adult work plays a crucial role. It is this exclusion that simultaneously exaggerates teenagers' dependence on peers for approval and eliminates the possibility of their obtaining funds to support their intensive, leisure-time social activities. The disrespectful

treatment students receive in school depends on their low social status, which in turn reflects their lack of employment. In late adolescence and early adulthood, their fear that this lack of employment will persist into adulthood evokes anxiety over achievement of traditional male gender role expectations, especially among males in the lower levels of the working class, thus contributing to a high level of violence.

What is significant about these accounts is that they permit us to connect up the data on schools and the earlier evidence regarding the persistent emergent problem of youthful employment. A policy which addresses the patterns of poor school performance as these relate to delinquency in all probability must come to grips with the employment backdrop which gives meaning to such educational data. Putting it another way, what poor school performance is about, ultimately, is employment, and a responsible strategy will be one which simultaneously addresses both educational and employment issues.

Some Issues of Delinquency Prevention Policy in Nonmetropolitan Areas

The development of a coherent delinquency prevention policy requires both some understanding of the nature of the problem and then the resources available to approach that problem. What has been stressed up to this point has been the combination of factors that are involved in the educational and work experiences made available to youth. If the problem of delinquency is viewed as the other side of the coin from positive youth development, the impact of scarcity of employment and educational opportunities becomes clear. From a youth development perspective the primary focus of analysis shifts from questions of why individuals become deviant to issues of why people conform and how normal or nondeviant maturational processes occur. Although even the most enlightened delinquency control or diversion program can only help some youth avoid problems of labeling which may contribute to spoiled (or illegitimate) identities, strategies of youth development attempt to create opportunities for all youth (deviant and nondeviant) to develop positive identities.

In describing aspects of adult life that tend to foster commitment to conforming behavior, Polk and Kobrin (1972) have identified four major components of what may be called a legitimate identity. These components—competence, potency, belongingness, and usefulness—are derived in postindustrial societies primarily from our participation in conventional institutions. While our occupation of roles in such institutional arenas as politics, education, and the family may contribute substantially to the development of each of these aspects of legitimate identity, one's work role is probably the most essential basis of legitimacy and almost a necessary condition for access to other conventional roles. Without a job that at minimum provides some earning power, achieving a sense of control over those persons and institutions that appear to be controlling as (potency), acquiring a sense of performing some important service that others value (usefulness) and performing it well (competence), and developing a feeling of being part of some conventional enterprise (belongingness) become difficult tasks for most of us. It is exactly the salience of the work role to the development (and maintenance) of a legitimate identity that makes an assessment of the problem of the unavailability of such roles to most young people so essential to an understanding of the troublesome behavior of youth. The absence of a basis for at least a minimum commitment to conformity which a job might provide means that for many young people (especially those without the commitment that may come from the future status promise of doing well in school) there is little to lose by involvement in delinquent behavior.

The changing nature of the rural job market, the lower rate of nonmetropolitan educational attainment, the relative absence of educational alternatives, and the general scarcity of resources in nonmetropolitan areas may make these problems of developing legitimate identities especially difficult for nonmetropolitan young people in years to come. Policymakers attempting to deal with problems of delinquency in these regions must first address the issue of how positive institutional roles may be made available to rural youth, while remaining cognizant of the unique practical difficulties involved in implementing such youth development strategies outside urban settings.

Certainly, it is possible to make a powerful argument for the value of employment to young persons on the basis of some experiments which offer individuals with delinquent histories opportunities for employment (Pearl 1978; Pearl, Grant, and Wenk, 1978). Furthermore, a strong case can be made both that young persons are capable of performing useful tasks, and that when they do, they turn from social destructive behavior. At the same time, what this requires is an emphasis on the creation of jobs, especially jobs that offer decent and reasonable futures. It is not vocational skills and work habits training that deserves priority, but rather the creation of employment itself. Although this will ultimately require a fundamental realignment of educational and employment policy priorities, we can only add our voices to that of Arthur Pearl when he says:

> Unless we alter our social and economic policies to allow young people a variety of productive roles, youth unemployment will continue to grow. Accompanying that growth in youth unemployment is likely to be an increase in all forms of youth crime and misbehavior, as well as an increase in the resort to expensive official actions against youth. The monies we now

devote to the punishment, control, and rehabilitation of youth could be used to generate opportunities for youth to be employed in socially useful projects. We have only to decide which is the most desirable alternative. [1978:50]

Notes

1. Marion County Youth Study is supported by funds granted by the National Institute of Mental Health (Grant MHI 4806 "Maturational Reform and Rural Delinquency").

2. *Rural* here refers to those young men who resided in rural areas during high school and who remained in rural areas eight years later. *Urban* refers to small city youth who eight years later are also in urban environments.

3. Systematic bias and vulnerability of Uniform Crime Report arrest data to measurement error have been frequently acknowledged by criminologists (Wolfgang 1963; Kelly 1978). Based on police arrest records, these data are subject to the influence of such factors as inconsistencies and changes in police practices and record-keeping procedures, new laws (President's Commission 1967), number of police officers per capita (Wheeler 1967), and differential enforcement policies.

In spite of these limitations, Uniform Crime Report statistics remain the only continuous nationwide data available which provide the number of arrests in a given year along with the age, sex, and racial background of those arrested. For purposes of rural-urban comparisons, use of these statistics is less problematic because there is no strong a priori reason for suggesting that exogenous variables such as those mentioned above as influencing Uniform Crime Report statistics are nonrandomly distributed between rural and urban settings (Steffensmeier and Jordan 1978). Finally, confidence in Uniform Crime Report statistics is bolstered somewhat by recent studies that show at least a moderate correlation of these data with victimization survey data and indicate that measurement errors in the former apparently do not lead to false conclusions or to measurement specific inferences (Skogan 1974; National Crime Survey Report 1976).

4. Whenever referring to official statistics on female delinquency, account must be taken of the differential response of the juvenile justice system to adolescent males and females. This differential response has been explained as a consequence of the paternalistic nature of the juvenile justice system and its particular concern with controlling the sexual activity of female adolescents (Meda-Chesney Lind 1973, 1977; Conway and Bogden 1977). This situation may be particularly aggravated in rural areas (Adams 1961).

5. Copyright 1965, National Association of Social Workers, Inc. Reprinted with permission from *Social Work* 10, (January 1965):9.

References

Adams, William T. (1961). Delinquency among minorities in rural areas. Paper read at the American Society of Criminology Meeting, Denver, Colorado, December 19.

Adler, Freda (1975). *Sisters in Crime*. New York: McGraw-Hill.

Bender, Lloyd, Hobbs, Daryl, and Golden, James (1967). "Congruence between aspirations and capabilities of youth in a low-income rural area." *Rural Sociology* 32:278-289.

Chesney-Lind, Meda (1973). "Judicial Enforcement of the female sex role: the family court and the female delinquent." *Issues in Criminology* 8:51-70.

_____ (1977). "Judicial paternalism and the female status offender: training women to know their place." *Crime and Delinquency* 23:121-130.

Clark, John P., and Wenninger, Eugene P. (1962). "Socio-economic class and correlates of illegal behavior among juveniles." *American Sociological Review* 27:856-834.

Clinard, Marshall B. (1942). "The process of urbanization and criminal behavior." *American Journal of Sociology* 48:202-213.

_____ (1944). "Rural criminal offenders." *American Journal of Sociology* 50:38-50.

Cloward, Richard A., and Ohlin, Lloyd E. (1960) *Delinquency and Opportunity*. New York: Free Press.

Cohen, Albert K. (1955). *Delinquent Boys*. New York: Free Press.

Conway, Alan, and Bogden, Carol (1977). "Sexual delinquency: the persistence of the double standard." *Crime and Delinquency* 23:131-135.

Dentler, Robert A., and Monroe, Lawrence J. (1961). "Social correlates of early adolescent theft." *American Sociological Review* 26:733-743.

Elliott, Delbert S., and Voss, Harwin L. (1974). *Delinquency and Dropout*. Lexington, Mass.: D.C. Heath.

Fuller, Varden (1970). *Rural Worker Adjustment to Urban Life: An Assessment of the Research*. Ann Arbor: University of Michigan.

Galvin, James L. (1975). Youth culture and adult success. Ph.D. dissertation. University of Oregon, Department of Curriculum and Instruction.

Giordano, Peggy (1978). "Research note: girls, guys and gangs: the changing social context of female delinquency." *The Journal of Criminal Law and Crimninology* 69:126-132.

Governors's Task Force on Juvenile Corrections (1979). *Task Force Report*. Salem: Oregon Law Enforcement Council, Governor's Office (in press).

Greenberg, David F. (1978). "Delinquency and the age structure of society." In Arthur Pearl, Douglas Grant, and Ernst Wenk (eds.), *The Value of Youth*, pp. 69-70. Davis, Calif.: Responsible Action.

Haller, Archibald, and Sewell, William (1967). "Occupational choices of Wisconsin farm boys." *Rural Sociology* 32:37-55.

Hargreaves, David H. (1967). *Social Relations in a Secondary School*. London: Routledge and Kegan Paul.

Hines, Fred, Brown, David, and Zimme, John (1975). *Social and Economic Characteristics of the Population in Metro and Nonmetro Counties, 1970*. Agricultural Economic Report No. 272. Washington, D.C.: USDA Economic Research Service.

Hirschi, Travis (1969). *Causes of Delinquency*. Berkeley: University of California Press.

Juvenile Court Statistics (1974). Washington, D.C.: U.S. Children's Bureau, p. 14.

Kelly, Delos H. (1978). *Delinquent Behavior: Interactional and Motivational Aspects*. Belmont, Calif.: Dickenson Publishing Co.

Kelly, Delos H., and Balch, Robert W. (1971). "Social origins and school failure: a reexamination of Cohen's theory of working-class delinquency." *Pacific Sociological Review* 14:413-430.

Lentz, William P. (1956). "Rural-urban differentials and juvenile delinquency." *Journal of Criminology and Police Science* 47:331-339.

Levanthal, Gloria (1977). "Female criminality: Is women's lib' to blame?" *Psychological Reports* 41:1179-1182.

Marshall, Ray (1976). "Problems of rural youth." In *From School to Work: Improving the Transition*, pp. 227-253. Washington, D.C.: U.S. Government Printing Office.

Miller, Walter B. (1958). "Lower-class culture as a generating milieu of gang delinquency." *Journal of Social Issues* 14 (November):5-19.

Mueller, B. Jeanne (1974). "Rural family life style and sons' school achievement." *Rural Sociology* 39:362-372.

National Crime Survey Report (1976). *Criminal Victimization in the United States, 1973*. Washington, D.C.: U.S. Department of Justice, National Criminal Justice Information and Statistics Service.

Nelson, Joel (1973). "Participation and college aspiration: complex effects of community size." *Rural Sociology* 38:7-16.

Noblit, George, and Burcart, Jane (1976). "Women and crime: 1960-1970." *Social Science Quarterly* 56:650-657.

Pearl, Arthur (1965). "Youth in lower class settings." In Muzafer Sherif and Carolyn W. Sherif (eds.), *Problems of Youth*. Chicago: Aldine Publishing Co.

_____ (1972). *The Atrocity of Education*. St. Louis: New Critics Press.

_____ (1978). "Employment dilemmas of youth." In Arthur Pearl, Douglas Grant, and Ernst Wenk (eds.), *The Value of Youth*, p. 50. Davis, Calif.: Responsible Action.

Pearl, Arthur, Grant, Douglas, and Wenk, Ernst (eds.) (1978). *The Value of Youth*. Davis, Calif.: Responsible Action.

Pearl, Arthur, and Riessman, Frank (1965). *New Careers for the Poor*. New York: Free Press.

Polk, Kenneth (1971). "Middle-class delinquency." *Youth and Society* 2 (March):333-353.

_____ (1974). *Teenage Delinquency in Small Town America*. Research Report 5. Bethesda, Md.: National Institute of Mental Health, DHEW Publication No. (ADM) 75-138.

_____ (1975). "Schools and the delinquency experience." *Criminal Justice and Behavior* 2 (December):315-338.

Polk, Kenneth, and Halferty, David (1966). "Adolescence, commitment, and delinquency." *Journal of Research in Crime and Delinquency* 4 (July):82-96.

Polk, Kenneth, and Kobrin, Solomon (1972). *Delinquency Prevention through Youth Development*. DHEW Publication O.SRS 73-26013. Washington, D.C.: U.S. Department of Health, Education and Welfare, U.S. Government Printing Office.

Polk, Kenneth, and Pink, William (1971). "Youth culture and the school: a replication." *British Journal of Sociology* 22 (June):160-171.

_____ (1972). "School pressures toward deviance: a cross-cultural comparison." In Kenneth Polk and Walter E. Schafer (eds.), *School and Delinquency*, pp. 129-141. Englewood Cliffs, N.J.: Prentice-Hall.

President's Commission on Law Enforcement and Administrative Justice (1967). *Task Force Report: Crime and Its Impact*. Washington, D.C.: U.S. Government Printing Office.

Riessman, Frank, Gartner, Alan, and Kohler, Mary (1971). *Children Teach Children: Learning by Teaching*. New York: Harper and Row.

Rhodes, A. Lewis, and Reiss, Albert J., Jr. (1969). "Apathy, truancy and delinquency as adaptations to school failure." *Social Forces* 48 (September):12-22.

Sanders, Irwin T. (1977). *Rural Society*. Englewood Cliffs, N.J.: Prentice-Hall.

Schwarzweller, Harry K. (1976). "Scholastic performance, sex differentials and the structuring of educational ambition among rural youth in three societies." *Rural Sociology* 41:194-216.

Short, James F., Jr., and Nye, F. Ivan, (1957). "Reported behavior as a criterion of deviant behavior." *Social Problems* 5 (Winter):207-213.

Simon, Rita James (1975). *Women and Crime*. Lexington, Mass.: Lexington Books, D.C. Heath.

Skogan, Wesley (1974). "The validity of official crime statistics: an empirical investigation." *Social Science Quarterly* 55 (June):25-38.

Slocum, Walter (1967). "The influence of reference group values on educational aspirations of rural high school students." *Rural Sociology* 32:269-277.

Smart, Carol (1976). *Women, Crime and Criminology: A Feminist Perspective*. London: Routledge and Kegan Paul.

Steffensmeier, Darrell J., and Jordan, Charlene (1978). "Changing patterns of female crime in rural America, 1962-75." *Rural Sociology* 43:87-102.

Stinchcombe, Arthur (1964). *Rebellion in a High School*. Chicago: Quadrangle Books.

Sugarman, Barry (1967). Youth culture, academic achievement, and conformity in school." *British Journal of Sociology* 18 (June):151-164.

Uniform Crime Reports (1971-1976). U.S. Federal Bureau of Investigation, U.S. Government Printing Office.

U.S. Department of Commerce, Bureau of the Census (1975). Social and Economic Characteristics of the Metropolitan and Non-Metropolitan Population: 1974 and 1970, pp. 3, table A; 5, table E; 15, table P; 16, table R; 54, table 9.

Vaz, Edmund W. (1965). "Middle-class adolescents: self-reported delinquency and youth culture activities." *Canadian Review of Sociology and Anthropology* 2:52-70.

Vaz, Edmund W. (ed.) (1967). *Middle-Class Juvenile Delinquency*. New York: Harper and Row.

Vinter, Robert D., and Sarri, Rosemary C. (1965). "Malperformance in the public school: a group work approach." *Social Work* 10 (January):3-13.

Wheeler, Stanton (1967). "Criminal statistics: a reformulation of the problem." *Journal of Criminal Law, Criminology, and Police Science* 58:317-324.

Wolfgang, Marvin (1963). "Uniform crime reports: a critical appraisal." *University of Pennsylvania Law Review* 111:708-738.

Wolfgang, Figlio, and Sellin, Thorsten (1972). *Delinquency in a Birth Cohort*. Chicago: University of Chicago Press.

Female Delinquency

Rose Giallombardo

Introduction

The sociological data and theories relating to juvenile delinquency are voluminous, but a review of this literature reveals that almost all the theories that have been propounded about delinquent behavior are focused on males. Sociologists have persistently directed their attention to male delinquency and have overlooked the involvement of females in the study of delinquent behavior. The reason for this presumably lies in the fact that female delinquency is less frequent and serious than male delinquency, hence the delinquent female is criminologically less interesting. With rare exception, the existing literature on female delinquency is of doubtful significance. Conceptually and methodologically limited, these studies provide nothing more than pseudoscientific assumptions about the female's inherent biological and psychological dispositions to explain delinquent behavior. Indeed, because the field is virtually unexplored, there is a dearth of scientific data necessary to compare the behavior of female and male delinquents. Yet this is precisely what is required if we are to gain an understanding of female and male delinquency that goes beyond the so-called facts, namely, that the public is less willing to report female offenders, the police are less likely to arrest them, and the judicial process is more lenient to them. Presumably, these processes result in an arrest and admission ratio in which the volume of arrests and the volume of admissions to institutions is considerably greater for males than for females.

In recent years, the female delinquent has become the subject of increasing interest because changes in the traditional patterns of female delinquency can be seen both by the numbers of females arrested and institutionalized, and by the types of delinquency activity engaged in by females. Although this concern stems mainly from the statistics indicating a growing female participation in crime, to some extent it is influenced by the women's liberation movement. Popular explanations of the rise in female arrests, for example, maintain that increased female assertiveness is reflected in more aggressive, violent, and serious crimes.

The aim of this chapter is to review briefly the literature on the subject of female delinquency and the theoretical concepts that have been utilized to explain female delinquency; to present some recent statistical data on female involvement in criminal activity and to compare juvenile females and males regarding their relative contribution to total crimes committed; and, finally, to examine the relationship of sexism and the administration of justice.

Theories of Delinquency Causation

Biological and Psychological Factors

Although delinquency is a legal and not a physical status, there has been considerable research into the physical concomitants of female delinquency, the biological factors of bodily development, menstruation, and personality maladjustments. Unlike the studies of male delinquency, the female's delinquent behavior is rarely discussed and analyzed within a framework of social conditions. Even the recent studies of female delinquency typically view the female's delinquent behavior as the result of individual characteristics of a physiological or psychological nature. These studies are noteworthy for their fragmentary evidence and speculative knowledge of the personal and social factors in the development of females that presumably lead to delinquent behavior.

Social research into the organic bases of criminal and delinquent behavior was given its first important emphasis in the studies of Cesare Lombroso (1876, 1906, 1920), who first asserted the influence of body build on behavior. Lombroso began with the assumption of the biological nature of human behavior and emphasized the necessity to study individual offenders. Through his anatomical research of prisoners he concluded that the criminal was a unique physical type—the born criminal—characterized by asymmetries and anomalies reminiscent of lower mammalian species. Criminal men and women were an atavistic reversion to primitive humans, and hence were incapable of adjusting to civilized society. In his later work, however, he concluded that criminal behavior to some extent was influenced or modified by various environmental influences, and he added three other criminal types—the occasional, the passionate, and the insane. Lombroso believed that there are fewer females who are born criminals. The female offender is more likely to display the characteristics of the occasional offender, although she is more "diabolical" than the male offender.[1] Lombroso's methodology and theoretical generalizations of hereditary criminal transmission have been discredited. Yet his influence is important. By shifting the focus of emphasis from causal factors in the environment to causal factors in individuals, the basis was laid for our present precedure of diagnosis and treatment of individual delinquents that views delinquency in terms of individual abnormality or psychological maladjustment.

Some evidence has been presented that associates physical overdevelopment with delinquency, especially sex delinquency in females. Healy and

Bronner (1926) found that 70 percent of the delinquent girls from the Chicago sample exceeded their age norms in weight. Their findings, however, are not corroborated by Burt's study (1925) of delinquent girls. Burt found that only 5 percent of the girls, contrasted to 12 percent of the boys, deviated from physical norms for given ages. Moreover, the girls were overweight and the boys were underweight. Ten percent of the female sample exhibited "precocious" sex development. In the same study, Burt cites evidence for a relationship between the menstrual cycle and delinquent behavior in females. Of eighty-seven reported thefts, 34 percent occurred during the menstrual week. In a later study, Middleton (1933) pursues the same theme and cites cases of girls who engaged in compulsive theft of useless objects during the menstrual period. Such works are characterized by a simple biological determinist perspective, and ignore altogether the findings of biological and medical science. In spite of the fact that convincing empirical evidence to substantiate such hypotheses is lacking, biological explanations of female delinquency and criminality continue to be pressed into service (Pollack 1961; Dalton 1961; Gibbens and Price 1962).[2]

In his study, *The Unadjusted Girl*, William I. Thomas (1923) viewed the sexually delinquent girl as an unadjusted and amoral individual who used sex to satisfy her basic wishes for security, recognition, new experience, and response. Thomas argued that females have an inherently greater need for emotional response and love than males. According to Thomas's view of human motives, solutions to the delinquency problem presumably may be reached by modifying the individual's definition of the social situation. Our current individualized treatment methods of offenders are based on this general principle.

Also within the psychological tradition is Konopka's descriptive study of delinquent girls (Konopka 1966). Like Thomas, she relies upon individual case histories and anecdotal evidence to account for the loneliness experienced by the adolescent girls she interviewed. She reports that the girls were characterized by poor self-images, a deep sense of isolation, fear and distrust of adults, and communication problems with others. Additional clinical and impressionistic observations of the delinquent girl's special need for affectional relationships may be found in the work of Webb (1943), Abel and Kinder (1942), and Kaufman Makkay, and Zilbach (1959).

Social Factors

Deficient family relationships of various kinds and their resolution through delinquency, especially sex delinquency and running away, receive particular emphasis in the literature on female delinquency, although many of the early studies of juvenile delinquency also stressed the broken home as a major causal factor for male delinquency. Indeed, there seems to be little recognition in the research done between 1900 and 1950 that delinquency between the two sexes is a different phenomenon, although it is true that the focus is much more on the delinquent boy than the delinquent girl. Thomas Monahan's comprehensive review of the literature between 1900 and 1933 (1957) revealed that an association between the broken home and juvenile delinquency was usually reported. Thus Monahan asserted that "early writers saw broken homes to be an important if not the greatest single proximate factor in understanding juvenile delinquency" (Monahan 1957:250). Monahan's study, involving 44,448 delinquents of both sexes, indicated that both female and male delinquents are less likely to come from intact family backgrounds than their nondelinquent counterparts. However, the data show that the broken home was differentially related to delinquency, affecting "girls most damagingly." According to Monahan, "among the females, the proportions from incomplete families are so high (42 percent for white girls and 68 percent for black girls) that there can hardly be any doubt as to the importance of parental deprivation to them (Monahan, 1957:258).

Although the research on the broken home and male delinquency has yielded inconsistent findings, the relationship between the broken home and female delinquency has been consistently supported. Ruth Morris (1964) conducted a study in Flint, Michigan, of fifty-six delinquent girls and fifty-six delinquent boys between the ages of thirteen and sixteen matched with fifty-six nondelinquent girls and fifty-six nondelinquent boys for age, intelligence, school grade, and social class. The delinquent girls were found to come from broken homes in significantly higher proportions than the control group of nondelinquent girls. Moreover, the homes of the delinquent girls were characterized by more intrafamily tensions. The interviewers rated the delinquent girls as being lower in personal appearance and poorer in grooming than the nondelinquent girls. The findings indicated that the differences in all these dimensions were greater between the delinquent and nondelinquent girls than was found to be the case between the delinquent and nondelinquent boys and between the delinquent girls and delinquent boys. Other studies that have found the broken home to be more important for female than male delinquents include Weeks (1940), Wattenberg and Saunders (1954), and Gibbons and Griswold (1957).

Barker and Adams (1962), however, found that broken homes were equally common among institutionalized males and females in Colorado training schools. Over 60 percent of the male and female delinquents were from broken homes. Other indicators of family disharmony were also common to both groups; most of the male and female delinquents had parents who were alcoholic or criminalistic. Differences between the two groups did appear, however, in the offense patterns. More females than males were involved in school misbehavior or had become school dropouts. Most of the females had been incarcerated for incorrigibility, sex offenses, or running away, in contrast to the male offenders who had been involved in burglary, robbery, and car theft. Barker and Adams reasoned that the deviant acts of males represent attempts to gain status by deviant means; therefore, many of them may be seen as attempts to demonstrate masculinity through acts of daring. The delinquencies of girls, on the other hand, were expressions of hostility toward parents or efforts to obtain needed gratification such as affection.

Wilkinson (1974) has pointed to several major problems with studies of the broken home and delinquency. First, the concept of broken home has been defined very broadly, making it ambiguous and vague; it requires careful definition in order to be scientifically useful. Second, it is important to clarify the extent to which cultural bias has been influential in assessing the significance of the broken home. As Smith (1955) has pointed out, the high rate of delinquents from broken homes may reflect the differential treatment of these children by the police and court personnel. It is often assumed that children with one parent are in need of greater control while those with two parents are thought to be adequately supervised. This is especially true in the case of the adolescent girl who is often institutionalized "for her own protection."[3] The problem of differential treatment suggests that self-report and other unofficial sources of data be utilized in addition to official data.

Hidden Female Delinquency and Social Class

All the studies leave the reader with the impression that delinquency is a highly abnormal phenomenon that affects only a small segment of the lower-class population. Much emphasis is placed on poverty and the economic and psychological disadvantages of the adolescents' homes. The data strongly suggest that delinquent females are relatively uncommon compared to delinquent males and are often dealt with informally when they do come to the attention of the police; however, those who are most delinquent are processed through the juvenile court, and some are committed to juvenile institutions. Since it is apparent that the official figures may be seriously incomplete or biased, it is important to determine the nature and extent of delinquent behavior committed by adolescents.

There have been several attempts to correct the deficiencies of official statistics by utilizing self-reported estimates of delinquent behavior to determine the extent of hidden delinquency, particularly among middle-class adolescents. In an early study of hidden delinquency, Short and Nye (1958), using three western and three midwestern small cities (with populations of ten thousand to thirty thousand), studied high school students to ascertain the extent of admitted involvement in a large variety of acts of misconduct. Comparisons of males and females indicated a higher proportion of males committing nearly all offenses. With few exceptions, such differences were statistically significant. Offenses for which significant differences between the sexes were not found consisted of those offenses for which female adolescents are most often apprehended: running away from home, defying parental authority, incorrigibility, and drinking. The fact that significantly higher proportions of males reported engaging in heterosexual relations and the fact that females are most often referred to court for such activities led the authors to conclude that this "presumably reflects society's greater concern for the unsupervised activities of girls." Short and Nye do not discuss the double standard of morality that is applied by the police and other judicial system personnel to create the differences in the rates for which females and males are referred to the court for engaging in heterosexual relations.

Using an interview method designed to probe into the details of self-reported delinquent behavior, Martin Gold (1966, 1970) in his study of a random sample of over five hundred students, thirteen to sixteen years of age in Flint, Michigan, found that at all status levels, for whites and for nonwhites, the nature of female delinquency was similar to that of the male sample, but at a significantly lower rate. The frequency rate of female delinquency was two to four times lower than that for boys except for the acts of running away and striking their parents, leading Gold to conclude that the differences between the two groups are too pronounced to be attributed to concealment. The lower female crime reported in studies of self-reported delinquency is consistent with the lower rates of female involvement that are shown by official delinquency figures.

In an attempt to correct the deficiencies of official statistics concerning middle-class delinquency among girls, Nancy Wise (1967) conducted an investigation of 1,079 sophomore and junior high school students in a predominantly middle-class Connecticut suburban community; the community also contained a large number of upper-middle-class and upper-class families. All the students completed a self-report questionnaire consisting of thirty-five delinquent acts; an equal number of typically working-class and middle-class delinquent acts were included. The boys and girls who were categorized as middle class included 589 approximately equal numbers of boys and girls ranging in age from fifteen to eighteen. Wise was particularly interested in disproving the assertion that girls commit predominantly sexual offenses by comparing the self-reported offenses of the two groups to the official statistics. Wise found, however, that "with few exceptions significantly more boys than girls reported committing each offense." Her research findings indicate that 50.1 percent of the boys and

49.9 percent of the girls committed sexual offenses, and 50.8 percent of the boys and 49.2 percent of the girls reported alcohol offenses. None of the girls acknowledged involvement in drug use; 15 percent confessed to vandalism; 14 percent reported they had run away; 21 percent reported acts of assault. Sex and alcohol offenses were the only offenses in which there was equal participation. For all other offenses, the middle-class boys admitted committing more delinquencies than did the girls, but the difference between the sexes was not as great as is claimed in official statistics. In general, the study showed that for the most part, the acts of lawbreaking were petty and inconsequential. Moreover, it is seriously questionable whether this study actually accounts for the discrepancy between official statistics and self-report figures as far as sexual offenses are concerned.

Like all self-report studies, Wise's research has serious limitations and possible distortions that cannot be disregarded in assessing the findings. First, it is important to note that her original checklist contained thirty-five delinquency items which were considered delinquent acts under Connecticut law, but since school authorities objected to items inquiring directly about sex, two items were substituted which presumably implied sex delinquency, although we are not told what they were. Thus we cannot determine to what extent social reality has been constructed by the researcher, or to what extent the findings actually represent the empirical state of affairs as far as the girls and boys are concerned. Clearly, hidden delinquency studies cannot compensate for the way in which the research subject defines the social situation of the reseach procedures and techniques and reacts accordingly.

Ruth Morris (1965) discovered that female delinquents feel greater shame over delinquent acts than male delinquents, as measured by their unwillingness even to admit to offenses known to the police. This suggests their awareness of the greater social disapproval of female delinquency. By contrast, the male delinquents were inclined to boast about their delinquent acts, as measured by questions relating to the degree of pride felt about a delinquent act. Delinquents, more than nondelinquents, were found to have friends who participated in delinquent activity, but more boys participated in delinquent activity than girls. Differences between females and males also existed in general attitudes toward delinquency. Delinquents were more tolerant of delinquent behavior than were nondelinquents, but boys appeared to be more tolerant of delinquency than girls. Morris suggests that all females—delinquents and nondelinquents—are faced with a relative absence of cultural and subcultural supports for delinquency, and greater social disapproval of delinquency than are boys.

Morris's study, however, has major methodological limitations. First, males and females were asked different questions to test attitudes toward delinquency, although it was claimed that the questions had equivalent relevance for obtaining information about deviant behavior. The males, for example, were asked how they felt about violence and car theft, but the females were asked about promiscuous sexual relations. Morris argues that the purpose of the different questions was to test the double standard of morality, but since she assumed at the outset that sexual behavior would have a different significance for females and males, the double standard was actually imposed by Morris before the attitude test began.

To summarize briefly, the literature reveals that many myths abound in studies of female delinquency. Most studies have probed into the biological factors of female delinquency or the personality maladjustments and special "needs" of the female that presumably are linked to delinquent behavior. The scanty evidence that is presented serves to raise more questions than to provide answers about the subject of female delinquency. This is due mainly to the unscientific nature of most studies, the serious methodological shortcomings, and the fact that male delinquency is the major focus of most studies and female involvement is usually discussed as an afterthought and receives superficial analysis.

Arrest Trends: Change in the Traditional Patterns?

Since the assumptions and theories that prevail in studies of female delinquency are usually derived from or related to the official criminal statistics, it is necessary to examine the official statistics in order to determine to what extent the pattern of female and male delinquency rates differ on the basis of arrest data. It is recognized that arrest rates are not a perfect measure of delinquency, but they are the most comprehensive and systematic source available.[4]

The statistics on arrests compiled by the Federal Bureau of Investigation reveal that there has been a steady decline in male arrests from 88.92 percent in 1960 to 83.71 percent in 1975. However, there has been a small but upward trend in female arrests from 1960 to 1975. Females comprised 11.08 percent of total arrests in 1960, but in 1975 female arrests were 16.29 percent of total arrests. In 1976, for the first time since 1960, male arrests increased to 84.09 percent, whereas the total female arrests actually decreased to 15.91 percent. Whether the arrest figures for 1976 signal a reverse trend for males and females than that which characterized the period from 1960 to 1975 cannot, of course, be determined at this time. The statistics for total arrests are gross tabulations, and we are particularly interested in the contribution to the total arrests made by female and male juveniles under eighteen years of age. The Uniform Crime Reports provide a breakdown of arrest trends only from the year 1960. The complete distribution of the total arrests by sex and age for the years 1960 through 1976 is shown in table 4-1.

Table 4-1
Total Arrests by Sex, 1960-1976

Year	Total Arrests	Under 18 Males Number	Percent	Under 18 Females Number	Percent	Over 18 Males Number	Percent	Over 18 Females Number	Percent
1960	2,313,368	275,788	11.92	47,145	2.04	1,781,302	77.00	209,133	9.04
1961	3,242,434	405,095	12.49	74,626	2.30	2,468,536	76.13	294,177	9.07
1962	3,242,181	431,845	13.32	79,033	2.44	2,442,347	75.33	288,956	8.91
1963	3,693,869	541,021	14.61	97,650	2.64	2,735,018	74.04	320,180	8.66
1964	4,107,392	688,804	16.76	130,191	3.16	2,934,292	71.43	354,105	8.62
1965	4,453,698	783,215	17.36	160,515	3.60	3,136,487	70.42	373,481	8.38
1966	4,475,895	845,257	18.88	177,328	3.96	3,087,807	68.98	365,503	8.16
1967	4,918,702	982,919	19.98	214,652	4.36	3,317,664	67.45	403,467	8.20
1968	5,261,206	1,113,572	21.16	251,170	4.77	3,465,857	65.87	430,607	8.18
1969	5,167,450	1,075,101	20.80	274,675	5.32	3,376,317	65.34	441,357	8.54
1970	5,922,688	1,182,666	19.96	321,736	5.43	3,877,286	65.46	541,000	9.13
1971	6,321,047	1,265,944	20.02	363,791	5.75	4,103,650	64.92	587,662	9.29
1972	6,399,094	1,282,463	20.04	374,032	5.84	4,149,837	64.85	592,751	9.26
1973	6,158,514	1,274,978	20.70	355,744	5.77	3,937,621	63.92	590,171	9.58
1974	5,170,544	1,138,922	22.11	306,412	5.94	3,182,627	61.55	542,583	10.49
1975	6,593,238	1,409,358	21.36	380,067	5.76	4,112,133	62.35	691,680	10.49
1976	6,957,080	1,387,424	19.94	380,622	5.47	4,463,190	64.15	725,844	10.43

Source: *Uniform Crime Reports*, 1960-1976 (Washington, D.C.: U.S. Department of Justice, Federal Bureau of Investigation.)

The data presented in table 4-1 indicate that the gap for total arrests in 1960 for male and female juveniles is narrower than for males and females who are over eighteen years of age (hereafter referred to as adults). In 1960, the ratio of juvenile male and female arrests was approximately 6 to 1, whereas for adult males and females, the ratio is approximately 8.5 male arrests to 1 female arrest. In addition, the ratio between juvenile males and females narrows to 5 to 1 in 1964 and to 4 to 1 in 1967, but remains relatively stable until 1971 when a slight increase in arrests of juvenile females during the period 1971 through 1976 decreases the ratio to approximately 3.5 male arrest to 1 female arrest. Comparing the total arrests for male and female juveniles, it can be seen that more female juveniles were arrested in 1976 than a decade earlier. The data indicate that the gap between male and female juveniles has narrowed to a greater degree than it has for male and female adults. Nevertheless, it is important to note that the contribution of male and female juveniles to the total arrests in any year remains relatively small. The vast majority of persons arrested are over eighteen years of age. As table 4-1 shows, the ratio of 8.5 adult males arrested to 1 adult female in 1960 continues until 1970 when the ratio narrows to 7 to 1, and then changes in 1974 to 6 to 1.

Important differences to be noted within the juvenile and adult groups of males and females include the following: First, for the female juveniles, there is a steady rise in arrests from 1960 through 1972, and arrests remain relatively stable during the period 1972 to 1976. By contrast, arrests for male juveniles show a steady rise in arrests from 1960 through 1968; there is a slight decline in arrests during 1969 and 1970, and again there appears to be a trend toward declining arrests for male juveniles in 1975. For the male and female adults, a different picture altogether emerges. The statistics for adult males indicate that from 1960 through 1975, there is a gradual decline in arrests from 77 percent of the total arrests in 1960 to 62 percent in 1975. In 1976 arrests for adult males increased to 64 percent of all arrests. From 1960 through 1968 there is a slight decline in arrests for adult females from 9 percent to 8 percent, but in 1969 we see a gradual increase in arrests from 8.5 percent to 10 percent in 1976.

Is there any validity to the popular belief that the women's movement is contributing to increased female delinquency and that female delinquency is more aggressive in nature? Is there a trend toward increased violent crimes for female juveniles? Are females being arrested more often at the present time for committing property crime than in the past? Table 4-2 presents data that compare crime index arrest trends for violent and property crime for the five-year period from 1972 to 1976. The crime index offenses for violent crime include murder, forcible rape, robbery, and aggravated assault; property crime includes offenses of burglary, larceny theft, and motor vehicle theft.

Table 4-2
Crime Index Arrests by Sex, 1972-1976

Offense	Total Arrests	Males				Females			
		Over 18	Percent	Under 18	Percent	Over 18	Percent	Under 18	Percent
1972									
Violent crime[a]	191,994	135,549	70.6	36,866	19.2	15,278	8.0	4,301	2.2
Property crime[b]	784,107	299,790	38.2	320,015	40.8	89,185	11.3	75,117	9.6
1976									
Violent crime[a]	252,605	178,808	70.8	46,933	18.6	20,995	8.3	5,869	2.3
Property crime[b]	1,149,274	458,639	39.9	431,370	37.5	156,821	13.6	102,444	8.9

Source: Adapted from table 29, *Uniform Crime Reports*, 1976 (Washington, D.C.: Federal Bureau of Investigation, U.S. Department of Justice).
[a]Violent crime includes murder, forcible rape, robbery, and aggravated assault.
[b]Property crime includes burglary, larceny theft, and motor vehicle theft.

It is readily apparent that there is very little change in the period 1972 to 1976 in the arrests of juvenile and adult fèmales. Arrests of juvenile and adult females for violent and property crime remain relatively few in number compared to arrests of juvenile and adult males. Moreover, the gap between the adult and juvenile females is much wider for arrests of violent crime than it is for adult and juvenile males. Yet for males and females of all ages, there is very little change in arrest patterns from 1972 and 1976. For male juveniles, there is a slight decrease in arrests for violent crime from 19.2 percent in 1972 to 18.6 percent in 1976, and also for property crime there is a decrease from 40.8 percent in 1972 to 37.5 percent in 1976. For adult males, on the other hand, the arrest rate was relatively stable for 1972 and 1976.

For adult and juvenile females, the arrest data for violent crime indicate no change for 1972 or 1976. Adult females accounted for 8 percent of all arrests for violent crime in 1972 and 1976; juvenile females, 2 percent. In short, women had a 10 percent involvement in violent crime in 1972 and in 1976. As far as property crime is concerned, arrests of female juveniles actually declined in 1976 to 8.9 percent compared to 9.6 percent in 1972. For adult females, arrests for property crime increased slightly in 1976 to 13.6 percent compared to 11.3 percent in 1972. For both adult and juvenile females, property crime arrests were mainly for larceny theft.

On the basis of the statistical data presented, it cannot be said that social change has had a significant impact on the incidence or the character of female delinquency. There continues to be a qualitative as well as a quantitative difference in the numbers and types of crimes committed by adult and juvenile females. The most well-documented feature of female delinquency that emerges from the available statistical data is the relatively few numbers of females who engage in what is legally defined as crime. The extent to which males exceed females in rates of delinquency in official arrest rates and in all the research studies is so great that despite some inadequacies in the statistics and methodology there can be little doubt about the trends. The official statistics reflect the extent to which female delinquency constitutes a problem for society. All the available evidence indicates clearly that females cause much less damage to society than males do. A broad generalization can be made that females are indeed more law-abiding than males. When they do break the law, their delinquencies are less aggressive and socially destructive than those of males.

The proportion of females who engage in crime, however, varies considerably according to the offense. In the case of larceny theft, for example, females accounted for 31 percent of all arrests for this offense in 1976—a higher involvement than for any of the other index offenses. On the other hand, the number of female offenders who are apprehended for motor vehicle theft comprise only a very small percentage of total arrests for this of-

fense. Adult and juvenile females exceed the number of males who are apprehended and arrested for shoplifting, but they rarely commit burglaries
(Cameron 1964).[5] The reason for the female's lack of criminal involvement
in burglaries is usually explained in physiological terms—her lack of
strength. A more convincing argument, however, may be made for her lack
of skills to execute the task. Females do not possess the technical skill, for
example, to commit the types of burglary that would require deactivating
sophisticated electronic devices or circumventing even simple alarm
systems. Moreover, since criminal activity of this type requires cooperation
among a group of individuals, females must learn to relate to other females
(or indeed males) in instrumental terms in order to play a more prominent
role in the statistics for burglary. The same may be said for other deviant
acts that require a highly developed organizational structure for successful
completion.

How can we account for the vast differences in arrest rates and criminal
activity between males and females? A plausible explanation lies in their differential expectations and socialization in American society. General
features of American society with respect to the cultural definitions and
content of male and female roles function to determine the focus of the
female's participation in criminal activity (Giallombardo 1966, 1974).[6]
Socialization patterns constitute powerful social forces that affect both
males and females. Both sex-role expectations and processes of social control serve to channel behavior in predictive ways and to create differences in
structural opportunities for female delinquency. Females are not only more
closely supervised than males, but they are also socialized to be more
passive and gentle, whereas males are expected to be aggressive and active.
Females conform more to societal norms because they are taught to believe
that the social consequences of delinquent behavior are more serious for
females than for males; hence they tend to fear social disapproval more
than males. The differential social consequences for the female are sometimes reflected in the wording of legal statutes and the behavioral acts for
which females receive judicial determination, particularly in the category of
sex offenses and other status offenses for which a greater number of
females than males are brought before the juvenile authorities and for
which they are more strictly disciplined.

Shoplifting, the pattern of theft in which females figure so prominently,
is closely related to the differential expectations of male and female role
behavior. It is consistent with the widely held norm that females should not
engage in violence or be overly aggressive. The forms of larceny theft engaged in by females neither require physical force nor the aggressive daring
that may be necessary for certain types of burglaries. In addition, shoplifting often consists of clothing, cosmetic, and other items that will enhance
physical appearance, again closely related to the differential content of male

and female roles. The thefts of the male, on the other hand, often consist of items such as cars, radios, and television sets that can be readily converted to cash, or, in the case of cars and guns, that can be useful in committing other crimes. Now although it is true that there are differences in the patterns of male and female thefts, it is not at all clear why male thefts are so often analyzed in economic terms but not female. Both male and female delinquents seek to enhance their status, but the means they use to achieve the goal differ in ways that are consistent with the differential expectations and content of male and female roles in American society, and we see this reflected in their patterns of theft. Nevertheless, the female delinquent's shoplifting is certainly related to the lack of financial resources at her disposal, a fact that is analytically distinct from the fact that she steals items that will improve her appearance.

Sexism and the Administration of Justice

Both police arrests reported by the Federal Bureau of Investigation and juvenile court cases—the extent to which the court is used to deal with juvenile delinquency—show a remarkable similarity in their long-range trends, despite differences in definitions and units of count. Because the reporting bases for the *Uniform Crime Reports* and the *Juvenile Court Statistics* differ,[7] the data are not directly comparable, but they are presented here to indicate the extent to which the disparity between male and female delinquency court cases is narrowing. The number of delinquency cases for females disposed of by juvenile courts has been rising faster than cases for delinquent males every year since 1965. The distribution of delinquency cases processed through the courts from 1957 to 1974 is shown in table 4-3.

As shown previously for police arrests, delinquency cases handled by courts also remain primarily a male problem, but the gap between the number of male and female delinquency court cases is narrowing. For many years, four times as many cases for males were disposed of by juvenile courts compared to those involving females. Because of the recent increase in female cases, however, the case ratio of males to females has decreased to 3 to 1. As table 4-3 indicates, the case ratio remained stable from 1972 to 1974, when for the third consecutive year 26 percent of the cases were females and 74 percent were males. Between 1964 and 1974, delinquency cases of females increased by 129 percent, while cases of male delinquents increased by 67 percent. The percentage increase in the total number of delinquency cases in 1974 was 9 percent for both males and females (U.S. Department of Justice, 1974: 6). In contrast to males, however, females are disproportionately processed through the juvenile justice system for status offenses. Only a few examples can be discussed here, but they will suffice to direct attention to the nature of the problems involved.

Table 4-3
Number and Percent Distribution of Delinquency Cases Disposed of by Juvenile Courts, by Sex, United States, 1957-1974

Year	Boys		Girls	
	Number	Percent	Number	Percent
1957	358,000	81	82,000	19
1958	383,000	81	87,000	19
1959	393,000	81	90,000	19
1960	415,000	81	99,000	19
1961	408,000	81	95,000	19
1962	450,000	81	104,500	19
1963	485,000	81	116,000	19
1964	555,000	81	131,000	19
1965	555,000	80	142,000	20
1966	593,000	80	152,000	20
1967	640,000	79	171,000	21
1968	708,000	79	191,000	21
1969	760,000	77	228,000	23
1970	799,500	76	252,000	24
1971	845,500	75	279,500	25
1972	827,500	74	285,000	26
1973	845,300	74	298,400	26
1974	927,000	74	325,700	26

Source: *Juvenile Court Statistics, 1974*, U.S. Department of Justice, p. 17.

An understanding of sexism in the administration of justice must begin with an examination of the legal definitions outlined in the juvenile codes and the provisions established in statute and case law to govern the juvenile court for such behavior as incorrigibility, promiscuity, truancy, running away from home, curfew violations, and other status offenses that are not violations of the law for adults. All of the fifty states as well as the District of Columbia include status offenders within the purview of the juvenile court; half of the states have a separate category for children, persons, or minors "in need of supervision."

As Davis and Chaires (1973) and Riback (1971) demonstrate, juvenile deinquency laws clearly discriminate against females (Temin 1973). Some juvenile court statutes are written in such a way that they are sexually discriminatory on their face, thus making it possible for judges to apply the double standard of morality with impunity. Other statutes that are apparently sex neutral on their face are unspecific and vague as to meaning; hence, they may be applied differently by judges on the basis of sex. These statutes usually include a broad or vague provision enabling the juvenile court to obtain jurisdiction over a youth who engages in socially unacceptable behavior such as lewd or immoral conduct. In summing up the problem of the vagueness and overbreadth flaws of juvenile statutes, Riback states:

Juvenile morals statutes . . . are unconstitutional because they give no
ascertainable standards as to what is punishable behavior and in addition
are so broad that almost every child could at some time be held to have
violated them. The overbreadth and vagueness of the statutes give rise to a
situation ripe for discriminatory enforcement against female juveniles. By
virtue of the nature of American culture and its view of sex roles, the same
behavior which goes unpunished in males may subject females to extended
periods of confinement. The fact that the statutes create a great potential
for discrimination and, in addition, unconstitutionally punish a status,
should be enough to condemn them. [1971: 341][8]

The result may be violations of the Fourteenth Amendment equal protection clause when female juveniles are awarded longer sentences than
male juveniles under the guise of "protection of the female." Although the
statutes are general in potential application against both males and females,
they are in fact often directed against female juveniles. Challenges that affect the processing of female status offenders are especially important
because this category includes 45 to 75 percent of the female offenders in
each state (Giallombardo 1974: 39). Until recently the New York Person In
Need of Supervision (PINS) law provided that females who were "persons
in need of supervision" could be institutionalized until the age of eighteen
whereas the upper limit for males was sixteen. This law was held unconstitutional and struck down by the New York Court of Appeals, as it violates the
equal protection clause (*In re Patricia A.* 1972). The court recognized the
purpose of the PINS statute to be rehabilitation and treatment, but held
that this purpose was insufficient to justify differentiation between males
and females since no factual differences between males and females could
be found in support of such differential treatment. A similar law, concerning length of confinement has been held to be unconstitutional in Connecticut (*Sumrell* v. *York* 1968). In some states, statutes framed in terms such
as "moral depravity," or "in danger of becoming immoral," have been
struck down as vague, as in California (*Gonzales* v. *Maillard* 1971).

The double standard of morality may lead to longer periods of incarceration for females than males committing the same acts, particularly
sexual delinquencies, running away, curfew violations, and other status offenses. Females are prosecuted almost exclusively for prostitution. The
prostitute's customer is not prosecuted in most jurisdictions, although some
states have enacted customer laws. New York, for example, has enacted a
law stating that patronizing a prostitute is a violation having a penalty of a
maximum sentence of fifteen day's imprisonment. However, the penalty for
the prostitute in New York is a maximum sentence of three months—a
dramatic example of the operation of the double standard of morality.

Andrews and Cohn's study (1974) of the functioning of the "ungovernability" jurisdiction in the New York Family Court indicates that 62 percent

of the cases were females in mid-adolescence and disproportionately non-white. The families were poor, large, and often headed by a single parent. Moreover, they found that there was considerable evidence of judicial over-reach, with the court misapplying the statute to 37 percent of the females, classifying them as ungovernable when they were in fact neglected, in order to expedite processing. Females, in particular, are disproportionately detained and committed to residential facilities than are males (Gibbons and Griswold 1957). The ungovernability jurisdiction provides less protection against the intrusion of the judge's personal predilections than do other legal proceedings that consider narrower issues.

Conclusion

Female delinquency is importantly related to the differential cultural definitions and expectations of sex roles in American society. Through the socialization process both males and females are taught to respond in appropriate ways, and we see this reflected in differences in types of delinquent behavior engaged in by males and females. Differential socialization and the application of social control measures for males and females both function to limit structurally determined opportunities for females to commit specific categories of delinquent behavior. In addition, some forms of female delinquency are a function of the legal statutes that facilitate processing and identification of certain forms of behavior as delinquent or criminal for females but not for males.

It has been predicted that as equality of opportunity between males and females increases, female crime rates will approximate or equal male crime rates. Thus far the greater participation of females in social, political, and business life has not had a corresponding rise in the delinquent and criminal activities of females. The view that sees women's economic, social, and political emancipation as reflected in increased delinquent and criminal behavior on the part of females takes for granted the direction of social change, and it presumes that other features of American society will not affect delinquent behavior in the future. It does not take into account the social and cultural forces that define the preferential behavioral content of social roles. It assumes that females will imitate males in their behavior, including delinquent and criminal activity, without considering whether such behavior could be role enhancing to the female.

Changes in female sex-role behavior to not encourage violation of the existing laws. Indeed, as the major socializing agents in American society, females may be an instrumental force to deemphasize violence in American life on the basis that it is not role enhancing for males and females alike. The far-reaching effects of such socialization practices may in the long run function to decrease male crimes of violence. As socialization practices work to create symmetry in sex-role behavior, preferred behavioral expectations will apply to both males and females. Hence, this process may be reflected in a decrease in crimes by males in all categories. On the other hand, as statutes that stress sexism are eliminated, there will be fewer females appearing in the official statistics for promiscuity and related status offenses.

Notes

1. Otto Pollack (1961), a more recent investigator, maintains that the criminality of females is largely masked behind the ordinary female social roles that are common to their social function in society, although no evidence is provided to substantiate this claim.

2. See Carol Smart (1976) for a good discussion of the application of the biological determinist perspective in studies of female criminality.

3. In Rose Giallombardo's comparative study of institutions for female juvenile delinquents (1974:39), it was reported that running away from home, incorrigibility in school and at home, or habitual truancy appears as the first offense cited for 72.7 percent of the inmates from eastern states, 72.6 percent of inmates from central states, and 42.1 percent of inmates from western states.

4. Hazards of using arrest statistics as a reliable source of data to determine actual crime rates have been well documented. See especially Sellin (1951) and Wolfgang (1963).

5. Cameron found that the younger the shoplifter was, irrespective of sex, the more likely that the individual would be in a group. Adults were almost uniformly alone, but male and female juveniles were usually in the company of one or more persons of the same sex when apprehended. Shoplifting for female juveniles consisted of taking small leather goods, jewelry, and clothing for personal use; the merchandise stolen by male juveniles included mainly small leather goods and gadgets such as cigarette lighters, flashlights, and cheap cameras. See Cameron (1964:102-103).

6. The remarkable difference in the structural form of the inmate social system developed by males and females in the prison setting can only be understood in terms of the differential cultural definitions ascribed to male and female roles in American society. See Giallombardo (1966, 1974).

7. Data are not collected by the national juvenile court statistical reporting program on the types of offenses for which juveniles are referred to the courts. However, the *Uniform Crime Reports* does provide some indication for the types of offenses for which juveniles are arrested. These include arrests for offenses that would be crimes if committed by adults as well as the juvenile status offenses of running away and curfew violations.

8. "Juvenile Delinquency Laws: Juvenile Women and the Double Standard of Morality," *UCLA Law Review* 19 (2):341. Reprinted with permission.

9. This study indicated that almost half of the male and female juveniles were released from court custody without formal action; however, of those retained by the court, twice as many females as males were committed to correctional institutions (25.8 percent compared to 11.3 percent).

References

Abel, Theodora M. and Elaine F. Kinder (1942). *The Subnormal Adolescent Girl*. New York: Columbia University Press.

Andrews, Jr., Hales, R. and Cohn, Andrew H. (1974). "Ungovernability: the unjustifiable jurisdiction." *The Yale Law Journal* 83:1383-1409.

Barker, Gordon H., and Adams, William T. (1962). "Comparison of the delinquencies of boys and girls." *Journal of Criminal Law, Criminology and Police Science* 53:470-475.

Burt, Cyril (1925). *The Young Delinquent*. New York: Appleton.

Cameron, Mary O. (1964). *The Booster and the Snitch*. Glencoe: Free Press.

Dalton, K. (1961). "Menstruation and crime." *British Medical Journal* 2: (part 2, December 30).

Davis, Samuel M., and Chaires, Susan C. (1973). "Equal protection for juveniles: the present status of sex-based discrimination in juvenile court laws." *Georgia Law Review* 7:494-532.

Giallombardo, Rose (1966). *Society of Women*. New York: Wiley.

_____ (1974). *The Social World of Imprisoned Girls*. New York: Wiley.

Gibbens, T.C.N., and Prince, J. (1962). *Shoplifting*. London: ISTD.

Gibbons, Don C., and Griswold, Manzer J. (1957). "Sex differences among juvenile court referrals." *Sociology and Social Research* 42:106-110.

Gold, Martin (1966). "Undetected delinquent behavior." *Journal of Research on Crime and Delinquency* 3:27-46.

_____ (1970). *Delinquent Behavior in an American City*. Belmont: Brooks/Cole.

Healy, William, and Bronner, Augusta F. (1926). *Delinquents and Criminals, Their Making and Unmaking*. New York: MacMillan.

Kaufman, Irving, Makkay, Elizabeth S. and Zilback, Joan (1959). "The impact of adolescence on girls with delinquent character formation." *American Journal of Orthopsychiatry* 29:130-143.

Konopka, Gisela (1966). *The Adolescent Girl in Conflict*. Englewood Cliffs, N.J.: Prentice-Hall.

Lombroso, Cesare (1876). *L'Uomo Delinquente*. Torino: Bocca.

_____ (1906). *Crime: Its Causes and Remedies*. Boston: Little, Brown.

_____ (1920). *The Female Offender*. New York: Appleton.

Middleton, Warren (1933). "Is there a relation between kleptomania and female periodicity in neurotic individuals?" *Psychological Clinic* (December):232-247.

Monahan, Thomas P. (1957). "Family status and the delinquent child: a reappraisal and some new findings." *Social Forces* 35:251-258.

Morris, Ruth R. (1964). "Female delinquency and relational problems." *Social Forces* 43:82-89.

_____ (1965). "Attitudes toward delinquency by delinquents, nondelinquents and their friends." *The British Journal of Criminology* (July):249-265.

Pollack, Otto (1961). *The Criminality of Women*. New York: A.S. Barnes.

Riback, Linda (1971). "Juvenile delinquency laws: juvenile women and the double standard of morality." *UCLA Law Review* 19:313-342.

Sellin, Thornsten (1951). "The significance of records of crime." *Law Quarterly Review* 67:489-504.

Short, James F., Jr., and Nye, F. Ivan (1958). "Extent of unrecorded delinquency: tentative conclusions." *Journal of Criminal Law, Criminology and Police Science* 49:296-302.

Smart, Carol (1976). *Women, Crime and Criminology*. London: Routledge Kegan Paul.

Smith, Philip M. (1955). "Broken homes and juvenile delinquency." *Sociology and Social Research* 39:307-311.

Temin, Carolyn Engel (1973). "Discriminatory sentencing of women offenders: the argument for ERA in a nutshell." *American Criminal Law Review* 11:353-372.

Thomas, William J. (1923). *The Unadjusted Girl*. Boston: Little, Brown.

U.S. Department of Justice (1974). *Juvenile Court Statistics*. Washington, D.C.: U.S. Government Printing Office.

Wattenberg, W.W., and Saunders, F. (1954). "Sex differences among juvenile offenders." *Sociology and Social Research* 39:24-31.

Webb, Mary L. (1943). "Delinquency in the making: patterns in the development of girl sex delinquency in the city of Seattle." *Journal of Social Hygiene* (November):502-510.

Weeks, H. Ashley (1940). "Male and female broken home rates by types of delinquency." *American Sociological Review* 5 (August):601-609.

Wilkinson, Karen (1974). "The broken family and juvenile delinquency: scientific explanation or ideology?" *Social Problems* 21:726-739.

Wise, Nancy B. (1967). "Juvenile delinquency among middle-class girls." In Edmund W. Vas (ed.), *Middle-Class Juvenile Delinquency*, pp. 179-188. New York: Harper and Row.

Wolfgang, Marvin W. (1963). "Uniform crime reports: a critical appraisal." *University of Pennsylvania Law Review* 111:708-738.

Delinquency and the Changing American Family

John W.C. Johnstone

The public is greatly concerned with family breakdown. It is disturbed at the rising divorce rate. It is alarmed at reports of the increasing rate of juvenile delinquency. It is disposed to hold parents responsible for the delinquency of children and to blame the parents of young couples if their marriage disintegrates. It advocates legislation to punish parents for their children's delinquency   —Ernest Burgess

This assessment of the state of American public opinion would be almost as accurate today as it was in 1954 when Ernest Burgess reported it to the American Orthopsychiatric Association. And it could well have been a valid reflection of American public opinion in 1854 or even 1754. Historically, the function of social control over the young in our society has been the domain of family government: in colonial New England in 1670, public officials would visit homes to ensure that parents were properly discharging their responsibilities for the moral and cognitive development of their offspring (Krisberg and Austin 1978: 12). Our society traditionally has assigned major credit for the successful socialization of the young to parents, and has pointed the causal finger of blame at parents when youngsters get into trouble.

In view of this heritage, it is somewhat surprising that one of the most predictably recurrent issues in American social science should be the role of the family in the etiology of juvenile delinquency. During the past fifty years, this question has generated an enormous volume of attention, so much in fact, that currently one can locate not only a literature on the topic but also an emergent literature on the literature itself. As part of a presidential commission, Rodman and Grams (1967) compiled 161 social scientific references on the topic, beginning in the twenties and thirties with the work of such familiar figures as Burt, Healy, Thrasher, Park and Burgess, Shaw and McKay, and the Gluecks, and culminating with 84 citations for the period 1960 to 1967. And more titles could be added for the current period.

Just as this literature is voluminous, so too is it inconclusive. In it one can discover positions ranging from the view that the family is the single most important determinant of delinquent behavior to the view that although some empirical association may exist, there is no basis on which to posit any direct causal connection between the two. Unlike many scholarly fields, the family-delinquency literature shows little crescive development: over and over investigators tackle the question de novo, and there are few studies built on the outcomes of preceding investigations. Although the topic has been explored more than once during each decade since the twenties, however, it has been much more salient during some periods than others. In a review essay on the literature, Wilkinson (1974) charts periods of acceptance and rejection of the status of the broken home in explaining delinquency, and suggests that investigators' values regarding the sanctity of the nuclear family explain these variations better than any objective evidence on the question. The issue, in short, has been and continues to be a heavily value-laden one, both for social scientists and for the society at large.

During the current decade, analysts have begun to use earlier delinquency studies as sources of data for critical reexamination. In one such study, Rosen (1970) recalculated statistical relationships for eleven different studies of broken homes and male delinquency conducted between 1932 and 1968 and discovered a surprising degree of uniformity in the results. Despite variation in time, locale, study design, operational definitions, sampling procedures, and populations, virtually all the studies yielded very weak positive relationships between broken homes and delinquency, relationships of the type that social scientists might say show statistical but little practical significance. Interestingly, secondary analysis of evidence linking social class to delinquency has resulted in a similar outcome. Tittle, Villemez, and Smith (1978) reexamined 363 sets of relevant data from the crime and delinquency literature and found that the mean level of association (*gamma*) was just −.09. Relationships this weak preclude serious consideration of class position as the foundation of any theoretical interpretation of delinquent or criminal behavior. Currently, it would appear that at least two of the more time-honored explanations of juvenile delinquency—lower-class position and broken homes—require factory recall.

It is questionable whether the public at large assigns much credibility to the conclusion that family factors have little bearing on delinquent behavior. This view is ideologically incompatible with our national heritage and values. Today, fewer and fewer social scientists claim the family as a major determinant of delinquency among American children and adolescents. Yet fewer still are the professionals or officials who deal with delinquent youngsters who are not impressed by aberrant features of their family circumstances. Popular notions prevail that weak familes produce troublesome (or troubled) youngsters. In 1968, 59 percent of American adults believed that faulty upbringing was the main reason for criminal behavior. Only 16 percent attributed it either to poverty or environmental circumstances (Law Enforcement Assistance Administration 1975). The mass media reinforce these impressions regularly. For example, in the cover story of its July 11, 1977, issue, *Time* attributed the major cause of the contemporary youth crime plague to the breakdown of the American family. It would be an instructive empirical exercise to record systematically the number of newspaper accounts which do *not* describe delinquents as the products of disrupted families.

Why should the social science evidence on this question differ so sharply from the views held by most other people in our society? This chapter will address this question and point to several features of the research literature which may have obfuscated rather than illuminated the issue. I will argue that the inconclusiveness stems not so much from investigator bias, though indeed that may have existed, but from several more systematic sources of bias related to variations in research design, in the family factors taken into consideration, in the conceptualization and measurement of delinquency, and in the rigor with which relationships have been tested. I will also argue that a different assessment of the impact of the family on delinquency will be obtained when the family is viewed as part of a wider social environment than when it is treated as an isolated social system unto itself. To begin, however, several recent changes in the nature of the American family require attention, for these have important ramifications both for the direction of future scientific inquiry and for public policy.

The Changing American Family

If concern over the impact of family structure on delinquency runs in cycles, then the time is ripe for an upsurge of national attention on this issue. During the 1970s dramatic shifts occurred in the family situations in which American children were being raised. Most notably, there was a sharp and unexpected rise in the prevalence of single-parent female-headed families in the population. Between 1970 and 1976, the percentage of American children under eighteen living in single-parent households increased from 11.8 to 17.1. In the white population the increase was from 8.7 to 13.0 percent; in the black, from 31.6 to 41.6 percent (U.S. Bureau of the Census, 1978:26). By 1976, more than half, 50.3 percent, of all black children born in the United States, and as many as 7.7 percent of white, were born to single women. Most of these births were to teenagers (National Center for Health Statistics, 1978:17).

These last statistics are both alarming and puzzling: alarming because of the substantial economic deprivations and other disadvantages many of these young mothers and children face; and puzzling because of the recent legalization of abortion and because birth rates have actually been declining in both the married and unmarried segments of the white and black female populations. Demographically, the shift is accounted for by a number of interrelated factors: greatly increased numbers of unmarried women in the population; a more rapid decline in the birth rate among married than un-married women; high rates of divorce; and an increase in the average age of first marriage. Sociologically, the trends may reflect other factors: changing standards regarding premarital sexual conduct; changing views of the sanc-tity of marriage; greater economic independence of women due to increased participation in the labor force; and within the black population, increasing polarization between a growing and increasingly affluent black middle class and a persistently large economically depressed and alienated black urban underclass.

To some degree the trend also reflects the continuation of strains that American society has experienced in absorbing the largest single cohort of new members in its history, the offspring of the post-World War II baby boom. During the sixties, these strains were visible primarily in the high schools and colleges, in a full-blown student movement, and in the juvenile courts—where the number of delinquency cases processed more than doubled between 1960 and 1970 (Corbett and Vereb 1974: 167). During the seventies, the strains have moved on to the institutions of young adulthood and are most visible in the labor force and the family. Current trends in na-tional statistics show simultaneous increases in the prevalence of single-parent families, which overwhelmingly are female headed, and in the numbers of youngsters processed by the courts. These trends cannot help but be interpreted by many as further evidence of causal links between the two.

Yet these statistics tell only part of the story. For one thing they do not specify who the adults are who actually rear the children. In the case of the black family, this deficiency seriously underestimates the role of extended kin networks. Following Moynihan (1965), a number of social scientists (Billingsley 1968; Staples 1971; Hays and Mindel 1973; Stack 1974) have focused in depth on these networks. Some researchers suggest that extended kinship is a more important phenomenon in the black population than in the white, and all argue that the American black family is a good deal stronger than previously recognized. Billingsley (1968) estimated that ap-proximately a quarter of black families in the United States are of the ex-tended variety, with relatives other than the child's natural parents (or parent) present in the household and presumably sharing in parenting responsibilities. Many of these families are of the attenuated extended type, consisting of a single, abandoned, legally separated, divorced or widowed woman living together with her own children plus other relatives. Still others are of the attenuated augmented type, consisting of the child's mother plus unrelated adults who also may share in the parenting.

What is significant here, of course, is that no one has ever examined the relationship between these types of family structure and delinquency. The literature simply has ignored the fact that there are different types of broken families, and the possibility that different structures may have a different impact on the behavior of the youngsters growing up in them.

A second way in which national statistics on family composition are misleading is that they ignore differences among two-parent families. For example, they group together intact families, where children live with both of their natural parents, and restructured nuclear families, where a stepparent has entered the family nexus. Figures on the prevalence of restructured families are hard to obtain. It is possible, however, that as many as a third of all first marriages in the United States now terminate in divorce. Furthermore, about three-quarters of divorced women and five-sixths of divorced men eventually remarry, on the average within three years (Glick 1977). Since about half to two-thirds of those who remarry remain married to the same spouse through their joint survival, it is evident that substantial numbers of American youngsters today are being raised in two-parent families made up of one natural and one stepparent. In 1972 only 6 percent of a statewide sample of Illinois adolescents reported family situations of this type (Johnstone 1977), but there may well be more today.

Little is known about the quality of intergenerational relations in families of this type, and even less is known about the delinquency of the children who live in them. In one study, however, Johnstone (1977) compared parent-youth relationships in intact, single-parent, and restructured families and found that parents in restructured families had greater difficulty having their authority accepted as legitimate by their adolescent offspring.

Isolated reports also abound of other forms of alternative parenting structures, such as lesbian women or homosexual men raising children in homosocial households, or of group or communal marriages and parenting arrangements. Virtually nothing is known about the prevalence of such arrangements or about the behavior of the youngsters reared in them.

For all of these reasons, then, there is a good chance that the relationship between family structure and delinquency has been obscured in the delinquency literature. Since it now appears beyond dispute that the family situations of American children are changing rapidly, it is time that delinquency researchers realized that there are different types of both intact and broken families.

Systematic Sources of Confusion

As a field, delinquency research today finds itself with neither a coherent theoretical position nor consistent empirical evidence regarding the relationship between family factors and delinquent behavior. There are a number of reasons for this, the first of which is variation in research design. Studies tracing the backgrounds of court-adjudicated delinquents (Jenkins and

Hewitt 1944; Glueck and Glueck 1950) have generally accorded family factors the more significant causal role. Self-report studies of representative samples of young people (Nye 1958; Hirschi 1969), on the other hand, have tended to turn up comparatively weaker relationships and, as a result, have interpreted the impact of the family more cautiously.

One reason for this discrepancy, as suggested by Nye (1958) and others, is that the juvenile justice system is more likely to process a young offender when there is no intact or stable family situation to which to return him. Because of differential selection, then, youth who become official delinquents tend disproportionately to be from less stable family backgrounds—so-called broken families or intact but large and economically depressed families. Unless a control group is matched on family characteristics, then, there is little chance that significant differences in family backgrounds will show up in studies of this type.

More generally, the research literature has failed to isolate the unique role of the family in the two processes differentiated by Williams and Gold (1972): the impact of the family in generating or preventing delinquent behavior in their children, and the influence of the family on the process by which children who do commit delinquent acts become transformed into official delinquents. On this point, secondary analysis by Johnstone (1977) of a large set of data on Illinois youngsters confirmed suspicions that family structure is still considered important in the juvenile justice system. Family structure was a better predictor of how far youthful offenders had been processed through the courts than of the behavior that brought them to the attention of the authorities in the first place.

A second source of confusion emerges when investigators fail to isolate different components of family systems, an oversight which serves to reinforce the assumption, widely held both in the juvenile justice community and by the public at large, that family structure implies family functioning. This assumption is usually based on one or more of the following beliefs: (1) that intact nuclear families offer the child a richer affective or emotional environment; (2) that single-parent families are either less able or less willing to discipline, set limits on, or otherwise control the behavior of their children; and (3) that when fathers are absent form the household boys will have no role model from which to learn appropriate masculine behavior and will emulate the excessively aggressive masculinity visible in the peer culture of the street. Remarkably, these beliefs have survived without any solid evidence to support them. Indeed, the little hard evidence there is (Nye 1958; Browning 1960; Johnstone 1977) suggests that family intactness by itself does not indicate either the psychological climate or the effectiveness of a family.

This issue is clearly an important one today in view of the apparent increase in the divorce rate. What is not clear, however, is whether the current divorce statistics imply that interpersonal relationships in marriages have deteriorated over what they were at some earlier time, or simply that couples whose relationships sour no longer feel any obligation to remain married. If the former is true, then it is possible that the quality of the nurturant environment experienced by the average American child has worsened: but if the latter is the case, one might prefer to conclude just the opposite.

Family Functioning

The preponderance of scholarly opinion is that delinquent behavior is related more strongly to internal family functioning than to family structure. Yet the evidence on which these opinions rests is difficult to assess: in the main it consists of zero-order relationships of low to moderate strength between delinquent behavior and a disparate array of measures which tap one or another facet of family dynamics. Many of the studies seem to have been uninformed by any prior theoretical considerations regarding how family systems are organized or work.

In their literature review, Rodman and Grams (1967) organized the relevant evidence on this question under three categories: the quality of relationships between parents—marital adjustment; the quality of relationships between parents and their children—the closeness of affectional ties across generations; and the nature, style, or consistency of disciplinary and childrearing methods. Delinquent outcomes have been linked to all three: to poor marital relationships; to weak affectional ties between parents and children; and to lax, inconsistent, or harsh discipline. Most investigators, however, have focused on just one of these classes of elements, or if they have looked at elements from more than one set, they have analyzed them one at a time rather than in combination. Virtually no studies have examined the interaction of different family dimensions. One exception is a study by McCord and McCord (1964) of the conditional impact of different mixes of affection and discipline. They found that when strong affectional ties existed between boys and both of their parents, different methods of discipline had no effect on delinquency. When affectional ties were strong with just one parent, however, erratic or lax discipline resulted in higher levels of delinquent behavior. Investigations focused on the inner workings of family systems are all too rare in the delinquency field, however, and it is perhaps safe to conclude that no one yet has utilized multivariate analysis effectively to sort out the elements of family systems that relate to delinquency.

As is the more general case with delinquency theory and research, the bulk of the family-delinquency literature deals only with males. Where both genders have been studied, the evidence is contradictory. For example, Nye (1958) found that family tension and quarrelling affects the delinquency of girls more than the delinquency of boys, whereas Johnstone (1977) concluded that disrupted family conditions, if anything, affect boys more than girls.

In overview, the research literature on this question has suffered from a surfeit of empirical measures and a dearth of theoretical focus. Although most of the elements which have been identified as important relate either to the affective or the instrumental solidarity of a family, it is not possible to say which of these dimensions is the more critical. Is delinquent behavior more a result of weak authority and control within a family, or more an issue of weak affectional ties? Does it stem more from lack of love or lack of discipline? Although these questions have been asked for a long time, about the best answer one can give on the basis of available evidence (Nye 1958; Hirschi 1969; Jensen 1972; Thomas et al. 1974; Johnstone 1977) is that both seem to be important. Nonetheless, it does seem clear that these aspects of families have more to do with delinquent behavior than do external properties such as family composition, family size, or the ordinal position of the child.

Measuring Delinquency

Still another source of ambiguity in the literature stems from the fact that delinquent behavior has been conceptualized and measured so differently. Many clinical studies, for example, develop typologies of delinquents or of delinquent acts, often connecting different expressions of delinquent behavior to differences in family structure or family functioning. Field studies of delinquency, on the other hand, have often measured delinquent behavior by means of some type of composite behavior index, or by simply lumping together all youngsters who end up in the juvenile court. These latter measurement strategies may err in assuming a unidimensional continuum of behavior that does not exist. It is not at all clear that different types of delinquent acts—offenses against persons or property, so-called victimless crimes, utilitarian and nonutilitarian delinquency, or defensive and adventuresome deviant acts (Lofland 1969)—share the same etiology. Moreover, Cohen (1974) has noted that the same delinquent act, vandalism, can take a variety of distinct forms depending on the meanings that participation has for the actors. Some types of delinquent expression, in short, may be intimately linked to tensions generated in the family; for other forms the family situation may be totally irrelevant. Empirical evidence supporting this position is found in Browning (1960) and in Johnstone (1978a).

More generally, then, there has been a poor fit in the delinquency literature between the richness of detailed afforded by careful clinical observation, and the representativeness afforded by scientific field studies. Where clinical investigators have had difficulty linking the behavioral distinctions they observe with adequate measures of the environmental or social forces which may generate them, field researchers, with some notable exceptions (Short, Tennyson, and Howard 1963; Cloward and Ohlin 1960) have not adequately investigated the impact of the family situation on different varieties of contranormative expression. Neither tradition, in short, has effectively addressed the possibility that the family may influence some types of delinquent behavior and not others.

The Community Context

A final weakness in the family-delinquency literature is that most studies have assumed, at least implicitly, that families operate as autonomous, independent social units rather than as elements of a wider social system. This oversight can be seriously misleading. For example, it can easily be demonstrated that there are more single-parent families in economically depressed urban areas than in economically more viable ones. It is also a long-established finding in ecological studies that official rates of delinquents are higher in communities of the former type. If a relationship is found between broken homes and delinquency, then, it is the responsibility of the analyst to establish that it cannot be explained away simply by the fact that delinquency is higher among youngsters from both stable and broken families in certain kinds of communities. Otherwise, there is the risk of interpreting a spurious relationship as causal.

In general, the family-delinquency literature has simply ignored this problem, as well as the general perspective that families, like individuals, function within a social context. It is likely, however, that family systems are strongly influenced by environmental circumstances, and that the family itself may have a different relationship to delinquency in different types of social environments. That these contingencies are in fact the case has been established by Johnstone (1978a), who examined the simultaneous effects of environmental and family factors on differeent forms of delinquent behavior. In that study, adolescent behavior, both conventional and deviant, was viewed as the end product of three sets of forces: peer-group influence, family influence, and community norms and pressures. Community pressure, conceptualized as "environmental press," was measured by three characteristics of the census tracts in which youngsters lived—the prevalence of poverty-level families, the unemployment rate, and the number of single-parent female-headed households with children under eighteen years of age. The economic position of the adolescent's own family was measured separately, and measures of family integration, attachment to a delinquency-prone peer group, and participation in law violations were all measured by questionnaire responses from adolescents themselves. This type of analysis allows effects stemming from the family to be identified independently of effects stemming from other sources. The logic of a contextual approach insists that if family characteristics are causal, empirical relationships must persist after the effects of the environment and of the peer group have been controlled.

Viewed in this light, several new insights emerged, some contrary to popular wisdom. The contextual analysis showed that the influence of the family varied both with the type of norm-violative behavior in question and with the community setting in which the adolescent lived. There was an inverse relationship between the seriousness of an offense pattern and the importance of the family in accounting for it. Weak family integration had a definite positive effect on less serious types of norm violation—status offenses, drug infractions, and property violations—but virtually no power as a predictor of protocriminal delinquency (burglary, larceny, and robbery) or of nonutilitarian violence. It was precisely on these latter types of behavior, moreover, that environmental press had its strongest effect. Both offense patterns, the criminal and the violent, were predicted better by community characteristics than by characteristics of the family. In other words, adolescent participation in heavy delinquent pursuits had no connection at all with the quality of family life experienced, but was rooted in the wider social environment. On the other hand, family malfunctioning predicted several less serious forms of delinquent expression. Status violations, drug use, offenses against property, and, to a degree, automobile offenses were all better interpreted as reactions to family problems than as reactions to a hostile external environment. Indeed, community characteristics had almost no relationship at all to these forms of law violation.

These patterns suggest a shifting balance between the role of the family and the role of the community in explaining contranormative behavior. Where the external environment is stable and provides a modicum of safety and security, disrupted family conditions can and do generate delinquent outcomes. Where communities are crowded and deteriorated, and where the economic press of life is constant and ubiquitous, however, the net added impact of a bad family situation is minimal. Paradoxically, it may not be in the heart of the inner-city slum that family disintegration has its most significant role in the etiology of delinquency. Deteriorated families seem to have a stronger impact on youngsters in benign than in hostile ecological settings.

Conclusions and Implications

Despite voluminous attention to the topic, the relationship between family factors and juvenile delinquency is still not well understood. It has been obscured by three main oversights: (1) a failure to clearly isolate how the major components of family systems relate to delinquent behavior; (2) a failure to discriminate the types of youthful misbehavior influenced and not influenced by the family; and (3) a failure to study the family in the context of the wider community.

Although the bulk of available evidence does suggest that the family has a disposing influence on delinquency, it may no longer make sense to interpret that influence as situationally invariant. The impact of the family on delinquency seems to vary directly with the quality of the immediate social environment. Efforts to establish policy regarding the family which do not recognize these wider social forces are subject to what Scheuch (1969) called the "individualistic fallacy," a frame of reference that ignores the possibility that individuals with similar characteristics may behave differently in different types of social environments. Just as ecological studies fail to explain why some young persons within an area become delinquent while others do not, studies or policies which isolate individuals or families from their social contexts will be impervious to situational variation. It has been shown elsewhere (Johnstone 1978b) that the contextual frame of reference helps clarify the relationship between social class position and delinquency, and further study of the joint impact of family and community systems on the behavior of children and adolescents also seems worthwhile.

The contextual perspective described here fits well with the needs hierarchy frame of reference (Maslow 1954). The failure to satisfy higher-order social and affiliational needs in family life may have a bearing on delinquency only in contexts where lower-order needs for survival and security have been met. Although families in poverty-stricken communities are more disrupted than families in other areas, they may not play the major role in determining delinquency. In those settings, pressures from the street and from the ubiquity of poverty may far overshadow negative influences from the home. In stable and more affluent communities, on the other hand, poor family relationships may constitute the worst social experiences in a child's life, and may therefore have a much more proximal impact on behavior. Before pointing to family malfunctioning as the source of all delinquent behavior, then, it is important to know that the critical cause is not what happens to the child outside the family. In hard-core poverty areas, family problems, though real, may not be the first order of business.

Current national policy regarding delinquency control stresses deinstitutionalization of delinquents, diversion of status offenders from the juvenile justice system, and a more balanced mix between prevention and correction. Finestone (1976) describes the period since 1970 as one in which the major responsibility for delinquency control has shifted from institutions to the community. Given this trend, a considerably stronger role for the family can be anticipated in programs related both to prevention and correction. The relevant question today is not *whether* the family has a role in delinquency control, but *how* families are to be involved.

If the impact of the family on delinquency cannot be separated from the community setting in which families function, then it follows that programs of delinquency control which involve the family should not be either. This implies that intervention with families should be targeted at different problems in different types of communities. Intervention focused on the internal dynamics of family systems, for example, has a much better chance of success in situations where family malfunctioning has a more direct impact on delinquent behavior. A treatment modality such as family therapy may be the only intervention necessary when the acting-out youngster comes from a stable community, or when the acting-out behavior is less serious. In disorganized communities, on the other hand, intervention focused exclusively on family dynamics is not likely to be effective except in isolated instances. In those settings the more pressing need is to help families combat the pressures of the external environment since it is those pressures that impact most directly on the behavior of their offspring. When the environmental press is strong, families with youngsters need to be in touch with other families who face similar problems so that together they can more effectively communicate their needs to the education, law enforcement, and other public and private agencies whose responsibility it is to provide services for youth and to combat juvenile crime. In other words, efforts to help families deal better with the external community should precede efforts to help them deal better with themselves. In disrupted communities, efforts to organize block clubs, citizens' committees, parent uniforms, and parent self-help organizations could all have positive payoffs in this regard, and could also serve the important secondary function of breaking down the isolation that many families in these settings are known to experience. Organizing a disrupted community is not a simple task, but it is the most direct way to combat juvenile delinquency in a high-crime area.

The upshot of the contextual perspective, then, is that the mode of intervention should fit the situational needs of the family. It should be obvious, therefore, that intervention either at the family systems level or at the community organization level is feasible only if basic survival needs are being met. Intervention focused on basic survival, via family assistance, logically supersedes any other intervention. In the hierarchy of needs perspective basic economic needs come first; control of the social environment comes next; and intervention with the family system itself should in most instances occur only when problems at these other levels are being dealt with. The paradox here is that if economic and community problems are in fact brought under control, then malfunctioning family relationships will become the more proximal stimulus to delinquent behavior. A sound social policy regarding the family's role in delinquency control, then, has to take all these levels into consideration. None can be neglected. At issue is the number of levels at which intervention is necessary.

Given the increasing prevalence of unmarried teenage mothers in the population, there is also a clear-cut need for training in parent effectiveness—programs focused on both affective and instrumental aspects of parenting, and on techniques of setting limits on children's behavior. High school outreach programs, community public health facilities, and the mass media could all be utilized in providing these services.

There is ample evidence from the research literature that family structure by itself is of little importance in explaining delinquent behavior. Structural characteristics are associated with how far youthful offenders are processed through the juvenile justice system, but they do not account well for the actions that bring youngsters to the courts in the first place. It is likely that many single-parent families, and in particular black families with extended kinship, are a great deal more effective than they often are assumed to be. Those persons, such as youth officers and judges, who are responsible for decisions as to whether a child is put on probation, goes to a correctional institution, or gets a lecture and sent home, would be well advised to look more carefully at the total family system. Too often in the past these decisions have been based on a superficial evaluation of a family, in combination with stereotypes and biases. The tendency to look only at family structure, and to ignore the quality of life in the family, has led to grave injustices and inequalities in juvenile justice. This issue is of critical importance today in view of the changing structure of the American family.

References

Billingsley, Andrew (1968). *Black Families in White America*. Englewood Cliffs, N.J.: Prentice-Hall.

Browning, C.J. (1960). "Differential impact of family disorganization on male adolescents." *Social Problems* 8:37-44.

Burgess, E.W. (1954). "Family breakdown." *American Journal of Orthopsychiatry* 24:462-470. Portions reprinted with permission. © 1954, The American Orthopsychiatric Association, Inc.

Cloward, Richard A., and Ohlin, Lloyd E. (1960). *Delinquency and Opportunity*. Glencoe, Ill.: Free Press.

Cohen, S. (1974). "Breaking out, smashing up and the social context of aspiration." *Working Papers in Cultural Studies* 5 (Spring):37-63.

Corbett, J., and Vereb, T.S. (1974). *Juvenile Court Statistics, 1972*. Washington, D.C.: U.S. Department of Justice, National Institute for Juvenile Justice and Delinquency Prevention.

Finestone, Harold (1976). *Victims of Change: Juvenile Delinquents in American Society*. Westport, Conn.: Greenwood Press.

Glick, P.C. (1977). "Updating the Life Cycle of the Family." *Journal of Marriage and the Family* 30 (February):5-14.

Glueck, Sheldon and Glueck, Eleanor (1950). *Unraveling Juvenile Delinquency*. Cambridge: Harvard University Press.

Hays, W.C., and Mindel, C.H. (1973). "Extended kinship relations in black and white families." *Journal of Marriage and the Family* 35 (February):51-57.

Hirschi, Travis (1969). *Causes of Delinquency*. Berkeley: University of California Press.

Jenkins, R.L., and Hewitt, L. (1944). "Types of personality structure encountered in child guidance clinics." *American Journal of Orthopsychiatry* 14:84-94.

Jensen, G.F. (1972). "Parents, peers, and delinquent action: a test of the differential association perspective." *American Journal of Sociology* 78 (November):562-575.

Johnstone, J.W.C. (1977). "The family and delinquency: a reappraisal." Chicago: Institute for Juvenile Research, mimeographed research report.

_____ (1978a). "Juvenile delinquency and the family: a contextual interpretation." *Youth and Society* 9 (March):299-313.

_____ (1978b). "Social class, social areas and delinquency." *Sociology and Social Research* 63 (October):49-72.

Krisberg, Barry, and Austin, James (1978). *The Children of Ishmael*. Palo Alto: Mayfield.

Law Enforcement Assistance Administration (1975). *Sourcebook of Criminal Justice Statistics, 1974*. Washington, D.C.: U.S. Government Printing Office.

Lofland, John (1969). *Deviance and Identity*. Englewood Cliffs, N.J.: Prentice-Hall.

McCord, J., and McCord, W. (1964). "The effects of parental role model on criminality." In R. Cavan (ed.), *Readings in Juvenile Delinquency*. Philadelphia: Lippincott.

Maslow, A. (1954). *Motivation and Personality*. New York: Harper.

Moynihan, D.P. (1965). *The Negro Family: The Case for National Action*. Washington, D.C.: U.S. Department of Labor, Office of Planning and Research.

National Center for Health Statistics (1978). Final Natality Statistics, 1976. Monthly Vital Statistics Report, 26, No. 12 (March 29). Washington, D.C.: U.S. Government Printing Office.

Nye, F. Ivan (1958). *Family Relationships and Delinquent Behavior*. New York: Wiley.

Rodman, H. and Grams, P. (1967). "Juvenile delinquency and the family: a review and discussion." In The President's Commission on Law Enforcement and Administration of Justice. *Task Force Report: Juvenile Delinquency and Youth Crime.* Washington D.C.: U.S. Government Printing Office, pp. 188-221.

Rosen, L. (1970). "The broken home and delinquency." In M.E. Wolfgang et al. (eds.), *The Sociology of Crime and Delinquency.* 2d ed. New York: Wiley, 489-495.

Scheuch, E.K. (1969). "Social context and individual behavior." In M. Dogan and S. Rokkan (eds.), *Quantitative Ecological Analysis in the Social Sciences.* Cambridge: MIT Press, pp. 133-155.

Short, J.F., Jr., Tennyson, R.A. and Howard, K.I. (1963). "Behavior dimensions of gang delinquency." *American Sociological Review* 28 (June):411-428.

Stack, Carol B. (1974). *All Our Kin: Strategies for Survival in a Black Community.* New York: Harper and Row.

Staples, R. (1971). "Towards a sociology of the black family: a decade of theory and research." *Journal of Marriage and the Family* 33 (February):19-38.

Thomas, Darwin L., Gecas, V., Weigert, A., and Rooney, E. (1974). *Family Socialization and the Adolescent.* Lexington, Mass.: Lexington Books, D.C. Heath.

Time (1977). "The youth crime plague." July 11.

Tittle, C.R., Villemez, W. J. and Smith, D.A. (1978). "The myth of social class and criminality: an empirical assessment of the empirical evidence." *American Sociological Review* 43 (October):643-656.

U.S. Bureau of the Census (1978). *Characteristics of American Children and Youth: 1976.* Current Population Reports, No. 66, Series P-23. Washington, D.C.: U.S. Government Printing Office.

Wilkinson, K. (1974). "The broken family and juvenile delinquency: scientific explanation or ideology?" *Social Problems* 21 (June):726-739.

Williams, J.R., and Gold, M. (1972). "From delinquent behavior to official delinquency." *Social Problems* 20 (Fall):209-227.

The Educational Experience and Evolving Delinquent Careers: A Neglected Institutional Link

Delos H. Kelly

Introduction

Traditionally, attempts at explaining the rise of delinquent or deviant activity have relied on the presumed importance of social class. The works of Merton (1938), Cohen (1955), Cloward and Ohlin (1960), and Miller (1958) provide representative statements of this position. Most of these efforts, moreover, are primarily structural in nature. What this generally means is that pressures toward deviation are located within specific types of societal conditions and not within individuals. Merton, for example, focuses on structural strain, Cohen on status frustration, Cloward and Ohlin on blocked opportunity, and Miller on the structure of the household. Presumably, intervening factors such as these operate in such a manner as to produce behavior that can be labeled as deviant, delinquent, or criminal. And while this may be the case, the actual empirical support for the class-bound theories and perspectives has been anything but convincing. Not only this, but the results that have emerged indicate that factors in addition to social class will have to be invoked, particularly if we are to approach a more complete understanding of those conditions that may produce acts of youth rebellion and delinquent activity, as well as delinquent careers. The major evidence in support of this position has been generated by what can be appropriately termed the Oregon school. (Representative examples of this school of thought will be cited throughout this chapter.)

Specifically, the bulk of research produced by the Oregon school indicates that various types of school factors, independent of status origins consideration, are especially important in the initiation and perpetuation of many deviant, delinquent, and, eventually, criminal careers (Polk 1975); those factors which appear most potent are linked to school failure (broadly conceived). Observations such as this also point to the need for analyzing the structure and process of schooling, and especially those elements and conditions that invariably guarantee the production of selected categories of "misfits" (Kelly 1978c). Even though this important requirement has been briefly acknowledged by some writers and investigators, it is still safe to conclude that very little research has actually been conducted in terms of analyzing institutional components and their negative impact upon students. More specifically, even though many would acknowledge the fact that school factors often stand out in the backgrounds of delinquents, the educational institution has not been regularly or systematically subjected to a critical organizational scrutiny.

A central thesis developed in this chapter is the notion that in spite of past theorizing efforts, as well as the new strands of theorizing that are either slowly evolving or currently being "discovered" (the Marxist, conflict, and labeling statements), none is systematically focused on educational structures and processes. As a result, not only do the topics of educational processing and its effects remain rather neglected concerns, but the actual organizational structure of the school remains relatively unresearched. In this chapter I will, in view of these specific neglects, present and outline an existing perspective (the organizational) that can be used to approach a more complete understanding of how various types of deviant and delinquent careers become initiated and perpetuated within the American educational system—careers which, most assuredly, have important ramifications for other domains such as the community and the world of work. I will also, where appropriate, draw upon my own theorizing and research efforts. Even such a brief analysis as this should help to move the search for causes away from an exclusive concern for such factors as social class, poverty, and race per se to an examination of how institutional structures and components relate to these factors and others (for example, personal identity) to produce the career of the delinquent. In this respect, then, the institution must also become a direct object of study.

The Class-Bound Argument

Many influential theorists have argued exclusively for the theoretical importance of social class. Presumably, and in an intervening sense, low social class gives rise to certain conditions such as status frustration that in turn produce motivations toward deviant and delinquent activities. One of the most famous examples of this general position can be found in Albert K. Cohen's work, *Delinquent Boys* (1955). Not only is his theory predicated on the importance of social class, but he, unlike the other well-known theorists, also argues that a negative school experience can give rise to status frustration on the part of working-class males; this frustration can then be resolved in several ways. The status-frustrated males may, for example, drop out of school or become involved in delinquency and the delinquent subculture. Thus, in terms of Cohen's argument, understanding the rise of youth misconduct requires an analysis of how the class variable articulates with the nature of the school experience. Although Cohen does offer an interesting and plausible thesis relative to the school, it can be noted that very few attempts have been made to assess the empirical adequacy of his theory. My efforts (Kelly 1972; Kelly and Balch 1971; Phillips and Kelly 1979) probably represent the major, systematic attempts to do so. A brief description of one of these studies follows, particularly those aspects that have a direct bearing upon my evolving concern with the organizational perspective.

In our examination of the rebellious and delinquent patterns of 1,227 male sophomores in the Pacific northwest, we actually found little support for the class argument (Kelly and Balch 1971). Our results, however, did sensitize us to the effects that a negative school experience, in general, may produce; this was most evident in terms of how the school factors operated. Specifically, instead of serving as major intervening variables between social class and the dependent concerns (as suggested by Cohen's theory), the school variables exhibited independent associations with school avoidance and deviant behavior. As far as the actual measures involved (grade-point average, academic self-evaluation, affect, and activities), grade-point average emerged as the strongest correlate of truancy, dropout, smoking, drinking, cruising, and delinquency. The effect of the class variable was both weak and inconsistent for selected indicators, particularly for the three measures of official delinquency (court contact, frequent delinquency, and serious delinquency). The data in table 6-1 support these patterns.

The major finding that emerged from this study and subsequent ones (Kelly 1971; Kelly and Pink 1971, 1972a,b, 1973, 1974, 1975) was the consistently strong association between school failure and youth misconduct, delinquency included. In more general terms, the results indicated that most

Table 6-1
School Avoidance and Deviant Behavior, by Social Origins and Academic Performance (percent)

| | Grade Point Average | | | |
| | High | | Low | |
	Middle Class	Working Class	Middle Class	Working Class
Truancy	27	26	47	51
Dropout	2	4	28	34
Smoking	11	18	38	41
Drinking	14	19	29	31
Cruising	51	62	78	82
Delinquency	19	22	44	35
Frequent	6	7	26	20
Serious	9	13	24	22

Source: D.H. Kelly and R.W. Balch, "Social Origins and School Failure: A Reexamination of Cohen's Theory of Working Class Delinquency," *Pacific Sociological Review* 14 (1971):423. Reprinted with permission.

students, regardless of their status origins, are likely to respond to failure in similar ways. Although such an observation may not appear especially startling, it did seem to corroborate partially the pioneering efforts of a few sociologists (Elliott 1966; Hargreaves 1967; Polk 1969; Schafer and Polk 1967; Schafer and Olexa 1971), most notably their arguments to the effect that the school experience requires careful analysis. And in a more specific fashion, the findings also provided support for those few (Hargreaves 1967; Kelly 1970; Schafer and Olexa 1971) who had called for a systematic examination of the school's status allocation process (and associated outcomes)—a primary focus of the Oregon, or "school status," viewpoint.

The School Status-Tracking Argument

A major argument also advanced by the proponents of the school status perspective is the notion that if one is to approach a better understanding of the major antecedents of youth crime in specific domains such as the school, then a prior analysis of existing structures must be conducted. The work of Hargreaves and Schafer and Olexa represent two of the more systematic attempts along this line.

Hargreaves, in his year-long study of streaming (tracking) in an English secondary school for boys, observed a strong association between stream position and school misconduct. Those students in the low streams, when compared with those in the high streams, exhibited the highest rates of misconduct and petty delinquency. Although Hargreaves did not control for social class (a potentially important selection factor for student placement), he did offer some impressionistic data suggesting that his results may be relatively unaffected by social class. Schafer and Olexa's study of the American tracking system parallels Hargreaves's in many ways.

Unlike Hargreaves's research, however, Schafer and Olexa's investigation of tracking in two midwestern, urban high schools exhibits a striking pattern of bias in terms of track assignment—a pattern that holds when controls are introduced for IQ and past achievement. Specifically, both blacks and low-income students (as measured by father's occupation) are more likely to be found in the low or basic tracks. Their research indicates further that even with such factors as IQ, father's occupation, and past performance controlled, tracking is still significantly linked to various outcomes. The low-track students, when compared with the high-track, were more likely to receive low grades, to drop out, and to become tagged as official delinquents.

Several of my recent studies (Kelly 1973, 1974a,b, 1975a,b, 1976a,b,c,d, 1977a,b,c,d,e, 1978a,b,c,d) have not only generally replicated and extended Schafer Olexa's research but have also examined the potential interpretive effect of selected variables such as self-esteem, school commitment, and peer affiliation. The overall results of these studies present a very clear pattern: track position, independent of various selection and interpretive factors, bears a significant relationship to youth misconduct. Some representative data in support of this general observation are contained in tables 6-2 and 6-3. The information in table 6-2, it can be noted, is drawn from my study of 173 juniors and seniors (both males and females) attending a school in a rural setting in western New York State; the evidence in table 6-3 comes from my study of 496 senior males and females attending a school in an urban setting in eastern New York State. Both sets of data exhibit a generally strong, independent association between tracking and juvenile misconduct.

The Evolving Organizational Perspective

The consistent finding that track position, a structural-organizational variable, is significantly related to youth misconduct provided further support for my feeling that we should examine institutional structures, not only in terms of their basic organizational components but also in terms of how the institution in its actual operation initiates and perpetuates deviant and delinquent careers. Again, relatively little work has been conducted in this area. The most systematic, as well as insightful, research has been done by Cicourel and Kitsuse (1963, 1968).

Cicourel and Kitsuse claim that the educational institution can be characterized in terms of its career lines, both the deviant and the nondeviant. To support their notion, they locate and describe three major careers: (1) the academic, (2) the emotional, and (3) the delinquent. A major observation concerns the way in which school personnel, especially the counselors, applied nonacademic criteria in selecting students for placement in the deviant careers (the delinquent and emotional careers). For example, violating school rules and regulations increased one's chances of being placed in the delinquent career line, suggesting that teachers and administrators are, in fact, most sensitized to those acts of deviance which occur within the confines of their jurisdiction; this finding has been corroborated by recent work (Balch and Kelly 1974; Kelly 1977d).

Cicourel and Kitsuse offer another extremely useful insight that has a direct bearing upon the origin of an institution's deviant career lines. In particular, they describe the process whereby guidance counselors, in a conscious and deliberate effort to justify their own position in the academic hierarchy, as well as in an attempt to carve out a permanent niche for themselves, began to identify emotional problems among the students where none has existed before. Predictably, this strategy not only produced

Table 6-2
Reported Delinquent Involvement, by Selected Predictor Variables
(Yule's Q)

Type of Misconduct	Zero-Order			First-Order[a]	
	Sex	Social Class	Track Position	Track Position with Sex Controlled	Track Position with Class Controlled
Drank alcohol	−.14	+.13	−.45*	−.43*	−.48*
Skipped school	−.24	−.24	−.45*	−.41*	−.41*
Drove without license	−.28	+.09	−.39*	−.35*	−.43*
Smoked cigarettes	+.06	−.02	−.57*	−.57*	−.60*
Shoplifted	−.14	+.07	−.46*	−.44*	−.50*
Drove under the influence	−.22	−.06	−.58*	−.55*	−.60*
Bought alcohol	−.45*	+.06	−.48*	−.31*	−.52*
Violated curfew	−.19	+.01	−.32*	−.30*	−.34*
Disturbed the peace	−.26	−.12	−.51*	−.49*	−.51*
Drunk in public	−.53*	+.01	−.67*	−.63*	−.70*
Stole book from library	−.21	+.08	−.39*	−.36*	−.43*
Trespassed (private residence)	−.43*	+.19	−.12	−.06	−.18
Smoked marijuana	−.09	+.22	−.39*	−.37*	−.39*
Ran away from home	−.12	−.08	−.40*	−.39*	−.40*
Used obscene language in public	−.13	−.27	−.62*	−.62*	−.62*
Made obscene phone call	−.10	+.07	−.87	−.86	−.87
Went "joy riding"	−.37	+.42*	−.45*	−.38	−.45*
Sold marijuana	−.54*	+.28	−.44	−.39*	−.44
Expelled from school	−.60*	−.10	−.66	−.70	−.66
Placed on school probation	−.07	+.07	−.52	−.69	−.52
Broke into a private residence	−.75*	+.01	−.80	−.79	−.80
Received ticket for speeding	−.70*	+.11	−.44	−.39	−.44
Stole a bicycle	−.76*	−.23	−.71*	−.69*	−.71*
Destroyed property	−.89*	−.04	−.62*	−.54*	−.62*
Involved in gang fighting	−.57*	+.08	−.61*	−.58*	−.61*

Source: D.H. Kelly, "*Track position* and *delinquent involvement*: a preliminary analysis," *Sociology and Social Research* 58 (1974):383. Reprinted with permission.

Note: * indicates statistical significance ($P \leqslant 0.25$).

[a]To obtain the first-order partials, a weighting system known as direct standardization was used (Anderson and Zelditch, 1968: 175-179). For an alternative method, see particularly Davis (1971).

Table 6-3
School and Youth Misconduct, by Selected Predictor Variables and Controls
(Yule's Q)

Types of Misconduct	Zero-Order			First-Order[a]		
	Sex	Status Origins	Track Position	Status Origins with Sex Controlled	Track Position with Sex Controlled	Track Position with Status Origins Controlled
Deliberately cut classes	−.10	−.10	−.14	−.10	−.17	−.06
Deliberately skip school	−.10	−.14	−.25*	−.12	−.28*	−.25*
School misconduct	−.46*	−.30*	−.05	−.31*	−.16	−.03
School probation	−.23	−.38	−.60*	.00	−.66*	−.60*
School expulsion	+.01	+.12	−.61*	+.09	−.67*	−.65*
Drink under age	−.32*	−.09	−.07	−.09	−.12	−.09
Smoke marijuana	−.18	−.24	−.47*	−.23	−.51*	−.46*
Arrested	−.44	−.40	−.40	−.21	−.46*	−.37
Juvenile court contact	+.09	−.18	−.26	−.34	−.34	−.26

[a]To obtain the first-order partials, a weighting system known as direct standardization was used.

Note: *Q is statistically significant ($p \leqslant .025$).

Source: D.H. Kelly "Comparing college-bound and non-college-bound students in terms of deviant behavior," *College Student Journal* 10 (1976):22. Reprinted with permission.

a new career line, but it also guaranteed a reserve of appropriate clients. Educational processes such as these, as well as others, also present us with a rather clear pattern: Many educators in their positions of power play a very important part in the evolution of various types of deviant careers; they also play a critical role in selecting out students for placement in careers. Furthermore, many of the students chosen are not only more susceptible or vulnerable to processing as deviants because they violated some rule or regulation, or exhibited presumed emotional problems, but they frequently lack the power and resources (for example, if they come from low-income or minority backgrounds) necessary to structure an effective counter definition of the situation. This general pattern also holds for parents and guardians who, unfortunately, rarely question the decisions that are made on behalf of their children or wards.

In one of my recent studies (Kelly 1976c) I examined the critical role that institutional personnel (specifically, teachers) can play in the initiation and perpetuation of deviant adolescent careers. I was also fortunate to be in a position where I could systematically analyze the evolution of a new deviant career line: the remedial reader.

Similar to Cicourel and Kitsuse's initial research, I was able to locate and describe three rather distinct career lines: (1) the academic, (2) the emotional-troublemaker, and (3) the vocational. Of equal significance was the observation that a clearly defined, six-level track system existed. This system, however, could be effectively collapsed into two major career lines: (1) the academic (track levels one and two) and (2) the nonacademic (track levels three to six). The evidence also indicated that a new subtype had evolved during the period from 1974 to 1976. I termed this career the "vocational-remedial," as it was available primarily to students situated in tracks three to six, and particularly those students who were destined for either a vocational career or who exhibited reading problems. I also noted that a great deal of stigma surrounded the new remedial reading program.

These initial observations gave rise to the second phase of my study. This aspect was concerned specifically with examining how students were actually chosen for placement in the remedial reading program. In September 1974, I was given complete access to the school records for all sixth- and seventh-grade students attending a middle school (grades five through eight) in an urban setting in western New York State. I then asked all teachers who had actually taught the sixth and seventh graders to nominate those students they felt should be placed in remedial reading. All teachers returned the nomination form and its instructions; however, and as might be expected, none of the teachers who had taught track level one and two students (the highest tracks) nominated any students. The teachers' nominations were then compared with the reading specialist's list of students. (A small portion of these findings are contained in tables 6-4 and 6-5.) Some clear patterns emerged: (1) Many of the students nominated for the program did not meet the minimal criteria for placement (as based on standardized reading tests); this was most evident from the observation that fifteen out of the forty nominees (or 37.5 percent) did not qualify for placement (table 6-4). (2) If students had experienced prior contact with a stigmatizing program (for example, previous remedial reading experience), this increased their chances of being nominated for the current program, even though their reading scores did not warrant such a nomination. Some of these observations are evident in table 6-5. It should be noted, additionally, that similar to Cicourel and Kitsuse's observations, many teachers were invoking nonacademic criteria in the selection process. This study has been recently replicated (Kelly 1977c) and the same general results obtain. Specifically, an examination of remedial reading placement for four grades indicates that stigmatizing experiences and contacts, as well as past instances of academic failure, increase a student's chances of being typed negatively and placed in a deviant career line.

Analyzing Institutional Structures

As the evidence reviewed thus far suggests, very little research has actually been directed toward an in-depth analysis of the educational institution; this

Table 6-4

Frequency of Teacher Nominations Compared to Reading Specialist Evaluations

Number of Teachers Recommending Student Placement in Remedial Reading Program	Reading Specialist Evaluations			
	Criteria Met	Criteria Possibly Met	Criteria Not Met	Total
Fifth-grade teachers	2	6	9	17
Sixth-grade teachers	7	10	6	23
Total	9	16	15	40

Source: D.H. Kelly, "The role of teachers' nominations in the perpetuation of deviant adolescent careers," Education 96 (1976):214. Reprinted with permission.

situation continues to hold, even in view of the repeated observation that educational factors such as school failure, low-track position, and counselor-teacher selection processes are significantly related to such outcomes as alienation, dropout, school misconduct, youth rebellion, and delinquent activity. The evidence also supports the notion that selected institutional personnel, with their monopoly of power and resources, frequently play a critical role in selecting out prospective clients for placement in the institution's existing, as well as evolving, deviant career lines—hence, the notion of the initiation of deviant and delinquent careers.

It should be noted, too, that once selected for placement in a specific career, the actor is expected, thereafter, to become committed to his or her new status and its associated roles. In fact, various types of institutional structures, mechanisms, controls, and sanctioning patterns operate in such a fashion as to virtually guarantee compliance on the part of the institu-

Table 6-5

Selected Student Attributes, by Nomination Status and Grade Level

Student Attribute	Sixth Grade		Seventh Grade	
	Nominees	Nonnominees	Nominees	Nonnominees
Reading score (mean)	79	81	77	80
IQ (mean)	106	103	98	102
Years failed (mean)	.33	.36	.81	.61
Past enrollment in remedial reading (proportion)	1.00	.40[a]	.65	.31[a]

Source: D.H. Kelly, "The role of teachers' nominations in the perpetuation of deviant adolescent careers," Education 96 (1976):214. Reprinted with permission.

[a] $p \leqslant .01$

tionally labeled deviant. The plight of McMurphy in *One Flew over the Cuckoo's Nest* (Kesey 1962) serves as an excellent case in point—a case with general principles that can be readily extrapolated to other institutions and domains.

Specifically, not only was McMurphy defined as being mentally ill, but the institution and its personnel expected him to act in accordance with their definition of him; however, he continually rejected his sick role. Thus what transpired was a running battle between Big Nurse (the institution's duly authorized representative) and McMurphy (the institution's perceived legitimate client or ward). Even the application of various types of institutional sanctions failed to bring McMurphy's behavior into line with the appropriate institutional expectations. And in the end it becomes a matter of debate as to who really won the battle, the institution or the individual. Still, the example, as well as my preceding analysis, is useful in terms of sensitizing one to the way in which institutions not only initiate but also perpetuate deviant careers. The example, and particularly the prior evidence on tracking and the selection of clients, also provides content to the thesis that not only do institutions require study, but we also need to carefully examine how an institution's organizational components (deviant career lines) may articulate with individual factors (an actor's rejection of a deviant label and its associated status and roles). For the actual elements and processes involved, several leads can be offered.

Theory of the Office and Diagnostic Stereotypes

Explicit in the work of Cicourel and Kitsuse and others (Kelly 1976c, 1977a,c,e, 1978a,b,c, 1979) is the notion that any institution can be characterized in terms of its theory of the office, or working ideology. In general terms, this refers to "what the institution or agency is about." For example, the police are expected to maintain order and enforce the law; the school is expected to educate children. Embedded within an institution's theory of the office are various types of conceptual packages, or diagnostic stereotypes, that are used in the identifying and classifying of clients or potential clients (Scheff 1966). The police, for example, become familiar with the existing "normal crimes" (Sudnow 1965); these then become important criteria as far as making initial sense out of an event such as a case of child molestation they may encounter. The categories of normal crimes also frequently suggest some likely attributes of the offender, as well as some possible reasons as to why the act was committed. Similarly, within the school, counselors, teachers, and administrators hold certain diagnostic stereotypes that are applied to students; this was perhaps most evident in the way Cicourel and Kitsuse's guidance counselors typed students for placement in the emotional and delinquent career lines. It was also apparent in terms of how some of the teachers in my research invoked nonacademic criteria in their selection process. What evidence such as this indicates is that the school's theory of the office is solidly predicated on the presumption of differential ability (Kelly 1977a,e, 1978c). Or, more specifically, the underlying philosophy is founded on the idea that a few students have ability, some little ability, and others no ability. Such an ideology means, predictably, that certain students are destined for success, others for failure. In fact, these specific notions are firmly entrenched within the very organizational structure of the school. The formal student stratification systems such as ability grouping and tracking provide clear examples of this. Structural conditions such as these offer us an absolute guarantee: As long as deviant career lines (and their associated diagnostic stereotypes) comprise an integral component of the school's organizational structure, educational personnel will continue to select out various categories of students (frequently, those who are perceived as lacking power and resources) for placement in these career lines. That is, and as I have argued elsewhere (Kelly 1978c), the school will continue to manufacture a certain amount of "misfits" for us. Logically, no other conclusion is warranted.

Some Institutional Components and Processes
that Require Examination

Throughout this chapter, certain components and processes have been commented upon, some extensively; this has been deliberate and is in line with my contention that not only do institutional structures require examination, but analyses also need to be conducted in terms of how structural and individual factors interact to produce deviant and delinquent careers.

As far as conducting an institutional analysis, several initial questions and concerns, which flow from my comments, need to be addressed: (1) How can we describe or characterize the institution's theory of the office or working ideology? Is it, like the school's, for example, predicated upon the presumption of differential ability? (2) What can we learn from the content of the existing diagnostic stereotypes that are embedded within the theory of the office? Are selected categories of individuals (blacks, Mexicans, Indians, low-income personnel, and those who generally lack power and resources) more likely to be perceived and responded to in a negative fashion? (3) How is the institution's theory of the office reflected in the existing careers or career lines? Is there, similar to the school's tracking mechanisms, a system of deviant and nondeviant career lines? (4) In terms of the actual selection process, how do institutional representatives actually apply the existing diagnostic stereotypes, as well as individual notions, to various categories of clients or prospective clients? Are the objects of negative stereotypes for example, blacks, Mexicans, Indians, low-income people, and those who generally lack power and resources more likely to be selected out for institutional typing and processing as deviants, criminals, or delinquents? (5) How does institutional processing affect the client's identity or self-image at various stages? Do the clients (delinquents) willingly accept the label and status being imputed to them? do they ignore it? or do they consciously try to reject it? Another neglected area that needs to be addressed concerns the way in which institutional members become socialized into the institution's existing culture and traditions. Specifically, what are the formal and informal social, psychological, and symbolic mechanisms that virtually guarantee that prospective members will not only become familiar with the system's theory of the office (and associated diagnostic stereotypes and career lines), but will also generally act in accordance with it? For example, formally, in the educational arena, we have teacher training and certification programs; informally, we have teacher lounges (Balch and Kelly 1974).

Summary and Implications

Most social scientists, by virtue of their rather exclusive and traditional concern with linking such variables as social class and race to delinquent activity, have generally neglected to consider directly how various factors articulate with institutional components and processes. I also contend that very little direct attention has been placed upon dissecting the institutions themselves, particularly in terms of how organizational components and institutional personnel initiate and perpetuate deviant and delinquent careers. I provided substance to these claims by directing my analysis primarily upon the sorting and processing aspects that continually take place within the American educational system. My comments suggest some important policy implications.

Initially, the educational institution needs to be carefully analyzed in terms of those elements and processes outlined. Once this has been accomplished, some concrete steps can be taken—measures which, if successfully implemented, will reduce the number of deviants, delinquents, and "misfits" manufactured by the school (Kelly 1978c). To begin with, the school's theory of the office needs to be radically altered. Instead of "presuming differential ability," the philosophy should be to the effect that all students are capable and have ability; this change in ideology must be accompanied by an elimination of the deviant career lines that are firmly entrenched within the organizational structure of the school. This also entails changing the content of the diagnostic stereotypes that are invariably applied to especially vulnerable students. Altering the theory of the office, doing away with deviant career lines, and changing the diagnostic stereotypes, however, is not enough. The basic substance and content of teacher training and certification programs must be revamped to reflect these changes. Prospective teachers, administrators, parents, and the students themselves must become critically aware of how society's institutions, in this case the schools, initiate and perpetuate the career of the deviant or misfit; they must also become attuned to the fact that, although institutions are most systematic and efficient in bestowing negative tags upon individuals, they are notoriously unsystematic and inefficient in removing such labels and their associated stigma. There is, thus, always a "lingering of traces" (Simmons 1969).

Obviously, making these basic changes will not begin to eliminate all cases of delinquency or deviance. Individuals will, for various reasons, continue to violate deviant categories in other settings, and they will be typed and selected out by social control agents to play the role of the deviant—processes that will not only frequently initiate but also perpetuate the career of the social deviant (Kelly 1979). Nonetheless, the structural changes discussed (which can be extrapolated to other institutions and settings) can reduce the number of misfits produced by the school. Quite obviously, too, the school will continue to be a critical domain, and academic success or failure will hold certain direct or indirect ramifications for other settings and experiences.

References

Anderson, Theodore R., and Zelditch, Morris, Jr., (1968). *A Basic Course in Statistics*. New York: Holt, Rinehart and Winston.

Balch, R.W., and Kelly, D.H. (1974). "Reactions to deviance in a junior high school: student views of the labeling process." *Instructional Psychology* 1:25-38.

Cicourel, A.V., and Kitsuse, J.I. (1968). "The social organization of the high school and deviant adolescent careers." In E. Rubington and M.S. Weinberg (eds.), *Deviance: The Interactionist Perspective*, pp. 124-135. New York: Macmillan.

————— (1963). *The Educational Decision-Makers*. Indianapolis: Bobbs-Merrill.

Cloward, R.A., and Ohlin, L.E. (1960). *Delinquency and Opportunity*. New York: Free Press.

Cohen, A.K. (1955). *Delinquent Boys*. New York: Free Press.

Davis, James A. (1971). *Elementary Survey Analysis*. Englewood Cliffs: Prentice-Hall.

Elliott, D.S. (1966). "Delinquency, school attendance and dropout." *Social Problems* 13:307-314.

Hargreaves, D. (1967). *Social Relations in a Secondary School.* New York: Humanities Press.

Kelly, D.H. (1970). Social class, school status, and self-evaluation as related to adolescent values, success, and deviance. Doctoral Dissertation, University of Oregon.

_____ (1971). "School failure, academic self-evaluation, and school avoidance and deviant behavior." *Youth and Society* 2:489-503.

_____ (1972). "Social origins and adolescent success patterns." *Education and Urban Society* 3:224-235.

_____ (1973). "Track assignment and student mobility patterns as barriers to equality of educational opportunity: a review of recent research." *Contemporary Education* 45:27-30.

_____ (1974a). "Student perceptions, self-concept, and curriculum assignment." *Urban Education* 9:257-269.

_____ (1974b). "Track position and delinquent involvement: a preliminary analysis." *Sociology and Social Research* 58:380-386.

_____ (1975a). "Tracking and its impact upon self-esteem: a neglected dimension." *Education* 96:2-9.

_____ (1975b). "Status origins, track position, and delinquent involvement: a self-report analysis." *Sociological Quarterly* 16:264-271.

_____ (1976a). "Analysis of the expected correlates of curriculum assignment patterns in a high school." *Contemporary Education* 47:74-78.

_____ (1976b). "Comparing college-bound and non-college-bound students in terms of deviant behavior." *College Student Journal* 10:20-27.

_____ (1976c). "The role of teachers' nominations in the perpetuation of deviant adolescent careers." *Education* 96:209-217.

_____ (1976d). "Track position, school misconduct, and youth deviance: a test of the interpretive effect of school commitment." *Urban Education* 10:379-388.

_____ (1977a). Conceptions, diagnostic stereotypes and the processing of delinquents. Paper written for the National Council on Crime and Delinquency.

_____ (1977b). "The effects of legal processing upon a delinquent's public identity: an analytical and empirical critique." *Education* 97:280-289.

_____ (1977c). "How the school and teachers create deviants." *Contemporary Education* 48:202-205.

_____ (1977d). "Labeling and the consequences of wearing a delinquent label in a school setting." *Education* 97:371-380.

_____ (1977e). *The Organizational Creation of Social Deviants: An Examination of the Educational Processing of Students.* Los Angeles: Trident Shop.

_____ (1978a). "Conceptions, definitions, and the measurement of delinquency and delinquent involvement." In D.H. Kelly (ed.), *Delinquent Behavior: Interactional and Motivational Aspects*, pp. 18-40. Belmont, Calif.: Dickenson (Wadsworth).

_____ (1978b). *Delinquent Behavior: Interactional and Motivational Aspects*. Belmont, Calif.: Dickenson (Wadsworth).

_____ (1978c). *How the School Manufactures "Misfits."* Rowland Heights, Calif.: Newcal Publications.

_____ (1978d). "Track position, peer affiliation, and youth crime." *Urban Education* 13:397-406.

_____ (1979). *Deviant Behavior*. New York: St. Martin's Press.

Kelly, D.H., and Balch, R.W. (1971). "Social origins and school failure: a re-examination of Cohen's theory of working-class delinquency." *Pacific Sociological Review* 14:413-430.

Kelly, D.H., and Pink, W.T. (1971). "School commitment and student career flows." *Youth and Society* 3:224-235.

_____ (1972a). "Academic failure, social involvement, and high school dropout." *Youth and Society* 4:47-59.

_____ (1972b). "Social origins, school status, and the learning experience: a theoretical and empirical examination of two competing viewpoints." *Pacific Sociological Review* 16:121-134.

_____ (1973). "School commitment, youth rebellion, and delinquency." *Criminology* 10:473-485.

_____ (1974). "High school dropout: a longitudinal analysis of post-school career flows." *Contemporary Education* 46:5-12.

_____ (1975). "Status Origins, youth rebellion, and delinquency: a re-examination of the class issue." *Journal of Youth and Adolescence* 4:339-347.

Kesey, K. (1962). *One Flew over the Cuckoo's Nest*. New York: Viking.

Merton, R.K. (1938). "Social structure and anomie." *American Sociological Review* 3:672-682.

Miller, W.B. (1958). "Lower class culture as a generating milieu of gang delinquency." *Journal of Social Issues* 14:5-19.

Phillips, J.C., and Kelly, D.H. (1979). "School failure and delinquency: Which causes which?" *Criminology* 17:194-207.

Polk, K. (1969). "Class, strain and rebellion among adolescents." *Social Problems* 17:214-224.

_____ (1975). "Schools and the delinquency experience." *Criminal Justice and Behavior* 2:315-338.

Schafer, W.E., and Olexa, C. (1971). *Tracking and Opportunity*. San Francisco: Chandler.

Schafer, W.E., and Polk, K. (1967). "Delinquency and the schools." In *Task Force Report: Juvenile Delinquency and Youth Crime*, pp. 222-277. Washington, D.C.: U.S. Government Printing Office.

Scheff, T.J. (1966). "Typification in the diagnostic practices of rehabilitation agencies." In M.B. Sussman (ed.), *Sociology and Rehabilitation*, pp. 139-144. Washington, D.C.: American Sociological Association.

Simmons, J.L. (1969). *Deviants*. Berkeley: Glendessary.

Sudnow, D. (1965). "Normal crimes: sociological features of the penal code." *Social Problems* 12:255-270.

Gangs, Groups, and Serious Youth Crime

Walter B. Miller

There is an intensified concern with those forms of illegal violence and predation commonly known as "street crime." The role of youth in such crime is a major element of this concern. It is widely held that the numbers of youths involved in crimes of violence or theft have increased, that the kinds of crimes they commit have become more serious, and that the age of offenders has become lower. Although such contentions are supported by the evidence, knowledge of the actual character of youthful involvement in serious crime remains fragmentary and imprecise.

One area where knowledge is particularly poor concerns crimes committed by youths acting in concert—the area of collective youth crime. How common is such crime? What forms does it take? How serious is it relative to crimes committed by individuals? How does one go about gathering information about it? Should there be special methods for dealing with it, or should one ignore the collective character of the offense in dealing with offenders? Current knowledge with respect to all these issues is extremely primitive.

It is paradoxical that knowledge in this area is so poor. The notion that the bulk of youth crime is collective is accepted as conventional wisdom by most workers in the field. Over and again one hears that lone offenders—particularly with respect to serious offenses—represent a minority, and in all probability a small minority, of all offenders. But coupled with this conviction is a curious reluctance to pursue its implications in any systematic fashion. With some exceptions the individual remains the primary focus of concern—in record keeping, in criminal justice processing, and in programs of control, reform, and rehabilitation.[1] This reluctance to exploit systematically the collective nature of most youth crime extends, for some, to a studied effort to minimize its importance, and to play down both the amount and significance of serious youth crime which involves multiple offenders acting in concert (Klein 1971:8-11; Hindelang 1976).

One consequence of the dearth of systematic attention to collective youth crime is that no satisfactory unit of analysis has ever been developed for this area. During the past fifty years, the major concept used to guide the examination of this phenomenon has been that of "gang." This concept has become increasingly unsatisfactory as the years have passed. At no time has there been anything close to consensus as to what a gang might be—by scholars, by criminal justice workers, by the general public.

Although there has been very little scholarly work on this subject for almost twenty years, in the late 1950s and early 1960s a fair amount of work was done in this area. Scholarly efforts during this period were characterized by a high level of disagreement—much of it attributable to definitional problems. Prominent among these were a confusion of the concepts of gang subculture and gang delinquency, and difficulties in trying to distinguish between "true," or "real," gangs and "pseudo," or "near," gangs (see Miller 1976:92).

One might have expected that a period of intensive scholarly concern with gangs would have led to an upgrading of the concept—making it more precise, more refined, and more useful as a basis for analyzing and coping with collective youth crime. Instead, the opposite seems to have occurred. The concept emerged from its brief period under the academic spotlight in worse shape than when it went in. Moreover, a set of social and historical developents during this period combined to infuse the concept of gang with strong pejorative connotations—connotations which had been weaker or absent in earlier usages. The concept of gang, in most current usages, thus suffers the unhappy fate of being at the same time conceptually confused and connotationally contaminated.

A major deficiency of the term lies in its scope, or semantic domain. It is applied very broadly, very narrowly, and in all degrees in between. Such elasticity makes the term highly susceptible to manipulation, for political and other purposes. In general, police departments in large cities apply the term quite narrowly, police in smaller cities and towns less narrowly, most media writers more broadly, and most distressed local citizens very broadly. Insofar as large city police can define as few as possible of the thousands of problem youth groups in their jurisdictions as gangs, to that degree is their "gang problem"; for which they are generally held quite directly accountable, minimized. Perhaps the most restrictive definition of all is that used by the Philadelphia police, who designate as a gang only those youth groups which claim control over a specific territory and defend that claim by force. At the other end of the spectrum are residents of local comunities who are upset by cliques of fifteen or sixteen year olds who congregate nightly in local parks, and who complain to the police that the commnity is being terrorized by savage groups.

Unfortunately from the viewpoint of the citizens, those most directly responsible for dealing with these problems—primarily the police, courts, and local governmental agencies—generally use the most restrictive definitions. This has led to a radical underestimation of the amount of street crime attributable to youth collectivities. When the only major form of collective youth crime subject to systematic consideration is gang crime, and when only those groups which are large, well organized, named, and highly visible are designated as gangs, it becomes possible to discount the hundreds of thousands of smaller and less formalized cliques, bands, rings, crowds, networks, and assemblages whose members are responsible for so massive an amount of violent and predatory crime. It is not so much that the collective nature of such crime goes unrecognized, but rather that these groups are so often dismissed as loosely knit or casual, and thus, by implication, not to be taken very seriously. The term gang, then, presents serious disadvantages as the major concept for dealing with collective youth crime, since, as generally used, it provides an easy way to exclude from systematic consideration the tens of thousands of youth groups who do not readily qualify as gangs, and for representing their criminal activities as random or adventitious.

Moreover, as will be shown, gangs as commonly defined are almost exclusively a phenomenon of large cities. The fact that there are few or no gangs in most medium or smaller-sized cities and suburban or rural communities makes this concept particularly inappropriate as a basis for examining collective youth crime as a national phenomenon. What is needed, then, is a unit of analysis which will provide a more satisfactory basis for examining problems of collective youth crime, and a precise specification of the relationship of the term gang to this unit. This paper will propose such a unit, and illustrate some of its applications to issues of information gathering and policy.

Most of the data underlying both the conceptual and empirical materials presented here were collected in the course of a federally sponsored survey of collective youth crime in twenty-four major United States cities. Cities were located in all regions of the country, and included the ten largest. Interviews were conducted with 445 staff members of 160 agencies representing a broad spectrum of youth-service organizations—public and private, criminal justice, and social service. Included were police officers, community outreach workers, judges, criminal justice planners, probation officers, prosecutors, defenders, educators, city council members, state legislators, ex-prisoners, past and present members of gangs and groups, and others. Approximately one-half of those interviewed were members of three major minority groups—Hispanics, blacks, and Asians. Interviews were based on an interview guide including approximately sixty items, not all of which were asked in all interviews. A report based on information gathered in the first twelve cities surveyed was published by the U.S. Department of Justice. A second report, based on the twenty-four-city survey, is in preparation (hereafter, the larger report), and much of the material in the present chapter is abstracted directly from that report (Miller 1975, 1979).

The Law-Violating Youth Group: A
Unit of Analysis

The present chapter proposes that the concept of the law-violating youth group, rather than the concept of the gang, be used as the major unit of analysis in the study of collective youth crime. The concept is defined as follows: A law-violating youth group is an association of three or more youths whose members engage recurrently in illegal activities with the cooperation and moral support of their companions.

Each of the terms of this definition is discussed in some detail in the larger report, *Crime by Youth Groups and Gangs in American Cities.* The term *law-violating* is used in preference to *deviant* or *delinquent* because the notion of deviance encompasses much too wide and heterogeneous a range of behavior for present purposes, and the term "delinquent," in most usages, applies only to offenses by persons sixteen, seventeen, or younger. Since the ages of most members of law-violating youth groups range from approximately ten to twenty-one, their illegal activities, as classified under law, include both crimes and delinquencies. The age range of those designated as youths thus corresponds roughly to the period of social adolescence—approximately ten or twelve to twenty or twenty-one.

Of several usages of the term *group*, the definition employs that usage which makes no assumptions as to the degree of solidarity, cohesion, direct interaction, or esprit de corps. Although some or all of these elements may be present, *group* in the present usage refers to a type of association whose members may be related to each other in a variety of ways; for example, in the case of group types designated as networks, crowds, or casual cliques, relations among group members may be indirect, temporary, or casual, as well as close and persisting. The term *recurrent* does not yield readily to precise specification on a general level due to wide variations in frequency of group offenses. For practical purposes, however, it is not difficult to ascertain whether illegal activities by particular groups represent one-time occurrences or part of repeated occurrences; the determination of recurrency must also take into account differing standards of different communities.

The choice of three as the minimum size for a group reflects the fact that this number was chosen as the lower limit for gangs by more survey respondents than any other, that triads are generally regarded as groups in popular usage, and that three-boy cliques represent one of the most prevalent forms of law-violating collectivities.[2]

The terms *whose numbers, cooperation,* and *moral support* are used to convey the idea that to be considered group related illegal activity does not have to involve simultaneous participation in particular ventures by all or most group members. In many instances, in fact, acts of group illegality represent cooperative rather than simultaneous-participation ventures, with selected group members playing different parts in their execution, including functions such as planning.

Further, acts such as hits by single assailants against rival gang members, while executed by one person, are clearly group related in that they arise out of collective planning. To qualify as group related it is necessary only that illegal acts by one or more individuals be executed with the moral support and cooperation of their colleagues. Thus, a mugging by two members of a six-boy clique condoned by the others would be considered an act of members of a law-violating youth group; if, on the other hand, the act was condemned by the others, and was nonrecurrent, the group would not be considered law-violating.

Central to any attempt to gauge the size, scope, and character of collective youth crime problems in the United States is a delineation of the most prevalent types of law-violating youth groups, based on systematic principles of categorization. Such a typology is presented in the larger report, which includes a discussion of the principles on which it is based, a delineation of types at several levels of generality, a method for categorizing specialized and diversified types, an empirical examination of the criteria used for distinguishing gangs from other types of group, and detailed descriptions of the form, character, age, and sex composition, and modus operandi of each type. For purposes of the present paper, one of the major typology listings is presented; those interested in more detail are referred to the larger work (Miller 1979).

Table 7-1
Types and Subtypes of Law-Violating Youth Groups

Number	Designation
1	Turf gangs
2	Regularly-associating disruptive local groups/crowds
3	Solidary disruptive local cliques
4	Casual disruptive local cliques
5	Gain-oriented gangs/extended networks
6	Looting groups/crowds
7	Established gain-oriented cliques/limited networks
7.1	Burglary rings
7.2	Robbery bands
7.3	Larceny cliques and networks
7.4	Extortion cliques
7.5	Drug-dealing cliques and networks
7.6	Fraudulent gain cliques
8	Casual gain-oriented cliques
9	Fighting gangs
10	Assaultive cliques and crowds
10.1	Assaultive affiliation cliques
10.2	Assaultive public-gathering crowds
11	Recurrently-active assaultive cliques
12	Casual assaultive cliques

Adapted from chart 2, ch. 25, Walter B. Miller (1979b), *Crime by Youth Groups and Gangs in American Cities.*

The delineation of eighteen types and subtypes of law-violating youth groups in table 7-1 provides a basis for a systematic examination of the numbers of such groups in designated areas (for example, cities, towns, metropolitan areas, districts, counties), as well as the volume and types of crime they are responsible for. There is at present no locality in the United States for which such information is available; later sections will provide estimates of numbers of groups and group-related offenses for selected categories of cities. For present purposes it is sufficient to note that only three of the eighteen types and subtypes of youth collectivities in table 7-1 are designated as gangs. The others are designated as cliques, groups, bands, rings, networks, and crowds. Thus, at least in the context of a listing of a discrete number of common types of law-violating youth collectivities, groups distinguishable as gangs are clearly in a minority.

A Consensual Definition of Gang

Serious definitional problems with the term gang, some of which were noted earlier, underlie the present proposal to replace this concept with that of the law-violating youth group as the basis of a systematic typology. But the typology does not discard the term gang; rather it reduces it from the status of a major generic concept to that of one category among several categories. This means that the definitional problems associated with the term cannot be disregarded, since it is still necessary to be able to distinguish this particular type from other types as precisely as possible.

Most available definitions have been developed either by individual scholars or local police departments. Biases related to particular purposes of both of these occupational groups militate against the development of a definition suited to the more neutral purposes of a descriptive toxonomy. Most scholarly definitions are developed within the context of specific theoretical or ideological frameworks, and incorporate the special assumptions of these frameworks. Most police definitions, as noted, reflect considerations related to specific policy objectives, such as minimizing or, less often, inflating, the scope and seriousness of local gang problems.

The present definition does not reflect the special biases of any particular occupational group, since it is derived from definitions provided by many categories of practitioners engaged in a wide variety of service and informational pursuits in all parts of the United States. It thus provides, for the first time, a definition derived from the pooled conceptions of a large and diverse nationwide group. As part of the survey cited earlier, respondents were asked, "What is *your* conception of a gang? Exactly how would you define it?" A summary definition, based on responses by 309 respondents representing 121 agencies in twenty-six localities, was developed through the analysis of approximately 1,400 definitional elements provided by respondents.[3] Six major elements were cited most frequently—being organized, having identifiable leadership, identifying with a territory, associating continuously, having a specific purpose, and engaging in illegal activity. Combining these elements produces the following definition: A youth gang is a self-formed association of peers, bound together by mutual interests, with identifiable leadership, well-developed lines of authority, and other organizational features, who act in concert to achieve a specific purpose or purposes which generally include the conduct of illegal activity and control over a particular territory, facility, or type of enterprise.

There was a surprising degree of agreement as to the major elements of this definition by respondents of all age categories, both sexes, many occupations, in larger and smaller cities, in all regions of the country, of all races and ethnic categories, of gang members, former gang members, and nongang members. There was 85 percent agreement that the six cited elements represent the essential criteria of a gang, with agreement exceeding 90 percent for three of the six criteria.[4] The definition thus comes as close as anything available to representing a national consensus as to the characteristics of a gang.

Two-thirds of the definitional responses relate to the six major criteria just cited. The remaining responses relate to ten additional criteria, characterized in the analysis as minor. One of these concerns the size of gangs. Of those who specified lower size limits, the majority was willing to designate as a gang a group as small as three; however, the average size for a gang was given as twenty. The definitional findings thus indicate that the term gang, for most practitioners, refers to a group which averages twenty persons, operates according to formal organizational procedures, has a well-developed hierarchical authority, and is specifically structured for the purpose of engaging in criminal activity. It is quite obvious that groups with such characteristics—particularly with respect to size and organization—must make up only a small proportion of all groups which pose serious crime problems. These findings thus provide strong empirical support for the position that the term gang, as generally understood, is far too restrictive to serve as a satisfactory generic term for the study of collective youth crime.

Once having determined the basic features of respondents' conceptions of the term gang, it became important to specify its boundaries as precisely as possible. To this end, respondents were presented with a detailed description of a regularly congregating, disruptive local group ("hanging" or "corner" group) of the type designated in table 7-1 as a "solidary local clique." The group was represented as congregating regularly and engaging in a range of disruptive and other illegal activities, but lacking the established leadership, organization, and dedication to purpose seen by most respondents as essential features of a gang. Respondents were asked, "Do you consider this type of group to be a gang?'' Of 187 respondents providing answers, 51 percent said yes and 49 percent said no. There was a statistically significant difference between cities reporting more serious problems with collective youth crime and those reporting less serious problems; approximately 60 percent of respondents in the former, compared to 40 percent in the latter, were willing to grant the status of gang to the type of local group described. These findings document once again the inadequacies of the term gang; the fifty-fifty split among respondents as to whether such a group is a gang comes about as close to perfect nonconsensus as one can find. The good agreement among respondents as to the essential characteristics of a true gang thus deteriorated into disagreement when considering the status of a type of group having some of these characteristics but lacking others. Moreover, the fact that a strong majority (60 percent) in the lower-seriousness localities denied gang status to criminally involved neighborhood groups suggests that the concept of gang is even less appropriate for analyzing collective youth crime in smaller and thus more typical American cities than in the larger urban centers.

Seriousness of Crime Problems Posed by
Law-violating Youth Groups in Major Cities

A major objective of the national survey was to determine whether major United States cities were experiencing problems with criminal activity by members of law-violating youth groups, and if so, how serious those problems were. In the absence of officially recorded data, it was necessary to obtain information directly from those criminal justice, youth service, and other local practitioners in the survey cities who are most familiar with the local youth crime situation.

Respondents were asked, ''Are the problems with youth gangs or other types of law-violating youth groups in your city?'' Table 7-2 categorizes twenty-three of the survey cities with respect to reported problems with gangs or groups.[6] Three categories of cities are distinguished with respect to gang problems: those in which problems were reported by all or almost all respondents (90-100 percent); those in which problems were reported by a majority (50-90 percent); and those in which they were reported by a minority (under 50 percent). Nine cities, including the four largest, fall into the first category, eight into the second, and three into the third. The nine cities with unanimous or near-unanimous reporting of gang problems will be designated as gang cities.

There was strikingly high agreement in twenty-two of the twenty-three cities with repect to problems with groups other than gangs. Only two respondents (one in Newark, one in Houston) denied the existence of such

Table 7-2
Law-violating Youth Groups and Gangs as a Crime Problem in Major U.S. Cities, Respondent Reports for 23 U.S. Cities

(total population = 27.8 million)

Percent Respondents Reporting Problems with Gangs (23 cities average = 75.2; 298 respondents)			Percent Respondents Reporting Problems with Groups (23 cities average = 99.1; 228 respondents)		
90-100	50-90	Under 50	90-100	50-90	
(9 city average = 96.1)	(8 city average = 61.5)	(6 city average = 35.3)	(22 city average = 99.5)	(1 city, 75)	
New York	Baltimore	Houston	New York	Houston	
Chicago	Washington	Dallas	Chicago		
Los Angeles	Cleveland	Milwaukee	Los Angeles		
Philadelphia	Pittsburgh	St. Louis	Philadelphia		
Detroit	Denver	New Orleans	Detroit		
San Francisco	Minneapolis	Newark	Baltimore		
San Antonio	St. Paul		Dallas		
Boston	Ft. Worth		Washington		
Miami			Cleveland		
			Milwaukee		
			San Francisco		
			San Antonio		
			Boston		
			St. Louis		
			New Orleans		
			Pittsburgh		
			Denver		
			Minneapolis		
			Newark		
			St. Paul		
			Miami		
			Ft. Worth		

problems. Insofar as the twenty-three-survey cities represent the national
urban situation, it would appear that crime problems by youth groups are
almost universal.

Groups designated as gangs are less widely perceived as posing problems. However, it should be noted that although respondents reported the
existence of gang problems unanimously or almost unanimously in nine of
the twenty-three cities majorities reported gang problems in seventeen. In
only six cities did majorities agree that gangs did not pose problems.
Moreover, the nine-gang cities, while comprising a minority of the surveyed
cities (nine/twenty-three = 39 percent), contain approximately 70 percent
of their total population (19 out of 28 million). It thus appears that many
more cities experience problems with groups than with gangs, but that cities
with gang problems are more likely to be the most populous.

Reporting that one's city has problems with crime by gangs or groups
does not necessarily mean that such problems are considered to be serious.
Respondents were asked to rate the degree of seriousness of collective youth
crime problems on a scale of 1 to 10, with 10 representing the seriousness of
the most serious forms of violent crime—homicide, forcible rape, aggravated assault and armed robbery. Estimates of 1 to 3 were categorized as
low, 4 to 6 as medium, and 7 or more as high.[7]

Table 7-3 shows that problems posed by gangs were considered to be
very serious in three of the nine gang cities, Los Angeles, New York, and
Philadelphia, and moderately serious in the others. Problems with groups

Table 7-3
**Respondent Estimates of Seriousness of Crime Problems Posed by Law-violating
Youth Groups and Gangs in Major U.S. Cities**

Seriousness of Problems with Gangs (9 Cities[a]; 144 respondents)			Seriousness of Problems with Groups (18 Cities[b]; 213 respondents)		
High[c]	Medium	Low	High	Medium	Low
Los Angeles	Chicago		Cleveland	Denver	Houston
New York	Detroit		Miami	Ft. Worth	
Philadelphia	San Francisco		Washington	Minneapolis	
	Miami		Pittsburgh	Detroit	
	San Antonio		St. Paul	Milwaukee	
	Boston		Boston	St. Louis	
			Newark	Chicago	
			New Orleans		
			San Antonio		
			Dallas		

[a]Table 7-2, column 1.
[b]Estimates for 6 cities not obtained.
[c]See text for basis of classification.

were rated as very serious in ten of eighteen cities for which estimates were obtained, moderately serious in seventeen others, and of low seriousness in one, Houston. It thus appears that respondents in cities claiming problems with youth groups are more likely to consider these to be very serious than respondents in cities claiming problems with gangs. One probable reason for this, to be discussed further, is that groups are so much more numerous than gangs that the volume of crime they commit is much greater. What is most significant about these findings, however, is that respondents in one-half of a set of cities including most of the major urban centers of the nation consider criminal activities by gangs or groups to pose problems on the order of seriousness of homicide, rape, and armed robbery.

Numbers of Law-violating Youth Groups and Group Members

An understanding of the scope and seriousness of collective youth crime requires some notion of the numbers of law-violating youth groups and group members in the United States. No such figures have ever been published. A comprehensive set of statistics would include counts, or at least informed estimates, for each of the eighteen types listed in table 7-1 for a variety of geographical entities—the nation as a whole, each state, each region, all urban, suburban, and rural communities, all large, medium, and small cities, and so on. Since nothing remotely resembling information on this order of detail is currently available, the following sections will rely primarily on estimates based on the best available data and extend these through extrapolations based on what appear to be reasonable assumptions. Present enumerations will concentrate primarily on urban communities, principally cities of 25,000 and over.

Estimates of the numbers of gangs and gang members will be presented first. In addition to direct answers to the question, "Are there gang problems in your city?" one fairly reliable indication of the existence of gangs is the ability of local practitioners to provide specific estimates of the numbers of the gangs in a particular city, district, or neighborhood. When such estimates are provided with relative ease, this is usually a good indication that recognized gangs exist; conversely, when estimates can be provided only with difficulty, or not at all, this generally indicates the absence, or low development, of gangs. Thus, for groups which meet the criteria for gangs—that is, types 1, 5, and 9 in table 7-1, numbers are quite readily obtainable in gang-problem cities. Furthermore, police or sheriffs' departments generally keep official counts of the number of recognized gangs in the metroplitan areas of New York, Chicago, and Los Angeles.

Numbers of gangs and gang members in those cities where practitioners are in a position to furnish specific estimates vary from year to year—

sometimes negligibly, sometimes substantially. Figures presented in this section are based on two kinds of averages; averages of high and low estimates provided by different sources in given cities, and time-period averages for 1973 through 1977, the information-gathering phase of the collective youth crime survey.[8]

Groups categorizable as gangs under the present definition are found in about fifteen cities in the United States. In addition to the nine gang-problem cities of table 7-2, about six or seven others, not included among the twenty-four cities visited, appear from other evidence to have gang problems. These include El Paso, Buffalo, and Seattle. During the 1973-1977 period estimates indicate that there were about 1,300 gangs in these fifteen cities. This number remained fairly stable during the five-year period, with decreases in some areas (for example, New York) and increases in others (Los Angeles metropolitan area). Overall, the numbers of reported gangs dropped slightly (about 3 percent) during this period.

Five cities reported a hundred or more gangs for at least one year of the five-year period. These are New York, Chicago, Los Angeles, Philadelphia, and Boston. For the fifteen cities the total estimated number of gang members was approximately 52,000. This comes to an average of about twenty-five members per gang, although reported numbers ranged from about sixty per gang for New York and Los Angeles to about ten to fifteen for Boston and San Francisco. The total number of gang members is equivalent to about 3.5 percent of the male population aged ten to nineteen of the fifteen cities. It is important to note as well that approximately 43,000, or 80 percent, of the estimated number of gang members are found in the three largest cities. This supports the finding suggested earlier that gangs, unlike groups, are predominantly a large city phenomenon.

Estimating the number of law-violating youth groups other than gangs is considerably more difficult, since there is so little explicit recognition of such groups as distinctive types. Most of the data needed to derive even moderately well-informed estimates has not been collected. For present purposes, figures are given for only three of the fifteen types of nongang groups of table 7-1—types 2, 3, and 4. All three are designated "disruptive local groups," and are generally referred to as street or street corner groups, crowds, or gangs.[9]

As part of the twenty-four-city survey, respondents were asked to estimate the number of type 2, 3, and 4 groups or group hangouts in their city, district, or neighborhood. One hundred one respondents in thirteen cities with a combined population of 7 million furnished such estimates. These cities ranged in size from 287,000 (St. Paul), to 816,000 (Dallas), with an average size of 530,000. Since no city of 1 million or more is included, the figures are based on estimates from the middle range of the large cities rather than the very largest. Respondent estimates provide the basis of a figure of approximately 8,000 disruptive local groups in the thirteen cities—an average of about 615 per city, or about 1.2 groups per 1,000 residents. Respondents were also asked to estimate the average size of these groups. Estimates ranged from a high of twenty-three per group or hangout in Miami to a low of nine in Cleveland and St. Louis, with an all-city average of about fifteen members per group. These figures produce a total of about 120,000 group members in the thirteen cities, or about 19 perent of the male youth aged ten to nineteen in the population.

Extrapolating these ratios to the fifteen gang cities (total population 21 million) produces a figure of something over 25,000 disruptive local groups with a total membership of about 380,000 members. Extrapolating the same ratios to the approximately nine hundred cities in the United States with populations of 25,000 or more produces a total of about 105,000 groups with a membership of about 1.6 million. This figure is equivalent to about 25 percent of the male youth (10-19) population of these cities.[10] Recall that the estimated number of gangs (types 1, 5, and 9) was about 1,300, and the number of gang members about 52,000. On the basis of these figures, there are about twenty times as many disruptive local groups as gangs, and about seven times as many group members as gang members in the fifteen gang cities. For all cities of 25,000 or more the ratios are eighty groups for every gang, and thirty group members for every gang member.

Note that these figures are based on only six of the eighteen types of law-violating youth groups delineated in table 7-1. When new data make it possible to include estimates for the remaining twelve types—particularly burglary rings, larceny cliques, and robbery bands—both the numbers of group members and the proportion of urban youth affiliated with such groups will undoubtedly be higher.

Criminal Activity by Law-violating Youth Groups

With estimates indicating that urban membership in about one-third of the types of youth group delineated here runs to about 1.5 million, or about one-quarter of the male population, the question arises: How much serious youth crime may reasonably be attributed to members of these and other types of group? The total volume of such crime is, of course, unknown and unknowable. For present purposes three major measures will be used to derive estimates—each of which represents a different method of compiling some portion of a theoretically complete population of criminal events. These are, first, arrests recorded by local police departments and reported to the Federal Bureau of Investigation ("arrests"); second, offenses known to the police (via citizen complaints and police discovery) and reported to the FBI ("known offenses"); and third, reports by victims of selected crimes affecting urban individuals, households, and commercial establishments compiled by the Census Bureau and reported through the Department of Justice ("victimization reports") (FBI 1972-1977; U.S. Department of Justice 1974-1976, 1977).

In light of the fact that there is far more explicit recognition of gangs as a type of criminally oriented unit than is the case for groups, one might expect that information concerning gang crime would be quite readily available. In fact, of the approximately fifteen gang cities, only three, New York, Chicago, and Los Angeles, provide such information.[11] Arrest data supplied by the police in these three cities indicate approximately 13,000 yearly arrests of gang members during the 1973-1974 period, including approximately 6,000 arrests for the more serious forms of violent crime. These figures are equivalent to about 10 percent of arrests of male youths (under eighteen) for all offenses, and about 30 percent of arrests for serious violent offenses, including homicides.[12] Since members of police-recognized gangs made up approximately 5 percent of the male youth (ten to nineteen) population in the three cities, it would appear that gang members overcontributed to arrests for all offenses by a factor of 2, and to serious violent offenses by a factor of 5.

The most serious of the violent crimes is homicide. During the five-year period between 1972 and 1977, approximately 1,000 gang-related killings were reported for the six largest gang cities. While yearly totals for the individual cities varied considerably during this period, all-city totals remained quite stable. The figure for 1972 was 174; for 1977, 189. The yearly average was 170.[13]

Although it is quite clear that members of recognized gangs contribute disproportionately to youth arrests, particularly in the case of the more violent forms of crime, it should be noted that the number of arrests of persons not recognized as gang members far exceeds the number of those who are. For the 1973-1974 period in the three largest cities, approximately 90 percent of arrests for all offenses and 70 percent of arrests for serious violent offenses involved youths who were not members of recognized gangs. These nongang members comprise three logical categories: those who are in fact gang members but are not so recognized; those who are affiliated with law-violating youth groups other than recognized gangs; and unaffiliated offenders. The next section attempts to provide some notion of the amount of serious crime attributable to the last two categories.

How much crime is attributable to members of groups other than gangs? This question is probably more important to basic policy issues than any of the others addressed here; unfortunately it is also the most difficult question to answer because of the paucity of relevant information.

For gang-member crime, despite the fact that the quality of available information is considerably less than ideal, data at least are gathered on a routine basis in the three largest cities; moreover, as noted, these cities contain approximately 80 percent of members of recognized gangs. By contrast, no city or other agency routinely collects crime data on the basis of group membership, and because of this it is necessary to use a different method of estimating the volume of such crimes.

Gang-member arrest statistics are based on lists of the names of gang members compiled by the police or other agencies. When the name of a youth who is arrested appears on such a list, the offense is recorded as having been committed by a gang member. This means that crimes committed by gang members acting alone or with one or two others are categorized as gang related, which corresponds to the usage of the present study. Since no such lists are compiled for groups, this method cannot be used to categorize crimes as group related.[14] What is possible on the basis of existing data is the derivation of estimates of how much youth crime is collectively executed. This is not the same as the amount of crime committed by members of groups.

As noted earlier, a substantial amount of crime by gang and group members is actually committed by individuals or pairs, and although such crimes may occur with the cooperation or moral support of the group, there is no way of knowing on the basis of routine records whether these individuals or pairs are affiliated with groups. The present section will attempt to estimate first how much youth crime involves collective participation, and then use these figures as a basis for estimating how much of this crime, whether or not collectively executed, may reasonably be attributed to persons affiliated with groups.

Before presenting such estimates, however, it will be useful simply to cite, without elaboration, the kinds of offenses most commonly committed by members of groups. These are: petty theft (minor burglaries, robberies, larcenies), serious theft (major burglaries, robberies, larcenies), looting, small-scale extortion, disorderly congregation, drunkenness and illegal drinking, drug use, drug dealing, simple assault (fighting, brawling, assault by missiles), aggravated assault, vandalism (damage by missiles, fire setting), harrassment, exclusionary occupancy of public facilities, ilegal gambling, disruption by violence of public gatherings, rape.[15]

It should be noted that these offenses range from those generally considered to be of low seriousness (disorderly congregation) to those considered to be extremely serious (armed robbery). In general, there is a rough inverse relationship between frequency and seriousness; the less serious offenses are most comon, the more serious least.[16]

Present estimates of the amount of crime attributable to groups are based primarily on statistics relating to five of the offenses categorized as "most serious" by the FBI.[17] These are robbery, burglary, aggravated assault, motor vehicle theft, and forcible rape. In 1976 3.3 million offenses in these categories were reported to police departments in cities of 25,000 or more. Approximately 65 percent of those arrested for these five categories of offenses in the same year were aged twenty or under. If we make the assumption that the ages of those who committed these crimes were the same as those arrested for them, we obtain a figure of 2.2 million offenses by city youths in 1976.[18]

Data are also available as to the proportion of various offenses by youth which are collective—that is, committed by two or more participants. For each offense category a percentage figure was obtained which indicates how often the commission of the offense involves two or more youths. These percentages were obtained from a variety of sources, principally the victimization reports compiled by the Census Bureau.[19] The percentages are: burglary, 80; motor vehicle theft, 75; robbery, 60; aggravated assault, 55; rape, 21. Applying these percentages to the number of youths estimated to have committed these crimes produces a figure of 1.6 million collectively executed offenses, or almost exactly one-half of all offenses reported for the five categories. These calculations thus provide one basis for estimating that just about half of the more serious crimes are collectively executed by youths.

As already noted, the proportion of crimes which are collectively executed is not the same as those which are committed by members of law-violating youth groups, since the "two or more" criterion used as the basis of most of the collective proportion percentages includes pairs, some of which are not affiliated with any larger group. However, it is possible to derive an estimate of the number of offenses which are committed by members of groups as here defined by making the following assumptions.

1. One-third of the single offenders are affiliated with at least two others.
2. Two-thirds of all collectively executed youth crimes are executed by pairs, one-third by three or more.
3. Three-quarters of all pairs are affiliated with at least one other person.
4. All crimes executed jointly by three or more youths are by definition group crimes.[20]

These assumptions applied to the figures just presented produce the following: approximately 1.5 million of the 3.3 million serious offenses reported for cities over 25,000 are committed by members of law-violating youth groups other than gangs. This is equivalent to 47 percent of all these offenses, and 71 percent of youth offenses. The estimates for group-member offenses and collectively executed offenses are thus quite close; just about half of the offenses were collectively executed, while something under half were executed by members of groups.[21]

It should be noted once again that the data necessary for accurate answers to most of the questions posed in this section are simply not available, but that the importance of gaining some notion, however rough, of the contribution of youth groups to the total volume of serious crime is sufficiently great as to justify the use of estimates based on those data which are available. At each state of the estimation process, assumptions have been made, most of which are supported at least by partial information, and each of these assumptions has been made explicit. However, the conclusions presented here are valid only insofar as the assumptions are valid. If future research demonstrates the invalidity of one or more of the assumptions, the conclusions will have to be modified accordingly.

Summary and Policy Implications

Despite intensification of concern with serious youth crime, very little systematic attention has been devoted to a crucial characteristic of such crime—that it is predominantly a collective phenomenon, executed by members of various kinds of identifiable youth groups. Among urban male youth in particular, serious crime by unaffiliated individuals is relatively uncommon. Although most workers in this field are well aware of the group nature of most serious youth crime, virtually no effort has been made to utilize this knowledge in any systematic fashion in gathering information, developing programs, and formulating policy. A major reason for this is that no satisfactory scheme for identifying and characterizing different kinds of law-violating youth groups has been available. Traditionally, the major approach to this phenomenon has been that of the gang—a concept with serious deficiencies as a unit of analysis. Between the units of the gang and individual lies a vast conceptual wasteland—with the thousands of cliques, crowds, bands, rings, networks, and so on which play so important a role in youth crime essentially ignored for purposes of record keeping and program development. The failure to systematically take into account the existence and activities of these distinctive units has resulted in a substantial underestimation of the amount of crime attributable to law-violating youth groups.

This chapter proposes and defines a new concept, the law-violating youth group, as the basis of the examination of collective youth crime, and delineates eighteen distinctive types and subtypes, including three types of gang. The major characteristics of gangs as distinct subtypes, derived from an analysis of conceptions of practitioners in all parts of the country, are presented, and the boundaries between gangs and related types of youth groups, also based on practitioner conceptions, are specified.

Based on the distinction between gangs and nongang groups, the paper attempts for the first time to estimate the numbers of law-violating youth collectivities in urban America, and to specify the seriousness of the problems they pose in major cities. Gangs as commonly conceived are seen to be predominantly a large-city phenomenon, while nongang groups are ubiquitous. About fifteen cities have problems with gangs, numbering about 1,300, with approximately 52,000 members, or about 3.5 percent of the male youth population. These same cities have an estimated 105,000 disruptive local groups with a membership of about 1.6 million, or about 25 percent of the male youth population.

In over half of the survey cities, crime problems posed by gangs or groups were judged to be on the order of seriousness of crimes such as armed robbery and aggravated assault. Problems with gangs were judged to be very serious in three of nine gang-problem cities, while problems with groups were characterized as very serious in ten of eighteen survey cities; it thus appears that cities reporting problems with groups are more likely to see these as very serious than those reporting problems with gangs.

Data were presented as to the volume and proportions of crime by gang members in the three largest cities. In the middle 1970s, arrests of gang members were equivalent to about 10 percent of juvenile arrests for all offenses, and about 30 percent of arrests for the most serious forms of violent crime. An attempt was made, also for the first time, to estimate the volume and proportion of serious crime by youth collectivities of all kinds in United States cities. Estimates based on a series of extrapolations and assumptions indicate that in cities of 25,000 or more, between 45 and 50 percent of serious offenses by persons of all ages are committed by members of youth groups, and about 70 percent of serious offenses by youths. During a five-year period, approximately 1,000 gang-related killings were reported for six of the gang-problem cities—a yearly average of about 170 killings per city.

What are the implications of these findings for crime prevention and control? Even if the present finding—that youth groups in American cities are responsible for about one-half of all serious crime and 70 percent of serious youth crime—overestimates the actual proportions by as much as 10 or 15 percent (there is also a good possibility of underestimation), the data suggest strongly that one characteristic of serious youth crime—its collective or group-related nature—must be taken into account explicitly and systematically in developing policy aimed at the reduction of serious crime.

The primary objective of this paper has been to present evidence in support of its major conclusions. However, it might be useful in addition to suggest briefly a few of the policy implications of these conclusions. Implications will be cited for six criminal justice areas—record keeping, community prevention and control programs, arrest policies, placement decisions, probation policies, and aftercare policies.

Implications for record keeping are most obvious. In addition to the current practice of maintaining records on individuals, information should be compiled on a routine basis that would indicate as precisely as possible the group membership status of offenders. Such data would involve more than the "apprehended with" type of information currently available in most police record systems, and more than the "usually or always commits crimes with others" type of information generally collected in self-report studies, and more than the "collective offender" type of information provided by the victimization reports. This information should be based on a systematic mapping of the numbers, locations, and particularly the types of law-violating youth groups in given jurisdictions (robbery bands, turf gangs, disruptive local groups, and so on), periodically updated to keep pace with the fluid nature of group affiliation.

Such information would provide an invaluable data base for policy decisions in a variety of criminal justice areas. For community-based programs of prevention and control, information as to the extent and type of group-related crime is an essential prerequisite to planning. Projects whose methods explicitly incorporate a recognition of the group nature of youth crime have traditionally faced three program options: recognize the group membership of clients for purposes of diagnosis, but ignore it for purposes of treatment; recognize the group and work to redirect the activity patterns of the unit as a whole; recognize the group, but work explicitly to weaken group bonds and/or separate members from the group. Although each of these options has been tried, systematic research knowledge as to their relative efficacy and the circumstances under which each might be more or less effective is still fragmentary and inconclusive (Klein 1971: ch. 2; Wright and Dixon 1977).

With respect to arrest policies involving groups of offenders, at least two conflicting positions have been advanced. One side contends that lone offenders should be arrested more readily than group offenders, since as loners they are less affected by group standards and are thus more likely to be disturbed, unpredictable, and dangerous; the other side argues that group offenders should be more readily arrested, since their criminal activity is embedded in, and reinforced by, an established set of group norms and values, making it more entrenched and less amenable to change. The lone offender is seen to be more readily weaned away from his criminality since it is not collectively supported and reinforced. Another issue concerns *which* of a group of collective offenders to arrest and charge (a situation frequently faced by police)—the leaders or key members only, followers only, or both? Here again, decisions faced repeatedly by arresting officers are generally uninformed by base data as to group membership and intragroup status, let alone knowledge as to which choice is likely to produce the best results (Cohn 1954; Dressler 1951).

With respect to placement decisions, one phenomenon has been well documented. When members of established big-city gangs are incarcerated together in traditional types of facilities, gang ties are used and expanded to create centers of power which provide a solid base for strong and often devastatingly effective opposition to prison administrations (Jacobs 1977; Conrad and Dinitz 1978). But to what extent do similar processes occur, on a smaller scale, when gang or group members are placed together in non-traditional facilities? Should members of neighborhood groups be systematically separated from one another in group homes, half-way houses, and the like, so as to minimize peer group influences, or should they be kept together so as to minimize differences from their normal community lifestyles, and facilitate reintegration into the community?

Issues respecting probation policies are similar to those cited for community programs. Should groups rather than individuals be taken as clientele units for probation services, and if so, under what circumstances? Aftercare involves another traditional dilemma. Many jurisdictions forbid parolees to associate with other offenders; in most instances such other offenders are in fact the parolee's fellow group members. How feasible are such structures (most offenders who return to their groups are continually violating the conditions of parole), and what is the evidence that such regulations do in fact serve to inhibit recidivism?

These are only a few of the more specific types of policy issues; others relate to policy at higher levels, including broad questions of resource allocation at the federal level. There is no guarantee that more specific recognition of the group nature of most serious youth crime would solve the kinds of problems just discussed. But one thing is quite certain. There is at present *no* systematic effort, at local, state or federal levels, to develop policy which is geared to the fundamental reality that about half of all serious crime, and almost three-quarters of serious youth crime, is the product of distinguishable types of law-violating youth groups. Recognition of this fact, and the accompanying realization of the importance of information as to the prevalence, types, and activities of such groups in different kinds of communities as well as the experiences of group members at different stages of the criminal justice process, is critically important. Without such recognition, policymakers will have deprived themselves of an absolutely essential component of an effective strategy for coping with serious youth crime.

Notes

1. An earier version of this chapter was presented at a symposium entitled "The Serious Juvenile Offender." The choice of the phrasing "*the* offender," instead of "offenders," attests to the pervasiveness of conceiving a predominantly collective phenomenon in individual terms.

2. This usage also conforms to that of police departments in several major cities. An official of the Gang Crimes Investigation Division of the Chicago Police Department stated, "We are interested in any group of three or more"; the gang intelligence unit of the Los Angeles Police Department defined a "gang incident" as "any legal infraction involving three or more juveniles."

3. The discussion based on the analysis of these elements is quite extensive, and comprises the bulk of ch. 3 of Miller (1979), "Conceptions, Definitions, and Images of Youth Gangs." The twenty-six communities used in the definitional analysis include two counties (Montgomery and Prince George, Maryland) in addition to the twenty-four surveyed cities.

4. See table I, Miller (1979).

5. In the actual interviews information with respect to this question was obtained through a series of more specific subquestions. See "Gang Survey Interview Guide," appendix A, Miller (1975), items I.1 through I.1.B.1., p. 77.

6. San Diego is omitted from this tabulation. See Miller (1975), p. 3.

7. See Miller (1975), p. 77, items I.1.A and I.1.B.1. Estimates provided by all respondents in each city were ranked (total estimates = 283), and the median value taken as the city rating.

8. Methods used to obtain estimates of the number of gangs and gang members are described in Miller (1975), pp. 15-16, and in appendix B, along with a discussion of some of the methodological problems involved.

9. Detailed characterizations of each of these three types are presented in Miller, (1979), ch. 5, "Types of Disruptive Youth Groups."

10. Population data are based on federal Census Bureau figures as reported in the 1975 edition of Statistical Abstract of the United States (U.S. Bureau of the Census, 1975). See especially tables 24 and 25, p. 23. Figures on the number of male youths ten to nineteen in the various cities in 1975 were obtained directly from the Census Bureau.

11. The Philadelphia Police Department also compiles information on gang crimes, but dissemination is restricted to internal departmental use. Detroit Police began to collect such information in 1976, but, like Philadelphia, does not make it available outside the department.

12. See Miller (1975) tables 18 and 19, p. 32.

13. See Miller (1975) table 15, and accompanying discussion. Figures for Los Angeles for 1977 are for the metropolitan area, which includes adjacent portions of Los Angeles, Orange, and San Bernadino counties.

14. The only known exception is the Group Identification Program of the St. Louis Police Department conducted during the 1960s and 1970s—in conjunction, during its later years, with a team counseling program for groups of delinquents. Officers filled out several forms relating to youth groups, including a detailed Field Investigation Report (FIR), which con-

tained information on the group affiliation of offenders. These data were analyzed by a computer program which detected and identified the major law-violating youth groups in the city. Police and treatment program officials were thus provided access to currently updated membership lists of active law-violating youth groups. See City of St. Louis (1972), and City of St. Louis (n.d.).

15. Detailed discussions of each of these offense categories are included in Miller (1979) ch. 5, 6, 7.

16. See Miller (1979) for further discussion of this relationship, and the criteria used to rate "seriousness."

17. The seven offense categories designated index crimes in the Uniform Crime Reports are considerd to be the most serious. These are criminal homicide, forcible rape, robbery, aggravated assault, burglary, larceny, motor vehicle theft. See Federal Bureau of Investigation, 1972-1977.

18. There are grounds for questioning the validity of this assumption. For example, some evidence indicated that youths who commit crimes such as robbery or burglary are more likely to be arrested than adults, who, as a result of experience, are more likely to avoid arrest for such crimes. However, the likelihood of a fairly close correspondence between the age of those who commit crimes and those who are arrested for them is high, and in the absence of substantial evidence to the contrary, the assumption seems tenable.

19. Sources include United States Department of Justice (1974-1976, 1977), Hindelang (1976), Pope (1977), and arrest printouts of several urban police departments.

20. Reliable information relative to assumptions one through three is virtually nonexistent. For the most part, they represent estimates based on over twenty years of research by the author in the area of collective youth crime. One source of these estimates are data contained in Miller (1979) in those chapters which utilize field observation as a basis of analyses of patterns of participation in criminal activity by Boston gang members. For example, table 7, "The Collectivity of Theft" in ch. 11 shows that of 184 incidents of burglary, robbery, and larceny engaged in by members of seven gangs, participants were single individuals in 39 percent of the incidents, pairs in 13 percent, and groups of three or more in 48 percent. Since all participants were known to be members of gangs, and since indirect evidence indicates that the bulk of thefts in the study area during this period were committed by members of gangs or groups (Miller 1969), the 39 percent figure provides one basis for the one-third estimate in the first assumption. A good example of a crime committed by a pair who actually were members of a larger group occurred in New York in 1978, when two youths murdered a well-known professional. Because of the eminence of the victim, police devoted unusual energy to solving the crime (over a hundred detectives

worked for three days), and discovered that the two killers were in fact part of a group of at least four which had been active as a unit prior to the murder but had split into pairs shortly before (*New York Times* 1978). Under ordinary circumstances the participants would have been recorded as a pair rather than as members of a group.

21. An official affiliated with the Group Identification Program of the St. Louis Police Department reported, in 1975, that "65 percent of all juvenile felonies in St. Louis are committed by members of youth groups." Since the extensive body of data on which this percentage is based is probably unique, the figure is of particular significance.

References

City of St. Louis (1972). Metropolitan Police Department. *Field Interview Report Information Manual.* 3d ed.

_____ n.d. *Group Identification Program.*

Cohn, Y. (1954). "Criteria for probation officers recommendation to the juvenile court judge." In D. Kelly, ed., *Delinquent Behavior: Interactional and Motivational Aspects.* Belmont, California: Dickenson, 1978.

Conrad J., and Dinitz, S. (1978). "The prison within a prison: discipline at the impass." *Academy for Contemporary Problems* Columbus, Ohio (March).

Dressler, D. (1951). *Probation and Parole.* New York: Columbia University Press.

Federal Bureau of Investigation (1972-1977). *Uniform Crime Reports.* Annual Reports. Washington, D.C.: U.S. Government Printing Office.

Hindelang, M. (1976). "With a little help from their friends: group participation in reported delinquent behavior." *British Journal of Criminology* 16:2.

Jacobs, J. (1977). *Stateville: The Penitentiary in Mass Society.* Chicago: University of Chicago Press.

Klein, M. (1971). *Street Gangs and Street Workers.* Englewood Cliffs, N.J.: Prentice-Hall.

Miller W. (1969). "White gangs." *Transaction* 6 (September).

_____ (1975). *Violence by Youth Gangs and Youth Groups as a Crime Problem in Major American Cities.* Office of Juvenile Justice and Delinquency Prevention, U.S. Department of Justice, Law Enforcement Assistance Administration. Washington, D.C.: U.S. Government Printing Office (December).

_____ (1976). Youth gangs in the urban crisis era." In J. Short (ed), *Delinquency, Crime and Society.* Chicago: University of Chicago Press.

_____ (1979). *City Gangs.* New York: John Wiley (in preparation).

_____ (1979). *Crime by Youth Groups and Gangs in American Cities.* Office of Juvenile Justice and Delinquency Prevention, U.S. Department of Justice. Washington, D.C.: Law Enforcement Assistance Administration (in press).

New York Times (1978). "Police arrest two teen-agers in slaying of designer." December 5.

Pope, C. (1977). *Crime-specific Analysis: An Empirical Examination of Burglary Offender Characteristics.* Analytic Report, Utilization of Criminal Justice Statistics Project:11. SD-AR-11, U.S. Department of Justice. Washington, D.C.: U.S. Government Printing Office.

Short, J. (ed.) (1976). *Delinquency, Crime, and Society.* Chicago: University of Chicago Press.

U.S. Department of Justice (1974-1976). *Criminal Victimization in the United States.* Washington, D.C.: U.S. Government Printing Office.

_____ (1977). *Criminal Victimization Surveys.* SD-NCS-C-7 through 19, July. Washington, D.C.: U.S. Government Printing Office.

U.S. Bureau of the Census (1975). *Statistical Abstract of the United States.* 96th ed. Washington, D.C.: U.S. Government Printing Office.

Wright, W., and Dixon, N. (1977). "An evaluation of community prevention and treatment of juvenile delinquency." In N. Johnston and L. Savitz (eds.), *Justice and Corrections.* New York: John Wiley and Sons, 1978.

8

The Dangerous
Two Percent

Simon Dinitz and
John P. Conrad

As part of the revisionism of the 1970s, some call it backlash against the
silent revolutions and traumas of post-World War II America, nearly all
human services and agencies have come under attack. Voters, as often as
not, reject school bond issues; the middle-class taxpayer revolt is in full
flower, welfare is seen as wasteful and outrageous. The rebirth of the central city is in doubt, the health care institutions out-of-control, the pension
and retirement systems—both public and private—in chaos. The general
disaffection of the populace with piecemeal attempts to plug so many holes
in the leaky public sector has coalesced around the criminal justice
system—the bête noir of our time. Crime in the streets, next to the bread-
and-butter issues of inflation, unemployent, and property taxes, has come
to dominate public consciousness to a degree unprecedented in U.S. history.
While hardly the moral equivalent of war, the war on crime, if not on the
conditions which spawn antisocial conduct, has become an umbrella issue
which is sufficiently ambiguous to cover all sorts of conflicts (racial, sexual,
class) and crosscurrents in American life.

No matter that the perception of the occurrence and danger of crime is
grossly overstated; no matter that our penalty structure is such as to in-
carcerate ten or more times as many persons per 100,000 population as
Holland and three times as many as the United Kingdom; no matter that
our prisons and training schools are ancient and inadequate; no matter that
our jails are as bad as nearly any in the world. The public demands safe
streets at almost any social and economic cost. To that end, it demands safe
cells where common crime transgressors are locked away for as long as
necessary under humane conditions but with the fewest possible amenities
(Bentham's principle of less eligibility).

More and more informed opinion, to say nothing of lay attitudes, is
convinced that rehabilitation, even if not a myth, is an unattainable goal.
Conrad put it well in his paper, "We Should Never Have Promised a
Hospital" (Conrad 1975). Critics like Wilson (1975), van den Haag (1975),
von Hirsch (1976), Fogel (1975), and many others (Andenaes 1974) have
revived classical goals such as punishment, incapacitation, and deterrence
as substitutes for treatment, reform, and rehabilitation (Rennie 1978).

No segment of the criminal justice system (a widely circulated idea
which is clearly misleading in that the diverse criminal justice elements con-

stitute anything but a system as the term is conventionally used) has been battered any worse than the juvenile side. Around the statehouses, various voices have been raised in support of the draft standard of the American Bar Association to integrate the juvenile and adult criminal courts. Here and there, bills (New York, for example) have been introduced or recommendations made to lower the age eligibility to fourteen, fifteen, or sixteen for entry into the adult system; to extend control over juveniles for longer periods of time; to make juvenile court waiver into the adult system easier; to increase the power of prosecutors and lessen that of juvenile court judges in regard to the processing of juveniles; to impose mandatory institutionalization for aggravated offenses—in short, to transfer and treat the dangerous and chronic juvenile as an ordinary violator without regard for his age.

Most of these proposals reflect disenchantment with the juvenile court system—its informality, focus on the youth, and quasi-welfare approach that serves neither justice nor treatment. Juvenile justice—the special police bureaus, the court with its referees and judges, and the dispositional alternatives—is too open-ended from the standpoint of the law enforcement community and from that of civil libertarians seeking due process and other constitutional guarantees.

There is also the matter, and a not so small one, that juveniles are arrested for about one-quarter of all violent crimes reported to the police; they are especially prominent in the commission of aggravated or felonious robberies (Uniform Crime Reports 1973-1976). The violent juvenile, with or without companions, has terrorized entire areas of central cities; forced the closing of low-income housing developments and the conversion of others to senior-citizens-only developments; threatened, injured, and abused classmates and teachers, forcing some schools, already financially strapped, to employ security guards for the protection of all; and preyed on elderly, handicapped, and defenseless victims (U.S. Congress 1976).

It is pointless to quote ancient Greek philosophers to the effect that the young have always been troublesome and lacking in all the pieties we would want. It is useless to suggest that the perception of the problem of youthful violence (and of criminal involvement of all types) much exaggerates the reality. And it is meaningless to think that the changing age composition (the graying of America) will solve the juvenile violence and juvenile justice system problems.

Just how real is the problem of dangerous and violent juveniles? Is there anything to the idea that the judicious incapacitation of a small proportion of the youth population will alleviate both the fear and the actuality of significant juvenile involvement in personal injury and other types of crime? Before any more legislatures respond blindly and emotionally to the pressures of their constituents (and then regret their haste for years to come), a careful evaluation of prevalence, onset, progression, and cessation of juvenile violence is warranted.

The Columbus Study

Antecedents

Nearly everything criminologists know about the dangerous and repetitively violent juvenile delinquent comes from one of two sources. First are clinical studies of small numbers of such youths at various points in the criminal justice process—usually as part of the presentence report or at the institutional workup on a temporary or permanent commitment to a state institution. Clinical studies in the United States date back to the early years of this century and to the pioneering efforts of Healy (1915), Alexander and Healy (1935), Friedlander (1947), and Menninger (1968).

The second source of information has come from empirical research using both official and unofficial information (self-reporting of offenses and victimizations and, in the case of gangs and street corner groups, participant observation). The research of Sheldon and Eleanor Glueck (1934, 1940, 1950, 1968) despite its methodological shortcomings, represents the benchmark work. Their approach involved a comparison of matched delinquents and nondelinquents. (Ferracuti and Dinitz, 1975). Almost without exception, the results indicated serious family, personality, school, and related deficits on the part of the delinquents. Additionally, hundreds of personality trait studies (comparing delinquents to the norm) found some deficits. So did studies of self-concept, the internalization of nondeviant norms, obedience to authority (compliance), and other measures. The basic unanswered question in all these investigations concerned the determination of cause and effect. Was a disturbed emotional state the cause or effect of the handling of delinquents, poor school grades, truancy, assault on schoolmates or teachers? For this and other reasons—the loss of faith in the ability of such investigations to delve into etiology—a new style of research has emerged which refocuses the problem. I refer to the birth cohort approach, long known and used in Scandanavian countries in studies of depression, schizophrenia, and identical twin delinquency. This approach was employed by Wolfgang, Figlio, and Sellin (1972) in their Philadelphia study of delinquency. In this highly innovative work, Wolfgang et al. chose a birth cohort of nearly 10,000 boys born in 1945 who lived in Philadelphia throughout their adolescent years, actually ten to seventeen. Using official records from various sources, Wolfgang found that (1) 35 percent were known to (had contact with) the police during their growing up, (2) that each successive offense increases the probability of yet another, (3) that 6 percent of the boys or 18 percent of the offenders (627 youths in all) had committed five or more offenses, (4) that these "chronics" were responsible for over half of all the crimes officially committed by the cohort and about two-thirds of the serious crimes attributed to the entire cohort, and (5) race and socioeconomic status were the most significant variables associated with initial as well as serious and persistent involvement in delinquency.

Other studies such as those of Reckless and Dinitz (1972) of "good" and "bad" boys reached much the same conclusions, albeit using a cross-sectional rather than a cohort format. In short, by whatever method employed, fifty years of research have tended to address, if not verify, some common lay assumptions:

1. A small proportion of age-eligible youth are disproportionately delinquent and violent.
2. These chronic offenders are poor, black, and quite young.
3. These youths are the monsters who terrorize their neighborhoods and communities across the land.
4. These monsters are heartless and seemingly without guilt. They are psychopaths and antisocial personalities for whom there is no adequate treatment.
5. The earlier a child embarks on a delinquent career, the longer that career is likely to last.
6. There is a progression from less to more serious crimes over time.
7. Delinquents, particularly violent ones, tend to persist in their speciality, whether aggravated crimes, rape, robberies, or assaults.
8. Dispositions tend to reflect a balanced judgment based on considerations of criminal history, the gravity of the index offense, and the social history of the violent offender.
9. Whatever its problems, incarceration tends to slow down the criminal activity of the youthful offender.

The Study Group

Five birth cohorts (1956-1960) in Columbus, Ohio, were selected for study because they include juveniles who would have completed their careers in 1977 (Hamparian et al. 1978). Of these five cohort years, the principal results are based on all juveniles arrested for violent crimes who were born in the years 1956-1958. All the subjects had been arrested at least once as juveniles for the commission of a violent crime which, by our definition, includes the sexual imposition offenses.

The universe of juveniles who had committed at least one violent crime was obtained form the juvenile records of the Columbus, Ohio, Police

Department Juvenile Bureau. These microfiche records—many thousands of which were searched—contain the complete police folders for all juveniles against whom a complaint had been filed.

The folder on each subject contains a case record or investigative report for every arrest. These case records are inserted chronologically so that it is possible to assess the arrests from earliest to most recent with minimum shuffling of reports. Each form contains the following data which were extracted for later coding and analysis: name, address, sex, race, age, date of birth, place of birth, charge or charges (this arrest), arrest time, date and location, arresting officer's name, names and addresses of parents or legal guardian, charge found guilty of, disposition, and previous record. There is space for the name of the school attended, the school grade level, and whether the juvenile arrestee had been placed in detention. The rest of the case record is devoted to a statement of the facts in the case.

An additional source of data were the Ohio Youth Commission commitment records. These records, on three-by-five cards, alphabetically arranged, were made available to the research project. A juvenile earns a separate card for each commitment. These cards contain the following information (which was recorded, coded, and analyzed): month and year of commitment and month and year of return to the community.

The Offenders

A total of 1,138 juveniles born in 1956-1960 was arrested for at least one violent crime in Columbus before January 1, 1976. All told they had been arrested for 4,499 as of that date. These 4,499 offenses include not only the required one violent offense per youth but a variety of other and usually less serious crimes as well.

Of these 1,138 juveniles, 811 were born in the 1956-1958 period and thus completed their juvenile careers. These 811 subjects had 3,393 arrests. Again, most of these arrests were for nonviolent crimes.

On the demographic side, these 811 subjects, who had been arrested for one or more violent crimes, constituted 1.6 percent of all age-eligible youth in the community. The figure for the boys was 2.3 percent.

Of the 205 census tracts from which the subjects could have come, 10 tracts, with 7.8 percent of the population, contributed nearly a third of the subjects. These tracts and the other major contributing census tracts had a population whose median income was less than 80 percent of median family income in the county; these same tracts were also very heavily black.

Of the 811 arrestees, over 84 percent were boys, over 54 percent black (against 15.4 percent in the age-eligible population) and only half came form two-parent families and a third from female-based households. One-eighth of the subjects (145 of the entire cohort) had at least one sibling who was also part of the research study. There were sixty-two pairs of siblings and seven sets of three sibs—a remarkable record considering the age span of roughly ten to seventeen inclusive. The probability of such great sibling involvement is quite low. The obvious conclusion is that some family settings are so detrimental to the well-being of the young that they produce and socialize offspring who become delinquents and commit violent acts much as other families produce professionals.

The Offenders and Their Offenses

This 1956-1958 cohort of 811 subjects constitutes the sum total of all arrestees for violent crimes in the age-eligible population. This number is laughably small when compared to similar cohorts in the south Bronx, north Philadelphia, east Los Angeles, south Chicago, and other celebrated cores of poverty and disorganization. The lesson here is that most criminological speculation, investigation, and policy recommendations derive from perhaps no more than thirteen cities in the United States—those studied by Miller (1976), for example, in his persistent quest for tracking gang behavior across the country.

Overlooked in most criminological analyses and in the media is the fact that the universe we generated is typical of communities of from 0.5 million people to about 1 million or more, accounting for some 30 million people according to figures in the 1970 census. These communities include Seattle, Denver, Minneapolis, Milwaukee, Indianapolis, Louisville, Atlanta, Pittsburgh, and points in between as well as south and east. Criminological theory must take into account the rest of America and not be blinded by the horrendous conditions described so forcefully by urban ethnographers. In this sense, the Columbus data are probably more typical of the juvenile crime problem in America than is the situation in Bedford-Stuyvesant so often discussed in the *New York Times*.

Looking at Columbus, the 811 youths were arrested for 985 violent crimes (1.2 per subject) and charged with 1,087 violent offenses (1.3 per youth) during the entire course of their adolescent and teenage years.

Of the 811, over 83 percent or 677 cohort subjects were arrested just once for a violent offense; 103 or 12.7 percent were arrested twice; 31 or nearly 4 percent had three or more such arrests. The top was six (in one case) and consisted of a series of robberies.

The violent arrests included 270 for aggravated crimes such as murder, manslaughter, forcible rape, armed robbery, and aggravated assault; 366 for robbery (no weapon used); and 455 for molesting and assault, the latter sometimes involving acts no more violent than a schoolyard fight.

Nor were the violent acts, except in the 31 repetitive cases, part of a repetitive and specialized pattern of criminal involvement. If anything, our delinquents were "no pattern" offenders, and even more commonly, first and only offenders. For the cohort, the range of all arrests was 1-23; the mean number, 4.2; and the more stable median value, 3.4.

Nearly 30 percent of the cohort was arrested just once (that for the violent crime). Considering their life circumstances, this significant dropout from delinquency is well worth noting. About 16 percent more dropped out after the second arrest, 10 percent after the third, and nearly 11 percent after the fourth. One-third continued on to further arrests, but the percentage decreased for each succeeding arrest. Part of this pattern can be explained by maturation out of the juvenile justice system of each subject as he or she reached eighteen. Undoubtedly, many continued on to arrests as adults.

Boys, blacks, and lower socioeconomic status subjects were overrepresented in the more than one repetitive violent crime category. They also had a generally longer history of involvement with the juvenile justice system.

The Major Findings

A short survey chapter can hardly do more than enumerate some of the more significant results obtained in an investigation of this magnitude. The areas to be covered are these: the monster myth, the chronic offender, desistance, age and progression, disposition, and velocity.

The Monster Myth

Of the estimated 50,875 age-eligible youths born in 1956-1958, ony 811 had been arrested for at least one violent crime while they were under eighteen. Of the 811, only 22 had been apprehended for two or more aggravated crimes of violence. Either the police were unusually inept in clearing crimes—a position hard to sustain—or the juvenile monster is more common as a myth than as a reality. Even these 22 monsters, 2.7 percent of the violent cohort, hardly compare to the uncontrollable and psychopathic juveniles who daily make the press. The monsters generally started as youngsters on or even before age thirteen. Their depredations, and police intervention and incarceration, generally followed a classic pattern of increasing gravity, increasing intervention, and still greater involvement. Their ultimate violence, murder, rape, robbery, was mostly clumsy and inadvertent. One of the monsters stabbed a tormentor who was taunting him about his obesity. The wound was in the shoulder; the victim needlessly bled to death. Another of these monsters hit a girl with an iron bar in his attempt to rape her. Before succeeding in his attempt, a passerby called the police. The event took place on the steps of a public building. However, much of this monster violence was in connection with mostly impulsive, target-of-convenience robberies.

Chronic Offenders

Although monsters are fortunately in short supply in our cohort and in the Columbus metropolitan area, chronic juvenile offenders, who have also committed at least one violent act for which they were arrested, are all too plentiful. Following Wolfgang et al. (1972), chronics were defined as those youths who had been arrested five or more times. In these terms, chronics constituted a third of the subjects (272 of 811) and accounted for more than two-thirds of all cohort member arrests. Over a fifth of the chronics had accumulated their five arrests before turning fourteen. Finally, the chronics were responsible for nearly 40 percent of the aggravated offenses and nearly 45 percent of all index crimes against the person. The saddest part of this picture is that, although others finally desisted at some point short of their eighteenth birthdays, the chronics kept right at it to the end. A followup study would undoubtedly show that these adults are now probably part of our burden in the correctional system (Collins 1976).

Desistance

There is a tendency in the field to focus on those offenders whose activities begin earlier, are more severe, and extinguish later rather than sooner. Thus, recidivism is studied more intensively than success after treatment (no matter how defined). The system seems to revel in its failures to the disregard of its successes. Thus, the 272 chronics seem more impressive than the 239 youths who, having been arrested once, never reappeared as policy statistics. Yet all sorts of research suggest that radical nonintervention (leave them alone until the nth offense, unless the crimes are sufficiently injurious to invoke the might of the state) may be the most effective of all management techniques (Schur 1975).

The termination of a delinquent career is always difficult to document. Using the clearance data, however, 534 of the 811 subjects were still being arrested in their sixteenth and seventeenth years. Of this number, 240 began their delinquencies during those years and had not previously been heard from. On the other side, more than half of the longer delinquent careers ended before the latter years of adolescence. Of the youths who first became delinquent in their thirteenth and fourteenth years, about half were arrested for the last time in their sixteenth or seventeenth years. (The exact percentages are 53.0 percent for the thirteen-year-old beginners, and 51.2 percent for the fourteen year olds.) No one can safely argue that youths whose last recorded arrests occurred before the age of sixteen are safely on the side of law and order. Despite this margin of uncertainty, there is an important inference here: there is nothing inevitable in the course of a delinquent career. Whether it is maturation, which is doubtful, or redirection, or the influence of incarceration, a substantial number of delinquents manage to extricate themselves from the malignant careers on which they had been embarked. More needs to be known about how this outcome can be facilitated by correctional strategies.

Age and Progression

The results suggest two major conclusions about age and progression in delinquent careers. First, the early onset of a first arrest, for whatever offense, is related positively to a long but not necessarily serious offense history. Early teenage onset (thirteen to fourteen) seems to engender a momentum of its own.

Onset during the fifteenth to seventeenth year is usually of a more serious nature but shorter duration. Crimes like robbery predominate rather than the assault offenses of the younger group. The most difficult group consists of those whose contacts with the police begin when they are six to twelve years old. They not only compile long but also accumulate some very grave offenses before they "max out" of the system of eighteen. They are likely to become our state-raised youths and are unusually likely candidates for adult careers. Nonintervention on behalf of some of these youths can be a form of criminal negligence. But even here, differentiating those who should be left alone from those who should not require predictive ability now beyond the state of the art.

Second, the data on the repeaters among the 811 subjects suggest that there is no point in their careers when they are more likely to commit their violent crime. For a third of the cohort, it came early—almost at the start of their contacts with the law. For another third, it came during the years of transition (thirteen to fifteen) and the loosening of family and neighborhood controls. For these subjects, there were earlier and more minor police involvements before the index event. In many instances, they logged later arrests. For the remainder, there was no official evidence of violence until they reached sixteen to seventeen years of age. Earlier arrests were for property and public order crimes and for simple assaults. The index event was either a grave injury to another or a spree of robberies. Like a summer thunderstorm, there was a lot of light and noise and then, for many, it was over.

In sum, violent acts resulting in arrest are most predictive of later problems when they occur before the teenage transition. For the cohort as a whole, this violence occurred more or less randomly (by age) in the careers of the 811 offenders.

Disposition

The most significant finding in this work concerns the disposition of our subjects by the police and juvenile court. In all, over ninety specific dispositions (reprimand and release, restitution, afterschool work assignment) were given the subjects. These condensed into four categories: commitment to a state training school, mail detention or some alternative, formal supervision (probation), and informal supervision (most of the ninety options used). In human terms, 214 of the 811 subjects served some time in an Ohio Youth Commission training school facility. About half of the 214 were confined once; 58, twice; 36 had three commitments; 10 were sent away four times; and five served five sentences each. The commitment rate for all 811 was 0.49; for the 214, the rate was 1.85.

Analysis of variance and related statistical tests led to these generalizations regarding disposition. The unit of measure was the event (crime-arrest). First, except for the most aggravated offenses which were committed by 203 boys and 15 of the girls, the action of the court cannot be accurately predicted from such objective criteria as the nature of the offense, the number of prior offenses, or the race, sex, age, or socioeconomic status of the individual arrested, including the interactions among these variables ($R^2 = 0.28$). There is reason to conclude that judicial intuition, within the discretion allowed to the courts, and the estimate by court personnel of the quality of the individual's family life are the two most influential factors in disposition decisions. These variables do not lend themselves to quantitative manipulation. The inclusion of these considerations on disposition in the form of a case variable is evident in the dramatic increase in explained variance—from 28 to 53 percent. The role of discretion, for better or worse, is very evident in these data.

Second, the recidivism of those committed to state institutions was quite high. More than half of the 214 so committed were recommitted for new offenses. Of those returned to state custody, half recidivated again. About 62 percent of the first recidivists recidivated again; 27.8 percent of the second recidivists returned; 40 percent of the third recidivists returned; and 25 percent were five-time recidivists. These percentages are minimal. Death, departure from Ohio, aging out of the system, and occasional inadequate recording all have the effect of understating recidivism. There is little in our data to indicate a positive effect of incarceration in a state facility. There is no way of knowing how many of the cohort would have recidivated without the threat of return to an institution. But one of our principal findings is that commitment to a state facility or to other formal control agency will increase the speed with which individuals return to serious delinquency. What is referred to as the velocity of delinquent acts accelerates with the kinds of official action now administered.

Third, as the number of delinquencies recorded increases, the patience of the court is obviously exhausted. Relatively minor charges sometimes result in a custodial commitment when a judge has three previous appearances in court to consider. Conversely, of course, the aggravated offense will result in an institutional commitment with only a relatively brief history before the court, or no history at all. After the first commitment, any future appearance in court will probably result in another commitment, regardless of the nature of the offense. This generalization is plausible enough, but still it does not account for much of the variance in disposition.

Velocity

The last analysis and findings to be reported concern the effects of incarceration and the other categories of disposition on the speed with which the next arrest occurs after expiration of the sanction. The measure is "street time" in months between any pair of arrests, one to two, six to seven, twenty-three to twenty-four. The independent variable is the nature of the disposition; the method of analysis a general linear models procedure.

Proponents of social defense contend that incarceration serves a vital social function outweighing economic costs and occasional injustices (van den Haag 1975). It restrains adjudicated serious offenders in situations where they cannot perpetrate new crimes on the street, and in doing so, it deters an unknowable number of potential offenders. Anyone familiar with American penal facilities, particularly those to which juvenile offenders are consigned, must doubt that custodial care is anything more than a transitory expedient of limited value either to the youth or to the community (Bartollas, Miller, and Dinitz 1975). Critics of institutional care, as it prevails in Ohio as well as most other states, argue that in these facilities the resident is better prepared for life inside than outside the compound. But whether a youth training school is a school for crime or for life is not the issue. Public opinion overwhelmingly favors incarceration of the dangerous juvenile, and legislative and judicial responses to the clamor are evident in budgets for expanded correctional programs.

The only question addressed here is based on the record of paired arrests. Controlling for such variables as arrest sequence number, type of offense, age, race, sex, and socioeconomic status, how does the sanction imposed for the first of any pair of offenses affect the velocity of the commission of the second in terms of street time before the next arrest? Exceptions must be made in our analysis for the single events (23.9 percent of the 811), and for the dismissals and incomplete cases (about 16 percent). In neither category does velocity enter into the analysis.

With this constraint, what can be said about the impact of various intervention modalities? One of the most significant findings in this study is that with all else controlled, there is a moderate to high inverse relationship between the severity of the sanction for the first in every pair of crimes and the arrest for the second in the pair. Institutionalization increases the velocity (reduces the street time) to the second arrest; informal supervision retards it most (increases the street time). The consistency of this finding throughout the analysis is almost enough to make it suspect in this area in which results are rarely so clear. However, we checked the results in several other ways with exactly the same outcome. Institutionalization tends to speed up the velocity or time to the next arrest for every pair of offenses (whether these are the first and second or the fifth and sixth). Jail and detention and like alternatives also increase the velocity, but less so; formal supervision has a more modest impact on street-time crime velocity. Only the mildest intervention, informal supervision, retards the speed of arrest of the next crime. For all pairs of offenses, the net street time between one arrest and the next was 9.33 months.

The variables measured against street time were type of offense (first arrest of pair) and disposition of first arrest of pair. In net street time an aggravated first crime increased street time by 2.33 months and a robbery by 1.00 months while a property crime increased street time for the pair by only 0.34 months. The first of a pair of arrests for assault and battery increased street time by a whopping 4.83 months. This is consistent with our prior findings, which indicate that assault and battery crimes are not treated as very serious. A property crime arrest is both perceived and treated as predictive of a more intense criminal history yet to come.

The main effects of the interventions were even more dramatic: incarceration reduced the net time to next arrests by 4.81 months; jail detention by 1.23 months; and formal supervision by 0.80 months. Only the least intrusive alternatives, grouped together here under the heading of informal supervision, increased street time. The figure was 2.71 months. Age and crime sequence number also affected street time. The younger the subject, the fewer the prior offenses, and the longer the street time. Race, socioeconomic status, and other demographic variables were not important in this respect.

There are three explanations possible for the observed result that the more formidable the sanction, the less time on the street to the next arrest. Without extended discussion these alternative interpretations are: (1) The judge intuitively singles out the potentially more troublesome youths for training school incarceration and jail detention. (2) The crime school thesis says that what the boy didn't know or feel before incarceration, he soon learns in the training school. (3) The stigma of a commitment alerts the police, neighbors, teachers, and employers to the dangerousness of the release. They become subject to more careful scrutiny. Labeling makes return to a normal life more difficult.

Conclusion

It is impossible to summarize, let alone interpret, as much information as has been presented in this short chapter. First, whatever else it is, the juvenile crime problem is only minimally a problem of violence. Most juvenile offenses, even those committed by youths who have also committed a violent crime, typically involve property or public order. Second, the youthful monster idea is just that. For three birth cohorts of violence offenders (811 subjects in all), just 22 youths could be classed as unusually violent, that is, media monsters. Third, the shortage of monsters is more than compensated by the large proportion of chronic offenders (272 of the 811), many of whom became chronic (five or more arrests) before reaching their fourteenth birthday. Fourth, police and court dispositions are unpredictable no matter what the criteria of evaluation. It is doubtful that intuition or seat-of-the-pants dispositions do much credit to our system of justice or have any noticeable deterrent effect, general or specific. Fifth, the harsher the penalty, the less the street time before the next arrest.

Much has been made of the magnitude of juvenile violence across the nation (Conrad and Dinitz 1977). Yet nearly all that is known about it comes from two sources: official data from historically violent sections of major cities (Philadelphia, Chicago, Los Angeles, New York) and testimony from police, prosecutors, and court personnel (Vera Institute of Justice 1976). This chapter suggests that middle-sized cities are far more safe and tranquil. To generalize from the south Bronx to most communities is absurd (Vera Institute of Justice 1976). In a city of the size and composition of Columbus, juvenile violence, as measured by arrests, is modest and manageable although it is and will continue to be a growing social problem. But even in these more manageable cities—from Seattle to Miami—the juvenile system is not rehabilitative, punitive, or incapacitative as such. The best that can be said is that it is in transition. It is to be fervently hoped that whatever its transformations, the system will emerge as more rational and equitable in its dealings with youthful offenders, a percentage of whom have committed violent crimes.

We close this chapter with a discussion of five principles which the architects of the emerging juvenile justice system might do well to incorporate. These five principles of system intervention, based on our research with the violent two percent, are:

1. There must be an adverse consequence for every delinquent act. It should follow that intervention must never be nominal; the message should be clear at every stage of a delinquent's career that his situation will get worse with every new delinquency. Of course, intervention should be mild at the beginning. A probation order with regular probation contacts, usually directed at problem solving for the probationer and his family, but communicating to all concerned that this is a serious situation which can get better with appropriate conduct but much worse with any further lapse into delinquency.

2. At every stage, decision makers must be governed by the principle of minimum penetration of the system. Once a consequence has been set in convincing manner, a limit must also be set. The juvenile and his family must be likewise convinced that there is a way out of the mess he is in. It must be a credible route to constructive behavior, and it must not be dependent on long-term control by agents of the juvenile justice system. It may be necessary to provide for extended services such as a foster home placement, a group home, or even a boarding school under private auspices, not specifically directed at a delinquent population. But if these services are to be paid for from public sources, they should be arranged by the system as an advocate for the child, not under the direct auspices of the system.

3. At all ponits, the disposition of the juvenile offender should be the least severe possible, consistent with public safety. If possible, the child should remain at home. If he must be removed, he should not have to go any farther away than necessary from the community in which he lives. If he must be committed to a state facility, it should be for as brief a period of time as is consistent with his safe restoration to the community.

4. At all points, there is a responsibility on the part of all agents of the system and contractors for service to identify strengths in the child on which building toward citizenship can be grounded, and unsatisfactory conditions of health, education, and socialization which can be remedied.

5. There must be a recognition that for certain chronic offenders, especially those who have exceeded a minimum level of seriousness in the nature of their delinquencies, extended restraint will ordinarily be necessary. This restraint may be in a correctional facility; it may also be a heavily programmed community-based control. The evidence we have presented leaves little doubt that the chronic youthful offender is also the most frequent and the most serious violator of the law. We are confronted with a need for the restraint of more such young people than we can handle in incarcerative facilities as we know them now. It is particularly important that social invention be directed toward less drastic and more constructive alternative methods of control.

If we can put these principles into effect consistently for all apprehended juvenile offenders, the criminal justice system will have filled its tallest order yet. There is no doubt that such a program will be responsive to the problem it is supposed to solve, but officials and staff of juvenile justice agencies will have to be far more innovative than they have ever been before.

What do these principles mean for the routine functioning of the system? I think we should give special care to both ends of the juvenile offender population. The very young offender and the first offender of all ages should be given the benefit of the statistical doubt. We know that most of them will not go on to further offenses; unless the offense is grave indeed, the consequence should be minimal. The bleak future ahead for a recidivist should be outlined convincingly, a probation or community service order should be made by the court, and it should be enforced to the letter. Recidivists should experience what was predicted to the first offender, a fairly massive intervention in the shape of close supervision accompanied by provision of any services needed to remedy social deficiencies. Finally, chronic offenders should get more of the same, with the likelihood of some form of custodial control for those who do not respond favorably to community services. For those, like our 811 cases, whose offenses are violent or repetitively serious, we should be planning for extended custodial restraint, perhaps in the form of special facilities for offenders who, though chronologically still minors, must be treated as adults. Such facilities must be small, intensively programmed for a variety of activities, and meshed with appropriate community services after release.

If this sounds like more of the same ineffectual system that we now have, we have failed to communicate the challenge. What we have now is rather like an electric switch. Occasionally it is turned on and something happens. Most of the time we pretend to turn it on, and nothing happens. All of this pretense is in the name of individualizing the offender. What actually happens is that the system tells the offender that his risks are minimal; the chances are that nothing serious will happen, no matter what he does. We do what we do because we fancy that we can predict the boy's future conduct, and in our optimistic society, we choose to suppose that both we and the boy will be fortunate. We will be spared any further trouble with him if we give him another chance, and he will stay out of further delinquency. But the record is pretty clear. We cannot predict the boy's further conduct, but we can make a rough calculation of the risks. The switch will probably not be flipped next time, either. What we need is a rheostat, a gradual intensification of each response of the system to the boy so that he can predict that the next consequence will be even more unfavorable than the present one.

The plan should be embodied in legislation which will authorize the judge to impose a graded series of sanctions, and in the creation of an apparatus which will be engaged in activities more useful than the presentence investigations which all too often justify less than sufficient intervention. Such an apparatus should be intended for realistic control and credible advocacy. The basis of the intervention will be the seriousness of the offense and the record; the basis of the advocacy will be the nature of the identified need. All of this is to be legitimized and enforced by a determinate order in court, specifying the duration of the intervention, the requirements that must be satisfied, and the services that will be provided.

This program will be expensive, but so is the present system, as ineffective as it now seems. It may take advantage of a child's most impressionable years to impress on him that the consequences of a delinquent career are serious, distressing, and avoidable. After all, these are the considerations that keep the rest of us out of trouble.

References

Alexander, Franz, and Healy, William (1935). *Roots of Crime*. New York: Knopf.

Andenaes, Johannes (1974). *Punishment and Deterrence*. Ann Arbor: University of Michigan Press.

Bartollas, Clemens, Miller, Stuart, and Dinitz, Simon (1976). *Juvenile Victimization: The Institutional Paradox*. New York: Sage-Halsted-Wiley.

Collins, James J. (1976). Chronic offender careers. Paper presented at the American Society of Criminology, Tucson, November 4-7.

Conrad, John P. (1975). "We should never have promised a hospital." *Federal Probation*, 34:3-9.

Conrad, John P., and Dinitz, Simon (1977). *In Fear of Each Other*. Lexington, Mass.: Lexington Books, D.C. Heath.

Ferracuti, Franco, Dinitz, Simon, and Acosta de Brenes, Esperanza (1975). *Delinquents and Nondelinquents in the Puerto Rico Slum Culture*. Columbus: Ohio State University Press.

Fogel, David (1975). ". . . *We Are the Living Proof* . . ." Cincinnati: Anderson.

Friedlander, Kate (1947). *The Psychoanalytic Approach to Juvenile Delinquency*. New York: International Universities Press.

Glueck, Sheldon and Glueck, Eleanor (1934). *One Thousand Juvenile Delinquents*. Cambridge: Harvard University Press.

_____ (1940). *Juvenile Delinquents Grown Up*. New York: Commonwealth Fund.

_____ (1950). *Unraveling Juvenile Delinquency*. New York: Commonwealth Fund.

_____ (1968). *Delinquents and Nondelinquents in Pespective*. Cambridge: Harvard University Press.

Hamparian, Donna, Schuster, Richard L., Dinitz, Simon, and Conrad, John P. (1978). *The Dangerous Few*. Lexington, Mass.: Lexington Books, D.C. Heath.

Healy, William (1915). *The Individual Delinquent*. Boston: Little, Brown.

Menninger, Karl (1968). *The Crime of Punishment*. New York: Viking.

Miller, Walter (1976). Violence by youth gangs in major american cities. National Institute for Juvenile Justice and Delinquency Prevention. Washington, D.C.: U.S. Government Printing Office.

Reckless, Walter, and Dinitz, Simon (1972). *The Prevention of Juvenile Delinquency*. Columbus: Ohio State University Press.

Rennie, Ysabel (1978). *The Search for Criminal Man*. Lexington, Mass.: Lexington Books, D.C. Heath.

Schur, Edwin (1975). *Radical Non-Intervention: Rethinking the Delinquency Problem*. Englewood Cliffs, N.J.: Prentice-Hall.

Uniform Crime Reports (1973-1976). Federal Bureau of Investigation. Washington, D.C.: U.S. Government Printing Office.

United States Congress (1976). *School Violence and Vandalism*. Committee on the Judiciary, Subcommittee to Investigate Juvenile Delinquency. Washington, D.C.: U.S. Government Printing Office.

van den Haag, Ernest (1975). *Punishing Criminals*. New York: Basic Books.

Vera Institute of Justice (1976). Violent Delinquents. Unpublished Manuscript. New York: Vera Institute of Justice.

von Hirsch, Andrew (1976). *Doing Justice*. New York: Hill and Wang.

Wilson, James Q. (1975). *Thinking about Crime*. New York: Basic Books.

Wolfgang, Marvin, Figlio, Robert, and Sellin, Thorsten (1972). *Delinquency in a Birth Cohort*. Chicago: University of Chicago Press.

Revolution and Counterrevolution: Current Trends in Juvenile Justice

LaMar T. Empey

Remarkable changes in the American concepts of delinquency and juvenile justice occurred in the 1960s and 1970s. The reputation of the juvenile court has been badly tarnished; the rules that define delinquency have been altered; and faith in the concept of rehabilitation has been seriously eroded. In short, we are witnessing changes in our treatment of the young that are every bit as revolutionary as was the invention of the juvenile court in 1899, or the construction of prisons and reformatories almost a century before that.

The usual tendency is to assume that these changes represent progress. Absolutistic laws that overregulate the moral behaviors of children will be eliminated, the constitutional rights of the young will be protected, and new ways will be found for helping rather than stigmatizing them. A careful review of history, however, reveals that, if today's reforms do signal a better life for children, they may not be an unmixed blesssing. At the very least, one should be cautious about equating change with progress.

The Invention of Juvenile Justice

For much of Western civilization, it would not have occurred to people to utilize a special court for children. During the Middle Ages, infants were seen less as human beings than as strange and formless little creatures with whom strong emotional ties were to be avoided. And when they did survive infancy, children were regarded more as small or inadequate versions of their parents than as sacred beings in need of special protection. Consequently, many unwanted children were deliberately put to death, abandoned at birth, sold into prostitution, or used to pay debts. Meanwhile, those children who realized a better fate seldom received much nurturing from their parents, were apprenticed to others at about age seven, and were expected to be of service and to learn a trade appropriate to their station in life. Most parents, in short, were simply not much involved with their own children, except insofar as those children could help to preserve the family line or to serve some economic purpose (Ariès 1962; Bremner 1970; deMause 1974; Marvick 1974; Robertson 1974).

It was not until the seventeenth century that much attention was paid to

157

the development of children. During the next two centuries, however, the idea gained increasing acceptance that children, because they are fragile and guileless, require special protection and care: they should be raised and loved by their own parents, should attend school so that they can learn moral as well as secular principles, and should be quarantined from adult vices and associates until they mature (Ariès 1962:269-285; Bremner 1970: vol. 1, 72-102; Laslett 1972:1-89).

As might be expected, the process of incorporating such beliefs into the institutional structures of society was long and tortuous. As in Europe, several American colonies created schools for children in the seventeenth century, but these schools were largely dependent upon private support for their existence and covered only the first few grades (Bremner 1970: vol. 1, 72-102). Hence, only the children of the well-to-do received instruction beyond a rudimentary level. The children of the poor, by contrast, had to rely upon their parents, church-sponsored schools, and the apprenticeship system for whatever education they received. Indeed, it was not until after the Civil War that the majority of American states passed mandatory school attendance laws, and even then, such laws often proved ineffective (Hoffman 1974:51). In 1900, for example, one-third of all workers in Southern mills were children, more than half of the children in the industry nationwide were the children of immigrants (Bremner 1970: vol. 2, 601-604).

A crusade against child labor gathered steam late in the nineteenth century, led by lawyers, social workers, various charitable groups and even some industrialists (Bremner 1970: vol. 2, 601-604). By the dawn of the twentieth century, therefore, twenty-eight states had passed laws regulating child labor as well as those which mandated attendance at school.

Although such laws reflected the growing sentiment in favor of the idea that the prolongation and protection of childhood was essential to human progress, there were no special legal mechanisms by which to enforce such laws or to process children charged with crimes. Children tried for committing crimes were routinely processed primarily by lower municipal courts (Schultz 1974:248). They were also committed to houses of refuge, orphan asylums, and training schools for being "destitute of proper parental care, or growing up in mendicancy, ignorance, idleness, or vice" (Platt 1969:103). Many were also committed to adult jails and to prisons for the blanket charge of disorderly conduct, which might cover anything from assault with a deadly weapon to building bonfires in the street or playing on the railroad tracks (Lathrop 1916:2). Consistent with the growth of paternalistic sentiments, however, changes also began to appear in the legal processing of children.

In 1870, Boston began holding separate court hearings for juveniles under sixteen, as did New York in 1877. Massachusetts also passed a law, in 1869, requiring agents of the State Board of Charities to attend the trials of children to protect their interests and to make recommendations to the judge (Caldwell 1961:400). Finally, in 1898, the Illinois Conference of Charities culminated over a decade of effort by proposing the most radical step of all—a special court just for children. The conference drafted a model court act, the Chicago Bar Association threw its support behind the act, and the Illinois legislature passed it in 1899 (Lathrop 1925). Within twenty-five years, moreover, similar laws were passed in every state but two. Along with laws regulating child labor and mandating attendance at school, the juvenile court had become a part of the institutional fabric of American society.

Functions of the Juvenile Court

The juvenile court was a creation of revolutionary significance and represented a response, not merely to evolutionary changes in the status of children, but to the momentous events and institutional upheavals of the nineteenth century. As such, it was expected to fulfill many functions.

Enforcing the Modern Concept of Childhood

The beliefs and aspirations which led to the creation of the juvenile court are best understood as an ideology—as a kind of visionary theorizing about children and the best way to nurture and to protect them. This ideology, in turn, rests heavily upon assumptions derived from the modern concept of childhood—the concept which had been growing in stature since the sixteenth century (Skolnick 1973:316-321):

1. Children go through several stages of development which require that their entrance into full adulthood be postponed until their twenties or even later.
2. Throughout the various stages of development, children are qualitatively different from adults: "Adults work and are responsible, children play and are irresponsible; adults are controlled and rational, children are emotional and irrational; adults think abstractly, children think concretely; adults are sexual, children are asexual; and so on" (Skolnick 1973:316).
3. Until their full emotional, moral, physical, and rational skills are cultivated, children should be quarantined from adult voices, activities, and responsibilities. Though this quarantine may be reduced gradually as children proceed through the developmental process, it should not be lifted entirely until adulthood has been achieved.

The school attendance and child labor laws of the late nineteenth century, as well as the creation of the juvenile court, represented an embodiment of these assumptions in the legal as well as the cultural fabric of society. That is why, until almost the present day, children have been referred to court not only for violating the criminal law, but for idle conduct, for intractibility, for knowingly associating with lewd or lascivious persons, for being truant, for being alone with someone of the opposite sex at night, or for one of a host of other possible offenses. Legal definitions of child deviance were simply the obverse of the moral principles inherent in the modern concept of childhood; namely, that the ideal child should be obedient, submissive, self-controlled, hardworking, modest, and chaste (Aries 1962:114-119; Gillis 1974:21). A paternalistic court was expected to ensure that children were stringently safeguarded, that they received an education, and that they did not behave as adults until they had outlived the quarantine associated with childhood.

Surrogate for Family and Community

The second function of the juvenile court was closely related to the first. Its creators firmly hoped that it could become a benevolent surrogate for ineffective families and corrupt communities. That is why the first juvenile court act in Illinois specified that the law should be "liberally construed to the end . . . that the care, custody and discipline of a child shall approximate . . . that which should be given by its parents" (Revised Statutes of Illinois 1899, Sec. 21).

By way of illustrating this expectation, the Educational Commission of Chicago complained, in 1899, that its Compulsory School Attendance Act was not adequate to ensure schooling for marginal children caught in the vortex of cultural conflict and social change: "They cannot be received or continued in the regularly organized schools; . . . their parents cannot or will not control them; teachers and committees fail to correct their evil tendencies and vicious conduct. What shall be done with them?" (Harpur 1899:161).

The answer was that they should be disciplined by the juvenile court. It would rescue them from their dissolute parents and see that they were properly educated: "The welfare of the city demands that such children be put under restraint . . . We should rightfully have the power to arrest all the little beggars, loafers, and vagabonds that infest our city, take them from the streets, and place them in schools where they are compelled to receive education and learn moral principles" (Harpur 1899:163-164). In short, the juvenile court would not only be a helpful parent but a stern parent, stepping in when all else failed.

Delinquency Prevention

By moving in where parents, teachers, and communities had failed, the juvenile court could not only keep children in school but could perform a much grander function: It could also prevent delinquency. As the Chicago Bar Association put it, the court should not have to wait until a child is "criminal in tastes and habits," or until he "is in jails, bridewells and reformatories" before it acts. Instead, it would "seize upon the first conditions of neglect or delinquency" and thereby prevent innocent children from treading the path that leads to criminality (Platt 1969:138-139). Furthermore, in fulfilling this role, the court should not be encumbered with all the inhibiting strictures of due process, since its primary goal was in pursuing good for children, not in punishing them for evil.

Decriminalizing Children

Besides using the juvenile court to prevent delinquency, reformers also believed that it could be used to decriminalize the conduct of young lawbreakers. In the past, as Judge Julian W. Mack (1910:293) put it, children were generally "huddled together" with older criminals in the station houses, jails, and workhouses of America. Thus, "instead of the state training its bad boys so as to make of them decent citizens, it permitted them to become outlaws and outcasts of society; it *criminalized* them by the methods it used in dealing with them" (emphasis added). The new juvenile court, by contrast, would decriminalize such children by calling them "delinquents" rather than "criminals."

Reformers saw little need to draw subtle distinctions among the neglected child, the rude and intemperate child, and the child who broke the criminal law. Rather, said Judge Mack (1910:29), it is the duty of the state not to ask whether a boy or girl has committed a specific offense, but "to find out what he is physically, mentally, and morally and then, if it learns that he is treading the path that leads to criminality, to take him in charge, not so much to punish as to reform, not to degrade but to uplift, not to crush but to develop, not to make him a criminal but a worthy citizen." Hence, in contrast to the efforts of today's reformers to draw sharp distinctions between delinquents and status offenders, those of the nineteenth century sought to make status offenders out of all misbehaving children, whether they were criminal or merely neglected and unruly.

Rehabilitation

The idea that juvenile crimes should be decriminalized and their perpetrators reformed was symptomatic of the growing popularity of the concept of rehabilitation during the nineteenth century. Indeed, there is striking evidence that growing concerns over the welfare of children had percolated upward and were being expressed as concerns over adults. Nineteenth century Americans, says Rothman (1971:66), "stripped away the years from adults and made everyone a child."

Reflective of this idea, the Cincinnati Prison Congress of 1870, from which the principles of rehabilitation were so remarkably well distilled, concluded that great good could be accomplished if adult criminals were made "the objects of generous parental care." Instead of being sentenced to suffering, they should be "trained to virtue" (Henderson 1910:40). "A prison governed by force and fear is a prison mismanaged, in which hope and love, the two great spiritual, uplifting, regenerative forces to which mankind must ever look for redemption, are asleep or dead" (Wines 1910:2).

It is scarcely surprising, then, that the concept of rehabilitation became a natural ally of the concept of childhood and was eagerly incorporated into the juvenile court philosophy. Ostensibly derived for the purposes of correcting criminals, the beliefs embodied in this concept were so like those embodied in the concept of childhood that they might be viewed as principles for raising children as well as for reforming criminals. Rehabilitation, not punishment, is the primary goal of penology; punishment only degrades, correctional practices should uplift; treat people, not crimes; apply scientific methods to the task of diagnosing, classifying, and treating offenders; replace peremptory with indeterminate sentences—the task of socializing people is a task of time; make use of all educational, emotional, and industrial resources in accomplishing this task; and ensure that offenders are assisted by a concerned parole officer when they return to the community (Henderson 1910:39-63). The only way that society can be protected from the evils of crime is to ensure that all offenders are socialized properly.

The only modern innovation which the Cincinnati Prison Congress failed to stress was probation. Instead, its members concluded that the most logical place to apply the principles of rehabilitation were in new, scientifically run reformatories (Brockway 1910). But, by the time the juvenile court was firmly established, this idea had lost some of its attractiveness:

> However good an institution may be, however kindly its spirit, however genial its atmosphere, however homelike its cottages, however fatherly and motherly its officers, however admirable its training, it is now generally

agreed . . . that institutional life is at the best artificial and unnatural, and that the child ought to be returned at the earliest practicable moment to the more natural environment of the family. [Hart 1910:12]

Early in the twentieth century, therefore, community treatment under the supervision of a probation officer became the philosophical ideal for the juvenile court. Probation, said Judge Richard Tuthill of Chicago, "is the cord upon which all the pearls of the juvenile court are strung" (Rothman 1978). Indeed, a discerning and consecrated probation officer, together with the judge, would operate the juvenile court like a medical clinic:

> The judge and the probation officer consider together, like a physician and his junior, whether the outbreak . . . was largely accidental, or whether it is habitual or likely to be so, whether it is due chiefly to some inherent physical or moral defect of the child, or whether some feature of his environment is an important factor; and then they address themselves to the question of how permanently to prevent a recurrence. [Baker 1910:322]

Whatever he needed, the unfortunate child would receive.

Triumphal Acceptance

Reactions to the invention of the juvenile court were overwhelmingly favorable. Though Roscoe Pound had warned, in 1913, that "the powers of the court of star chamber were a bagtelle compared with those of American juvenile courts," he described those same courts, in 1950, as "the greatest step forward in Anglo-American jurisprudence since the Magna Charta!" (Compare Rothman 1978 with National Probation and Parole Association 1957:127). Similarly, Judge Orman Ketcham of the District of Columbia remarked that "the first two decades of the juvenile court movement produced a wealth of philosophical comment so sound in conception and so modern in tone that it has sacrcely been modified or improved upon since that time" (1962:26).

For much of this century, then, most authorities have not been concerned with the possibility that the juvenile court might be overly patronizing and arbitrary, but with finding ways by which its functions might be made more effective. Conceived in an aura of benevolent paternalism, it would be law and social work, control and help, the good parent and the stern parent. It would be all things to all people (Rubin 1976a:66).

The Tarnished Superparent

The original philosophy of the juvenile court, if not all its practices, remained largely unchanged until well after mid-twentieth century, but by the late 1960s, its reputation had become badly tarnished. Today, it is being irrevocably altered. Why?

Enforcing the Concept of Childhood

Meeting in London in 1960, the Second United Nations Congress on the Prevention of Crime and the Treatment of Offenders recommended "that the meaning of the term juvenile delinquency should be restricted as far as possible to violations of the criminal law" (United Nations 1961:61). In 1967, the President's Commission on Law Enforcement and Administration of Justice (1967a:25) made the same recommendation. "Serious consideration," it said, "should be given to complete elimination of the court's power over children for noncriminal conduct"—such acts as staying out late, disobeying parents, engaging in premarital sex, playing truant, or running away from home.

On their face, such recommendations could be, and often were, interpreted as suggesting merely that other than legal procedures are the best means for socializing misbehaving children. But, in actuality, these recommendations signaled important changes in the moral standards governing childhood. In writing for the President's Crime Commission, Edwin Lemert (1967:97) pointed them out. "Individual morality," he said, "has become functional rather than sacred or ethical in the older sense. [Hence,] it has become equally or more important to protect children from the unanticipated and unwanted consequences of organized movements in their behalf than from the unorganized, adventious 'evils' which give birth to the juvenile court." It was not an exploitive and sinful world from which children now needed protection from paternalistic do-gooders. It was they who had now become the problem.

Lemert's remarks were prophetic. In 1971 the Twenty-sixth Amendment to the Constitution granted full political suffrage to young people at age eighteen rather than at age twenty-one (Coleman et al. 1974:42); a variety of higher court decisions have supported the rights of students to free speech in the public schools (*Tinker* v. *Des Moines Independent School District* 1969); child labor legislation has come under increasing attack, as have mandatory school attendance laws (White House Conference 1971; Coleman et al. 1974:43); several states have lowered the school-leaving age (Empey 1978:566-567); legal restrictions on drinking by people under twenty-one have been relaxed; values favoring chastity have been attacked; and the Supreme Court has ruled that a pregnant teenager, no less than adult women, has the right to an abortion without parental consent (*Los Angeles Times* July 5, 1976); and a child rights movement designed to liberate children has started.

At the cutting edge of this movement are such moralist reformers as Richard Farson (1974) and John Holt (1974) who would do away with childhood as we know it. Instead, they would enforce a new bill of rights for children. They would permit youngsters of all ages to decide whether they wish to live with their parents, with someone else, or in state-run child care centers; to choose and to design their own educational programs, including the right not to attend school; to use alcohol or drugs and to experience sex with no more restrictions upon them than those placed upon adults; to obtain employment; to manage their own money; to own credit cards; to enter binding contracts; to vote; and to share completely in the political process. In short, says Farson, "We are on the threshold of a new consciousness of children's rights, a dramatically new concept of childhood itself. The fundamental change will be a recognition of the child's right to live with the same guarantee of freedom that adults enjoy, the basic right being that of self determination" (*Los Angeles Times*, January 28, 1975).

Society, of course, is not yet ready to invest children with all the rights that adults enjoy; such an event, if it does occur, will be a long time in coming. Nonetheless, changing attitudes have had a marked impact on the power and functions of the juvenile court. The legal code of virtually every state has been altered so that status offenders can no longer be called delinquents. Instead, they are denoted by such euphemisms as "minor in need of supervision" (MINS), "person in need of supervision" (PINS) or "unruly child" (UC) (Rubin 1974:6-7). Such prestigious groups as the International Chiefs of Police, the National Council on Crime and Delinquency, and the framers of the Model Act for Family Courts have gone even further and argued that the jurisdiction of the juvenile court over status offenders should be eliminated entirely (National Task Force 1977:3). Federal legislation has mandated that each state must guarantee that status offenders will not be placed in secure detention or correctional facilities (Law Enforcement Assistance Administration 1974b:395). The state of California has followed the federal lead and made it illegal to place status offenders in detention (California Welfare and Institutions Code 1976). And the state of Washington has gone one step further—status offenders have been removed entirely from the jurisdiction of the juvenile court and placed under the Department of Health Services (Revised Code of Washington 1977).

It seems to be only a matter of time until the juvenile court will be out of business entirely of enforcing the traditional concept of childhood.

Surrogate for Family and Community

The role of the juvenile court as surrogate for family and community has also been attacked from almost every angle. For the first time in history, in 1966, this role was reviewed by the Supreme Court in the now famous *Kent v. United States* case. "While there can be no doubt of the original laudable purpose of the juvenile courts," the justices wrote, "studies and critiques in recent years raise serious questions as to whether actual performance measures well enough against theoretical purpose to make tolerable the immunity of the process from the constitutional guarantees applicable to adults.''

What the justices were referring to is the fact that detention facilities for juveniles existed in only about 7 percent of the nation's counties, serving only about 50 percent of its youth; the rest were being detained in adult jails (National Council on Crime and Delinquency 1967:122). Many judges had neither college nor legal educations, and most practiced on a part-time basis (President's Commission 1967b:6-7; Smith 1974). Many juvenile courts were operating a kind of assembly-line justice in which hearings were delayed for weeks or months, yet took only ten to fifteen minutes to conduct (Cohen 1975; President's Commission 1967b:7). Probation services in most courts were grossly understaffed or nonexistent. And many juveniles were still being confined in overcrowded and ineffective training schools (President's Commission 1967b; Rubin 1976b). Hence, said the Supreme Court, "there is evidence . . . that the child receives the worse of two possible worlds: that he gets neither the protections accorded to adults nor the solicitous care . . . postulated for children" (*Kent* v. *United States* 1966).

But this was only the beginning. Subsequent decisions of the Supreme Court also began to reflect the influence of the child rights movement. Hence, it ruled that traditional protections afforded to adults could no longer be ignored for children (*In re Gault* 1967; *In re Winship* 1970). "Juvenile court history," it said, "has again demonstrated that unbridled discretion, however benevolently motivated, is frequently a poor substitute for principle and procedures" (*In re Gault* 1967:28-29). Instead of a family surrogate, therefore, the juvenile court had to become a court.

Social science also had a telling effect. Based on a highly popular, but largely untested set of assumptions, labeling theorists had concluded that the processes of identifying, labeling, and stigmatizing of children by the juvenile court had only made their problems worse, not better (Tannenbaum 1938:19). Indeed, said Edwin Lemert (1967:96), "it would be well to delete entirely from [the laws of the land] pious injunctions that the care, custody, and discipline of children under the control of the juvenile court shall approximate that which they would receive from their parents." The only defensible philosophy for the juvenile court is one of judicious nonintervention. Quickly translated into policy, this injunction has now become a national fad; nonserious offenders are diverted to hundreds of agencies in lieu of being sent to court (Carter and Klein 1976; Klein et al. 1976). Meanwhile, those who end up in court are being processed by prosecutors, sworn witnesses, and defense attorneys, as well as by judges and probation officers. The benevolent assumption that the juvenile court should be society's superparent has been discredited and is being discarded.

Delinquency Prevention

For over sixty years, juvenile court judges operated upon the assumption that they could prevent delinquency by acting in a paternalistic way. Consequently, they were not inhibited by the requirements of due process in their dealings with children. As Judge Paul W. Alexander put it (1962:89), "the question is almost never 'Did he or didn't he?' but rather 'What is the best way to change his attitude and correct his unlawful behavior?' "

Today, by contrast, paternalism is suspect. Instead of a preventive role, the juvenile court is expected to model itself after the adult criminal court. Rather than informal and uncensored inquiry into a child's history and background, it must devote itself exclusively to the charges against him, to warn him of his rights, and to referee the adversary procedures conducted by prosecution and defense. It has become a justice court, and an arbiter of criminal proceedings, not a supposed preventer of future criminal acts.

Decriminalization

Current reforms have had an ironic effect in terms of the original notion that the juvenile court should serve the purpose of decriminalizing the acts of all children, whether they were status offenders or criminals. On the one hand, much is now made of the fact that steps are being taken to decriminalize the acts of status offenders. On the other hand, the concerted effort to draw sharp distinctions between them and juvenile criminals has had the paradoxical effect of recriminalizing the latter. Whereas the original juvenile court was expected to treat offenders, not offenses, such is much less true today. Instead, those juveniles who commit crimes are viewed as beings of a different type. Although they are supposed to have all the benefits of due process, authorities are expected to deal more formally with them and, above all, to avoid contaminating status offenders with them. Indeed, the current enthusiasm for keeping the two groups separate is reminiscent of the enthusiasm exhibited by nineteenth century reformers when they sought to have children separated from the contaminating influence of adult offenders.

Rehabilitation

By now, it should be obvious that the one remaining cornerstone of the juvenile court—the rehabilitative philosophy—is also in a shambles. The remarks of Norman Carlson (1975:1) before the American Academy of

Psychiatry and Law epitomize this shambles. "We cannot diagnose criminality," he said, "we cannot prescribe treatment, and we certainly cannot guarantee a cure." Past efforts to rehabilitate offenders have been fruitless.

Attempts to explain Carlson's despairing conclusion have been many and varied. Critics like Lemert (1967:96) have suggested that we either lack sufficient knowledge by which to change people or that deliberate efforts to do so simply will not work. Rather than the rehabilitative model, therefore, a more realistic model would be "midwifery." Judges, probation officers, psychiatrists, and counselors must leaven their arrogance with humility and recognize that, like midwives, they do not have the knowledge by which to diagnose problems and to prescribe cures. At best, they can only assist the process of maturation and cannot have much impact on its outcome.

In rebuttal to such criticisms, many judges, national commissions, and professional associations have maintained that the failure to rehabilitate children is due to a lack of resources: the continued detention of children in jails, poorly paid and unqualified judges, inadequate numbers of probation officers, few psychiatric services, inadequate foster homes and institutional care, and an absence of educational programs and occuaptional opportunities (National Commission on Law Observance and Enforcement 1931; White House Conference on Child Health and Protections 1932; President's Commission 1967b). The problem is not due to deficiencies in the rehabilitative concept but to the failure to implement it successfully.

Finally, the findings of science on the effectiveness of correctional programs have been inconclusive, at best, and devastatingly negative, at worst. Perhaps the most controversial issue, therefore, is how one should interpret existing findings. On the one hand, the most scientifically defensible experiments have tended to indicate that one correctional alternative is rarely found to be clearly superior to another in reducing overall recidivism rates. For example, while a series of experimental community programs have been shown to be at least as effective as incarceration in reducing recidivism, and usually much less costly, they are not clearly superior (Empey and Lubeck 1971; Empey and Erickson 1972; Ohlin et al. 1977; Palmer 1971). A major limitation of most of these studies, however, is that they fail to distinguish among types of offenders and to indicate whether, for some, different programs might have a beneficial impact. It is conceivable that were our knowledge greater, correctional programs could be better adapted to individual needs.

On the other hand, large surveys of correctional research, much of which is of questionable quality, have led those who conduct the surveys to conclude that "nothing works" (Martinson 1974:25). Correctional efforts have been a waste of taxpayers' money. Thus, when this kind of conclusion has been coupled with evidence of rapidly rising crime rates among juveniles

(Empey 1978), and with evidence that a disproportionate amount of crime is committed by a tiny proportion of all offenders (Wolfgang et al. 1972), it has led to policy recommendations which are highly contradictory.

One set of recommendations has been liberal in character, suggesting that juveniles should be left alone wherever possible (Schur 1973:155), or that correctional programs should be concentrated in the community for all but the most dangerous criminals (President's Commission 1967a; Smith 1973; Ward 1972). If correctional programs do not correct, then the best that can be done is to avoid making offenders worse. Thus, deinstitutionalization, like due process and diversion, has become a popular fad (Law Enforcement Assistance Administration 1974b).

A second set of recommendations has been advocated by those who favor a return to the classical and punitive concept of justice (van den Haag 1975; Wilks and Martinson 1976; Wilson 1975). According to this group, all sentences should be of determinate length and would be based upon offense seriousness and prior criminal history, not upon social and psychological background. Each time an offender is reconvicted, in fact, the length of his sentence should be increased—doubled, perhaps, for a second offense and tripled for a third. The goal would be to immobilize repeat offenders until they are in their thirties or forties, not to try to change them (van den Haag 1975).

For the most part, this latter set of recommendations has been applied more to adults than to children. Indeed, its advocates do not seem to have paid much attention to the fact that the preponderant majority of all traditional crimes are committed by juveniles and young adults. Thus, if they were fully implemented, they would require that a crime war be waged on the nation's youth. Nonetheless, it is significant that this point of view is beginning to appear more and more in policies set for children. The state of Washington, for example, has now begun administering a determinate sentence law for delinquents (Revised Code of Washington 1977). This law dictates that, except in cases where "manifest injustice" would be done, the only factors authorities are supposed to take into account in sentencing children are age, prior offense history, and current offense. Social background and mitigating circumstances, so important to the original rehabilitative goals of the juvenile court, rank far down in the list of factors to be used in determining sentence.

It would be foolhardy to suggest that these developments mean that the rehabilitative ideal has been totally discarded. It has not. Yet, the current emphasis upon formalistic procedures, and dispensing justice according to type of crime rather than to the needs of the offender, stands in striking contrast to the reforms of the nineteenth century. Whereas the latter were exceedingly optimistic and filled with benevolent hopes and pronouncements, today's reforms tend to be pessimistic and increasingly neoclassical. Indeed, the best thing that could be said about a benevolent optimist today would be to call him naive; at worst, he would be branded a fool.

Conclusions and Implications

Since today's reforms are usually promoted with the same fervent, even self-righteous, conviction that prior reforms were promoted, perhaps the most useful way to provide a brief critique of them is to play the devil's advocate. In addition to their possible benefits, what other factors might be considered in deciding whether they represent inevitable steps forward in the progress of humanity?

Child Rights Movement

Usually ignored is the fact that the child rights movement often finds itself in conflict with other contemporary movements—the civil rights movement, the women's movement, and the rights of the elderly. For example, children now interfere with the professional aspirations of not only the father but also the mother. Abortion, as a consequence, has become as common as infanticide was during the Middle Ages, the nature of family life is changing, and the birth rate is declining. Hence, as Judith Blake Davis, a demographer, puts it: "You won't find those sacrificial mothers any more" (*Time* February 28, 1977). Caught up in the conflict between a desire for personal autonomy and self-realization and the responsibilities of raising children, women as well as men now find the latter task increasingly onerous. Hence, it is not unlikely that their preoccupation with nurturing and protecting children will decline.

For the children of the well-to-do, this may not present a serious problem, but there is evidence that it will be keenly felt by those at the bottom of the economic heap. For example, "over 2 million children now live in single-parent (usually father absent) households, almost *double* the number of ten years ago. . . . The average income for a single parent family with children under six years of age was, in 1970, only $3,100, well below the official 'poverty line' " (Bronfenbrenner 1974; Monahan 1957, as cited by Wilson 1975:231). Since it is among these one-parent families where rates of school failure, venereal disease, teenage pregnancies, criminal victimization, and child abuse are the highest, it is obvious that there are glaring contradictions between the rhetoric of the child rights movement and actual reality.

The same is also true with respect to jobs. Despite the fact that unemployment is far higher among adolescents than among any other group, they now find themselves in increasing competition, not merely with adult men but with large numbers of married women and with the elderly. Thus, the right of the child to work is still "much farther from realization than [his] right to protection against certain kinds of work at too early an age" (Coleman et al. 1974:40). Once again, then, it is all too clear that the movement to grant greater freedoms to children is not yet matched by a set of institutional arrangements by which rights can become a reality. A basic question, therefore, is whether current reforms in juvenile justice will help to remedy them.

Decriminalization

The decriminalization of status offenses is supposed to liberate children from the restraints imposed by an outmoded set of morals and an antiquated juvenile justice system. Herman and Julia Schwendinger (1978) argue that, although decriminalization may reduce the harrassment of working-class children by the police, it might also do lasting harm to them. Working-class or single-parent families already have a difficult time controlling their children in the face of meager family resources, poor public schools, and the attractions of neighborhood gangs.

Former family court justice, Justine Wise Polier (1978) agrees. Such terms as "incorrigibility," "ungovernability" or "running away," she says, usually cover a multitude of problems as well "sins." Desperate parents often come to officials asking for help, not only because their children are truant, stay out late, or become pregnant, but because they are using hard drugs, are gang members, or are teenage prostitutes. But if status offenses are decriminalized, legal authorities cannot act unless there is evidence of a crime.

It is assumed, however, that agencies other than the juvenile court will handle these problems. But how can one assume that they are any wiser, or that they can ensure that children will receive needed legal protections as well as controls? Indeed, many higher courts still contend that legal jurisdiction by the juvenile court over status offenders is, or should be, constitutional. Consider the case of a thirteen year old who was out of parental control and refused to go to school:

> While the doctrine of *parens patriae* does not permit any unfairness in judicial procedure towards juveniles [it is the New York] Court's opinion . . . that the State has the power to perform the parental role of insuring the child's education and training, when the parent is unable to control him sufficiently to perform it. If children were permitted the same freedom of choice as adults, they might well be unequipped when they at-

tain adulthood to exercise *any* freedom of choice—specifically, without an education or training, they would be unable to choose to work in a job for which they in fact have the potential. Enforcement agianst the child of the compulsory school law appears still to be constitutional. [Paulsen and Whitebread 1974:46]

For the same reasons cited in this opinion, the Schwendingers, as well as Judge Polier, contend that, if decriminalization is combined with new laws granting children the right to ignore parental directives or to leave school at their own discretion, it would constitute yet another example of benign neglect, justified by high flown, but class-biased, principles. The chances of lower class children for integration into the opportunity structures of society would become even worse.

Diversion

Perhaps the most popular of current reforms is diversion—referring problem children to agencies other than the juvenile court for help and supervision. Yet, this practice has had some paradoxical consequences. In the first place, diversion is nothing new. For as long as data have been gathered, they show that police and probation officers have customarily counseled and released the majority of children they have taken into custody, to say nothing of those they have excused with a warning. As a result, only a small minority of potential court cases actually ever ended up there (Empey 1978: chaps. 15-16).

Second, diversion was supposed to reduce the number of children being referred to court. Thus far, however, it has not had that effect. Instead, those children who are being diverted tend to be the younger, less serious offenders whom the police used to counsel and release. As a consequence, the net of the juvenile court has not been reduced. Instead, those types of children who have always been processed legally are still being processed (Klein and Teilmann 1976; Nejelski 1976).

Third, diversion was supposed to increase indigenous community services for children, reduce stigma, and lessen the effects of legal and bureaucratic controls over them. Actually, it has not done this, at least so far. Not only has it created a new system of social control for less serious offenders but it seems to be dominated by the agents of the juvenile justice system, and their satellite set of counseling and rehabilitative agencies (Blomberg 1975; Graecen 1975; Klein et al. 1976; Kutchins and Kutchins 1973; Mattingly and Katkin 1975; Nejelski 1976).

Given these developments, several important questions remain. There is serious doubt that stigma for misbehaving children has been reduced and that they are actually reintegrated more effectively into such normal youth institutions as family, school, and work. Furthermore, the new system of social control is not subject to the legal safeguards and higher court reviews to which the juvenile court is subject. Thus, as Cressey and McDermott (1973:59-60) point out:

1. The faddist nature of diversion has produced a proliferation of diversion units and programs without generating a close look at whether the juvenile subject to all this attention is receiving a better deal.

2. So far as we know, no one has shown that the juvenile offender and his family perceive their handling as materially different under the auspices of a diversion than under a more traditional justice agency.

Like decriminalization, therefore, diversion has not proven to be a remedy for many of the problems for which the juvenile court was criticized, nor have its programs been particularly innovative in their approach to youth problems.

Due Process

The concept of due process is one that also enjoys almost universal support. Yet, this support means quite different things to different people. One group of reformers would like to have the best of two possible worlds; namely, a formal juvenile court which not only guards the rights of juveniles but which gives them tender loving care as well. In the *Gault* case (1967:21), for example, the justices of the Supreme Court maintained, "The observance of due process standards, intelligently and not ruthlessly administered, will not compel the States to abandon or displace any of the substantive benefits of the juvenile process. . . . Nothing will require that the conception of the kindly judge be replaced by its opposite."

The National Council of Juvenile Court Judges responded to this admonition by saying that it seemed to be inherently contradictory (Rubin 1976b:136). How can judges remain impartial with respect to proving the acts that juveniles commit and yet appear to be partial and kindly in the process? Who is to say that prosecutors and defense attorneys will behave differently in juvenile court than they do in adult court, where their goal is to win a case, not necessarily to see that the truth is discovered? To what degree will harm be done to impressionable children when they discover what the rules of this game are and how to take advantage of them?

Attempts to answer such questions are made no easier by the fact that the adult criminal court is often cited as a model for the juvenile court to follow. Yet, this court is characterized by a massive backlog of cases; about 90 percent of its charges are resolved by bargaining between prosecutor and defense attorneys and result in guilty pleas; and existing arrangements tend to favor the wealthy and to penalize the poor (Lefcourt 1971). Thus, if some more humane, yet just, model is to be sought for juveniles, it is by no means clear that the criminal court provides the answer.

A second group of reformers, by contrast, are not concerned with kindly care for young criminals but with making justice uniform for everyone, and administering punishment that is swift and certain (Morris 1974; Wilson 1975; van den Haag 1975). Their position is that society has been guilty of excessive leniency toward young hoodlums, has denied the needs of their victims, has helped to erode discipline and respect for authority, has made the costs of crime unbearable, and has threatened to destroy social order (Miller 1973:454-455). Hence, instead of protecting children the following reforms are recommended:

1. Lower the age of accountability for crime. Threats to the social order no longer justify allowing children to escape unscathed for their acts. Indeed, in support of this view, various states have lowered the age of accountability for crime from eighteen to sixteen, and now require that juveniles charged with serious felonies be sent automatically to adult court (California Welfare and Institutions Code 1976).

2. Abolish the juvenile court. Now that the Supreme Court has ruled that the juvenile court must become more formal, why retain it at all? It is a diseased organ that no longer performs any useful function (McCarthy 1977). Neglected children and status offenders may be handled by family courts, but young criminals, no matter what their age, should be tried by the criminal courts.

3. Punish and incapacitate criminals. Since the permissive philosophy of the juvenile court is a proven failure, justice demands an elimination of the individualized approach to criminals and a return to classical practices in which retribution and restraint are the governing principles (Morris 1974; Wilks and Martinson 1976; Wilson 1975; van den Haag 1975). It is futile to try to control crime by focusing on family background, poverty, or peer groups. The justice system is unable to prevent or to rectify them. Hence, its principal function should be that of administering equal justice and of ensuring that punishment is swift, certain, and uniform.

Given these conflicting images of justice for juveniles, it is by no means certain that current concerns over due process will result in an unqualified blessing for them. In light of recent increases in juvenile crime, and in levels of cynicism over all kinds of social programs, they may well result in a kind of justice that is more classical and retributive than rehabilitative.

Deinstitutionalization

Support for the fourth and final reform—deinstitutionalization—is certainly not new. It has existed among some reformers for over a hundred years. For the first time, however, it is becoming an established fact for status offenders. Yet, again, some crucial issues are unresolved.

Police officers, judges, and probation officers, for example, are often confronted with the seamy side of juvenile life—fourteen-year-old prostitutes, male and female, children who use drugs habitually, or youngsters who create havoc for others in school and neighborhood. Since these children often come from homes where parents are cruel and uncaring, authorities do not always feel that some type of secure, residential placement is the worst of all worlds for them, particularly for those who refuse to remain in voluntary placements. Yet, because secure placement is now precluded by federal and by an increasing number of state laws, more and more police and probation officers are disinclined to deal with such children when they encounter them. As a consequence, an incredulous president of the National Council of Juvenile Court Judges, Judge Margaret Driscoll, asks what their fate shall be: "If these children can't be brought to court," she questions, "what on earth is going to happen to them? Are they seriously telling us that when all else has failed they are simply willing to leave thirteen- and fourteen-year-old girls out on the street to fend for themselves?" (*Los Angeles Times* February 12, 1976). In light of current trends, the answer may be yes. Coercion for status offenders, however benevolently motivated, is out.

Deinstitutionalization for criminal youngsters is another matter. On the one hand, sentiments in favor of it grew markedly during the 1960s and early 1970s, and the state of Massachusetts even went so far as to close completely all of its juvenile institutions (Ohlin et al. 1977). On the other hand, concerns over rising crime rates and the counterrevolution favoring equal justice and punishment have served to seriously dampen the movement in recent years. This has occurred despite evidence that community programs cost less, do not increase recidivism, and may be more humane (Empey 1978:553-554; Ohlin et al. 1977). But since these programs rarely assuage public fears of crime and sometimes contribute to "deviant ghettoes" among a few contriving and habitual offenders, they remain suspect (Scull 1977:152-153). Furthermore, an all-or-none demand that every institution be closed, no matter what its size or character, or the contention that community programs can successfully deal with every offender, no matter how predatory he or she may be, simply do not make sense. In light of conservative trends, in fact, such contentions may detract from the considerable virtues of the deinstitutionalization movement and contribute to counter-demands favoring more determinate sentences and harsher punishments.

In summary, then, deinstitutionalization, like the child rights movement and other reforms, has been greeted with understandably mixed reactions, has had mixed results, and is by no means an unmixed blessing. Thus, it would seem that if we are to avoid the traditional trap into which virtually all reformers in the past have fallen, we should not only be asking whether current reforms represent clear-cut improvements over that which existed before, but whether they are superior to other possible alternatives. Given the uncertain consequences of our present endeavors, there are many reasons to believe that some additional alternatives might be desirable.[2]

Notes

1. M.G. Paulsen and C.H. Whitebread, "Juvenile Law and Procedure," National Council of Juvenile and Family Court Judges, 1974, p. 46. Reprinted with permission.
2. This chapter is a distillation of my much longer review of the history of childhood and juvenile justice. For a more complete account see, *American Delinquency: Its Meaning and Construction* (Homewood, Ill.: Dorsey Press, 1978).

References

Alexander, Paul W. (1962). "Constitutional rights in the juvenile court." In Margaret K. Rosenheim (ed.), *Justice for the Child*, pp. 82-94. Chicago: University of Chicago Press.

Ariès, Philippe (1962). *Centuries of Childhood* (translated by Robert Baldick). New York: Alfred A. Knopf.

Baker, Harvey H. (1910). "Procedure for the Boston juvenile Court." In Hastings H. Hart (ed.), *Preventive Treatment of Neglected Children*, pp. 318-327. New York: Charities Publication Committee.

Blomberg, T.G. (1975). Diversion: a strategy of family control in the juvenile court process. Tallahassee: School of Criminology, Florida State University (unpublished).

Bremner, Robert H. (ed.) (1970). *Children and Youth in America: A Documentary History*. 2 vols. Cambridge: Harvard University Press.

Brockway, Z.R. (1910). "The American reformatory prison system." In Charles R. Henderson (ed.), *Prison Reform and Criminal Law*, pp. 88-107. New York: Charities Publication Committee.

Bronfenbrenner, Urie (1974). "The origins of alienation." *Scientific American*, 231:48-59.

Caldwell, Robert G. (1961). "The Juvenile court: its development and some major problems." *Journal of Criminal Law, Criminology, and Police Science* 51:593-607.

California Welfare and Institutions Code (1976). Assembly Bill 3121. Ch. 1071:1-25.

Carlson, Norman (1975). "Giving up the medical model." *Behavior Today*, 6:1.

Carter, Robert M., and Klein, Malcolm W. (1976). *Back on the Street: The Diversion of Juvenile Offenders*. Englewood Cliffs, N.J.: Prentice-Hall.

Cohen, Lawrence E. (1975). *Juvenile Dispositions: Social and Legal Factors Related to the Processing of Denver Delinquency Cases*. Law Enforcement Assistance Administration. Washington, D.C.: U.S. Government Printing Office.

Coleman, James S., et al. (1974). Youth: *Transition to Adulthood*. Chicago: University of Chicago Press.

Cressey, Donald R., and McDermott, Robert A. (1973). *Diversion from the Juvenile Justice System*. National Assessment of Juvenile Corrections. Ann Arbor: University of Michigan.

deMause, Lloyd (ed). (1974). *The History of Childhood*. New York: Psychohistory Press.

Empey, LaMar T. (1978). *American Delinquency: Its Meaning and Construction*. Homewood, Ill.: Dorsey.

Empey, LaMar T., Erickson, Maynard L. (1972). *The Provo Experiment: Evaluating Community Control of Delinquency*. Lexington, Mass.: Lexington Books, D.C. Heath.

Empey, LaMar T., and Lubeck, Steven G. (1971). *The Silverlake Experiment: Testing Delinquency Theory and Community Intervention*. Chicago: Aldine.

Farson, Richard (1974). *Birthrights: A Bill of Rights for Children*. New York: Macmillan.

Gillis, John R. (1974). *Youth and History*. New York: Academic Press.

Graecen, John M. (1975). Pitfalls and possibilities in juvenile justice reform. Paper presented at the National Conference on Juvenile Justice, Los Angeles.

Harpur, W.R. (1899). *The Report of the Educational Commission of the City of Chicago*. Chicago: Lakeside Press.

Hart, Hastings (1910). *Preventive Treatment of Neglected Children*. New York: Charities Publication Committee.

Henderson, Charles R. (ed.) (1910). *Prison Reform and Criminal Law*. New York: Charities Publication Committee.

Hoffman, Edward (1974). "The treatment of deviance by the educational system: history." In William C. Rhoads and Sabin Head (eds.), *A Study of Child Variance*, vol. 3, pp. 41-56. Ann Arbor: Institute for the Study of Mental Retardation and Related Disabilities, University of Michigan.

Hold, John (1974). *Escape from Childhood*. New York: Dutton.

In re Gault (1967). 387 U.S. 1, 18L. ed. 2d 527, 87S. Ct. 1428.

In re Winship (1970). 397 U.S. 358, 25L. ed. 2d 368, 90S. Ct. 1068.

Kent v. *United States* (1966). 383 U.S. 541, 16L. ed. 2d 84,86S. Ct. 1045.

Ketcham, Orman W. (1962). "The unfilled promise of the American juvenile court." In Margaret K. Rosenheim (ed.), *Justice for the Child*, pp. 22-43. New York: Free Press.

Klein, Malcolm W., and Teilmann, Kathie S. (1976). *Pivotal Ingredients of Police Juvenile Diversion Programs*. Washington, D.C.: National Institute for Juvenile Justice and Delinquency Prevention.

Klein, Malcolm. W., Teilmann, Kathie S., Styles, Joseph A., Lincoln, Suzanne B. and Labin-Rosensweig, Susan (1976). "The explosion of police diversion programs." In Malcolm W. Klein (ed.), *The Juvenile Justice System*, pp. 101-120. Beverly Hills: Sage.

Kutchins, H., and Kutchins, S. (1973). Pretrial diversionary programs: new expansion of law enforcement activity camouflaged as rehabilitation. Paper presented at the Annual Meetings of the Pacific Sociological Association, Honolulu.

Laslett, Peter (1972). *Household and Family in Past Time*. Cambridge: Cambridge University Press.

Lathrop, Julia (1916). "Introduction." In Sophonisba P. Breckenridge and Edith Abbott (eds.), *The Delinquent Child and the Home*, pp. 1-15. New York: Free Press.

_____ (1925). "The background of the juvenile court in Illinois." In Julia Addams (ed.), *The Child, the Clinic and the Court*, pp. 290-297, 320-330. New York: New Republic.

Law Enforcement Assistance Administration (1974a). *Children in Custody*. Washington, D.C.: U.S. Government Printing Office.

_____ (1974b). *Indexed Legislative History of the Juvenile Justice and Delinquency Prevention Act of 1974*. Washington, D.C.: U.S. Government Printing Office.

Lefcourt, Robert (ed.) (1971). *Law against the People*. New York: Vintage Books.

Lemert, Edwin M. (1967). "The juvenile court: quest and realities." In President's Commission on Law Enforcement and Administration of Justice, *Task Force Report: Juvenile Delinquency and Youth Crime*, pp. 91-106. Washington, D.C.: U.S. Government Printing Office.

McCarthy, Francis B. (1977). "Should juvenile delinquency be abolished?" *Crime and Delinquency* 23:196-203.

Mack, Julian W. (1910). "The juvenile court as a legal institution." In Hastings H. Hart (ed.), *Preventive Treatment of Neglected Children*, pp. 293-317. New York: Charities Publication Committee.

Martinson, Robert (1974). "What works? Questions and answers about prison reform." *Public Interest* 35:22-54.

Marvick, Elizabeth W. (1974). "Nature versus nurture: patterns and trends in seventeenth century French child rearing." In Lloyd deMause (ed.), *The History of Childhood*, pp. 259-302. New York: Psychohistory Press.

Mattingly, J., and Katkin, D. (1975). The youth service bureau: a re-invented wheel? Paper presented at the Society for the Study of Social Problems, San Francisco.

Miller, Walter B. (1973). "Ideology and criminal justice policy: some current issues." In Sheldon L. Messinger et al. (eds.), *The Aldine Crime and Justice Annual, 1973*, pp. 453-473. Chicago: Aldine.

Monahan, Thomas P. (1957). "Family status and the delinquent child: a reappraisal and some new findings." *Social Forces* 35:250-258.

Morris, Norval (1974). "The future of imprisonment: toward a punitive philosophy." *Michigan Law Review* 72:1161-1180.

National Commission on Law Observance and Enforcement (1931). *The Child Offender in the Federal System of Justice*. Washington, D.C.: U.S. Government Printing Office.

National Council on Crime and Delinquency (1967). "Correction in the United States." In President's Commission on Law Enforcement and Administration of Justice; *Task Force Report: Corrections*, pp. 115-212. Washington, D.C.: U.S. Government Printing Office.

National Probation and Parole Association (1957). *Guides for Juvenile Court Judges*. New York: National Probation and Parole Association.

National Task Force to Develop Standards and Goals for Juvenile Justice and Delinquency Prevention (1977). *Jurisdiction: Status Offenses*. Washington, D.C.: National Institute for Juvenile Justice and Delinquency Prevention.

Nejelski, Paul (1976). "Diversion: the promise and the danger." *Crime and Delinquency*, 22:393-410.

Ohlin, Lloyd E., Miller, Alden D., and Coates, Robert B. (1977). *Juvenile Correctional Reform in Massachusetts*. Washington, D.C.: U.S. Government Printing Office.

Palmer, Theodore B. (1971). "California's treatment program for delinquency adolescents." *Journal of Research in Crime and Delinquency*, 8:74-92.

Paulsen, Monrad G., and Whitebread, Charles H. (1974). *Juvenile Law and Procedure*. Reno: National Council of Juvenile Court Judges.

Platt, Anthony M. (1969). *The Child Savers*. Chicago: University of Chicago Press.

Polier, Justine Wise (1978). "Prescriptions for reform: doing what we set out to do?" In LaMar T. Empey (ed.), *Juvenile Justice: The Progressive Legacy and Current Reforms*. Charlottesville: University of Virginia Press.

President's Commission on Law Enforcement and Administration of Justice (1967a). *The Challenge of Crime in a Free Society*. Washington, D.C.: U.S. Government Printing Office.

_____ (1967b). *Juvenile Delinquency and Youth Crime*. Washington, D.C.: U.S. Government Printing Office.

Revised Code of Washington (1977). *Title 13: Juvenile Courts and Juvenile Delinquents*. Pp. 66-90, 726-729.

Revised Statutes of Illinois, 1899, Sec. 21.

Robertson, Pricilla (1974). "Home as a nest: middle-class childhood in nineteenth century Europe." In Lloyd deMause (ed.), *The History of Childhood*, pp. 407-431. New York: Psychohistory Press.

Rothman, David J. (1971). *The Discovery of the Asylum*. Boston: Little, Brown.

_____ (1978). "The Progressive legacy: American attitudes toward juvenile delinquency." In LaMar T. Empey (ed., *Juvenile Justice: The Progressive Legacy and Current Reforms*, pp. 1-25. Charlottesville: University of Virginia Press.

Rubin, H. Ted (1974). Transferring responsibility for juvenile noncriminal misconduct from the juvenile courts to nonauthoritarian community agencies. Phoenix: Arizona Conference on Delinquency Intervention (unpublished).

_____ (1976a). *The Courts: Fulcrum of the Justice System*. Pacific Palisades: Goodyear.

_____ (1976b). "The eye of the juvenile court judge: a one-step-up view of the juvenile justice system." In Malcolm W. Klein (ed.), *The Juvenile Justice System*, pp. 133-159. Beverly Hills: Sage.

Sanders, Wiley B. (ed.) (1970). *Juvenile Offenders for a Thousand Years*. Chapel Hill: University of North Carolina Press.

Schultz, J. Lawrence (1974). "The cycle of juvenile court history." In Sheldon Messinger et al. (eds.), *The Aldine Crime and Justice Annual, 1973*, pp. 239-258. Chicago: Aldine.

Schur, Edwin M. (1973). *Radical Nonintervention: Rethinking and Delinquency Problem*. Englewood Cliffs, N.J.: Prentice-Hall.

Schwendinger, Herman, and Schwendinger, Julia (1978). "Delinquency and social reform: a radical perspective." In LaMar T. Empey (ed.), *Juvenile Justice: The Progressive Legacy and Current Reforms*. Charlottesville: University of Virginia Press.

Scull, Andres (1977). *Community Treatment and the Deviant: A Radical View*. Englewood Cliffs, N.J.: Prentice-Hall.

Skolnick, Arlene (1973). *The Intimate Environment: Exploring Marriage and the Family*. Boston: Little, Brown.

Smith, D.C. (1974). "A profile of juvenile court judges in the United States." *Juvenile Justice*, 25:27-38.

Smith, Robert L. (1973). *A Quiet Revolution: Probation Subsidy*. Youth Development and Delinquency Prevention Administration, HEW. Washington, D.C.: U.S. Government Printing Office.

Tannenbaum, Frank (1938). *Crime and the Community*. New York: Columbia University Press.

Tinker v. *Des Moines Independent School District* (1969). 393 U.S. 503.

United Nations (1961). *Report prepared by the Secretariat*. New York: United Nations.

United States Bureau of the Census (1955). *Current Population Reports.* Series R-25, No. 123. Washington, D.C.: U.S. Government Printing Office.

van den Haag, Ernest (1975). *Punishing Criminals.* New York: Basic Books.

Ward, David A. (1972). "Evaluative research for corrections." In Lloyd E. Ohlin (ed.), *Prisoners in America*, pp. 184-206. Englewood Cliffs, N.J.: Prentice-Hall.

White House Conference on Child Health and Protection (1932). *The Delinquent Child.* New York: Century.

White House Conference on Youth (1971). *Preamble.* Recommendations and Resolutions. Wahsington, D.C.: U.S. Government Printing Office.

Wilks, Judith and Robert Martinson (1976). "Is the treatment of criminal offenders really necessary?" *Federal Probation* 40:3-8.

Wilson, James Q. (1975). *Think about Crime.* New York: Basic Books.

Wines, Frederick H. (1910). "Historical Introduction." In Charles R. Henderson (ed.), *Prison Reform and Criminal Law*, pp. 3-38. New York: Charities Publication Committee.

Wolfgang, Marvin E., Figlio, Robert, and Sellin, Thorsten (1972). *Delinquency in a Birth Cohort.* Chicago: University of Chicago Press.

10 Punishment, Deterrence, and Juvenile Justice

Maynard L. Erickson and
Jack P. Gibbs

In the eighty years since the juvenile court was invented, juvenile justice policy in this country has been guided by the notion of "rehabilitation." During this whole period juvenile justice policy was intended to minimize punishment. In fact, even the use of detention and incarceration, which are ordinarily thought of as punitive, has been defended from a rehabilitative philosophy.

However, in recent years the rehabilitative approach has come under considerable fire (Lipton, Martinson, and Wilks 1975; Hirsch 1976; van den Haag 1975; Wilson 1975). In its extreme form it has been concluded that "nothing works" (Martinson 1974). As a consequence of the apparent failure of the rehabilitative approach, two alternative approaches have emerged. One of these has been referred to as the "hands off" approach (Empey 1978; Erickson 1979). Empey (1978:525-558) refers to this approach as the most recent revolution in juvenile justice and characterizes it in terms of four policy concerns (due process, decriminalization, diversion, and deinstitutionalization).

The second approach to emerge recently represents a return to a classical penal policy (Bentham 1962; Beccaria 1963) emphasizing punishment and deterrence. This movement can be characterized in terms of three major reforms: (1) lowering the age of accountability for crime from eighteen to sixteen, thus making adult penal sanctions applicable; (2) abolishing the juvenile court; and (3) punishing or incapacitating offenders (Empey 1978: 584-585). The significant movement toward the extended use of punishment in dealing with juvenile offenders is evident in many states. For example, major statutory changes have already been made in Washington and California.

In Washington a new system of mandatory sentences has been adopted for juvenile offenders (Revised Criminal Code of Washington 1977: title 13, 66-90).

The research reported in this chapter was conducted under support from PHS research grant MH22350, NIMH (Center for Studies of Crime and Delinquency). The authors express their gratitude to all the project staff over the years. We owe a special debt to James Galliher for his assistance in completing this aspect of the project.

183

In that code, the ten purposes of the code are spelled out. The four listed first are as follows:

1. Protect the citizenry from criminal behavior.
2. Provide for determining whether accused juveniles have committed offenses as defined by this chapter.
3. Make the juvenile offender accountable for his or her criminal behavior.
4. Provide for punishment commensurate with the age, crime, and criminal history of the juvenile offender.

The above is only illustrative of the kinds of changes that have been made or are being contemplated in other states. Obviously, it is too early to assess the impact of such statutory changes on the rate(s) of delinquency.

The best that can be hoped for at this time is a tentative exploration of the following general question: What might be the outcome of attempts to reduce the volume of delinquency by implementing a policy which emphasizes punishment or incapacitation? Any answer cannot be free of speculation; nonetheless, the question should be confronted, if only because it is reasonable to expect that such policies are likely to be proposed by more and more critics of other juvenile justice policies such as rehabilitation and "hands off."

The Promotion of Deterrence in Juvenile Justice

The deterrence doctrine is a far cry from a systematic theory, and that consideration creates all manner of problems in attempting to bring evidence to bear on the doctrine (Gibbs 1975). Nonetheless, there are certain points of agreement among those writers who have taken tentative steps toward stating the deterrence doctrine as a systematic theory. Perhaps the most important point is that the doctrine must be stated so as to recognize the role of perception in deterrence. So construed, one of the central ideas reduces to the following general proposition: Legal punishments deter crime and delinquency to the extent that potential offenders perceive those punishments as certain, severe, and swift.

No attempt is made here to realize a definitive test of the foregoing proposition; rather, the focus is primarily on findings pertaining to the perceptions of legal punishments by Arizona juveniles. An analysis of those perceptions is not a test of the deterrence doctrine, but it does bear on the possible outcomes of attempts to promote deterrence in the juvenile justice system. To illustrate, the idea of promoting deterrence by adjudicating juveniles as adults would be dubious if juveniles perceive the statutory penalties in the criminal code as most uncertain (Erickson 1979).

At first glance it may appear that there is nothing in the deterrence doctrine that would make it any more or less applicable to juveniles than to adults. On the whole, that is the case; but observe that an attempt to promote deterrence among juveniles may follow one of two strategies: (1) all juveniles charged with crimes (not status offenses) could be adjudicated as adults, or (2) such juveniles could be adjudicated as juveniles with judges selecting treatment modes that are presumptively more punitive than those now commonly applied. The immediate question in the case of the first alternative strategy is: How do juveniles perceive the severity of adult penalties? In the case of the second strategy the immediate question is somewhat different: Are there any existing treatment modes for juvenile delinquents that juveniles perceive as especially severe? If the answer to the latter question is no, then that would be a basis for construing the first strategy as essential for promoting deterrence among juveniles. However, the first strategy presumes that juveniles perceive adult penalties as severe.

Despite the national clamor for tough penal policies, it is probably true that public opinion is still inclined toward less severe punishments for juvenile offenders, even those charged with a serious criminal offense. The general point is that a policy to promote deterrence among juveniles should recognize a limit as to what the public will tolerate in the way of punishing juvenile offenders. In that connection there are two strategic questions. (1) What penalties do members of the public prefer for juvenile offenders? (2) In what way (if any) do those preferred penalties differ from those now prescribed for adults? Those questions are all the more important because legislators and judges are sensitive to public opinion (though undoubtedly some much more than others) when it comes to the adjudication of juvenile cases, and that is so independent of any particular concern with deterrence.

Data Sources

The findings reported in this chapter are based on two series of surveys in Arizona, one of students in six high schools—three in a metropolitan area and the only school in each of three small towns. The other surveys focused on adult residents of four places, the metropolitan area's central city and the three small towns.

In the survey of students, a questionnaire was administered either to all students (especially in the case of the small towns) or to all students attending a particular class on a particular day (with the class deemed to be representative of the student body as a whole). The only known bias in the selection of students is underrepresentation of persistent truants and (in the case of some schools) those students whose parents declined permission to have their children participate in the survey.

All adult respondents in the survey were selected through a random sampling of households from an ostensibly complete list for each of the four places. Approximately 80 percent of the attempted interviews were successful, with the remaining 20 percent representing refusals or instances where no adult could be contacted at the residence in any of three visitations.

Since the surveys were concerned with a very general topic—community tolerance of deviance—a variety of instruments (questionnaires and schedules) were employed. In some of the instruments, questions were asked about hypothetical juvenile offenders, and in others, about hypothetical adult offenders. To avoid intolerably long interviews, respondents could not be asked questions about more than four types of crimes or delinquencies, with the types varying from one set of schedules to the next. So the project encompassed a series of distinct surveys over 1974-1976. The principal data for this chapter were gathered during 1974-1975, but the sample numbers for the statistics reported here vary so much that a complete account is not feasible. It must suffice to say that the minimum number for any datum pertaining to the survey of students is 3,145, and the minimum number for any datum pertaining to the adult survey is 480.

Only a few of the numerous questions posed in the surveys are relevant for present purposes; namely, those having to do with the perceived severity of various kinds of legal punishments or reactions to offenses (crimes or delinquencies), the perceived certainty of those punishments, public preferences as to legal punishments, self-reported offenses, self-reported instances of being the object of a legal reaction to an offense, and the degree of social (public) disapproval of particular types of offenses. The emphasis on perceptual questions stems from recognition that the deterrence doctrine is first and foremost a perceptual theory; that is, it asserts that punishments deter crimes to the extent they are perceived by the potential perpetrators as certain, swift, and severe.

With a view to assessing the juvenile population's perception of the severity of legal punishments, the high school students were asked a series of questions in the following form: "Now think how much you would dislike being arrested by the police, and give this a score of 100. What number best represents how much you would dislike each of the following: One month in county jail? Six months in county jail? One year in county jail? One year in prison? Five years in prison? Ten years in prison? Fifteen years in prison? Life in Prison?"[1] Similar questions about various other kinds of legal reactions (for example, commitment to a reformatory) were interspersed among those pertaining to jail and prison, but space limitations make it necessary to consider responses to questions about only a few kinds of legal reactions, jail and prison sentences particularly. Those questions are central because prison and jail sentences are perceived as the most severe statutory penalties that could conceivably be applied to juveniles if they are charged with a noncapital felony or a misdemeanor, prosecuted as an adult, and convicted. That is seldom the case, but a policy shift in juvenile justice to an emphasis on deterrence would probably entail an increase in the imposition of jail or prison sentences. In contemplating such a shift in policy, judges and legislators are unlikely to ignore the question: What severity of punishment of juveniles will the public tolerate? That question presupposes knowledge of the way that the public views conventional adult penalties, jail and prison sentences in particular. So in the surveys, adults were asked questions in this form: "If 100 represents how serious or severe it is to be sentenced to one year in the county jail, what number would you assign to (*designation of some other legal reaction*) to show how much more serious or severe it is than being sentenced to one year in the county jail?"[2] As in the case of the surveys of students, adults were asked questions about a wide variety of possible legal reactions and magnitudes of punishment; but again space limitations permit an analysis of only a few.

With a view to an assessment of public preferences in legal reactions to juvenile offenders, the adults were asked questions in the following forms: "If you had your say, would you sentence some, all, or no juveniles convicted of (*designation of a type of offense*) to (*type of penalty but without specification of magnitude*)?" If the respondent replied with either "some" or "all" the subsequent question was: "What is the maximum (*specification of the penalty*) that you would impose in such cases?"

Questions designed to elicit estimates by the high school students as to the certainty of particular types of penalties (ignoring magnitudes) or legal reactions for particular types of offenses by juveniles were worded as follows: "Out of the last hundred times that a juvenile committed (*designation of one offense*), how many would you guess resulted in (*designation of the type of penalty or legal reaction*)?" Questions were asked about several types of penalties or legal reactions, but only three types are considered here: arrest, court referral, and being sentenced to a reformatory.

Although the deterrence doctrine is first and foremost a perceptual theory, if it were nothing more than that it would have no particular implications for penal policy. The point is that the doctrine comprises propositions about the empirical relation between properties of prescribed (statutory) or actual punishments and the perception of punishment by potential offenders. One of those propositions is fairly simple: the greater the objective certainty of legal punishments, the greater the certainty of those punishments as perceived by potential offenders. In attempting to bring evidence to bear on that proposition, objective certainty can be estimated by computing the ratio of actual legal reactions (arrests, prison sentences imposed) to the number of offenses reported in official statistics or some other official number deemed indicative of incidence. Needless to say, there are grave doubts about the extent to which official statistics are indicative of incidence, and the problem is accentuated in the case of juvenile delinquency. Specifically, those official statistics that are conventionally taken as indicative of the incidence of juvenile offenses actually pertain to legal reactions (arrests of juveniles or court referrals). The point is not just that there are doubts about the extent to which official reactions are indicative of the incidence of juvenile delinquency (especially so in the case of offenders without victims and status offenses in general); additionally, if arrests of juveniles are taken as indicative of the incidence of offenses by juveniles, then the objective certainty of arrest is unity (that is, 100 percent) because the two variables (estimated incidence and official reactions) are the same. Accordingly, in this research the objective certainty of three types of legal reactions (arrest, court referral, commitment to a reformatory) is estimated by computing the ratio of instances where a student reports having been the object of a type of reaction (for example, self-reported arrests) to the number of self-reported violations. Data on self-reported instances of legal reactions were gathered in the student survey by posing questions in the following form: During the last twelve months how many times did you (*designation of a type of offense*)? How many times were you caught and (*designation of a type of legal reaction*)?

In recognition that public tolerance of the punishment of juvenile offenders is to some extent a function of the type of offense, the adults were asked: If I give 100 points to show how much you disapprove of petty theft, what number would you give to (*designation of some other type of offense*) to show your amount of disapproval? Since the willingness of the police to arrest and further the prosecution of juveniles may depend to some extent on the seriousness of the offense, a sample of police officers was asked the same questions. The corresponding question posed for high school students was: "Now, in the following list the number 100 is used to indicate how serious stealing something worth less than $100 is. What number would you give to (*designation of another type of offense*)?"

Rightly or wrongly, the foremost concern for both officials (legislators in particular) and the public at large appears to be the relation between the policies of the juvenile justice system and the incidence of offenses by juveniles. Any attempt to answer that question is haunted by doubts as to the extent that arrest and court statistics are indicative of the true incidence of offenses by juveniles. Accordingly, with a view to obtaining unofficial incidence figures, the high school students were asked questions of this form: During the last twelve months how many times did you (*designation of a type of offense*)? The argument is not that there are no particular problems in interpreting figures on self-reported offenses (quite the contrary) or even that such figures are necessarily more reliable than official figures (arrests of juveniles, court referrals) that are commonly construed as indicative of true incidence. Rather, the self-reported figures are simply an alternative to official figures, and they do have one advantage over official figures. In addition to using self-reported figures to compute the equivalent of the conventional offense rate (the mean number of offenses),[3] they can be used (unlike official incidence figures) to compute the repetitive rate, the mean number of offenses excluding individuals who ostensibly have not committed the offense. The conventional rate or its equivalent is not particularly informative, as it does not distinguish between two situations: (1) virtually all members of a population commit the offense at least once but seldom more than once, and (2) a few members of a population commit the offense several or many times.

The Perceived Severity of Various Kinds of Legal Reactions

The findings in table 10-1 should make it clear that adults view some of the currently common kinds of reactions to juvenile offenders (for example, small losses of money, short-term probation, expulsion from school, and early curfew) as little more than the proverbial "slap on the wrist," judging them to be not more than one-fourth as severe as being sentenced to one year in the county jail. Conversely, the legal punishments that are least likely to be applied to juvenile offenders—death or life imprisonment—are perceived as very severe relative to the standard (being sentenced to one year in jail), 100 times in the case of death and 10 times in the case of life imprisonment. To be sure, it is most unlikely that passing death or life imprisonment sentences on juveniles will become common for any type of offense. Yet the findings in table 10-1 clearly suggest that the regular imposition of even fairly short jail or prison sentences on juvenile offenders would be viewed by adults as a dramatic increase in the severity of reactions over those that are now conventional.

How would such a change in the juvenile justice system be perceived by the juveniles themselves? There is no obvious and clearly indisputable answer. The figures in table 10-1 suggest that juveniles do not view even the death penalty as truly awesome, certainly not in the sense that adults view it; however, not a great deal should be made of that comparison. That is the case because the results of experimentation with questions pertaining to subjects other than the severity of penalties seem to indicate that juveniles tend to give much smaller magnitude ratios regardless of the units of comparison. In brief, although the issue remains controversial, it appears that, in comparison to adults, juveniles simply do think in terms of big numbers.[4]

Nonetheless, it is significant that juveniles do not perceive a sentence of one year in jail as more severe than currently common types of reactions

Table 10-1
Perceived Severity of Various Kinds of Possible Legal Reactions to Offenses, Arizona, 1975

Reaction	Magnitude	Median Perceived Severity Values	
		Juvenile Perceptions	Adult Perceptions
Probation	1 year	84[a]	25[a]
	5 years	110[a]	75[a]
	10 years	190[a]	100[a]
Fine	$ 100	60[a]	10[a]
	$ 500	100[a]	30[a]
	$2,000	180[a]	60[a]
Death		500[a]	10,000[b]
Prison	1 year	150	175
	5 years	350	541
	10 years	400	878
	Life	500[a]	1,000[b]
Expelled from school		100[b]	25[b]
7 P.M. curfew	1 month	100[b]	10[b]
Loss of spend- ing money	1 month	100[b]	10[b]

[a]Standard used to judge severity: Being arrested by the police = 100.

[b]Standard used to judge severity: Sentenced to one year in the county jail.

to juvenile offenders in the juvenile court. Some of those types of reactions not shown in table 10-1 (because comparable data on adults are not available) include placement in a foster home, counseling once a week, and special work assignments. Since those reactions are not perceived by juveniles as less severe than being sentenced to one year in jail, it might appear that deterrence can be furthered only through resorting to reformatory or prison longer than a year. However, the findings are surely puzzling, as one might well ask: How could a student possibly perceive being sentenced to one year in jail as no more severe than, say, a 7 P.M. curfew for one month? So much more research is needed on the subject before any policymaker would be justified in arriving at a conclusion. Even so, the present findings suggest a most significant possibility: the incarceration of juveniles (especially those in the middle class or upper class) has become so rare that juveniles scarcely have any experiential basis (vicarious or otherwise) for assessing the severity of incarceration.

Prison and Jail Sentences for Particular Offenses

As previously suggested, the findings in table 10-1 indicate that the regular imposition of prison sentences in the juvenile justice system would be likely to satisfy the most ardent proponent of law and order. If one-year prison sentences are not deemed sufficient, then the perceived severity values in column 3 of table 10-2 are surely convincing evidence that the maximum prison sentences which could be imposed on juveniles are viewed by adults as extremely harsh, at least 3 times that of a one-year jail sentence for all types of offenses listed in the table and over 56 times as harsh for several of the offenses. For that matter, advocates of either the retributive doctrine or the deterrence doctrine might well take comfort in the severity of maximum statutory prison sentences as perceived by the students. No significance can be attached to the difference in the severity values of the students and the adults, if only because it appears that students tend to give lesser values than adults in response to virtually any magnitude question, whatever the subject. In any case, juveniles evidently view the maximum prison sentences for any offense listed in table 10-1 as more than twice as severe as being arrested, whereas the median of the severity values assigned by students to one year of probation is less than being arrested.

Needless to say, the argument can be made that a prison sentence of even one year is very rare in the juvenile justice system, but those who would attribute such leniency to judges have simply overestimated the willingness of the public (at least Arizona adults) to "get tough with juveniles." In particular, as shown in column 4 of table 10-2, only in the case of first-degree murder would even a majority (56.3 percent) of the adults impose a prison sentence of any length on a juvenile offender. The fact that a majority of adults do not advocate really harsh measures in juvenile justice is all the more significant since many of the tough-minded adults would impose prison sentences only in some cases. What do the adults prefer, if not prison? Regardless of the type of offense, many of the adults voice a preference for jail sentences, others fines, still others probation, and on and on. Indeed, the lack of consensus among adults may be more important than their seeming reluctance to invoke really harsh measures; that is, no policy in the juvenile justice system is likely to please even a majority of adults.

The foregoing interpretation is consistent with still another set of findings—the sentences preferred by adults who would imprison juvenile offenders, as shown in column 5 of the same table. Those preferred sentences are much less than the maximum that could be imposed on juveniles (that is, the statutory maximum; compare columns 2 and 5).

It is pointless to assume that the findings merely reflect a liberal tradition in Arizona; to the contrary, the state has a reputation for being conservative. Nor can the findings be rightly construed as reflecting an unwillingness to advocate the harsh punishment of any offender, regardless of age. Other findings clearly show that Arizona adults prefer much harsher punishments for adult offenders.

Table 10-2
Statistics Pertaining to Prison and Jail Sentences, Arizona, 1975

Type of Offense	Prison					Jail				
	Statutory Maximum for First Offense (Months)	Value of Maximum[a]		Proportion of Adults Who Prefer a Prison Sentence for Juvenile Offenders[b]	Median Prison Sentence Preferred by Adults for Juvenile Offenders (Months)	Statutory Maximum for First Offense (Months)	Value of Maximum		Proportion of Adults Who Prefer a Jail Sentence for Juvenile Offenders[b]	Median Jail Sentence Preferred by Adults for Juvenile Offender (Months)
		Perceived by Juveniles	Perceived by Adults				Perceived by Juveniles	Perceived by Adults		
First-degree murder	Life	615	5662	.563	241	12	197	90	.371	36
Voluntary manslaughter	10 years	308	962	.369	119	12	197	90	.413	18
First-degree rape	Life	615	5662	.285	60	12	197	90	.398	12
Armed robbery	Life	615	5662	.185	37	12	197	90	.398	12
Second-degree rape	Life	615	5662	.142	48	12	197	90	.285	12
Aggravated assault	5 years	250	564	.096	24	12	197	90	.275	12
Robbery, unarmed	Life	615	5662	.100	24	12	197	90	.227	12
First-degree burglary	15 years	348	1312	.079	26	12	197	90	.244	12
Grand theft	10 years	308	962	.104	24	12	197	90	.258	6
Permanent auto theft	5 years	250	564	.092	24	12	197	90	.256	12
Causing an abortion	5 years	250	564	.142	37	12	197	90	.250	12
Homosexuality	5 years	250	564	.025	13	12	197	90	.048	8
Second-degree burglary	5 years	250[c]	564[c]	.067	13	12	197	90	.231	6
Simple assault				.048	12	3	141	34	.183	6
Possession of marijuana	10 years	308	262	.058	12	12	197	90	.171	6
Adultery	3 years	215	380	.017	16	12	197	90	.075	6
Temporary auto theft	[c]	[c]	[c]	.029	13	6	166	55	.137	6
Petty theft	[c]	[c]	[c]	.017	8	6	166	55	.081	3
Shoplifting	[c]	[c]	[c]	.019	11	6	166	55	.085	6

[a]See text for description of data and procedure used to compute the values.
[b]For "some" or "all" juvenile offenders.
[c]No prescribed prison sentence for first offenders.

Jail Sentences

Turning now to columns 6-10, at first glance it may appear that a compelling argument could be made for the imposition of jail sentences in juvenile justice. With a view to furthering deterrence, considerable significance attaches to the high severity values that the high school students assigned to jail sentences relative to being arrested (see column 7), and the vast majority of adults view a one-year jail sentence as much more severe than probation or any other common legal reaction applied to the offenses of juveniles. Moreover, the maximum statutory jail sentences (column 6) are fairly consistent with the length of sentences preferred by adults (see column 10).

The findings that cast doubt on the utilization of jail sentences appear in column 9. Observe that for no offense, not even first-degree murder, do a majority of the Arizona adults prefer a jail sentence for some or all juvenile offenders. That is not to say that adults really prefer a less harsh reaction to juvenile offenders; indeed, many of them prefer a prison sentence (at least for several types of offenses). Nonetheless, the fact remains that there is very little consensus among the adults as to the use of jail sentences in juvenile justice.

Perceived Severity and Deterrence

None of the findings in tables 10-1 and 10-2 answer this question: What is the relation between the severity of a threatened punishment for a type of offense as perceived by the juveniles and the frequency with which juveniles commit that offense? That question bears on the deterrence doctine, and the relevant findings are shown in columns 1, 2, and 3 of table 10-3.

Observe that for eleven of the types of offenses in table 10-3 there is a value entry in each of the three columns (1-3), and the deterrence doctrine implies that there should be an inverse relation among those eleven types between the incidence rate and the perceived severity of the maximum statutory punishment (prison or jail) as perceived by juveniles. Consistent with that expectation, the rank-order coefficient of correlation (*rho*) between column 1 and column 3 is $-.55$ ($p = > .05$), and *rho* for column 2 and column 3 is $-.18$ (not statistically significant).

Granted that the relation between the values in each of the two sets of incidence rates is in the direction anticipated by the deterrence doctrine, only in the case of columns 1 and 3 is the magnitude of *rho* moderately high and statistically significant. Moreover, it could be argued that the relation, not even a truly close inverse relation between the values in question, would corroborate the deterrence doctrine, the rationale being that the maximum statutory punishment for a type of offense reflects the degree to which the

Table 10-3
Additional Findings, Arizona, 1975

Type of Offense	Self-Reported Instances by Juveniles		Median Severity of Maximum Statutory Punishment as Perceived by Juveniles	Objective Certainty of Arrest for Juveniles	Mean Certainty of Arrest as Perceived by Juveniles	Mean Certainty of Court Referral as Perceived by Juveniles	Mean Certainty of Reformatory as Perceived by Juveniles	Median Disapproval or Seriousness Values		
	Mean Rate	Repetitive Rate						Given by Juveniles	Given by Adults	Given by Police
Burglary	1.398	10.521	299	2.99	41.471	33.135	17.083	105	225	449
Shoplifting	4.968	13.386	166	1.16	31.586	23.051	10.594	100	100	100
Grand theft	.390	5.583	308	11.67	46.932	38.322	23.567	150	300	400
Petty theft	2.234	10.680	166	0.46	36.416	26.553	12.560	100	100	100
Aggravated assault	1.826	10.541	250	1.57	29.120	21.710	12.025	110	300	497
Fighting	3.061	9.966	141	1.77	19.371	12.724	6.124	75	150	150
Armed robbery	.214	8.265	615	8.17	48.051	39.307	25.508	200	499	799
Unarmed robbery	.714	10.525	615	1.09	31.486	22.754	11.514	120	200	500
Truant	10.253	19.242	b	0.72	12.252	6.365	2.795	30	50	50
Runaway	.275	2.359	b	14.77	31.434	25.426	11.772	75	75	100
Defiance	32.764	52.269	b	0.47	12.228	8.455	4.531	50	100	102
Drinking	41.438	57.684	b	0.12	21.945	14.006	5.561	50	65	50
Drunkenness	24.943	43.349	b	0.17	27.654	18.146	7.323	60	a	a
Auto theft	.710	6.317	208	6.54	41.877	33.697	18.958	130	249	350
Marijuana	34.073	83.390	308	0.07	33.494	25.681	13.494	90	100	150
Other drugs	4.256	28.356	b	0.78	38.676	31.112	19.918	125	a	a
Vandalism	2.003	8.563	b	0.80	27.947	20.074	9.391	100	a	a
Fornication	a	a	b	a	11.898	7.339	4.120	50	75	50
Homosexuality	a	a	250	a	12.411	10.214	7.417	150	100	100
Smoking	58.181	126.670	b	0.09	8.227	4.469	2.103	25	25	20

Note: See text for a description of the data and procedures used to compute the values.

ᵃQuestion not asked in survey.

ᵇNo prescribed (statutory) prison or jail sentence, either because the offense is a status offense or has no specific equivalent in the Arizona criminal code.

offense is socially disapproved (by adults and juveniles alike), and the incidence of a type of offense (whether juvenile offenders or adult offenders) is an inverse function of the degree of social disapproval. If that argument is accepted, the inverse relation between the perceived severity values in table 10-1 and either of the incidence rates reflects the differential social disapproval of offenses, not deterrence.

Note that even if the reported correlations are construed as evidence of deterrence, the perceived severity of threatened punishments appears to have a greater impact on restrictive deterrence than on absolute deterrence (Gibbs 1975). In the case of restrictive deterrence, individuals do not entirely refrain from the type of offenses in question, but they do curtail their violations to reduce the chances of legal punishment. By contrast, in the case of absolute deterrence, individuals have contemplated the offense at least once but refrained in all such instances out of the fear of punishment. Since the repetitive rate in table 10-3 (column 2), is more indicative of restrictive deterrence than is the mean rate (column 1), the difference between the two previously reported correlation coefficients suggests that insofar as the perceived severity of threatened punishments deters at all, it is more likely to prompt individuals to refrain from the type of offense entirely than it is to prompt individuals to curtail their violations.

The possibility just alluded to has real policy implications because the public is especially likely to demand the threat of a harsh punishment for juveniles who repeat an offense time and again. Yet the findings indicate that such an offender is the least likely to be deterred by the threat of a harsh punishment.

The Certainty of Punishment

In response to the foregoing findings, the counter argument of defenders of the deterrence doctrine could be that the doctrine implies a close inverse relation between the perceived severity of a threatened punishment for a type of offense and the incidence rate for that offense only insofar as the punishment is perceived by potential offenders as certain. The first set of relevant figures for assessing that counter argument is the percentage of self-reported offenses that resulted in an arrest (also self-reported). Those percentages, designated as the objective certainty of arrest, appear in column 4 of table 10-3.

Observe that for all types of offenses the objective certainty of arrest is less than 15 percent and less than 2 percent for twelve types. Accordingly, one must surely wonder how substantial deterrence could possibly be realized with such low levels of the certainty of punishment, but that consideration does not refute the deterrence doctrine. After all, the doctrine does not imply that legal punishment is certain for any type of offense in any jurisdiction, let alone all types in all jurisdictions. Rather, the deterrence doctrine asserts that the consequences of a low level of objective certainty in punishment is a low level of perceived certainty and a high incidence of offenses. Consistent with the doctrine, many of the values in columns 1 and 2 of table 10-3 (rates of self-reported offenses) could hardly be described as negligible. No less important and again consistent with the deterrence doctrine, there is a very close inverse relation between the incidence rates (columns 1 and 2) and the objective certainty of arrest (column 4). *Rho* for columns 1 and 4 is $-.90$ ($p = > .001$), and it is $-.93$ ($p = > .001$) for columns 2 and 4.

The findings are impressive, but they cannot be construed as verifying the deterrence doctrine if only because the doctrine itself clearly asserts that the objective certainty of punishment is related to the offense rate through the perceived certainty of punishment. Briefly it is not the objective certainty of a punishment that deters but, rather, the certainty of the punishment as perceived by potential offenders. So attention shifts to the perceived certainty values in columns 5-7 of table 10-3.

The immediate consideration is the enormous difference betwen the objective certainty of arrest and the perceived certainty of arrest. Observe that for all types of offenses the perceived certainty is at least twice that of objective certainty, and for several of the offenses it is more than 30 times as great. Yet those differences neither confirm nor disconfirm the deterrence doctrine, for it could be that (consistent with the doctrine) the perceived certainty of punishment is directly related to the objective certainty of punishment and inversely related to the offense rate. That is the case, with *rho* being $+.54$ ($p = > .01$) for columns 4 and 5, $-.68$ ($p = > .001$) for columns 1 and 5, and $-.54$ for columns 2 and 5. Observe that none of the correlation coefficients are truly substantial, and the coefficient for columns 4 and 5 casts some doubt on one of the central propositions in the deterrence doctrine—that the actual punishment of offenses (the objective certainty of punishment) determines the perceived certainty of punishent. Then one must surely wonder not only why the perceived certainty of punishment is not more closely related to the mean rate of self-reported offenses but also why it is related even less closely to the repetitive rate of self-reported offenses.

A no less important consideration is less obvious. Recall that the objective certainty of punishment (in this case arrest) is supposedly related to the offense rate through the perceived certainty of punishment; hence, the relation between columns 1 and 4 or between columns 2 and 4 should be less than the relation between columns 1 and 5 or between columns 2 and 5. That is definitely not the case; and so it appears that the close inverse relation between the objective certainty of arrest and the incidence rate is to some extent a statistical artifact and/or reflects some preventive mechanism of legal reactions other than deterrence (for example, incapacitation).

Defenders of the deterrence doctrine could respond to at least one of the foregoing doubts by pointing out that the only moderate relation between the perceived certainty of arrest and the incidence rates may reflect the fact that an arrest is not perceived as sufficiently severe to deter. The merits of that argument can be examined by considering the relation between the perceived certainty of commitment to a reformatory (a legal reaction that the students do perceive as more severe than arrest) and each of the two incidence rates. Since *rho* for columns 1 and 7 (table 10-3) is only $-.69$ ($p = < .001$) and only $-.53$ ($p = > .01$) for columns 2 and 7, it does not appear that the perceived severity of legal reactions is decisive in determining the relation between the objective certainty of legal reactions and the incidence rate.

The possibility that it is the certainty of a type of legal reaction rather than its perceived severity has real policy implications, for it suggests that an attempt to further deterrence in the juvenile justice system by increasing the presumptive severity of legal reactions to juvenile offenders would be misguided. Yet an exclusive emphasis on increasing the objective certainty of legal reactions to offenses by juveniles would be questionable also, for that emphasis would ignore two crucial points: (1) the inverse relation between the objective certainty of arrest and the perceived certainty of arrest is by no means truly close, and (2) the same may be said of the inverse relation between the perceived certainty of arrest and the incidence rate. The second point could be viewed by advocates of a deterrent policy in juvenile justice as simply something beyond legal control, which is to say an admission that the incidence of juvenile delinqueny substantially reflects extralegal conditions. However, that admission does not speak to the first point, and it has some policy implications that can be appreciated only by contemplating the question: Why is the inverse relation between the objective certainty of arrest and the perceived certainty of arrest far from truly close?

A truly defensible and complete answer to the question cannot be offered here, but observe that a step toward an answer can be taken by pointing out that it is status offenses and other victimless offenses (drug use, including marijuana) that are the major exceptions to the inverse relation (i.e., least consistent with the relation). However, the implication of that observation (especially if confirmed in other research) is not just that a switch to a deterrence policy is unlikely to have any impact on the volume of status offenses and victimless offenses; additionally, attempts to prevent those kinds of offenses through the threat of legal reactions could undermine attempts to prevent serious crimes through the threat of punishment. An argument can be made that both adults and juveniles tend to perceive

the certainty of legal reactions diffusely, that is, without differentiating between the types of offenses. To the extent that this is the case and to the extent
that the objective certainty is the prime determinant of the perceived certainty, then the generally low levels of objective certainty of legal reactions
to status offenses and victimless offenses could eventually result in a decline
in the perceived certainty of the punishment for serious offenses. The same
argument extends to the severity of legal reactions. Specifically, there is no
reason to suppose that legal reactions to status offenses will never be
perceived as especially severe, and that perception may come to be
generalized to all legal reactions, including those to serious crimes.

The Social Condemnation of Offenses

Although it has never been recognized as a theory, running throughout the
literature of the social and behavioral sciences is the expressed belief that
the incidence of any type of act (be it criminal, delinquent, or otherwise) in a
population is an inverse function of the extent to which the members of that
population disapprove of the act. That belief has implications for juvenile
justice not only because it identifies an extralegal etiological condition but
also because it suggests a consideration that could be of importance in contemplating the difference between offenses by juveniles and offenses by
adults. If juvenile delinquency is truly a subcultural phenomenon of the life
cycle, then there could be considerable divergence between the social condemnation of juveniles and adults as regards particular types of offenses.
Correlatively, if the incidence of a type of act is an inverse function of the
extent of its disapproval, then a change to a deterrent policy in juvenile
justice may well have no appreciable impact on the incidence of offenses by
juveniles.

The findings in columns 8-10 of table 10-3 cast doubts on one of the
possibilities alluded to above—that adults and juveniles are markedly
divergent in their social condemnation of particular types of offenses.
Specifically, there is a close direct relation among the types of offenses in
the degree of disapproval by students and by adults, including the police.
Moreover, there is ample evidence of a general correspondence between the
properties of legal reactions (including perceptual properties) and the disapproval (seriousness) values that the students assigned to particular types of
offenses (column 8, table 10-3). *Rho* for column 8 and column 4 (objective
certainty of arrest) is $+.63$ ($p = < .003$), and for column 8 and column 5
(perceived certainty of arrest), *rho* is $+.77$ ($p = < .001$). Then observe that
the findings provide impressive support for the belief that the incidence of a
type of act is an inverse function of the extent of its social disapproval. *Rho*
for column 8 and column 1 is $-.77$ ($p = < .001$), and *rho* for column 8
and column 2 is $-.62$ ($p = < .003$). The difference between the two *rho*

values is hardly surprising if one assumes that an individual's intense social disapproval of some type of act is more likely to determine whether he or she commits the act at all than the frequency which she or he commits the act; and frequency is more nearly reflected by the repetitive rate.

The foregoing relations can be extended to an explanation of all other findings previously considered. First, there is an inverse relation among types of offenses between the objective certainty of legal reactions and the offense-to-offense rate by juveniles beccause the police are willing to press for an arrest in the case of offenses that they and juveniles disapprove of sharply, and the rate for that type of offense is likely to be low because juveniles disapprove of it. Second, juveniles scarcely have a basis for an accurate estimate of the certainty of legal reactions to each of various types of offenses; so they perceive certainty largely in terms of what it should be (that is, arrest should be certain for serious offenses), and those perceptions are directly related to the objective certainty of legal reactions and inversely related to the offense rate for juveniles. To be sure, there is no truly close relation between degree of social disapproval and all other properties of legal reactions or the juvenile offense rate; but a truly close relation is not necessary to maintain the argument that what appears to be evidence of deterrence is really a manifestation of the differential social disapproval of types of offenses.

Confronted with that argument, defenders of the deterrence doctrine could reply that legal reactions to offenses generate or at least sustain the social condemnation of offenses. There may be something to that point, but observe that the postulated mechanism by which legal reactions prevent offenses is normative validation, not deterrence. Moreover, if those who make policy in juvenile justice are to take the idea of normative validation seriously, they must surely entertain doubts about continuing attempts to reduce status offenses and other victimless offenses by the threat of legal punishment. No norm is likely to be validated if the punishment of transgressors is perceived as neither certain nor severe.

Summary and Conclusions

On the whole, the findings cast doubt on any attempt to further deterrence in the juvenile justice system. The immediate and less disputable consideration is that adults are unlikely to endorse the regular imposition of long prison sentences even if juvenile offenders are prosecuted as though they were adults. Should the national clamor for law and order reach a point where a truly punitive policy in juvenile justice is supported by the public, in implementing that policy it is likely to be discovered that the objective certainty of harsh punishments are most uncertain, if only because the objective certainty of arrest is very low for all types of offenses. True, it is conceivable that some policy changes and a massive investment of resources could raise the objective certainty of punishment for serious offenses substantially, but a marked increase for status offenses and victimless offenses is not likely. In fact, it is more likely that most states will decriminalize status offenses in the next decade. Washington State and California have already done so. For that matter, even if the objective certainty of punishment should be increased substantially for all types of offenses, the impact on the perceived certainty of punishment would be problematical, and that is a crucial consideration when contemplating the furtherance of deterrence in either the adult or the juvenile justice system. Finally, even if the relation between objective and perceived certainty is followed by a proportionate increase in perceived certainty, there is hardly any basis to anticipate that an increase in the perceived certainty of punishment will be followed by a proportionate decrease in the offense rate.

Perhaps most important of all, the present findings and several others pertaining to adults clearly suggest that what appears to be evidence of deterrence may only reflect the fact that some types of offenses are socially disapproved much more than others. Moreover, even if it is granted that legal reactions can generate or at least sustain the social condemnation of offenses, it is surely difficult to see how such normative validation can be realized when the legal reactions are most uncertain and not perceived by the public as severe, which is the case for most delinquent offenses (status offenses and victimless offenses in particular).

The foregoing conclusions are not an endorsement of what appear to be the predominant policies of juvenile justice in the United States. On the contrary, the system of juvenile justice is a hodgepodge, and the effective prevention of offenses by juveniles is not being realized by any mechanism, be it rehabilitation, incapacitation, deterrence, or normative validation. If the present findings mean anything, the message is this: No policy in juvenile justice is likely to be successful as long as attempts to prevent offenses by juveniles extend to status offenses and other victimless offenses. In this light what is being tried in California (assembly bill 3121, chapter 1071:1-24) makes sense. In this bill status offenses are decriminalized while at the same time juveniles sixteen and older who are accused of a selected list of felonies will be made more vulnerable to adult penal sanctions. The legal change seems to reflect an effort to implement deterrence but limits it to those offenses most likely to be deterrable by increased severity of punishments. This does not mean, of course, that statutory changes will work! First, the question as to whether the public (juveniles in particular) is knowledgeable of these changes needs to be answered. Second, one must surely ask whether the adult courts will be any more effective in deterring offenders, especially, given what we know about the methods used in adult courts to handle cases (for example, plea bargaining). But finally, none of these changes affect certainty of legal reaction. Given the low levels of certainty it is questionable whether deterrence can be effective no matter how severity (statutory or actual) is manipulated. This is especially true because the public is unlikely to approve of harsh punishment being imposed on juvenile offenders. Thus the final question remains: With a limit to possible increases in severity of punishments for juvenile offenders and the low levels of certainty of punishment (objective and perceived) is it likely that efforts to broaden deterrence in the juvenile justice system will be successful? Based on what we now know, the prognosis must be pessimistic.

Notes

1. Data were gathered concerning many other legal and extralegal penalties. Not all of these data are relevant in the present context. The method used in collecting these data is referred to as "magnitude estimation" (Hamblin 1974). The method has been widely used in assessing seriousness of offenses, but little work has been published that attempts to assess the perceived severity of reactions. In another study we have applied the method to legal penalties among adults and police officers (see Erickson and Gibbs 1979).

2. For a comprehensive treatment of a wide range of legal penalties using these methods see Erickson and Gibbs (1979).

3. For a detailed explication and analysis of conventional and special rates using self-reported data see Erickson, Gibbs, and Jensen (1977).

4. It appears that there may be differences in the juvenile and adult use of numbers in making magnitude estimates. It remains problematic whether these differences represent substantive findings or simply artifacts of the use of magnitude estimate methods using numbers. Work is presently being contemplated that would resolve this controversy. The goal would be to gather data on the seriousness of acts and severity of penalties using forms of magnitude estimation that do not depend on the use of reported numbers.

References

Beccaria, Cesare (1963). *On Crimes and Punishments*. Indianapolis: Bobbs-Merrill.

Bentham, Jeremy (1962). The Works of Jeremy Bentham (Bowring, ed.), Vol. 1. New York: Russell and Russell.

California Welfare and Institutions Code (1976). Assembly Bill 3121. Ch. 1071:1-24.

Empey, LaMar T. (1978). American Delinquency: Its Meaning and Construction. Homewood, Ill.: Dorsey.

Erickson, Maynard L. (1979). "Some empirical questions concerning the current revolution in juvenile justice." In LaMar T. Empey (ed.), *The Future of Childhood and Juvenile Justice.* Charlottesville: University Press of Virginia.

Erickson, Maynard L., and Gibbs, Jack P. (1979). "On the perceived severity of legal penalties." *Journal of Criminal Law and Criminology* 70(3):102-116.

Erickson, Maynard L., Gibbs, Jack P. and Jensen, Gary F. (1977). "Conventional and special crime and delinquency rates." *Journal of Criminal Law and Criminology* 68 (3):440-453.

Gibbs, Jack P. (1975). *Crime, Punishment and Deterrence.* New York: Elsevier.

Hamblin, Robert (1974). "Social attitudes: magnitude measurement and theory." In Hubert Blalock, Jr. (ed.), *Measurement in Social Science,* pp. 62-120. New York: Aldine.

Hirsch, Andrew von (1976). *Doing Justice.* New York: Hill and Wang.

Lipton, Douglas, Martinson, Robert, and Wilks, Judith (1975). *The Effectiveness of Correctional Treatment: A Survey of Treatment Evaluation Studies.* New York: Praeger.

Martinson, Robert (1974). "What works? Questions and answers about prison reform." *The Public Interest* 35 (Spring):22-54.

van den Haag, Ernest (1975). *Punishing Criminals.* New York: Basic Books.

Washington State (1977). Revised Criminal Code of Washington. Title 13: Juvenile Courts and Juvenile Delinquents.

Wilson, James Q. (1975). *Thinking about Crime.* New York: Basic Books.

11 Offense Patterns of Status Offenders

Solomon Kobrin,
Frank R. Hellum, and
John W. Peterson

Until very recently, the laws in the United States treated as delinquents not only youth who violated the criminal law but also all those who ran away from home, were incorrigibly disobedient, refused to attend school, violated local curfew regulations, and committed similar acts prohibited only for the young. These infractions have been designated "status offenses" since they apply only to the incumbents of youthful age status. Juvenile courts have commonly accorded status offenders much the same treatment given those who committed criminal offenses. They were frequently placed in locked detention facilities awaiting a formal court hearing, with the period of detention sometimes prolonged until the hearing date. When formally adjudicated as status offenders, many were committed to juvenile correctional institutions, where they were indiscriminately mixed with youth committed for criminal offenses.[1]

During the past decade, a deinstitutionalization movement of substantial strength has developed to provide a separate type of treatment for status offenders. Two kinds of arguments have been advanced in support of the status offender deinstitutionalization movement. The first has been based on legal and ethical doctrines. It asserts that there can be no justification for subjecting those who commit noncriminal acts to the same deprivation of liberty as is imposed on youth guilty of criminal violations. Quite apart from the effect that incarceration in detention facilities or correctional institutions may have on noncriminal youth, that is, whether such treatment deters or stimulates future misbehavior, the secure confinement of status offenders is judged to be both unwarranted and morally repugnant.

A second set of arguments marshalled in support of the movement rests on the perspective of labeling theory (Lement 1951; Becker 1963; Schur 1971). Proponents of this view have asserted that deviant identity becomes a fixed element of the person's self-concept primarily as a consequence of

Prepared under Grant Numbers 76-JN-99-0014, 76-JN-99-1004, and 77-JN-99-0018 from the National Institute of Juvenile Justice and Delinquency Prevention, Law Enforcement Assistance Administration, U.S. Department of Justice. Interpretations of data findings and points of view expressed in this chapter are those of the authors and do not necessarily represent the official position or policies of the U.S. Department of Justice.

being dealt with as a deviant by the agents of the official control institutions. The meaning of an act, and therefore its significance for the person's
self-concept, is defined by the response to the act on the part of those who
wield societal authority. Status offenders who are arrested and haled before
the court, like youthful criminal offenders, are subtly pressed to see
themselves as delinquents, however minor, transitory, or fortuitous their
status offenses might have been. In many cases, such pressures may induce
an adaptive response in which the young person seeks the companionship
and social support of those similarly stigmatized. This outcome is seen as
more likely if status offenders are held in detention facilities and committed
to correctional institutions where they are thrown into close association
with youth held for criminal offenses. However unintended, the result, the
argument runs, is to encourage the development of delinquent careers.
Youth whose initial deviance may have been confined to the status offenses
now expand their misbehavior to include the more serious offenses by virtue
of the exposure to institutional treatment.

In the past there has been little opportunity to investigate the claims of
the latter perspective with respect to the effect of institutional treatment on
status offenders. Specifically, two propositions are asserted. The first is that
there exists an identifiable population of young offenders who confine their
misbehavior to the status offenses, who endanger themselves rather than the
community, and who require a quite different treatment approach than that
accorded the young criminal offender. The second proposition implicit in
the labeling perspective is that there occurs a progression from status to
criminal offenses, resulting in part from the labeling process to which status
offenders are exposed and in part from their exposure to young criminal offenders in detention and correctional facilities.

Both of these assertions have been questioned, in particular the view that
there exists a group of juveniles who commit only status offenses. Among
the few studies that have examined this issue, the majority conclude that
status offenders cannot be distinguished from those who commit criminal
violations (Thomas 1976; Erickson 1979; Klein 1971). These findings have
been interpreted as supporting a versatile or cafeteria-style view of juvenile
offense patterns in which "today's status offender is tomorrow's burglar
and vice versa" (Klein 1979). There is, however, at least one study that
found status offenders to be a clearly discernible subgroup.

Clarke (1975) reported major differences among types of juvenile offenders in the Philadelphia birth cohort data (Wolfgang, Figlio, Sellin
1972). Among the 3,475 males who acquired a police juvenile record, 23.4
percent, or 812, first appeared for behavior that would not be criminal if
engaged in by an adult; they were classified as juvenile status offenders.
Comparisons with those who were first arrested for a criminal offense
reveal the following: (1) criminal offenders recidivated at over twice the rate

of status offenders (61 percent compared to 30 percent had committed at least two offenses); and (2) 21 percent of the initial criminal violators became chronic offenders (at least five offenses) in contrast to only 10 percent of the status offenders. The less serious nature of delinquency involvement among status offenders was apparent in additional measures reported by Clarke, and identical patterns were found among white and nonwhite males analyzed separately.

The contradiction between the findings reported by Clarke and the conclusions of the other studies may be explained by a number of factors. Beyond the common focus on offense patterning, these studies varied considerably in terms of the selection of research issues, the choice of research design, and even in the definition of major terms. For instance, possession of alcohol by a minor may have been counted either as status or as criminal offense; two studies examined birth cohorts as compared to cross-sectional data; and an interest in repeated violation of a specific statute (such as burglary) is a separate issue from that of concentration within broader categories of offense behavior or of movement toward nonrecidivism. Since these variations might have led to varying conclusions, it would seem appropriate to briefly review each of these studies for evidence bearing upon the issue raised in this research: are there youths who confine their offense behavior to status violations?

The earliest cited findings (Klein 1971) were gathered in evaluations of programs directed at gang delinquency in five major cities. In at least one site, Los Angeles, an attempt was made to determine the correlations between specific, officially recorded violations among individuals in five male gangs. The finding of "no systematic ordering of offenses" (Klein 1971: 125) supported the conclusion of versatility in offense behavior. While gang members in Klein's study had on occasion been charged with status offenses, the population was not representative of juvenile offenders, nor was an analysis reported of patterns or progressions involving the broader categories of status and criminal violations. In fact, it seems rather unlikely that a juvenile who committed only status offenses would be viewed as a bonafide gang member. The absence of offense patterning in this study might provide a benchmark for further research in establishing analogies between diverse juvenile populations, but it does not directly apply to the issue under consideration.

The previously discussed findings offered by Clarke (1975) are of limited value in ascertaining patterned offense behavior. A major limitation is the absence of females, who represent a substantial portion of the status offender population. For the male birth cohort, the data do show that initial status offenders are the least seriously delinquent group, and that 70 percent appeared only for a single status violation. However, there is no indication of the extent to which criminal offenders subsequently appeared for status violations, nor is it possible to determine the types of violations for which status offenders recidivate. The latter issue is of importance because it bears upon our second proposition, namely, that status offenders become involved in a progression toward more serious violations. In recomputing some of the reported information it is possible to suggest at least the direction in which status offenders progress.

An additional measure of seriousness examined in the study was the average number of index offenses attributable to the initial offender groups. These offenses consist of the more serious violations involving injury, theft, or property damage. This classification was also used to divide the initial criminal violators into two groups—index and nonindex offenders. In the total population the index offense average for the three initial groups consisted of the following: status (0.354), nonindex (0.727), index (2.053). If a progression toward more serious violations was evident in the data, then one would expect that the disparity among average number of index offenses would be substantially reduced for those in the initial groups who committed further law violations. In other words, the recidivists would appear to be much more similar in this respect than the initial offender groups. Recomputation of the average number of index offenses beyond the first offense for the recidivists in the initial groups yielded the following: status (1.191), nonindex (1.219), index (1.686). When examining only recidivism, there are a number of reasons for reduced disparity among the groups; the first index offense of the initial index offenders is automatically excluded, and the fewer number of repeat offenders in the initial status offenders group affects the average figure considerably. However, it does appear that when initial status offenders are involved in further violations, the seriousness of the behavior is comparable to that of the initial criminal offenders. In sum, the Philadelphia cohort data is at least suggestive of both a specialized status offender population and of some progression toward more serious violations.

Thomas (1976) examined offense patterns among 2,092 youths appearing in the juvenile court records of two cities during the years 1970 through 1974. From the analysis he concluded that the data provided "little or no support for those who have contended that status offenders are a distinctly different group of juveniles" (p. 454). Notwithstanding the nuances of the term *distinctly different*, the conclusion appears to be unwarranted, since the data contained in the published report of the study support an alternative interpretation. For the purposes of this review, the data suggest that in the earlier stages of their offense careers status offenders are readily distinguishable from criminal violators, but with further involvement their offense behavior seems to progress toward more serious violations.

In examining differences among types of offenders, Thomas divided the population according to their most serious charge at initial appearance in court records and obtained the following three groups: felony (467), misdemeanor (1,053), and status (572). Comparisons were then made of the offenses charged for as many as three reappearances. For the first reappearance, Thomas noted that initial status offenders did not differ in the expected direction toward fewer repeated violations (pp. 445-446). Status offenders were reported as having the highest rates of recidivism (status, 38 percent; misdemeanor, 22 percent; felony, 31 percent). However, inspection of the data reveals that this finding was entirely a function of the initial status offenders being more likely than any other group to have reappeared for a status offense. If first reappearance rates had been reported for criminal offenses only, the ordering of initial offender groups would have changed considerably (status, 20 percent; misdemeanor, 17 percent; felony, 28 percent). A major difference between the groups was that the initial status offenders, constituting approximately 27 percent of the total population, accounted for 63 percent of all status violations recorded at first reappearance. Similar figures can be obtained for the distribution of offenses at the second and third reappearances as well. In other words, contrary to Thomas's conclusion, the data indicate that status offenders differ from criminal offenders in that their subsequent offenses more often involve repeated status violations.

With regard to progression in offense careers, Thomas states that "evidence in support of the hypothesis that court appearances encourage movement toward more serious delinquency is difficult to find in any of the tables present in this analysis" (p. 449). It should be noted, however, that there are alternative methods of analysis which might have uncovered supporting evidence. One possibility would be simply to examine the relationship between types of initial and subsequent offenses to determine if there was a shift toward more serious violations at each level of increasing court involvement.

The necessary data can be abstracted from the published report (pp. 445-446) and are shown in table 11-1. The analysis shows that at first reappearance there is a moderate relationship between initial offense type and the type of offense at reappearance ($gamma = .45, p < .01$). This is consistent with the previous observation of differences between groups. At the point of first reappearance those who committed a second offense showed the highest percentage of involvement for the same type of violation as was initially charged: for returning felony offenders (147), 46 percent reappeared as felony violators; among the misdemeanor recidivists (227), 55 percent committed a misdemeanor; and for the reappearing initial status offenders (217), 46 percent returned for a status violation. If progression is suggested by the data, then it would be expected that the relationship between initial and subsequent offenses would decline with increasing reappearances

Table 11-1
Subsequent Offenses of Status and Delinquent Offenders
(percent)

	Type of Offense at Initial Appearance		
Type of Offense	Status	Misdemeanor	Felony
First reappearance[a]			
Felony	18	26	46
	(38)	(59)	(67)
Misdemeanor	36	55	43
	(79)	(125)	(63)
Status	46	19	12
	(100)	(43)	(17)
Total	100	100	100
	(217)	(227)	(147)
Second reappearance[b]			
Felony	20	40	37
	(22)	(42)	(26)
Misdemeanor	46	42	49
	(50)	(44)	(34)
Status	33	17	14
	(36)	(18)	(10)
Total	99	99	100
	(108)	(104)	(70)
Third Appearance[c]			
Felony	27	46	41
	(14)	(22)	(17)
Misdemeanor	38	44	49
	(20)	(21)	(20)
Status	35	10	10
	(18)	(5)	(4)
Total	100	100	100
	(52)	(48)	(41)

Source: Thomas (1976:445-446).
Note: Number is in parentheses.
[a]*Gamma* = .45, $P < .01$.
[b]*Gamma* = .29, $P < .02$.
[c]*Gamma* = .30, $P < .10$.

in court records (that is, knowledge of the initial offense would not predict the type of later offense because the groups had become more similar in their law-violating behavior). The test of this relationship at later reappearances shows evidence of progression toward more serious violations. At second reappearance the relationship is reduced considerably as the initial status offenders show a greater proclivity for criminal violations, but the differences between the groups are still statistically significant (*gamma* = .29, $p < .02$). By the third reappearance the measure of association remains stable, but the group differences are not statistically significant (gamma = .30, p < .10). In other words, the differences that were observed in their early offense careers appear to diminish with further juvenile court involvement as the recidivists among the initial offender groups become more heavily involved in criminal violations.

As a final comment on the Thomas study, an explanation should be attempted as to why a reanalysis of reported data could lead to conclusions that contradict those of the original author. An important clue can be found in the title of the Thomas study—"Are Status Offenders *Really So Different*" (italics added). This question seems to imply a standard of absolute difference in comparing juvenile offenders. According to this standard, Thomas's conclusions are absolutely correct. Even in their early offense careers *some* status offenders reappear for felony violations, and *some* criminal violators return for status offenses. It is also possible to maintain that there is an absence of pronounced homogeneity in offense careers (p. 447), that juvenile offenders are not bound to a single type of delinquency involvement (p. 448), and that the type of initial charge is an imperfect predictor of subsequent offense (p. 453). However, the present review of the Thomas data has focused on relative differences, and according to this standard status offenders do appear to be different from criminal violators, but the difference becomes relatively less pronounced with increased involvement in the juvenile justice system.

The most recently reported data on offense patterns appears in Erickson (1979) who offers an analysis of both self-reported and officially recorded delinquency in several populations of juvenile offenders. The data that are comparable to the studies reviewed here are drawn from the official records of a birth cohort including both males and females, and represents all violations for 2,843 juveniles in the years prior to their eighteenth birthday. The analysis of official offenses is quite dissimilar to the tracking of initial offender groups as undertaken by both Clarke and Thomas, and there are very few parallel findings that can be abstracted from the published data. Also, Erickson's data are largely reported as percentages of the total population, and therefore the following must be viewed as approximated figures.

Erickson reported that 50 percent of the cohort first appeared in court records as status offenders (p. 21). This represents an obvious disparity with the 23.4 percent figure in Clarke's data and the 27.4 percent from the Thomas study. Because none of these studies state the specific violations included in the classification of status offense, it is difficult to determine if the difference is a matter of definition or represents some other source of variation.

Erickson also indicated that criminal violators are less likely than status offenders to reappear for a second offense. In the total population, 38 percent were reported as one time offenders for either a felony or misdemeanor violation. Since the total population was evenly divided between status and criminal offenders, this means that 76 percent of the initial criminal offenders were nonrecidivists. For initial status offenders only 40 percent were reported as having never returned for a second offense. In other words, the data showed almost a complete reversal of the Clarke findings that 39 percent of the criminal offenders were nonrecidivists as compared to 70 percent of the status violators. Comparable figures from the Thomas study showed that 75 percent of the combined criminal offender groups never returned for a second offense, and that nonrecidivist status offenders accounted for 62 percent of the initial group (with the difference being attributed to repeated status offenses in the status offender group).

Erickson's analysis was primarily aimed at demonstrating the rarity with which juveniles were concentrated in the category of pure status offenders and that with increasing involvement in court processing the offense careers of juveniles assume an erratic-random pattern. Until the data are subjected to further analysis, it is impossible to determine if a progression toward more serious violations by status offenders is present in Erickson's data. The only difference noted by Erickson that would seem to favor specialized treatment of status offenders is found in his category of static careers. Here it was found that 15 percent of the total population having multiple offense careers persisted in the commission of a single type of offense. Within this category 11 percent of the total population committed only status violation with the number of offenses varying from as few as two and as many as twenty-seven in a single offense career. Relative to the 50 percent of the total population who first appeared for a status offense, this means that approximately two-thirds (62 percent) either did not return for a second time or reappeared only for status violation.

Thus, recent research offers reasonably strong evidence of the existence of a fairly large group of juvenile offenders who tend to restrict their violations to the status offenses, of whom a small subset recidivate as pure status offenders. Although some progression from status to delinquent offenses is apparent in the Thomas data, those who appeared initially as delinquents (misdemeanor or felony offenders) were significantly more prominent in the same subsequent offense categories than were those who appeared initially for status offenses. Similarly, status offenders on initial appearance showed much higher proportions of status than of delinquent offenses in their subsequent appearances. Status offenders may not be distinctly different from delinquent offenders, as Thomas asserts, but they are distinguished by a tendency to reappear in police and court records as status offenders in significantly higher proportions than are youth who commit misdemeanor and felony offenses. Finally, Erickson's data provide clear evidence of the very small proportion of all juvenile offenders who fall into the pure status offender group and underscore the prominence of versatility in juvenile offense patterns.

However, these findings may not be entirely relevant to the need for special programs to deal with the status offense problem. The opportunity and incentive to commit status offenses is generally available to all youth, including those with records of serious and persistent delinquency, minor and intermittent delinquency, and of no delinquency. Of all youth who at any juncture in their careers are arrested or cited for a status offense, it should be possible in principle to differentiate this population in terms of somewhat typical juvenile career patterns, each of which encompasses some degree of offense versatility. These may include, at a minimum, the heavies who are predominantly serious delinquent offenders, a category of lightweights made up of misdemeanants, and a group of predominantly conforming youth, whose misbehavior may occasionally come to the attention of the juvenile authorities. Each of these groups is in one sense made up of status offenders, but the meaning of the status offense differs for the members of each group, for the community, and for the juvenile justice system. For the heavies a status offense is likely to be a largely incidental event. For those given to minor and intermittent delinquent acts, for the possibly very small group which restricts itself to multiple status offenses, and for those who gain admission to a population recorded as having committed a status offense by an occasional outburst of rebellion against adult authority, the act may well be symptomatic of a set of problems unique to this group. Clearly, then the question of the potential usefulness of special programs of any kind, including a program for the deinstitutionalization of status offenders, will rest largely on the relative size of the second and third of the three groups identified.

These considerations suggest that in examining the evidence in support of the status-to-delinquency offense progression assumption, it is essential to focus on the latter two groups should it turn out that they are in fact discriminable. The hazard of escalation from status to delinquent offenses involves these groups principally. Youth whose records may include status offenses but whose delinquency is of the more serious variety raise other concerns.

An opportunity to examine these issues empirically has arisen during the past several years. In 1976, the Federal Office of Juvenile Justice and Delinquency Prevention (OJJDP) of the Law Enforcement Assistance Administration (LEAA) funded a large-scale program to encourage the deinstitutionalization of status offenders, as mandated by the Juvenile Justice and Delinquency Prevention Act of 1974 (Law Enforcement Assistance Administration 1975). Funding support was provided for eleven projects in various regions of the United States. Of these, eight projects were intensively examined in an evaluation study (Korbin and Klein 1979).

The programs were designed to encourage police agencies and courts to divert status offenders from detention facilities and correctional institutions by referring them for rehabilitative services to community-based youth service agencies. The data reported here are based on the evaluation study of the national program.

The Data

During the two-year period of federal funding of the national program, over 16,000 juveniles charged with status offenses were served by the eight programs. Demographic, socioeconomic, and family data were obtained on all juveniles referred to the program. In addition, treatment and both self-report and official offense data were collected on some 4,000 program clients constituting the evaluated sample. With the exception of self-report offense and treatment data, similar information was obtained on a comparable control group of status offenders dealt with in each program jurisdiction during the year prior to the establishment of the program. The preprogram comparison group consisted of approximately 3,000 individuals. Evidence for the existence of a discriminable population of status offenders, and of progression from status to criminal offenses was examined with reference only to the preprogram group, for which the special deinstitutionalization program was not yet available, and who therefore were more likely to be exposed to the threat or the experience of secure detention and commitment to correctional institutions.

The preprogram population in each site consisted of a sample of juveniles from the preprogram year who became eligible for selection into the sample upon their first status offense for that year.[2] This first status offense, for the period and not for the individual career, was defined as the instant status offense. The sample was selected as far as possible to match the program clientele at each site with respect to sociodemographic and offense characteristics. Court files were searched for the record of all offenses prior and subsequent to the instant offense, as well as the record of charges in police files which were available and accessible in all but one site. The record of subsequent offenses was compiled for two periods, yielding a six-month followup for approximately 75 percent of the evaluated sample, and a smaller twelve-month followup cohort, consisting of approximately 37 percent of the sample.[3] The research cohort was classified by four offense categories with respect to both prior and subsequent offenses: no offenses, status offenses only, mixed status and criminal (both misdemeanor and felony) offenses, and criminal offenses only. Those with prior records of mixed or criminal offenses will be referred to here as delinquents by way of distinguishing them from the pure status offenders.

The Status Offender Population

Two questions are addressed in examining the evidence for the existence of a population constituted predominantly by status offenders. First, is there a segment of the juvenile offender group that confines its infractions largely to the status offenses, and if so, what is its relative size? Second, do their age, gender, and ethnic characteristics differ from those of a population whose records contain substantial proportions of delinquent offenses as well?

As seen in table 11-2, those with no offenses of either kind recorded prior to their initial appearance in police and court files for a status offense constituted half (51.9 percent) of a population dealt with as status offenders at a given point in time. When the additional 11.2 percent of those whose prior offenses were only of the status variety is added, almost two-thirds (63.1 percent) of the population dealt with as status offenders had no official record as a prior delinquent, that is, criminal act.[4]

Two cautions must be observed in the interpretation of this finding. First, it is based solely on official records. Self-report delinquency studies have provided ample evidence of the large number of delinquent acts which result neither in apprehension nor court action (Erickson and Empey 1963; Gold 1966). On the other hand, it has also been noted that as concerns the more serious offenses against property and persons, the discrepancy between self-report and officially recorded offenses is substantially reduced (Empey 1978: 164). Hence the use solely of officially recorded offense data in assessing the distribution of offense patterns among those dealt with as status offenders is warranted when, as in the present study, interest centers on the shift from status to the more serious forms of delinquency. It is entirely likely that the offense record is incomplete with respect principally to the minor and occasional offenses commonly viewed by control agents as undeserving of their time, attention, and effort.

The second caution regarding the offense pattern of the preprogram sample concerns the effort to match it to the program clientele. The latter group was selected into the program on the basis of their referral by police, courts, schools, and others for a status offense. Criteria employed in determining eligibility for program services varied widely from site to site. In some instances eligibility criteria excluded the more persistent offenders, such as those with more than two prior status offenses, or those already on probation for a previous status offense. To the extent, then, that the match between preprogram and program subjects was successful, the preprogram group may well have been biased toward the selection of individuals less likely to include the mixed and criminal offense only category.

These cautions notwithstanding, the substantial proportion represented by those whose only prior offenses were of the status variety can suffer a

Table 11-2
Prior Offense Pattern of Preprogram Population by Age

Offense Type	Under Thirteen		Thirteen to Fourteen		Fifteen to Sixteen		Over Sixteen		Total		Offense Type
	Number	Percent	Number	Percent	Number	Percent	Number	Percent	Number	Percent	Percent
No offenses	173	11.1	510	32.7	738	47.3	139	8.9	1,560	100.0	51.9
Status only	19	5.7	122	36.3	178	53.0	17	5.1	336	100.0	11.2
Delinquent only	42	7.3	185	32.0	283	49.0	68	11.8	578	100.0	19.2
Mixed	30	5.6	171	32.1	295	55.5	36	6.8	532	100.0	17.7
Total	264	8.8	988	32.9	1,494	49.7	260	8.6	3,006	100.0	100.0

Note: $\chi^2 = 42.06$, df $= 9$, $p < .001$.

material corrective reduction and still constitute a very large proportion of all those dealt with by police and courts as status offenders. In brief, there does appear to be a substantial and identifiable group in the juvenile offender population whose infractions are largely restricted to the status offenses.[5]

Age and Gender Characteristics

Juveniles cited for status offenses among the preprogram group fell principally in the thirteen through sixteen-year-old age group (table 11-2), with half (49.7 percent) consisting of fifteen and sixteen year olds. About one-third (32.9 percent) were thirteen and fourteen years old, and a residual 17.4 percent were equally distributed between those under thirteen and over sixteen. With respect to age distribution, the question of interest is whether age level is related to differences in the proportion with prior delinquent offenses, a relationship that may have a bearing on an assumed progression from status to delinquent offenses. The percentage of those with no prior offenses, or with status offenses only, declines steadily from 72.7 percent in the group under thirteen years of age to 60.0 percent in the group over sixteen (table 11-3). However, when the no prior offense category is excluded from the sample, it becomes evident that there is virtually no relationship between age and prior delinquent offenses (table 11-4).[6] Even for those under thirteen years of age, over three-quarters had records of prior delinquent offenses. The proportion with such prior records remains remarkably stable through age sixteen.

The data on gender distribution confirms the prevailing impression that among status offenders females constitute a far larger proportion than among delinquent offenders (table 11-5). Approximately half of the total preprogram population (49.2 percent) are females, representing a 1:1 ratio. This is in striking contrast to the 4:1 ratio of males to females in the general delinquent population (Gottfredson et al. 1977: 487). Further, the data of table 11-5 disclose a perceptible difference between male and female status offenders in the age distribution across the four patterns of prior offense. Although there is a relationship between age and pattern of prior offense for both genders, it has a higher level of probability for males than for females ($p < .001$ vs. $p < .02$). This is seen even more clearly when the four prior offense patterns are collapsed to two: no offenses-status offenses only, and delinquent-mixed (table 11-6). Here, percentages are calculated for each age group. For females, the probability level of the relationship becomes nonsignificant, while for males it retains its definitive character ($p < .001$). These findings may be interpreted to mean that at every age level females in high proportions are found in the no offense-

Table 11-3
Major Type of Prior Offense Pattern by Age

Offense Type	Under Thirteen		Thirteen to Fourteen		Fifteen to Sixteen		Over Sixteen		Total	
	Number	Percent	Number	Percent	Number	Percent	Number	Percent	Number	Percent
No offense and status only	192	72.7	632	63.9	916	61.3	156	60.0	1,896	63.1
Delinquent and mixed	72	27.3	356	36.1	578	38.7	104	40.0	1,110	36.9
Total	264	100.0	988	100.0	1,494	100.0	260	100.0	3,006	100.0

Note: $\chi^2 = 13.95$, df = 3, $p < .01$.

Table 11-4
Prior Offense Pattern of Preprogram Population by Age, with "No Offense Priors" Excluded

Offense Type	Under Thirteen		Thirteen to Fourteen		Fifteen to Sixteen		Over Sixteen		Total
	Number	Percent	Number	Percent	Number	Percent	Number	Percent	
Status only	19	20.9	122	25.5	178	23.5	17	14.0	336
Delinquent only and mixed	72	79.1	356	74.5	578	76.5	104	86.0	1,110
Total	91	100.0	478	100.0	756	100.0	121	100.0	1,446

Note: $x^2 = 7.46$, df $= 3$, $p < .05$.

Table 11-5
Prior Offense Pattern of Preprogram Population by Age and Gender

Offense Type	Under Thirteen		Thirteen to Fourteen		Fifteen to Sixteen		Over Sixteen		Total		Offense Type
	Number	*Percent*	*Number*	*Percent*	*Number*	*Percent*	*Number*	*Percent*	*Number*	*Percent*	*Percent*
Male[a]											
No offenses	93	13.7	198	29.2	308	45.5	78	11.5	677	100.0	44.4
Status only	10	12.0	27	32.5	39	47.0	7	8.4	83	100.0	5.4
Delinquent only	30	6.8	130	29.6	218	49.7	61	13.9	439	100.0	28.8
Mixed	21	6.4	97	29.8	180	55.1	28	8.6	326	100.0	21.4
Total	154	10.1	452	29.6	745	48.9	174	11.4	1,525	100.0	100.0
Female[b]											
No offenses	80	9.1	310	35.3	429	48.8	60	6.8	879	100.0	59.6
Status only	9	3.6	95	37.5	139	54.9	10	4.0	253	100.0	17.1
Delinquent only	12	8.6	55	39.6	65	46.8	7	5.0	139	100.0	9.4
Mixed	9	4.4	73	35.6	115	56.1	8	3.9	205	100.0	13.9
Total	110	7.5	533	36.1	748	50.7	85	5.8	1,476	100.0	100.0

[a] $\chi^2 = 28.09$, df = 9, $p < .001$.
[b] $\chi^2 = 19.64$, df = 9, $p < .02$.

status offense only prior offense category. Among males, on the other hand, the proportion in this category declines with increasing age. Put another way, three-quarters to four-fifths of the females across the entire span of juvenile age may be found in the no offense-status offense only prior offense category, while the proportion of males in this category declines from about two-thirds in the youngest group to somewhat less than one-half in the older groups.

Ethnic Characteristics

The ethnic breakdown of the preprogram population indicates that in all patterns of prior offense white youth had the highest ratios, followed by blacks, Hispanics, and a residual other group, respectively (table 11-7). Since no data were obtained on the distribution of white and minority populations in the program jurisdictions, it cannot be determined which of these groups were disproportionately represented in the preprogram status offender sample. The Hispanic group in the sample included principally Mexican-American youth in program jurisdictions located in the west and southwest regions of the United States, and Puerto Rican youth in the midwest and eastern regions. The residual other category was drawn from native American and Asian groups at all sites.

With the exception of the last group, whose numbers were too small to yield a stable measure, the two major minority groups show relatively smaller proportions than white youth in the no offense and status offense only categories, and larger proportions in the delinquent only and mixed categories.

The relationship of ethnicity to prior offense pattern is more clearly seen in table 11-8, particularly with respect to the comparative distribution of the prior offense pattern for the black and Hispanic groups. The former showed a higher proportion in the no offenses-status offenses only category; the latter, in the delinquent only-mixed category.

Effects of Age, Gender, and Ethnicity

The differential effects of age, gender, and ethnicity on the probability of a prior pattern of delinquent offenses in a population of status offenders requires further assessment. A regression model was developed to measure the main and interaction effects on the likelihood of a pattern of criminal offenses (delinquent only plus criminal status) prior to the instant status offense.

Table 11-6
Major Type of Prior Offense Pattern by Age and Gender

	Under Thirteen		Thirteen to Fourteen		Fifteen to Sixteen		Over Sixteen		Total	
	Number	Percent	Number	Percent	Number	Percent	Number	Percent	Number	Percent
Male[a]										
No offense and status only	103	66.9	225	49.8	347	46.6	85	48.9	760	49.8
Delinquent and mixed	51	33.1	227	50.2	398	53.4	89	51.1	765	50.1
Total	154	100.0	452	100.0	745	100.0	174	100.0	1,525	99.9
Female[b]										
No offense and status only	89	80.9	405	76.0	568	75.9	70	82.4	1,132	76.7
Delinquent and mixed	21	19.1	128	24.0	180	24.1	15	17.6	344	23.3
Total	110	100.0	533	100.0	748	100.0	85	100.0	1,476	100.0

[a] $\chi^2 = 21.17$, df $= 3$, $p < .001$.
[b] $\chi^2 = 3.00$, df $= 3$, p not significant.

Table 11-7
Prior Offense Pattern of Preprogram Population by Ethnicity

Offense Type	White		Black		Hispanic		Other		Total		Offense Type
	Number	Percent	Number	Percent	Number	Percent	Number	Percent	Number	Percent	Percent
No offenses	1,115	71.4	326	20.9	79	5.1	41	2.6	1,561	100.0	51.9
Status only	213	63.4	95	28.3	21	6.3	7	2.1	336	100.0	11.2
Delinquent only	333	57.6	169	29.2	61	10.6	15	2.6	578	100.0	19.2
Mixed	300	56.4	164	30.8	61	11.5	7	1.3	532	100.0	17.7
Total	1,961	65.2	754	25.1	222	7.4	70	2.3	3,007	100.0	100.0

Note: χ^2 = 79.28, df = 9, $p < .001$.

Table 11-8
Major Type of Prior Offense Pattern by Ethnicity

Offense Type	White		Black		Hispanic		Other		Total	
	Number	*Percent*	*Number*	*Percent*	*Number*	*Percent*	*Number*	*Percent*	*Number*	*Percent*
No offense and status only	1,328	67.7	421	55.8	100	45.0	48	68.6	1,897	63.1
Delinquent and mixed	633	32.3	333	44.2	122	55.0	22	31.4	1,110	36.9
Total	1,961	100.0	754	100.0	222	100.0	70	100.0	3,007	100.0

Note: $\chi^2 = 67.13$, df $= 3$, $p < .001$.

The three variables were operationalized in the following manner:

1. Site was treated as a set of seven effect-coded dichotomous variables and entered into the equation prior to age, gender, and ethnicity.
2. Age from seven through eighteen was used as a straightforward interval level variable.
3. Gender was treated as a dummy variable, coded 1 for female, 0 for male.
4. Ethnicity was operationalized as a set of three dummy variables, reflecting a four-category classification, as follows: Hispanic = 1 if client was Hispanic, 0 otherwise; black = 1 if client was black, 0 otherwise; other ethnic = 1 if client was not black, white, or Hispanic, 0 otherwise; and white clients constituted the omitted category by the set of three dummy variables.[7]

Variables were entered into the regression in four stages as follows:

1. Seven site effect codes.
2. Additive versions of the client variables, namely, age, gender, and ethnicity.
3. Interaction terms, successively added to the base model established at stage 2. These included (a) multiplicative terms reflecting interaction between age and ethnic categories; (b) interaction of age and gender; and (c) interaction of gender and ethnic categories.
4. Based on the results of stage 3, a final regression equation was developed which included stage 2 variables plus the age-gender interaction term and the gender-ethnicity interaction terms.

Site location proved to be a substantial determinant of delinquent priors. The additive effects of site on the likelihood of a delinquent offense pattern prior to the instant status offense was found to explain approximately half of the variation in delinquent priors accounted for jointly by client characteristics and site.[8] This suggests that independently of age, gender, and ethnicity, the probability that the status offender will fall into the delinquent prior offense category is substantially affected by the jurisdictions in which he resides.[9] When the effects of age, gender, and ethnicity on the likelihood of a pattern of prior delinquent offenses were included, explained variance was increased to 19.5 percent (table 11-9).

More detailed information regarding the determinants of prior offense pattern is provided by an examination of interaction effects. The interaction of age and gender by itself has a significant effect on the probability of a pattern of prior delinquency. The age-ethnicity interaction was not found to be significant when added to the basic equation for additive effects alone. However, when the gender-ethnicity interaction is included in the basic

Table 11-9
Regression Coefficients of Prior Delinquent Patterns on Age, Gender, Ethnicity, and Two-way Interactions

Variables	Additive Model[a]		Interaction Model[b]	
	B	Beta	B	Beta
Male	.252	.261[c]	−.145	−.150
Age	.001	.037[d]	−.004	−.013
Black	.061	.054[e]	.035	.032
Hispanic	.097	.052[e]	.012	.006
Other ethnic	.083	−.026	.010	.003
Age × gender	—	—	.026	.398[e]
Other ethnic × gender	—	—	−.171	−.039
Hispanic × gender	—	—	.145	.061[e]
Black × gender	—	—	.052	.035
Constant	.309		.262	

Note: Site effect codes entered a controls, but not presented. N = 2993.
[a]$R^2 = .195$.
[b]$R^2 = .199$.
[c]$p < .001$.
[d]$p < .01$.
[e]$p < .05$.

equation, the explained variation for prior delinquent offense is significantly increased. These statistical tests indicated that although the age-ethnicity interaction has no significant effect in relation to prior delinquent offense pattern, both the age-gender and the gender-ethnicity interactions do.

While the effects of age, gender, and ethnicity on the likelihood of a prior delinquent pattern are significant in an additive model, their effects were found to fall below an acceptable level of significance ($p < .05$) when the interactions among these variables were included in the equation. On the other hand, interaction between age and gender is a significant determinant, as is the set of terms capturing gender-ethnicity interaction. Of the latter set, only the variable reflecting whether or not the youth is an Hispanic male is individually significant, indicating that they are more likely to show a pattern of prior delinquency than would be predicted by gender or ethnicity as separate variables. The age-gender interaction coefficient suggests that the likelihood of a pattern of prior delinquent offenses increases at a higher rate for males than for females with an increase in age. Furthermore, among the set of gender-ethnicity interaction coefficients, the only one that is individually significant is that for Hispanic males, indicating that they are more likely to show a pattern of prior delinquency than would be predicted by either gender or ethnicity alone.

Thus, as seen in the additive model displayed in table 11-9, the variables of age, gender, and ethnicity were positively and significantly related to the probability that a status offender in the preprogram sample would have a record of prior delinquent offenses. The main effects of the variables, along with information as to jurisdiction, accounted for 19.5 percent of the variation in the incidence of a prior delinquent offense pattern. Although quite modest, the 0.4 percent increment in explained variation due to the addition of age-gender and ethnicity-gender interaction terms is statistically significant, owing to the large sample size. Individually significant interaction terms suggest that being an older male or an Hispanic male raises the probability of a delinquent prior career beyond what might be predicted on the basis of age, gender, and ethnicity considered separately.

Progression from Status of Delinquent Offenses

Although the data revealed an identifiable population of juvenile offenders whose only recorded offenses prior to their identification were of the status variety, the question remains whether they tend over time to commit with increasing frequency the delinquent offenses (misdemeanors and felonies).

To assess this question, the officially recorded offenses of the preprogram group in the national status offender program were examined subsequent as well as prior to the instant status offense. As stated earlier, the instant offense was defined as the first occurrence of a recorded status offense during the preprogram year. The preprogram sample was classified by four types of prior offense: no offenses, status offenses only, delinquent (misdemeanor and felony) offenses only, and mixed status and delinquent offenses. The sample was then cross-classified by the same offense categories subsequent to the instant offense, utilizing a six-month and a twelve-month followup period. Since the instant offense could occur at any point during the preprogram year, it was necessary to eliminate from the followup cohorts those members of the sample who, by virtue of the date of their instant, were not at risk for six months in one case and for twelve months in the other. Consequently, each of the followup cohorts represents a reduced subset of the preprogram sample, larger for the six-month cohort, smaller for those having a twelve-month risk period.

As seen in table 11-10, six months after their first recorded status offense, most of the group in this followup cohort (68.7 percent) had no record of a subsequent offense. Of those with no prior offenses, a substantial 83.1 percent remained free of subsequent offenses of any kind. Very small proportions of those with no prior offenses turned up as having committed

Table 11-10
Subsequent Offense Pattern of Preprogram Sample at Six-month Followup

Subsequent Offenses	Prior Offenses									
	No Offenses		Status Only		Delinquent Only		Mixed		Total	
	Number	Percent	Number	Percent	Number	Percent	Number	Percent	Number	Percent
No offenses	1,302	83.1	191	56.7	335	57.8	245	46.0	2,073	68.7
Status only	130	8.3	80	23.7	66	11.4	89	16.7	365	12.1
Delinquent only	95	6.1	29	8.6	126	21.7	117	22.0	367	12.2
Mixed	40	2.6	37	11.0	53	9.1	82	15.4	212	7.0
Total	1,567	100.1	337	100.0	580	100.0	533	100.1	3,017	100.0

Note: $\chi^2 = 416.4$, df = 9, $p = < .001$.

status offenses (8.3 percent), and even fewer in the delinquency only (6.1 percent), and the mixed (2.6 percent) categories. The no prior offense subset in the twelve-month followup cohort exhibited substantially the same absence of subsequent offenses, with 75.9 percent remaining free of recorded offenses of any kind (table 11-11). It may thus be noted at the outset that there exists a very large group of youth of which, on a first citation for a status offense, from three-quarters to four-fifths are unlikely to commit further offenses of any kind during the following year. This finding raises the question whether the official intervention in a status offense case is warranted for the protection of either the person or the community, and supports the contention of those urging a "do nothing" approach in dealing with status offenders. At the same time, however, it cannot be determined from these data whether nonappearance for a recorded subsequent offense may be attributed to the deterrent effect of official intervention, to increased knowledge of how to avoid arrest, or to intensified information pressures from family members for conforming behavior, among other possibilities.

The issue of progression from status to delinquent offenses is best examined by excluding the large group for which no offenses were recorded either prior or subsequent to the instant offense. This procedure yields a 2 × 2 table in which the prior status only and delinquent/mixed categories are cross-classified by the same categories at six- and twelve-month followup. The sample may now be regarded as purified by the exclusion not only of those who had no prior offenses, but of those as well who had no subsequent offenses. The status offense only priors are now individuals for whom two or more status offenses were recorded (at least one of which occurred prior to the instant), and they may be viewed more appropriately as a pure status offender group. Furthermore, since those in the mixed category are known to have committed both delinquent and status offenses, their merging with those recorded as delinquent only creates a category of youth known to have committed delinquent offenses.

Almost half of those with status only prior offenses at both the six- and twelve-month followup had records of delinquent offenses (45.2 and 48.5 percent), respectively (tables 11-12 and 11-13). But notable in the same data is the distinction that persistently emerges between two groups in the preprogram sample: those whose offenses tend to remain predominantly in the status offense category, and those given principally to delinquent offenses. Approximately 70 percent of those with delinquent priors had only delinquent subsequent offenses, and approximately 50 percent of those with only status offense priors had only status offense subsequents. These seem to represent two discernably different groups with respect to offense pattern. A third group emerges, clearly apparent only when the no offense individuals in either their prior or subsequent offenses are excluded from the followup cohorts, constituted by a subset of status offenders of whom a

Table 11-11
Subsequent Offense Pattern of Preprogram Sample at Twelve-month Followup

Subsequent Offenses	No Offenses		Status Only		Prior Offenses Delinquent		Mixed		Total	
	Number	Percent	Number	Percent	Number	Percent	Number	Percent	Number	Percent
No offenses	555	75.9	85	45.2	130	46.1	99	35.6	869	58.8
Status only	76	10.4	53	28.2	30	10.6	57	20.5	216	14.6
Delinquent only	63	8.6	18	9.6	75	26.6	63	22.7	219	14.8
Mixed	37	5.1	32	17.0	47	16.7	59	21.2	175	11.8
Total	731	100.0	188	100.0	282	100.0	278	100.0	1,479	100.0

Note: χ^2 = 237.2, df = 9, p = < .001.

Table 11-12

Subsequent Offense Pattern of Preprogram Sample at Six-month Followup, with No Offense Priors and Subsequents Excluded

| Subsequent Offenses | Prior Offenses | | | | | |
| | Status Only | | Delinquent Only and Mixed | | Total | |
	Number	Percent	Number	Percent	Number	Percent
Status only	80	54.8	155	29.1	235	34.7
Delinquent only and mixed	66	45.2	377	70.9	443	65.3
Total	146	100.0	532	100.0	678	100.0

Note x^2 = 33.3, df = 1, $p < .001$.

substantial proportion show subsequent records of delinquency. In the six-month cohort, of the 146 juveniles with prior status offenses only, 45.2 percent had subsequent records of delinquent acts. The corresponding percentage among the 103 juveniles with prior status offenses only in the twelve-month followup cohort was 48.5 percent.

These findings offer some support for the progression thesis, if only with respect to a limited segment of a status offender population. However, the evidence is subject to an important qualification. In the light of the probable differential treatment of female status offenders, namely, their higher vulnerability to recording as delinquent offenders on the basis of probation violation, it is entirely possible that a very high proportion of the recorded subsequent delinquent offenses of prior status offenders may be ascribed to female probation violators.[10] Hence, the impression of progression from status to delinquent offenses suggested by the data of this study may be misleading. In addition, there is evidence for regression from delinquent to

Table 11-13

Subsequent Offense Pattern of Preprogram Sample at Twelve-month Followup, with No Offense Priors and Subsequents Excluded

| Subsequent Offenses | Prior Offenses | | | | | |
| | Status Only | | Delinquent Only and Mixed | | Total | |
	Number	Percent	Number	Percent	Number	Percent
Status only	53	51.5	87	26.3	140	32.3
Delinquent only and mixed	50	48.5	244	73.7	294	67.7
Total	103	100.0	331	100.0	434	100.0

Note: x^2 = 34.3, df = 1, $p < .001$.

status offenses as well as for progression from status to delinquent offenses. The data of tables 11-10 and 11-11 indicate that at six-month followup 19.6 percent of those with status only priors were recorded as having subsequent records of delinquency (delinquency only plus mixed). The corresponding percentage at twelve-month followup was 26.6. However, of those with delinquent only priors, 11.4 and 10.6 percent had status only subsequents at six- and twelve-month followup, respectively. This suggests, of course, the substantial degree of offense versatility exhibited by most juvenile offenders, repeatedly noted in prior research (Thomas 1976; Klein 1971; Wolfgang et al. 1973; Erickson 1979; Institute for Juvenile Research 1972).[11]

Discussion

Two major assumptions inform the current movement to deinstitutionalize status offenders by reducing and ultimately eliminating the power of police and courts to deal with them as they do with youth who commit criminal offenses. Supporters of the movement contend, first, that status offenders constitute a distinctive and identifiable category of juvenile offenders, largely free of involvement in criminal acts. It follows from this that the use of secure detention and commitment to correctional institutions has neither legal nor ethical justification. A second assumption holds that, by virtue of being accorded standard police and court treatment, status offenders tend increasingly to commit the more serious criminal offenses. Hence, the removal of status offenders from the jurisdiction of the juvenile justice system is expected over time to prevent delinquency.

Data obtained in conjunction with an evaluation study of a federally funded status offender deinstitutionalization program presented an opportunity to test the support for the empirically more accessible of these assumptions. Singled out for scrutiny was, first, the question whether there may be found a subset of infractious youth who confine their misbehavior to the status offenses and, if identified, its proportion among a status offending population, together with its age, gender, ethnic, and racial characteristics, and patterns of offense over time. The second question assessed was the extent to which progression from status to criminal offenses occurred in an identified population of status offenders.

Data analysis yielded, first, the unanticipated finding that, in any population identified by a citation for a status offense, by far the largest proportion is likely to be youngsters for whom there exists no official record of a prior offense of any kind. They fall principally between the ages of thirteen and sixteen, with approximately equal proportions of males and females. With reference to ethnicity, the black and Hispanic minority groups were found to have higher proportions of their prior offenses in the delinquent category than were whites. The group free of official records of offense prior to an arrest or citation for a status offense tend not to reappear either as status or delinquent offenders subsequently. It is likely that on the whole this group undergoes minimal penetration into the juvenile justice system and represents those customarily diverted by the police.

A second finding, less unexpected, was that, of those with offense records prior to a status offense arrest, about one in ten consist of youth who have committed only status offenses. Of this group, about one-quarter continue to confine their infractions to the status offenses, another quarter show a subsequent record of delinquent offenses, and approximately half remain free of recorded offenses.

In general, it appears that a population identified by an arrest or appearance before the juvenile court for a status offense contains two quite distinguishable groups. About two-thirds consist of a majority of youth virtually free of recorded prior offenses, and a minority show records of prior status offenses only. The prior records of the remaining one-third of this population designate either solely delinquent offenses or mixed delinquent and status offenses. That the distinction between the no offense-status offense only group and the delinquent only-mixed group remains relatively stable is attested to by the subsequent offenses of the two groups. The latter group remains disproportionately in the delinquency-mixed categories; the former in those of no offense-status offenses only.

Findings on gender differences indicate that females at every age level are very much more likely than males to acquire records of status offenses. Three-quarters of the female members of the sample had prior records of status offenses; one-half of the male members fell in this category.

Examination of the relative predictive utility of jurisdiction, age, gender, and ethnicity revealed jurisdiction to be an important determinant of the probability that a youth cited for a status offense would have a record of a prior delinquent offense. Certain combinations of age, gender, and ethnicity were found to increase this probability. Thus, the likelihood of a prior record of delinquent offenses increased with increasing age at a higher rate for males than for females. When this interaction is combined further with ethnicity, it was found that older Hispanic males had the highest probability of recorded prior delinquency.

On the basis of the data available for this analysis, the evidence for progression from status to delinquent offenses remains debatable. If the population under consideration are all youth cited for a status offense within a given time period, irrespective of the number of prior status offenses, the overwhelming majority within a twelve-month followup are found either to have no subsequent offenses or to confine their subsequents to the status offenses. On the other hand, if the population of concern are youth with two or more prior status offenses, there is virtual equal probability that their subsequent offenses will be either of the delinquent or of the status variety. In other words, youth marginally involved in status offense behavior are in little danger of moving into the more serious forms of delinquency. However, those for whom status offense behavior has become chronic appear to be as likely subsequently to commit misdemeanor and criminal offenses as they are to confine themselves to the status offenses.

But there remains strong and consistent evidence for the existence of three relatively separable groups, each of substantial size, and each distinguishable on the basis of the predominant character of their offenses. The first consists of status offenders with little tendency to commit the more serious delinquent offenses; the second includes juveniles whose records show a predominance of delinquent offenses. Finally, as a finding of some importance, the data revealed the third and largest group to consist of juveniles without records of either a status or a delinquent offense both prior and subsequent to the single incident that defined their membership in a status offender population.

Thus, only one of the basic assumptions of fact on which the status offender deinstitutionalization movement rests is provisionally supported by the evidence of the present study. Although its boundaries cannot be sharply drawn, there does appear to be a distinguishable population of misbehaving youth whose infractions are confined principally to the status offenses. Nor does it appear that they tend to commit the more serious delinquent offenses in increasing numbers and with increasing frequency. They thus constitute an identifiable group whose problem behavior may be sufficiently differentiated from that represented by acts in violation of the criminal law to warrant distinctive forms of response and treatment. There is little support for the notion that they tend in substantial proportions to become serious delinquents. What evidence there is in support of that assumption has reference only to that relatively small segment of a status-offending population consisting of chronic status offenders. They are as likely in time to engage in serious delinquent offenses as they are to remain status offenders.

Finally, nothing in the data of this study can throw light on the third basic assumption of the status offender deinstitutionalization movement asserting that traditional juvenile court processing increases the likelihood of progression from status to delinquent offenses. However, the evidence does indicate that contained within any population of juvenile offenders defined by a citation for a status offense are substantial numbers of delinquent offenders. Whether the use of secure confinement in the treatment of this group reduces their recidivism or increases community protection is a separate issue. But with respect to the group of status offenders that shows little inclination to engage in the more serious forms of delinquency, no form of secure confinement would appear to be warranted on either preventive or ethical grounds.

Notes

1. Surveys conducted during the decade, 1965-1974, in a variety of jurisdictions have found that half of all juveniles arrested for a status offense were placed in secure detention for periods ranging from several days to several months (Law Enforcement Assistance Administration, 1975:1-3). One-third of all juveniles in correctional institutions (training schools, group homes, half-way houses) were committed as adjudicated status offenders (Law Enforcement Assistance Administration, 1974).

2. The status offenses were runaway, ungovernability, truancy, curfew violation, and possession of alcohol by a minor. A residual other category was used to include types of behavior defined as status offenses in some but not other jurisdictions.

3. The two-year life of both the program and the evaluation study meant that the later during this period that juveniles were referred to the program, the less their availability for a twelve-month followup.

4. The data on prior offenses and gender are presented by age as a summary indication that age distribution does not differ materially as between those whose prior offenses do and do not include a substantial proportion of delinquent offenses.

5. Attention is directed to the fact that the records were entered in a search for instant status offenses. The number of those who were primarily status offenders in terms of their prior records constitutes 63 percent of the total as defined by our entry criteria. The same number of status offenders would constitute a far smaller proportion of the total arrested and adjudicated juvenile population. A project on delinquent or mixed offenders, using an anagous record entry procedure, would have yielded large numbers of predominantly delinquent or predominantly mixed offenders. A not unreasonable alternative in estimating the proportion of status offenders in the preprogram population is to exclude the 1,560 individuals with no recorded offenses prior to the instant on grounds that they are essentially nonoffenders. With their exclusion, the number is 1,446, of which 336, or 23.2 percent, have substantial prior records of status offenses only (see table 11-2). As will be seen, however, this proportion is further reduced when offenses subsequent to the instant at six- and twelve-month followup are taken into account.

6. The exclusion of the no prior offense category is warranted for present purposes since a large proportion in the category is likely to be one-time offenders. Thus, 43.2 and 37.5 percent, respectively, had no record of a subsequent offense of any kind at six- and twelve-month followup.

7. The dependent variable of delinquent priors was operationalized as a dummy variable, with 1 being the record of a delinquency prior to the instant offense; 0, no such record. Anticipating the objection that the use of dummy variables in regression equations violates the necessary assumption of homoscedasticity, it should be stated that in this instance the dichotomy is not badly skewed. In the 2,993 cases in the regression, the proportion in 1 was 37 percent; in 0, 63 percent.

8. This was ascertained in a special analysis of the independent effects of site location. Site terms were entered after the client variables, permitting assessment of their contribution to explained variance due solely to their addition.

9. With the data available to this study, it was not possible to determine the relative importance of various features of jurisdictions in the relationship. These include community tolerance for juvenile misbehavior, police and court policies with respect to the use of diversion practices, the statutory definition of status offenses, the adequacy of record keeping, accessibility of the records, and the diligence with which a search of the records may have been conducted.

10. Most jurisdictions treat violation of probation as a delinquent offense. Females were found to constitute approximately half of the preprogram sample. Since female status offenders are more likely than males on a first offense to receive probation because of concern over alleged sexual misconduct, they may be more likely to acquire a higher risk of probation violation, and therefore to being recorded for a delinquent offense.

11. Similar findings were reported by one large-scale study of youth behavior based on self-report data. However, their data did not identify a population similar to that found in the present study (Illinois Institute for Juvenile Research 1972).

References

Becker, Howard S. (1963). *Outsiders: Studies in the Sociology of Deviance.* New York: Free Press.
Clarke, Steven H. (1975). "Some implications for North Carolina of recent research in juvenile delinquency." *Journal of Research in Crime and Delinquency* 12(1):51-60.
Erickson, Maynard L. (1979). "Some empirical questions concerning the current revolution in juvenile justice. In LaMar T. Empey (ed.), *The*

Future of Childhood and Juvenile Justice, Charlottesville: University of Virginia Press.

Erickson, Maynard L., and Empey, LaMar T. (1963). "Court records, undetected delinquency, and decisionmaking." *The Journal of Criminal Law, Criminology, and Police Science.* 54 (December):456-469.

Gold, Martin (1966). "Undetected delinquent behavior." *Journal of Research in Crime and Delinquency.* 3 (January):27-46.

Gottfredson, Michael R., Hindelang, Michael J., and Parisi, Nicolette (1977). *Sourcebook of Criminal Justice Statistics.* Washington, D.C.: U.S. Government Printing Office.

Illinois Institute for Juvenile Research (1972). *Juvenile Delinquency in Illinois.* Chicago: Illinois Department of Mental Health.

Klein, Malcolm W. (1971). *Street Gangs and Street Workers.* Englewood Cliffs, N.J.: Prentice-Hall.

_____ (1979). "Deinstitutionalization and diversion of juvenile offenders: a litany of impediments." In Norval Morris and Michael Tonry (eds.) *Crime and Justice.* Chicago: University of Chicago Press.

Kobrin, Solomon, and Klein, Malcolm W. (1979). National Evaluation Study of the Status Offender Deinstitutionalization Program (forthcoming).

Law Enforcement Assistance Administration (1974). *Children in Custody: A Report on the Juvenile Detention and Correctional Facility Census of 1971.* Washington, D.C.: U.S. Government Printing Office.

_____ (1975). *Program Announcement: Deinstitutionalization of Status Offenders.* Washington, D.C.: U.S. Government Printing Office.

Lemert, Edwin M. (1951). *Social Pathology.* New York: McGraw-Hill.

Schur, Edwin M. (1971). *Labeling Deviant Behavior.* New York: Harper and Row.

Thomas, Charles W. (1976). "Are status offenders really so different?" *Crime and Deliquency* 22:438-455.

Wolfgang, Marvin, E., Figlio, Robert M., and Sellin, Thorsten (1972). *Delinquency in a Birth Cohort.* Chicago: University of Chicago Press.

12 Recurring Issues in the Evaluation of Delinquency Prevention and Treatment Programs

Delbert S. Elliott

The orientation of this chapter is a practical one, focusing upon a number of both conceptual and methodological issues which I have encountered repeatedly during the course of evaluating delinquency prevention and treatment programs. There will be no attempt to systematically summarize research findings relative to the success or failure of specific programs or approaches to delinquency prevention and treatment.[1] Neither is this chapter intended to present a systematic review of evaluation methods or procedures. Rather, the concern is over a number of specific recurring problems which affect the general validity and utility of such evaluations. These specific issues are discussed and some suggestions for dealing with them are offered, with the aim of making delinquency program evaluations more theoretically relevant, more sensitive to postulated effects, and more useful for policy formation and program development.

Conceptual Issues

Traditional descriptions of the developmental process for delinquency prevention or treatment program (CAR 1976; Klein 1979; Stanford Research Consortium 1976; VanMaanen 1979; Riecken and Boruch 1974; Cain and Hollister 1972) typically involve something like the following sequence:

1. A causal model or theoretical paradigm which identifies a set of variables (attributes, relationships or circumstances) connected by some logical process to delinquent behavior;

The author was the principal investigator for the national evaluation of programs funded by the Youth Development and Delinquency Prevention Administration, HEW, 1972-1973; the National Evaluation of programs funded by the Office of Youth Development (OYD), HEW, 1973-1974; a national evaluation of ten delinquency prevention projects funded by OYD, HEW, 1974-1975; project director for the national evaluation of LEAA's diversion initiative, 1976-1980; and the principal investigator for a sizable number of evaluations of independent local delinquency prevention-treatment programs. The author wishes to acknowledge the helpful comments of two colleagues, Frank Dunford and Brian Knowles, on an earlier version of this manuscript.

2. The identification of a set of program activities or interventions which are designed to manipulate these causal variables;
3. The implementation of the program with these manipulations operationalized as program objectives;
4. Information feedback during operation to determine if the program activities are, in fact, occurring and the objectives being met (process evaluation);
5. Feedback to determine if the realization of these program objectives is having the theoretically expected effect on delinquency (impact evaluation);
6. The modification of the theoretical paradigm or the program activities and objectives as suggested by the process and impact evaluations so as to increase the program's effectiveness in reducing delinquency.

This process involves an experimental approach to program development and evaluation.[2] This approach provides a logic for interpreting specific impact results, accumulating evidence relative to the validity and utility of the theoretical paradigm employed, and documenting the utility of specific program activities or interventions. If one or more of the first four of these elements is missing, the interpretation of impact evaluation results becomes problematic, there is no accumulated knowledge concerning the validity of the theoretical paradigm, and the utility of specific program activities remains unknown.

The experimental process described above is rarely utilized in current delinquency prevention program development and evaluation. The problem is not simply a failure to use this particular ordinal sequence, with its implied logic of moving from abstract theoretical ideas to specific program components, to process and impact evaluations, and back to modifications of the program or theoretical rationale as necessary. More importantly, it involves a nearly universal absence of any explicit theoretical rationale, either pre or post hoc, to serve as a guide for the identification of particular program activities which have some postulated relationship to delinquency.

Particular program activities and treatment modes have become so institutionalized that they are employed without clear reference to any particular theoretical paradigm, their own unique theoretical origins having been lost, forgotten, or discredited. They are employed because they have become proper and accepted things to do for youth in trouble, because they are relatively easy to implement, and because people are trained to provide this service or treatment. The implications of this situation for the evaluation of delinquency prevention and treatment programs are truly serious. The 1973 and 1974 national evaluations of delinquency prevention programs funded by the Department of Health, Education and Welfare illustrate this situation and the problems it poses for evaluation studies.

In 1971, the Youth Development and Delinquency Prevention Administration (YDDPA) published its national strategy for youth development and delinquency prevention as a general conceptual framework for developing delinquency prevention programs to be funded by HEW (Gemignani 1971, 1976; Elliott 1971; Cartwright 1971; Polk and Kobrin 1972). Programs funded by YDDPA and the subsequent Office of Youth Development (OYD) from 1972 through 1975[3] were to be guided by this general theoretical statement. The national evaluations of these programs conducted in 1973, 1974 and 1975 were designed to test a set of theoretical propositions derived from this National Strategy statement (BREC 1973, 1974; Elliott et al. 1975).

These evaluations revealed several significant findings relative to the theoretical orientations of programs funded to implement this strategy:

1. With the exception of project directors and persons responsible for writing the grant applications, project staffs knew little or nothing about OYD's national strategy for youth development and delinquency prevention and its general directives for delinquency programming.[4]
2. Although the orientation of the OYD national strategy was toward changing the structure of social institutions to facilitate positive youth development (reducing negative labeling practices and increasing access to conventional social roles), the orientation of project staffs was overwhelmingly a psychological, individual treatment orientation.
3. The vast majority of staff persons interviewed had no clear rationale connecting their immediate treatment objectives to a reduction in delinquent behavior (BREC 1974).

In retrospect, it is clear that many of the programs funded by YDDPA and OYD during this period were developed without reference to the theoretical orientation proposed by YDDPA or OYD. Older traditional treatment approaches were often dressed up in grant applications to look like they conformed to the new funding guidelines. In most cases, what was actually implemented under this new strategy was some form of individual casework or counseling. The vast majority of referrals to these projects received some type of personal or group counseling service.[5]

It was one thing to observe that the OYD national strategy was not serving as the theoretical paradigm for these delinquency prevention programs, and another to discover that, in most cases, no alternative paradigm was being utilized in its place. Interviews with project staffs revealed only vague and fuzzy notions about how their activities were related to a reduction in delinquency (BREC 1974). This is not to say that a rationale could not be made for these activities, but rather that few persons addressed this issue directly, and few were aware of any theoretical rationale that operated to guide their specific activities.

Even within specific programs, there was little consensus concerning the causes of delinquency and what specific interventions or changes were most likely to reduce an individual's delinquency involvement. Rarely did programs spend any time attempting to development a rationale. For example, counseling activities may be justified as an intervention strategy in delinquency prevention and treatment programs from several different theoretical perspectives: psychopathy, personality theory, reality therapy, social learning theory, control theory, and perhaps even strain or structural theories. But the specific objectives of the counseling activity vary according to which theoretical perspective is employed, and few programs were even aware of this issue. Some staff personnel admitted outright that they were not sure there was any direct relationship between program activities and delinquency reduction. In sum, most program staffs operated with an undirected approach to delinquency prevention programming.

Although the rationales connecting program activities to reductions in delinquency were vague and inconsistent, there was a clear and strong commitment on the part of program staff to particular treatment or intervention approaches. Program staffs were consistent in their belief that counseling, recreational activities, and tutorial-skill development classes were helping youth. The commitment was not to a theoretical model of delinquency prevention, but to a particular treatment mode or intervention technique that, in some largely unspecified way, was considered helpful to youth in trouble.

The absence of any clear theoretical rationale or conceptual framework for delinquency prevention-treatment projects is a very widespread problem. The example cited above is particularly noteworthy because it involved projects that were funded with a specific theoretical model proposed as a guideline for program development. But the problem is a general one, and the lack of any clear theoretical rationale undermines the evaluation of most delinquency prevention-treatment programs in several important ways.

First, the theoretical orientation influences the way in which immediate program objectives are conceptualized and operationalized. The situation described above produced a number of problems for the 1973 and 1974 national evaluations, which attempted to test the propositions contained in the OYD national strategy. The immediate treatment objectives of projects were often inconsistent with the OYD national strategy, and projects resisted the attempt of the evaluators to impose a set of treatment objectives which were logically consistent with this strategy. Even in those cases where there was general agreement about an immediate objective, there was often disagreement as to how that objective should be operationalized.

The objective of diverting youth from further penetration into the juvenile justice system was endorsed by most projects and was also logically derived from the OYD national strategy. Given the clinical orientation of project staffs, they viewed all youth referred to them from police or probation departments as instances of diversion. Yet, from the perspective of the OYD national strategy, diversion represented a change in the flow of youth through the juvenile justice system; that is, diversion represented a change in institutional processing practices—a willingness on the part of the police and probation departments to divert youth who, in prior times, would have been handled formally.

We thus proposed to measure diversion in a given community in terms of the reduction in maintenance probabilities of the police and probation departments, that is, a reduction in the probability that a suspected offender would be kept in the justice system by some formal action. An analysis of these maintenance probabilities before and after the implementation of projects typically indicated little or no change in police and probation processing practices. This was often the case, even though police were referring substantial numbers of youth to the newly created OYD projects.[6]

The way that diversion was operationalized thus created a serious strain between evaluators and project staffs. Often we observed a situation where the maintenance probabilities for the system remained unchanged, and yet the project served three or four hundred youth referred by the police during the course of a year. Some projects claimed that this constituted ample evidence of their diversion effectiveness. Yet from the system perspective, no substantial diversion was taking place, and youth being served by these projects would in all likelihood have been lectured and released had the projects not been available. The absence of any consistent theoretical rationale for these projects thus led to different perspectives on how even intermediary objectives should be operationalized.

Second, the lack of a clear theoretical rationale accounts for why so many delinquency prevention-treatment programs have relied upon recidivism as the single criterion for program success or effectiveness. Projects with a theoretical rationale can often identify multiple success criteria. These additional success criteria are typically intervening variables by which program activities are connected to a reduction in delinquency. The identification of such variables depends in large part upon the presence of some clear, explicit theoretical rationale. Projects operating without a rationale have no clear conceptual basis for identifying success criteria and use recidivism by default. Its appeal is practical: the data are readily available, the cost is minimal, and there is historical precedent for utilizing this outcome measure.

More will be said about the problem of using recidivism as a general outcome criterion in delinquency prevention programs, but for the present, the point is simply that identification of outcome measures ought to be tied to the theoretical rationale for the service activities provided. When there is no conceptual basis for identifying outcomes, the selection will be made on practical grounds. The historical precedent for recidivism is very strong, and alternative or additional success criteria are sometimes difficult to justify even when a strong theoretical argument can be made for them.

A third consequence of failing to operate with an adequate theoretical rationale is that the interpretation of evaluation outcomes becomes problematic. It is essential in any evaluation to determine that the immediate program objectives were, in fact, achieved. That is to say, that tutorial programs did improve participants' academic performance; that employment programs did find jobs for delinquent youth; and that counseling programs did have the postulated effect with respect to changing attitudes, perceived negative labeling, levels of alienation, and so on. This part of the total evaluation is typically called the process evaluation and is considered a test of program success, as distinguished from the impact evaluation, which is considered a test of the theory's validity. But these two aspects of evaluation are interdependent.

Assuming that immediate treatment objectives are in fact achieved (program success), it is still very difficult to interpret impact findings without the ability to specify a series of intervening variables linking that treatment objective to a reduction in delinquency. In a technical sense, this series of intervening variables provides some control for spuriousness. Even when experimental designs are utilized in evaluation studies, the fact that they are conducted in natural settings means that the type of control necessary to make a straightforward causal argument is simply not possible.

The failure to operate from an explicit theoretical model limits both the strength of any conclusions that may be drawn from an impact evaluation and the utility of the findings for subsequent program modification or development. Without an a priori theoretical rationale, causal interpretations of impact findings are not warranted (Hirschi and Selvin 1967), regardless of the outcome of the process evaluation and the magnitude of the pre and post change or difference observed between the experimental and the control group. A compelling causal interpretation requires a theoretical rationale.

For example, consider a tutorial program for delinquent youth. There is no explicit theoretical rationale, and the program contracts for a simple recidivism impact evaluation which finds no difference in recidivism between controls and participants after six months. What are we to conclude? Can we reasonably conclude that improving academic skills was unrelated to involvement in delinquent behavior (theory failure)? Can we conclude that the program was unsuccessful in achieving its treatment objectives (program failure)? Neither of these conclusions is warranted. Neither are there any clear and direct implications from this evaluation for changing the program (or the theoretical model) to increase its effectiveness.

Consider a second evaluation of this tutorial program based on a rationale derived from control theory. Specifically, improving academic skills (the immediate treatment objective) is viewed as a means for improving regular school performance, which is postulated to increase the youth's stake in conformity and his integration into the school (bonding variables), and thereby reduce his involvement in delinquent behavior and lower his subsequent risk for rearrest (recidivism). The process evaluation indicates that the program did improve participants' academic skills. The impact evaluation discloses that there were (1) no changes in the participants' school performance, (2) no changes in the participants' feelings of alienation from the school or the importance of academic success, (3) no changes in self-reported levels of delinquency involvement, and (4) no difference between participants and controls in recidivism.

The outcome of this recidivism analysis is thus identical to the first evaluation example, but much more is known. The program did, in fact, achieve its initial objective of improving academic skills. In this sense, the program was successful. On the other hand, improving academic skills did not appear to impact on either delinquent behavior or rearrest as hypothesized. Thus, the impact evaluation failed to provide support for the theoretical rationale.

However, these data from the impact evaluation provide some important feedback suggesting a number of new objectives or directions for the program. Improved academic skills did not result in improved academic performance. Perhaps this was due to prior labeling by teachers which negated the actual improvement in academic skills. Perhaps the time lag (six months) was insufficient for the improved skills to result in improved grades, and therefore a longer followup was needed.

Had the impact evaluation indicated an improved school performance, reduced alienation, increased value placed upon education, reduced involvement in delinquent behavior, and a reduction in arrests, the causal argument would be much stronger than it could possibly have been given the simple recidivism analysis in the first evaluation example. Likewise, had the second evaluation example shown positive change on all variables but recidivism, the conclusion of the two evaluations would be very different—inconclusive findings in the first instance, and both program success and theory support in the second.

Romig (1978) describes a study of an academic skill-development educational project that reported a significant reduction in recidivism. Yet data relative to academic performance failed to provide evidence that the program had any impact upon academic performance. If the recidivism impact analysis had been the only analysis undertaken, it would have appeared to support the conclusion that improving academic performance was related to reduction in delinquency—program success and theory support. The fact that data were collected relative to improved academic performance results in a very different interpretation of the recidivism findings: not only was the program unsuccessful in achieving its immediate treatment objectives, but also the recidivism outcome cannot be viewed as support for the postulated relationship between improved academic performance and reductions in delinquent arrests. Although it is logically possible that some unplanned and unidentified factors associated with program participation accounted for the observed reduction in recidivism, this reduction appeared unrelated to planned program activities.

In sum, evaluations based upon a theoretical rationale provide a better basis for interpreting results, better controls for spuriousness, and the potential for more compelling causal arguments. Unfortunately, the vast majority of delinquency program evaluations approximate the first evaluation example rather than the second.

A fourth consequence of the atheoretical nature of most delinquency prevention-treatment programs is a general resistance to evaluation on the part of program personnel and a failure to utilize evaluation findings in the ongoing operation of the program. In our national evaluation of HEW-funded programs, the imposition of a theoretical model on programs by the national funding agency and the national evaluators produced considerable strain and some outright hostility. Project personnel assumed that a negative evaluation would have some bearing on future funding from HEW.[7] They reacted, not unreasonably, to the imposition of evaluation objectives which were of questionable relevance to their actual program operation, or were conceptualized and measured in ways which they believed made their programs look bad (as in the case of diversion).

It is not surprising that most projects essentially ignored the recommendations contained in the final evaluation report. Given the atheoretical orientation of their programs and the feeling that the evaluation had little relevance to their treatment-service operation, project personnel could hardly be expected to have received the evaluation with positive attitudes or to have utilized evaluation findings for program modification. In fact, these findings were of value only to those who saw some relevance of the national strategy for their programs.

Many reviews of evaluation research (Weiss 1972; Riecken and Boruch 1974; Patton 1978; Etzioni 1960) argue that it is the poor quality of evaluation designs and methodology which accounts for the general failure to use evaluation findings in program planning. A few (Suchman 1972; Short 1975) suggest that it is the role of the evaluator and the type of evaluation (formative or summative) which influence the utility of evaluation findings. Our experience indicates that it is the absence of any explicit theoretical rationale for programs which is the major factor in the limited use of evaluation findings.

The atheoretical nature of most programs accounts, in large part, for the weak evaluation designs and poor methodology. The time of the feedback to programs (that is, whether the evaluation is formative or summative) is hardly relevant if the evaluation is conceptualized so poorly that its findings have no implications for program change to improve efficiency or effectiveness. On the other hand, our evaluation experience suggests that programs developed around an explicit theoretical model will make constructive use of evaluation findings, even very limited or tentative finds produced by quasi-experimental designs and limited measures of the relevant variables.

There is no easy solution to this difficulty. It seems clear that a post hoc theoretical model cannot be imposed upon programs. Although this may produce a better quality evaluation, it will have little final impact on program structures and objectives and, indeed, it is questionable that the findings are even relevant to the program under this condition.

One possible solution is to work with program personnel, prior to implementing the evaluation, in a joint effort to develop a theoretical rationale, even a crude one. If consensus and support for a rationale can be developed and a set of intervening variables or processes that link the treatment objectives to delinquent behavior can be agreed on, the scene has been set for a better evaluation design and a positive reception of eventual findings. The oft-cited tensions between evaluators and practitioners suggest this may be difficult to do (Hackler 1967; Weiss 1975; Campbell 1975).[8]

In general, practitioners do not understand or appreciate the relevance of theory. They view it as a purely academic interest that is totally removed from the reality of helping youth with their immediate problems. Even when they are familiar with the theoretical rationale for a particular type of service or treatment activity, they rarely understand the dynamic interplay between the rationale and the everyday service-treatment planning and decision making. However, they do not bear the responsibility for this failure alone. To a great extent, this difficulty lies with the theory builders who, by and large, have failed to specify clearly the practical program implications of their theories. There is a critical need for better communication and exchange between the basic research community and the criminal justice practitioner.

The translation of theoretical notions into operational concepts, variables and practices which have direct relevance for delinquency prevention-treatment efforts is a difficult task, and one which is often ignored by academics. Yet persons who can articulate clearly the program implications of various theoretical models are sorely needed if we are to deal effectively with this problem.

Sociological theories of delinquency, in particular, are not understood or implemented in contemporary delinquency prevention-treatment programs.

A few of the HEW projects operating under the national strategy made deliberate attempts to develop program components or strategies for changing general institutional processing practices within local schools and juvenile justice systems. In most instances, however, the structural orientation toward delinquency prevention in the national strategy was translated by program developers and project directors into individually oriented program components—youth advocacy programs, programs oriented toward improving educational and occupational opportunities for specific individuals, and so forth. Ultimately, even these programs regressed to individual, psychologically oriented counseling programs or were only thinly veiled casework or counseling programs from the start. In sum, in the area of delinquency prevention-treatment, there is a critical need for the clear articulation of sociological concepts and processes into specific change objectives and activities.

Design Issues

There is a general, widespread criticism of delinquency evaluation studies for their heavy reliance upon preexperimental and quasi-experimental designs, particularly upon nonrandomized post-test-only designs (Boruch 1975; Campbell and Stanley 1963; Riecken and Boruch 1974; Guttentag 1977; Struening and Guttentag 1975; Glass 1976). In part, the use of these designs is the result of the general atheoretical orientation of delinquency prevention-treatment programs as noted above.

In addition, our experience indicates that the failure to employ stronger designs is often the result of an assumed resistance to these designs which is unfounded. Our experience also indicates that the use of field experimental designs with random assignment is not a cure-all for evaluation studies: they do not guarantee unequivocal evaluation findings and interpretations. Thus, there is both an underuse of these designs in actual practice and also an overly optimistic view that, when they are used, they will provide definitive evaluation results.

In the first instance, there is a general reluctance on the part of many evaluators to argue strongly for randomized field experimental designs. Yet our experience suggests that such designs are often possible and, under some frequently encountered circumstances, a strong case can be made that they are more ethical and politically efficacious than quasi-experimental designs. Our observations are thus consistent with those of Boruch et al. (1978), who suggest that randomized field experimental designs are more feasible than commonly assumed by evaluators.

Our current national evaluation of programs funded under LEAA's diversion initiative is an important case in point. The formal program announcement by LEAA specifically indicated that the programs funded would be required to implement a random assignment procedure in connection with the evaluation. The extent to which randomization was assured by juvenile justice agencies in the local community was specifically listed as a formal selection criterion for awarding grants (LEAA 1976:113-114):

> *The extent to which randomization* is assured by juvenile justice agencies is assignment of youth to the range of dispositional alternatives outlined in the program. Randomization is possible because the resources of the diversion programs will not allow provision of services to all youth diverted. Random assignment of youth to services is therefore a reasonable and equitable procedure to follow in the allocation of limited resources. Among those youth determined to be eligible for diversion in this program, some will be referred for normal Juvenile Justice System processing, and tracked. Others will be diverted as program participants. Their dispositions will include: (1) Diversion with services. (2) Diversion without serivces.

This quote is of interest because it sets forth a requirement that projects implement a random assignment procedure. It also provides a rationale for this requirement.

The justification for random assignment in the program announcement is that the allocation of a limited set of resources (diversion services) will be most reasonable and equitable if all eligible youth have the same opportunity or chance of receiving these resources. This condition, that is, a limited availability of services given the eligible pool, is one which often characterizes delinquency prevention-treatment programs, and it thus offers an officially recognized justification for random assignment.

This same justification was used successfully in an evaluation of a youth work experience program in Oakland (Elliott and Knowles 1978). The Oakland project staff had considerable prior experience with youth work experience programs in Oakland and, in these earlier instances, had encountered criticism from community agencies and citizen interest groups over selection procedures and quotas. They were therefore quite open to our suggestion of using a random selection process and to the argument that this procedure was an equitable one which community agencies and interest groups would accept.

The project staff correctly anticipated approximately six hundred eligible youth applicants for this program, which could accommodate a maximum of two hundred participants. Applicants were told that the actual selection of participants would be made randomly by a computer, and that each person's chance of selection was the same, approximately one in three.

As part of the application procedure, each youth determined to be eligible completed an interview schedule which included measures of all the major evaluation variables. An O-type clustering technique was used to match subjects into pairs on this set of initial measures. One subject from each pair was then selected randomly for participation in the work experience program; the other was placed in the control group.

The project staff was very pleased with this selection procedure. No complaints were registered by groups in the community. Applicants appeared to understand the procedure and accepted it as reasonable and fair. To our knowledge, there were no challenges by applicants or others over specific selections or any aspect of the process.

Clearly, the local situation is not always conducive to this approach and rationale for participant selection. It is equally clear that this justification for random assignment is relevant to many program evaluations in which evaluators, assuming opposition from program personnel or powerful community interest groups, have employed less powerful designs.

In our national evaluation of programs funded under the LEAA diversion initiative, we attempted to obtain approval from police and juvenile court judges for a two-stage random assignment, from police or probation intake to: (1) the juvenile court or the diversion project, and (2) treatment or no-treatment alternatives at the project. Not all of the eleven funded projects were ultimately able to secure these approvals and implement this design. However, in most cases, random assignment at one of the above two stages was approved and implemented, and random assignment at both stages was implemented by four projects.

It should be noted that even after all parties involved in a program have formally approved a random assignment process, implementation problems remain. In the Oakland study, all assignments were made at one time. Often, however, the pool of eligible participants is generated over an extended period of time, which introduces some problems in maintaining the integrity of the assignment mechanism. Klein (1975) reports a situation in which agency persons had access to the operational mechanism for random assignment and, during the assignment period, deliberately manipulated it to obtain particular assignments for particular youth. In our national evaluation of diversion programs, we also had an extended assignment period and had to maintain a tight control over the assignment process in an effort to protect against this type of contamination.[9] The possibility of some manipulation always remains, and the evaluation design ought to include periodic checks of the procedure to ensure that it is working properly, particularly when it is used over an extended period of time.

The general position taken here is that opportunities for randomized field experiments are greater than many evaluators assume and appear particularly justifiable in the situations described. There may well be other circumstances and situations in which a randomized selection process is justifiable on ethical and practical, as well as scientific, grounds. Our concern is that evaluators often assume a resistance to these more powerful designs and settle for quasi-experimental designs, when a more aggressive, creative approach to the evaluation might result in some type of randomized field experiment.

At the same time, our experience with field experiments using random assignment has led to the realization that this is not a cure-all for evaluation studies. For example, it cannot compensate for an inadequate theoretical rationale, and it does not guarantee clear unequivocal research findings. However, this is certainly not an argument in favor of using quasi-experimental designs. We are inclined to agree with Gilbert et al. (1975) that some of the more frequently used quasi-experimental designs constitute a "fooling around with people" (p. 182). Rather, we are simply calling attention to the fact that the use of a randomized design does not resolve all methodological issues in evaluation studies.

Since evaluation studies almost invariably occur in natural settings, the precision and control which characterize the laboratory experiment is simply not possible. The primary difficulty is that of controlling for what Campbell and Stanley (1963) call history effects, that is, unplanned events occurring during the evaluation in addition to the intended treatment effect. In many instances, there is a related problem which involves an inability to control or manipulate the intended treatment experience. In neither case does random assignment control for these difficulties. The following examples illustrate these problems.

In our evaluation of the Oakland youth work experience program, youth were matched into pairs on impact variables, age, sex, and ethnicity. Then one member was randomly assigned to the work program and the other to the control group. The primary treatment in this program was on-the-job work experience for all youth participating in the program. In addition, participants were given some classroom training to improve basic educational and work skills, and they also participated in group activities designed to provide a positive social setting and group support for the work experience.

The theoretical rationale for this program viewed work as a social bond, integrating disadvantaged youth into conventional social roles and increasing their stake in conformity. The work experience lasted six months, at which point approximately half of the participants dropped out of the work program and the other half were placed in new work situations.

The design involved obtaining initial measures on evaluation variables prior to assignment; a six-month followup measure for both participants and controls, which coincided with termination from the program for half the participants; and a twelve-month followup for both participants and controls, which coincided with termination from the program for the remainder of the original participants.

At the six-month followup, we discovered that 75 percent of the youth in the control group had found work on their own and thus obtained some work experience also. This finding raised a number of questions about the design and the appropriate interpretations of comparisons between program participants and controls.

In this case, the design controlled for participation in the program, and comparisons between participants and controls measured the effects of program participation as compared with nonprogram participation; nonparticipation in this case meant whatever would have happened naturally in the absence of the work program. The treatment in this sense was participation in the program—not work experience per se. Yet from a theoretical viewpoint, the intended treatment was work experience. But the design did not allow for adequate control of this variable, and the participant-control comparison was contaminated with respect to work experience.

The general comparison indicated no statistically significant differences between participants and controls on any of the impact criteria at six months. There was no evidence here of any positive program impact. However, a pure case analysis limited to participant-control pairs in which controls reported no work experience in the six-month evaluation period revealed several significant differences favoring participants. This last finding provided partial support for the theoretical rationale and the postulated effects of work experience.

It is our view that this situation is likely to characterize many delinquency evaluation studies, that is, a situation where random assignment to program and control groups does not adequately control for the planned intervention or treatment. There are two reasons for this.

First, the treatment cannot be restricted to the program participants. The treatment often occurs within the control group as a result of parental action, self-selection, or any number of other operational influences which cannot be controlled by the program or the evaluator.

Unplanned treatment effects in the control group may be handled in the analysis if pretreatment measures are available as control variables, as was the case in the Oakland study. This solution may not be possible if the design involves a post-test-only design, even if a control group and random assignment are involved. Furthermore, controlling for this situation at the analysis level typically involves a reduced number of cases and, unless such an eventuality is anticipated, this may not be a viable solution. In the Oakland study, we anticipated some work experience among controls, but we clearly underestimated the proportion of controls who actually obtained work on their own. The resulting small number of pure cases generated special problems for the analysis.

Second, random assignment to a project may not be equated with random assignment to a specific treatment. Had the participant-control comparisons in the Oakland study revealed more favorable outcomes for participants, it would not have been possible to isolate the independent effects of the various program components (educational training, group support activities, and work experience) and argue that it was work experience that was responsible for the observed impact on outcome variables. Although the rationale of the program focused primarily upon work experience as the treatment variable, participation in the program involved more than work experience.

Depending on the objectives of the evaluation, one ought to randomly assign to the project or to specific treatments. However, this latter option is often not feasible or practical, due to small sample sizes within treatment categories and the frequent use of multiple treatments for individual participants. In the Oakland study, for example, all participants were exposed to all program components.

Our national evaluation of LEAA funded diversion programs provides another illustration of control problems. Youth arrested by the police and determined to be in the eligible pool were randomly assigned to the diversion project or were petitioned into the juvenile court. Those reporting to the diversion project were then randomly assigned to treatment or to no treatment. The three relevant groups for analysis were thus: (1) those petitioned to court, (2) those diverted with services, and (3) those diverted without services. We were aware of the fact that during the treatment period a proportion of youth assigned to each of these dispositions would be rearrested and reprocessed in the system. In some instances, we worked out an agreement with justice system officials whereby these youth would be referred back to their original assignment for all but very serious offenses. The basic problem remains, however, and experience in the justice system occurring after initial assignment will have to be controlled in the analysis. This case provides another demonstration that neither the program nor the evaluator has adequate control over the postulated treatment after initial assignment.

The inability to adequately control for history effects in randomized field experiments requires careful attention to the unforeseen events that can impact on the outcome variables of an evaluation. The first example discussed above, the Oakland study, involved history effects occurring within the control group. The second, the diversion study, involved history effects occurring in both treatment and control groups. Any unplanned and unforeseen events occurring during the study that affect study variables constitute a threat to the internal validity of the study, if not controlled.

The problem is thus a very general one, and it is not solved by the use of random assignment. In most cases, these problems are handled through careful observation and documentation of events occurring during the treatment period and through special data analysis techniques. However, there is no means of ensuring that some unplanned event will not contaminate the design, and evaluators must be prepared to assume some risk when employing randomized field experiments.

Another recurring design issue for evaluation studies involves the timing of observations or measures. Ideally, the timing of observations should be based upon some knowledge about the dynamics of the treatment relative to its postulated effects. The fact is that little is known about the dynamics of many treatment variables, and little attention is paid to the reasonableness of the timing of observations in evaluation designs.

If any justification for particular time lags is offered, it typically involves the reporting requirements of the funding agency, practical problems of tracking or locating participants, or the termination of participants from the project. It is not uncommon to see a single set of time lags employed in the evaluation of a project offering a wide variety of treatments and services which might be expected to have very different dynamics. For example, the effects of short-term family crisis counseling might reasonably be expected to occur over a shorter time period than the effects of an educational skill development program or a work experience program.

In the earlier cited example of a tutorial program which postulated that improved academic skills would result in improved school performance, increased integration into school activities, and ultimately a reduction in delinquent behavior and recidivism, a six-month postentry time lag is clearly unreasonable. It might not be unreasonable to assume that some improvement in academic skills should be observable after six months, or even that there might be some observable improvement in academic performance after six months. However, given the lengthy causal sequence postulated, a reduction in delinquent behavior and rearrests does not seem reasonable with a six-month time lag.

Estimating reasonable time lags is a difficult problem and one that is rarely addressed in delinquency program evaluations. Yet evaluations run the risk of missing or underestimating a true causal relationship by employing time lags which are either too short or too long. Pelz and Lew (1970) present evidence suggesting that, under some circumstances, an inappropriate time lag could even result in incorrect conclusions regarding the direction of the causal influence.

Here, again, an adequate theoretical model should provide some insight into what constitutes a reasonable time lag for specific postulated effects. Also, additional research may provide some empirical evidence on the dynamics of frequently employed treatment variables. In the absence of a theoretical rationale and empirical evidence, Pelz and Lew (1970) recommend that multiple observations (more than two) be built into the design, and that change or differences be measured as a function of measurement lag.

Measurement and Analysis Issues

In large part, measurement and analysis difficulties stem from the absence of explicit theoretical rationales and inadequate evaluation designs. An atheoretical orientation often results in a poor conceptualization of relevant objectives and outcome variables, and it accounts for the general lack of attention to the validity and reliability of measures employed in delinquency program evaluations. We have also argued that it explains the heavy reliance upon recidivism as a single criterion variable for program success.

From our perspective, it is unfortunate when the entire burden of a program's success and support for a theoretical approach to delinquency prevention rides on a recidivism analysis. In our experience, explicit theoretical arguments linking current treatment objectives to a reduction in delinquency are almost uniformly concerned with a reduction in delinquent behavior.

Recidivism, whether measured in terms of rearrests or reconvictions, reflects official law enforcement activity. These official actions are based upon a number of factors in addition to the presumed delinquent behavior, for example, personal attributes, such as age, sex, class, and race; the suspected offender's dress and demeanor; and prior official records. Furthermore, these actions are limited, for the most part, to those delinquent offenses which come to the attention of law enforcement agencies. Yet self-reported delinquency studies suggest that the great majority of delinquent acts never come to the attention of law enforcement agencies (Gold 1966; Empey 1978; Elliott and Voss 1974; Erickson and Empey 1963; Williams and Gold 1972). Given that official actions involve a number of factors in addition to delinquent behavior and reflect only a small fraction of delinquent acts committed, it is apparent that recidivism is neither a very pure nor sensitive measure of delinquent behavior.

In the first instance, we have reason to question the face validity of recidivism as a measure of delinquent behavior. Since the number and relevance of extrabehavioral factors increase with further penetration into the justice system, recidivism measures based on reconviction or recommitment are particularly problematic as measures of delinquent behavior.

In addition to questions of face validity, however, the insensitivity of recidivism to real changes in delinquent behavior renders this measure unsuitable for short-range evaluations of programs aimed at reducing delinquent behavior. Stated simply, it is quite possible for a treatment to have a significant impact on delinquent behavior which is not reflected in a recidivism analysis. Likewise, it is quite possible to observe a change in recidivism when there has been no change in delinquent behavior.[10]

In the absence of a clear theoretical rationale, there is often conceptual confusion between measures of delinquent behavior and measures of official responses to delinquent behavior, but the distinction is critical. For those programs employing individual treatment strategies with the objective of changing the participant's behavior, recidivism is a very poor criterion measure.[11]

A final issue involves the almost exclusive concern in evaluation studies with general overall comparisons between program participants and control groups, or those exposed to a particular treatment and those not exposed to this treatment. While these global findings present an overview of program or treatment success, they may obscure important findings regarding the differential impact of the program-treatment on particular subgroups of participants.

This is essentially a concern over the possibility of an interaction between participant types and types of treatment employed. The argument here is that the treatment may be effective for some participants and not others, or its effects may be positive for some participants and negative for others. In both cases, there is some support for program-treatment effectiveness, but evidence for such outcomes is often obscured by the evaluation design or the form of the analysis.

For example, analyses that focus upon general comparisons of treatment and control group means are likely to miss both of these possible outcomes, even when field experimental designs with random assignment are used. Assuming no through-time change for controls, the situation where the treatment is effective for some participants and not others is likely to produce some differences in treatment and control group means, although they may not be significant. However, where treatment effects are positive for some and negative for others, the comparison could logically result in no difference in pre or post means for the treatment group and no difference between treatment and control group post means. This would be the case whenever positive and negative gains offset one another.

Hood and Sparks report that "fewer than a dozen research projects have been undertaken . . . which permit testing of hypothesis concerning interaction effects" (1970:197). Furthermore, the results of those studies reviewed by Hood and Sparks were not particularly encouraging, as there was little evidence of any true interaction effects.

A major difficulty lies in the construction of reliable participant-offender typologies which have some theoretical relevance for different treatment modes. Admittedly, at the present time there is very limited knowledge about offender typologies, particularly those having some theoretical or empirical relevance for different treatment effects. In most of the studies reviewed by Hood and Sparks, the typologies employed were based upon the I-level (interpersonal maturity) index developed originally by Sullivan, Grant, and Grant (1957). While the available evidence has not demonstrated either the reliability or the utility of this particular typology (Hood and Sparks 1970; Lerman 1975; Beker and Heyman 1972), the fact remains that there have been few evaluations which have utilized offender typologies and looked for offender-treatment interactions.

In our longitudinal study of three diversion projects (Elliott, Dunford, and Knowles 1978), we developed a social-psychological offender typology based upon the OYD national strategy and tested for offender-treatment interactions and for offender-processing alternative interactions (lecture and release, diversion, court). Four offender types were identified using OYD national strategy variables in a multivariate classification analysis (WARD clustering and K-means analyses).

Over the eighteen-month followup period, the global analysis comparing those receiving program treatment with those receiving no treatment found significant diferences in perceived negative labeling. Those receiving treatment or services reported higher levels of perceived negative labeling. However, offender-type interaction effects were observed, indicating that this general effect was occurring for two specific types of youth and not for others. This latter finding constitutes an important qualification on the general finding and demonstrates the importance of designing evaluations and conducting analyses that test for interaction effects.

Conclusion

Although these few issues obviously do not provide a comprehensive or systematic review of delinquency program evaluation problem, they do include serious and frequent problems facing evaluation researchers and practitioners. Clearly, their satisfactory resolution would enhance both the quality and the utility of evaluation studies, and it is to this end that we have shared our experience and offered suggestions for dealing with these issues.

At present, the poor quality of delinquency evaluation studies precludes almost any firm, definitive conclusions about the effectiveness of any specific program or treatment. In this sense, Romig's conclusions (1978) regarding the effectiveness of specific treatments appear premature. In most cases, it is impossible to distinguish program failure from theory failure, and it is equally difficult to establish causal influence in those instances where favorable outcomes are observed for treatment-program groups.

However, we have been encouraged over the course of our own evaluation experience, and we believe that the future provides some promise for better quality evaluations—more explicit theoretical models, more frequent use of experimental designs, more sophisticated approaches to measurement and analysis, and more definitive conclusions.

Notes

1. For a recent review of specific treatment approaches, see Romig (1978).

2. There are those who take exception to this experimental approach and propose substantially different approaches to evaluation. For example, see Guttentag (1973) for an alternative model based upon decision theory.

3. The Delinquency Prevention Act of 1974 transferred the responsibility for delinquency programming from HEW to LEAA. OYD funding ended for most programs during 1975.

4. Klein reports on a site visit to an OYD-funded project where "the Director could not name, nor did he recognize, a single component of the (OYD) strategy" (1979:17).

5. Others have documented the almost exclusive reliance on counseling within delinquency prevention-treatment programs. See Dunford (1977), Klein (1979), Klein and Teilmann (1976), and Bohnstedt et al. (1975).

6. It was clear from the evaluation of these particular projects that a "widening of the net" was occurring, and that police and probation personnel were referring youth to diversion programs whom they would have lectured and released in the absence of that program. This was particularly true for the first year of operation for most of the projects we examined. There appeared to be an initial reaction upon the part of the police and probation personnel to new diversion programs, which resulted in their referring cases that they would otherwise have lectured and released. For those programs which survived for a longer period of time and developed good relationships with the police and court, there was evidence in many cases of an increasing willingness on the part of justice personnel to refer cases that they would have otherwise formally processed, that is, police maintenance probabilities tended to decrease and diversion increased as the programs became more established in the community.

7. It is our impression that the evaluations had little or no effect on future funding by YDDPA or OYD.

8. In several instances, we were able to work with HEW projects included in the 1973 and 1974 national evaluations in the development of theoretical rationales consistent with the OYD national strategy. Our success in this area appeared to be at least partly a function of the type of staffing philosophy utilized by the programs. Most programs hired persons with prior juvenile justice (often police or probation), or other social service agency, backgrounds and experience. Rarely were we successful in developing a theoretical rationale with these project staffs. Their focus was upon particular treatment modes and techniques which they were hired to deliver. They were generally threatened by any discussion of theoretical relevance. On the other hand, projects which hired recent college graduates, or persons

with little or no prior experience with justice or social service agencies, tended to be more open and willing to consider the relationship between program components and theoretical issues.

9. In the negotiation for random assignment, the specific mechanism proposed for obtaining random assignment was often critical, and evaluators ought to be armed with a number of different methods for obtaining randomization. In our national evaluation of diversion programs, the specific mechanisms employed varied by project and reflected the results of this negotiation process.

10. Several HEW-funded projects included in our 1973 and 1974 national evaluations had worked out special arrangements with the police whereby youth in their programs were referred directly back to the project, without arrest or official action, if apprehended for any nonviolent crime. The net effect of this informal arrangement between the projects and police was a reduction in recidivism rates for program participants, which was unrelated to any changes in their delinquent behavior.

11. It should be noted that arrest and processing measures are appropriate criteria measures for some delinquency prevention programs. For example, diversion projects which have a reduction in penetration as a program objective are directly concerned with changing official responses to delinquency—reducing the number or proportions of youth arrested, petitioned into court, and adjudicated delinquent. Processing measures based upon these specific decisions within the juvenile justice system are thus appropriate criteria for such programs.

References

Beker, J. and Heyman, D.S. (1972). "A Critical Appraisal of the California differential treatment typology of adolescent offenders." *Criminology* 10:3-59.

Bohnstedt, Marvin, et al. (1975). *The Evaluation of Juvenile Diversion Programs*. Sacramento: California Youth Authority.

Boruch, Robert F. (1975). "On common contentions about randomized field experiments." In Robert F. Boruch and Henry W. Riecken (eds.), *Experimental Testing of Public Policy: The Proceedings of the 1974 Social Science Research Council Conference on Social Experiments*, pp. 107-145. Boulder: Westview.

Boruch, Robert F., McSweeney, A. John, and Soderstrom, E. Jon (1978). "Randomized field experiments for program planning, development, and evaluation: an illustrative bibliography." *Evaluation Quarterly* 2:655-695.

BREC (1973). *National Evaluation of Youth Services System: Final Report.* HEW-SRS-72-72. Boulder: Behavioral Research and Evaluation Corporation.

_____ (1974). *National Evaluation of Youth Services System: Final Report.* HEW-OS-73-214. Boulder: Behavioral Research and Evaluation Corporation.

Cain, Glen G., and Hollister, Robinson G. (1972). "The methodology of evaluating social action programs." In Peter H. Rossi and Walter Williams (eds.), *Evaluating Social Programs*, pp. 109-137. New York: Seminar.

Campbell, Donald T. (1975). "Reform as experiments." In Elmer L. Struening and Marcia Guttentag (eds.), *Handbook of Evaluation Research*, vol. 1, pp. 71-100. Beverly Hills: Sage.

Campbell, Donald T., and Stanley, Julian C. (1963). "Experimental and quasi-experimental designs for research on teaching." In N.L. Gage (ed.), *Handbook of Research on Teaching*, pp. 171-246. Chicago: Rand McNally.

CAR (1976). *A Design for Youth Development Policy.* Contract No. HEW-105-75-2107. Boulder: Center for Action Research, University of Colorado.

Cartwright, Desmond S. (1971). "Conceptual issues in the national strategy for delinquency prevention." As summarized by Charles Taylor, in *National Strategy for Youth Development and Delinquency Prevention and Conceptual Issues*, pp. 27-62. Document No. 34. Boulder: Center for Action Research, University of Colorado.

Dunford, Franklyn W. (1977). "Police diversion: an illusion?" *Criminology* 15:335-352.

Elliott, Delbert S., Ageton, Suzanne S., Hunter, Margaret, and Knowles, Brian A. (1975). *Research Handbook for Community Planning and Feedback Instruments*, vol. I. HEW-OS-74-308. Boulder: Behavioral Research and Evaluation Corporation.

Elliott, Delbert S. (1971). "The prevention of delinquency through youth development: strategy and project evaluation." In *National Strategy for Youth Development and Delinquency Prevention and Conceptual Issues*, pp. 13-26. Document No. 34. Boulder: Center for Action Research, University of Colorado.

Elliott, Delbert S., Dunford, Franklyn W., and Knowles, Brian A. (1978). *Summary Report: Diversion—A Study of Alternative Processing Practices.* NIMH Grant No. MH26141. Boulder: Behavioral Research Institute.

Elliott, Delbert S. and Knowles, Brian A. (1978). "Social development and employment: an evaluation of the Oakland Youth Work Experience Program." In *Conference Report on Youth Unemployment: Its*

Measurement and Meaning, pp. 287-321. U.S. Department of Labor. Washington, D.C.: U.S. Government Printing Office.

Elliott, Delbert S. and Voss, Harwin (1974). *Delinquency and Dropout*. Lexington, Mass.: Lexington Books, D.C. Heath.

Empey, LaMar T. (1978). *American Delinquency*. Homewood, Ill.: Dorsey.

Erickson, Maynard L., and Empey, LaMar T. (1963). "Court records, undetected delinquency and decisionmaking." *Journal of Criminal Law, Criminology, and Police Science* 54:456-469.

Etzioni, Amitai (1960). "Two approaches to organizational analysis: a critique and a suggestion." *Administration Science Quarterly* 5:257-278.

Gemignani, Robert J. (1971). "National Strategy for Youth Development and Delinquency Prevention." In *National Strategy for Youth Development and Delinquency Prevention and Conceptual Issues*, pp. 1-12. Document No. 34. Boulder: Center for Action Research, University of Colorado.

_____ (1976). "Youth services systems." In Robert M. Carter and Malcolm W. Klein (eds.), *Back on the Street: The Diversion of Juvenile Offenders*, pp. 55-67. Englewood Cliffs, N.J.: Prentice-Hall.

Gilbert, J.P., Light, R.J., and Mosteller, F. (1975). "Assessing social innovations: an experimental base for policy." In Carl A. Bennett and Arthur A. Lumsdaine (eds.), *Evaluation and Experiment: Some Critical Issues in Assessing Social Programs*, pp. 39-194. New York: Academic Press.

Glass, Gene V. (ed.) (1976). *Evaluation Studies Review Annual*, vol. 1. Beverly Hills: Sage.

Gold, Martin (1966). "Undetected delinquent behavior." *Journal of Research in Crime and Delinquency* 3:27-46.

Guttentag, Marcia (1973). "Subjectivity and its use in evaluation research." *Evaluation* 1:60-65.

Guttentag, Marcia (ed.) (1977). *Evaluation Studies Review Annual*, vol. 2. Beverly Hills: Sage.

Hackler, James C. (1967). "Evaluation of delinquency prevention programs: ideals and compromises." *Federal Probation* 31:22-26.

Hirschi, Travis, and Selvin, Hanan C. (1967). *Delinquency Research*. New York: Free Press.

Hood, Roger, and Sparks, Richard (1970). *Key Issues in Criminology*. New York: World University Library, McGraw-Hill.

Klein, Malcolm W. (1975). *Alternative Dispositions for Juvenile Offenders*. Los Angeles: Social Science Research Institute, University of Southern California.

_____ (1979). "Deinstitutionalization and diversion of juvenile offenders: a litany of impediments." In Norval Morris and Michael Tonry (eds.), *Criminal Justice, 1978*. Chicago: University of Chicago Press (in press).

Klein, Malcolm W., and Teilmann, Kathleen S. (1976). Pivotal Ingredients in Police Diversion Programs. Report to the National Institute for Juvenile Justice and Delinquency Prevention, Office of Juvenile Justice and Delinquency Administration, Law Enforcement Assistance Administration.

LEAA (1976). Program Announcement: Diversion of Youth from the Juvenile Justice System. Office of Juvenile Justice and Delinquency Administration, Law Enforcement Assistance Administration, U.S. Department of Justice.

Lerman, Paul (1975). *Community Treatment and Social Control: A Critical Analysis of Juvenile Correctional Policy.* Chicago: University of Chicago Press.

Patton, Michael (1978). *Utilization: Focused Evaluation.* Beverly Hills: Sage.

Pelz, Donald C., and Lew, Robert A. (1970). "Heise's Causal Model Applied." In Edgar F. Borgatta and George W. Bohrnstedt (eds.), *Sociological Methodology, 1970*, pp. 28-37. San Francisco: Jossey-Bass.

Polk, Kenneth, and Kobrin, Sol (1972). Delinquency prevention through youth development. SRS 73-26013. U.S. Department of Health, Education and Welfare.

Riecken, Henry W., and Boruch, Robert F. (1974). *Social Experimentation: A Method for Planning and Evaluating Social Intervention.* New York: Academic.

Romig, Dennis A. (1978). *Justice for Our Children: An Examination of Juvenile Delinquent Rehabilitation Programs.* Lexington, Mass.: Lexington Books, D.C. Heath.

Short, James F., Jr. (1975). "The natural history of an applied theory: differential opportunity and 'mobilization for youth'." In N.J. Demerath III, Otto Larsen, and Karl F. Schuessler (eds.), *Social Policy and Sociology*, pp. 193-210. New York: Academic Press.

Stanford Evaluation Consortium (1976). "Evaluating the *Handbook of Evaluating Research.*" In Gene V. Glass (ed.), *Evaluation Studies Review Annual*, vol. 1, pp. 195-215. Beverly Hills: Sage.

Struening, Elmer L., and Guttentag, Marcia (eds.) (1975). *Handbook of Evaluation Research*, vol. 1. Beverly Hills: Sage.

Suchman, Edward A. (1972). "Action for what? A critique of evaluative research." In Carol H. Weiss (ed.), *Evaluating Action Programs: Readings in Social Action and Education*, pp. 52-84. Boston: Allyn and Bacon.

Sullivan, Clyde E., Grant, Marguerite Q., and Grant, Douglas J. (1957). "The development of interpersonal maturity: applications to delinquency." *Psychiatry* 20:373-385.

VanMaanen, John (1979). "The process of program evaluation." *Grantsmanship Center News* 5:29-74.

Weiss, Carol H. (1975). "Evaluation research in the political context." In Elmer L. Struening and Marcia Guttentag (eds.), *Handbook of Evaluation Research*, vol. 1, pp. 13-26. Beverly Hills: Sage.

Weiss, Carol H. (ed.) (1972). *Evaluating Action Programs: Readings in Social Action and Education*. Boston: Allyn and Bacon.

Williams, Jay R., and Gold, Martin (1972). "From delinquent behavior to official delinquency." *Social Problems* 20:209-229.

13 Primary Prevention of Juvenile Delinquency

Sarnoff A. Mednick

In March 1979 Attorney General Griffin B. Bell reported that FBI national crime statistics for 1978 indicate a 5 percent increase in violent offenses (*Los Angeles Times*, March 28, 1979). This is not welcome news, especially after the leveling off and decrease of the U.S. crime rate in recent years. Most disheartening is the focus of this increase in youngsters; more crimes are now being committed by children under fifteen than adults over twenty-five! In the past twenty years juvenile crime has increased 1,600 percent (Godwin 1978). These youngsters are not going to be rehabilitated over-night. They are walking time bombs with long careers ahead of them.

What has been society's response to this threat? In 1969 the Law Enforcement Assistance Administration began a program aimed at reducing crime. Over the subsequent eight years it expended over $5 billion. Unfortunately most of it (85 percent) was earmarked for state and local governments which (in the main) proceeded to buy hardware. The 500,000 or so uniformed police in the United States have enough guns, helmets, armored vehicles, and gas grenades to conquer and hold a medium-sized country. But they cannot do much about street crime. One critic has described the government's crime-fighting program as resembling "a doctor trying to treat a German measles epidemic by dabbing at the individual spots on his patients' skin." (Godwin 1978:350).

The analogy to the medical situation is not poorly taken. There are interesting parallels between medical science's struggles with controlling disease and society's struggles with controlling crime. Perhaps we can learn something from the shared failures.

The great successes of recent medical research are centered in techniques for treating and maintaining those already stricken with illness. Intensive care units are electronic marvels; we transplant hearts and kidneys. If we do not have a natural kidney at hand we can construct a machine. The wonder drugs have reduced the threat of some of the previous great killing diseases such as pneumonia.

But despite this success the medical bills of the developed nations increase annually almost geometrically. Much of this societal cost and investment has

The material in this chapter formed the essence of a talk given at the University of Southern California April 2, 1979. Mednick's work on this material is supported by USPHS grant No. MH 31352 and LEAA contract No. 78-NI-AX-0088.

little impact on rates of disease onset. The research effort is mainly responsive to already developed illnesses and is heavily invested in methods of maintaining the chronically ill. Paradoxically, the sheer magnitude of society's problems are being increased by our laudable success at prolonging the lives of the chronically ill. I would argue that along with this development of treatment technology we should allocate resources to research in the primary prevention of illness. Consider smallpox and polio.

Just as in medicine, our major efforts to control crime start with the individual already delinquent or criminal. We spend fortunes on developing mace, nicer jails, methods of rehabilitation, and faster court systems. Less effort is expended on the primary prevention of crime. I wish to suggest that along with efforts to deal with discovered criminality, we consider methods of early intervention to prevent the initial onset of criminal behavior.

I can imagine three avenues in which primary intervention might be explored: (1) Ecological alterations, (2) Systematic societal change, and (3) Individual intervention.

1. Ecological alteration. By ecological alteration I refer to environmental manipulation which discourages crime such as increasing street lighting, improving supermarket and department store security, and defensive architectural design. I will not consider this method further.

2. Societal change. In this century criminology has been dominated by sociological thinking—and for good reason. It seems quite clear that socioeconomic factors provide the reasons for crime for most criminals. Sociological thinking has suggested that the etiology of crime lies in the structure of society. It is expressly assumed that criminals are normal individuals who have been misshapen by an inappropriately arranged social system. If we improve this system this should prevent criminality.

3. Individual intervention. A critical assumption of this approach to primary prevention is the essential normality of criminals. To the extent that some criminals have deviant psychological or biological characteristics which help predispose them to antisocial behavior, societal manipulation alone will not be sufficient to prevent crime. Thus, in order to better plan the primary prevention of criminal behavior we must first consider evidence regarding the possibility that some forms of criminal behavior have individual psychological or biological predispositions.

I will review evidence which bears on this issue. First I will discuss genetic research, then physiological studies, and finally suggestive crime statistics. Then I will attempt to imagine how some specific biological factor might interact with social variables to increase the likelihood that an individual will fail to learn to behave morally.

Heritability of Antisocial Behavior

What is the point of examining the genetics literature? Only one, from my point of view. If it can be demonstrated that there is some genetic contribution to some forms of criminality, then consideration of a partial biological etiology for antisocial behavior would be forced on us. This would have implications for directions of research.

Two valuable strategies for studying the influence of genetic factors on behavior are the twin and adoption methods. In the adoption method we study individuals adopted at birth who later become criminal or psychopathic. Because environment and genetics are thus relatively well separated, we can evaluate the relative influence of these two factors by studying the criminality in the adoptee's biological and adoptive families. The twin method capitalizes on the fact that monozygotic (MZ) twins have essentially identical genetic structures, whereas dizygotic (DZ) twins are not more similar genetically than are siblings. If criminality within pairs of MZ twins is markedly more similar (or concordant) than is criminality within pairs of DZ twins, this may not be seen as evidence against a possible genetic influence. Conclusions from twin research related to genetics are somewhat weakened, however, by assertions that MZ twins have more mutually similar environments than do DZ twins (Christiansen 1977b). Thus environment as well as genetics may be more similar for MZ twins. On the other hand, environmental conditions during pregnancy, delivery, and postnatally may produce differences between MZ twins. Because of these factors the twin studies must be interpreted cautiously.

Twin Studies

In the first twin-criminality study, Lange (1929), found 77 percent concordance for MZ twins and 12 percent concordance for DZ twins. Subsequently, studies of twins (see table 13-1) tended to confirm Lange's results. About 60 percent concordance has been reported for MZ and about 30 percent concordance for DZ twins.

These eight twin studies suffer from the fact that their sampling was biased or even rather haphazard. They report too high a proportion of MZ twins. MZ pairs, concordant for criminality, are more likely to be noted. MZ twins prove easier to detect, especially if they end up in the same prison. All these factors tend to inflate MZ concordance in asystematic studies.

Christiansen (1977a) in Copenhagen overcame these sampling problems by studying all twins born in a well-defined area of Denmark between 1881 and 1910. Of 3,586 such twin pairs he found 799 pairs with at least one of

Table 13-1
Studies of Psychopathy and Criminality for Monozygotic
and Same-sexed Dizygotic Twins

		Monozygotic			Dizygotic		
Study	*Location*	*Total Pairs*	*Pairs Concor- dant*	*Percent Con- cordant*	*Total Pairs*	*Pairs Concor- dant*	*Percent Con- cordant*
Lange, 1929	Bavaria	13	10	77	17	2	12
Legras, 1932	Holland	4	4	100	5	1	20
Rosanoff, 1934	United States	37	25	68	28	5	18
Stumpfl, 1936	Germany	18	11	61	19	7	37
Kranz, 1936	Prussia	32	21	66	43	23	54
Borgstrom, 1939	Finland	4	3	75	5	2	40
Slater, 1953 (psychopathy)	England	2	1	50	10	3	30
Yoshimasu, 1961	Japan	28	17	61	18	2	11
Total		138	92	67.2	145	45	31.0

Source: Table adapted from Christiansen (1968) and Rosenthal (1972).

the twins registered for criminality or minor criminality. He reported a pairwise concordance rate of 36 percent for the MZ twins and 12.5 percent for the DZ. The MZ concordance is 2.8 times higher than the DZ concordance. Christiansen's study is now being extended to all twins born up until 1920 and will include all of Denmark. This will bring the number of twins up to approximately 14,000 pairs. This number should be sufficient for a more detailed analysis than has been possible before. Despite the cautions mentioned, this study does not argue against the existence of some genetic effect in criminality.

Dalgaard and Kringlen (1977) have recently completed a study in Norway which involved a representative, but small, population of twins born from 1921 to 1930. Their MZ pairwise concordance rate for serious criminality was 25.8 percent; their DZ pairwise concordance rate was 14.9 percent. This is the smallest MZ-DZ difference recorded in twin literature, but the results are in the same direction as all the other work.

I urge those interested to study Christiansen's detailed review of these twin studies (Christiansen 1977b). Despite the weaknesses of the twin method, we can certainly state that the reported findings do not argue for rejection of the hypothesis assigning a partial etiological role to genetic factors.

Adoption Studies

A weakness of the twin method for drawing conclusions relating to genetics is the fact that in the overwhelming number of cases the twins are raised together. Thus genetic and environmental factors are not well separated. A design which does a better job in this regard studies individuals adopted at birth. Fortunately, a register of all nonfamilial adoptions in Denmark in the years 1924-1947 has been established (Kety et al. 1968), at the Psykologisk Institut. There are 14,300 adoptions recorded including information on the adoptee and his biological and adoptive parents.

I will report two investigations completed on this material studying adoptees born in Copenhagen. I will also describe a U.S. study by Crowe. From 5,483 Copenhagen adoptees, Schulsinger (1977) identified 57 psychopaths from the psychiatric registers and police files. His definition of psychopathy was reliable and specified. Schulsinger also selected 57 non-psychopathic control adoptees matched for sex, age, social class, neighborhood of rearing, and age of transfer to the adoptive family. Despite the small sample, it is clear from table 13-2 that the heaviest weight of psychopathy in the relatives comes in the cell concerning the biological relatives of the psychopathic adoptees. Since the postnatal contact between the adoptee and the relative was in most cases nonexistent or at most minimal, environmental factors probably did not play a very important role in this relationship. The existence of some heritable factor seems the most reasonable interpretation.

Table 13-2
Psychopathy in Relatives of Psychopathic Adoptees and Control Adoptees

Relationship	Biological Relatives	Adoptive Relatives
Psychopathy in relatives		
Psychopathic adoptees	$\frac{12}{305} = 3.9\%$	$\frac{1}{131} = 0.8\%$
Control adoptees	$\frac{4}{285} = 1.4\%$	$\frac{2}{133} = 1.5\%$
Psychopathy in parents		
Psychopathic adoptees	$\frac{5}{111} = 4.5\%$	$\frac{1}{111} = 0.9\%$
Control adoptees	$\frac{1}{113} = 0.9\%$	$\frac{0}{114} = 0\%$
Psychopathy in fathers		
Psychopathic adoptees	$\frac{5}{54} = 9.3\%$	$\frac{1}{54} = 1.9\%$
Control adoptees	$\frac{1}{56} = 1.8\%$	$\frac{0}{57} = 0\%$

Note: The above contingency tables were constructed from data in F. Schulsinger (1972).

Using part of the same adoptee material, Hutchings and Mednick (1977) conducted a pilot study on the registered criminality of a sample of 1,145 male adoptees born in Copenhagen between 1927 and 1941. Of these 1,145 male adoptees, 185 or 16.2 percent had been convicted of a violation of the Danish Penal Code. Of these 185 criminals we were able to identify 143 for each of whom we were certain of the biological father's identity and where the fathers had been born after 1890 (since better police records were kept after 1890). To each of these 143 criminal adoptees we matched a noncriminal adoptive son for age of child and social class of adoptive father. For the criminal and noncriminal groups the age of parents and the age of child at adoption were examined; interestingly enough, they proved to be about the same, suggesting that these variables were not related to the child's later criminality. The amount of contact between the adoptee and the biological father was, in almost all cases, none at all. Table 13-3A indicates that the weight of the registered criminality in the fathers is in the cell of the biological fathers of the criminal adoptees. Again, we have evidence that genetic factors play some partial role in the etiology of registered criminality.

Table 13-3B presents this information in a different form, analogous to the cross-fostering paradigm. As can be seen in the lower right-hand cell, if neither the biological nor the adoptive father is criminal, 10.5 percent of their sons are criminal. If the biological father is not criminal but the adoptive father is criminal, this figure rises to only 11.5 percent. But, as is illustrated in the lower left-hand cell, if the biological father is criminal and the adoptive father is not criminal, 22 percent of the sons are criminal. The genetic influence is highly significant, and the direction and extent of the differences are clear. This seems to suggest that a partial genetic etiology

Table 13-3
Registered Criminality in Biological and Adoptive Fathers of Criminal Adoptees

	Biological Father	Adoptive Father
Criminal adoptive sons (143)	70	33
Control adoptive sons (143)	40	14

| | | Cross Fostering Analysis: Is Biological Father Criminal?[a] | |
		Yes	No
Is Adoptive Father Criminal?	Yes	36.2% (of 58)	11.5% (of 52)
	No	22% (of 219)	10.5% (of 333)

[a]Tabled values are percentage of adoptive sons who are registered criminals.

assumption may not be totally inaccurate. Note that in this table, the influence of the adoptive father's criminality is only statistically significant (36.2 percent versus 22 percent) in those sons with biological criminal fathers.

We have now extended this study to include all of the 14,300 adoptions in the Kingdom of Denmark from 1924 to 1947. Including the biological parents and adoptive parents gives us a population of over 70,000 individuals. The results shown in table 13-3 are strongly supported by preliminary analyses of the data of the extended study.

I must caution that simply knowing that the adoptive father has been a criminal does not tell us how criminogenic the adoptee's environment has been. On the other hand, just a second after conception the genetic influence of the father is already complete. Thus, as we have arranged the cross-fostering table, it is not a fair comparison between environmental and genetic influences.

There are a number of other difficulties with the adoption method which should be pointed out. The adoption agency consciously attempts to match the biological and adoptive parents. The adoptive parents are informed regarding criminal behavior on the part of the biological parents. Results of this study in Denmark should not be casually generalized to other nations without careful evaluation. (See Mednick and Hutchings, 1977 for further discusison of the limitations of the adoptee method.)

A third adoptee project has been completed by Crowe (1975) in Iowa. This investigation found forty-one female inmates of a reformatory who had given up their children for adoption. He selected controls from a state adoptions register and matched them to the experimental group for age, sex, race, and age of adoption. Eight of the index cases and two of the controls had arrest records. The index cases had eighteen records of arrest, the controls two arrests. Seven of the index cases had been convicted, only one of the controls. Crowe further notes an apparent similarity in the types of crimes of the biological mother and the index cases. This suggests the possibility of some form of specificity of genetic effect. At present, Hutchings and Mednick are extending the adoptee-criminality study to encompass the entire 14,300 adoptees and their adoptive and biological parents. From study of these individuals and Christiansen's 14,000 twin pairs, it should be possible to test a more precise question regarding the genetic specificity of type of crime.

The evidence of these twin and adoptee studies lends some credence to a hypothesis partially involving genetically influenced factors in the etiology of antisocial behavior. As suggested above, this implies rather forcefully that biological factors are, to some extent, involved in the etiology of antisocial behavior. There is no suggestion in these findings that biological factors predestine criminality in some inevitable, fateful manner. Rather, they suggest there must be some biosocial interaction at work.

These findings suggest that there are individual factors which partially determine the probability that a person will become a criminal. Perhaps societal manipulation will not be totally effective as a primary prevention method.

Physiological Factors

The twin and adoption studies urge us to search for biological differences between criminals and noncriminals. If we find such differences they may have implications for our choice of primary prevention methods.

My own involvement in criminology research came about through a longitudinal study of 311 Danish children who had schizophenic mothers and thus were themselves at high risk for schizophrenia (Mednick et al. 1974). In 1962 we examined the autonomic nervous system functioning of these children. A measure of special interest was skin conductance, a peripheral indicant of autonomic nervous system (ANS) activity. We noted and have published several papers on the autonomic reactiveness of children who later became schizophrenic (Mednick et al. 1974; Mednick 1979). But 36 of our subjects eventually became criminal. We checked and noticed that in 1962 when they were children, their ANS reactiveness was abornormally small and their recovery was very slow (Loeb and Mednick 1977).

The results are reminiscent of early work by Lykken (1957) who found that psychopathic individuals tend to be sluggish ANS responders. Since that time a number of investigators in England, Sweden, Denmark, the United States, and Canada have found the criminal or the psychopath to tend to evidence very low ANS responsiveness and slow ANS recovery (see review by Siddle 1977). Two studies are especially interesting. Wadsworth (1976) traced all the males registered for delinquency from a sample of 13,687 births which occurred in England, Wales, and Scotland between March 3 and 9 in 1946. When these individuals were eleven years old they had a school medical examination during which their pulse rate in response to a mild stress was measured. This pulse rate was abnormally low in those boys who became delinquent in the ensuing ten years.

Hare, in 1967, measured skin conductance in a group of prisoners at a maximum security prison in Canada. He found their skin conductance to be abnormally low if they were more serious criminals. Ten years later (1977) he checked to see how recidivistic these same prisoners had been. Those who had committed additional crimes had (in 1967) slower recovery. Thus in these two studies abnormally diminished autonomic reactiveness and slow recovery predicted criminality ten years later. This is impressive in the one case because of the representativeness of the population and in the other case because the discrimination could be made within a group of maximum security prisoners.

More recently we have ascertained the recorded delinquency of a group of Danish children we have followed now for eight years. Part of our original assessment of these children included a computer-scored electroencephalogram. These EEG data, taken at age eleven, predict rather well the later delinquency of the boys in this group.

All of these results suggest that there are individual biological variables that are characteristic of those who evidence antisocial behavior. Note also that in many cases these measures were taken well before the individuals embarked on a serious criminal career. Thus the measures could not be the result of the criminal career. In addition these measures are predictive and thus could conceivably form some part of a test battery to select those at high risk of delinquency for research on preventive intervention.

Heritability of ANS Recovery Rate

In view of the relationship between ANS variables and antisocial behavior and in view of our interest in better understanding the apparent genetic predisposition to antisocial behavior, we next turned to a study of the possible heritability of ANS behavior (Bell et al. 1977). Male twelve-year-old twin pairs were studied. Interestingly enough, among the physiological measures only ANS recovery proved to have significant heritability ($H = .89$). This finding suggested that part of the heritability of antisocial behavior might be related to the heritability of ANS recovery. Thus, ANS slow recovery might be a characteristic a criminal parent could pass to a biological son which (in combination with the proper environmental circumstances) could increase the probability of the child's failing to learn adequately to inhibit antisocial responses. Thus we would predict that criminal parents would have children with slow recovery.

Table 13-4 presents data on the electrodermal behavior of children with criminal and noncriminal fathers. As can be seen, results are consistent with the prediction regarding ANS recovery. It is interesting that the pattern of responsiveness of these children closely resembles that which we might anticipate seeing in their criminal fathers.

I will briefly mention one other indirect fact which suggests that individual factors may help determine the probability that a person will exhibit antisocial behavior. In an important study in Philadelphia, Wolfgang, Sellin, and Figlio have shown clearly that about 6 percent of the males are responsible for over 50 percent of the serious crimes in that city. We have observed the same effect in a study of a large birth cohort in Copenhagen. Farrington (1979) reports the same relationship for inner London. The concentration of the serious crimes in a very small subgroup of the population suggests that perhaps these highly active criminals have some individual

Table 13-4

Skin Conductance Behavior during Orienting Response Testing in Children with Criminal and Noncriminal Fathers

| Skin Conductance Function (right hand) | Mean Score | | F | df | p |
	Noncriminal Father	Criminal Father			
Basal level skin conductance	2.51	2.33	.09	1,193	n.s.
Amplitude (in micromhos)	.031	.016	.03	1,193	n.s.
Number of responses	2.79	1.55	8.51	1,187	.01
Response onset latency (in seconds)	2.11	2.18	.07	1,97	n.s.
Latency to response peak (in seconds)	2.05	2.38	5.32	1,95	.05
Average half recovery time (in seconds)	3.75	5.43	4.26	1,90	.05
Minimum half recovery time	2.26	4.33	8.80	1,90	.01

Note: During orienting response testing, the child was presented fourteen times with a tone of 1,000 Hz; n.s. = not significant.

characteristics which make their serious criminality more probable. (See Carlsson, 1977, for a detailed discussion of this idea.)

A Theory

Lawful behavior is moral behaivor. I would now like to close with a suggestion as to how a biological variable might interact with social forces to produce moral behavior.

Perhaps it would do no great harm to begin with a discussion of how I define morality. An early publication on this topic is summarized in table 13-5. Note that the major thrust of the message is negative, "Thou shalt *not* . . ." Although subsequent moral authorities have added *some* positive acts to elaborate the definition of moral behavior (for example, "love thy neighbor"), they have also retained the original, basic, inhibitory definitions of moral acts. There are very few who will denounce you if you do not love your neighbor; if you seduce his wife, steal from him, or kill him (and you are detected), however, you may be certain that your behavior will be classified as immoral. Thus, putting aside (for the moment) highly philosophical, poetic, or artistic musings on morality, we might admit to ourselves that the statements of moral behavior which are critical for everyday activities are essentially negative and inhibitory in character. The fact that someone took the trouble to enumerate these strictures and then carve them onto stone tablets, suggests that there must have been a strong need for the insistence on these inhibitions.

Table 13-5
The Ten Commandments

Thou shalt *not* have other gods before me.
Thou shalt *not* make any graven image.
Thou shalt *not* take the name of the Lord in vain.
Remember the Sabbath Day.
Honor thy father and thy mother.
Thou shalt *not* kill.
Thou shalt *not* steal.
Thou shalt *not* commit adultery.
Thou shalt *not* bear false witness.
Thou shalt *not* covet thy neighbor's home, wife, maidservant, ox, ass.

People must have evidenced and still do evidence a tendency to exhibit aggressive, adulterous, and avaricious behavior. In self-defense, society has set up moral codes and has struggled to teach its children to inhibit impulses leading to transgression of those codes.

How are these inhibitions taught to children? As far as I can see there are three mechanisms which might help parents teach children civilized behavior—modeling, positive reinforcement, and negative reinforcement. I believe that positive acts such as loving neighbors, helping old people across the street, and cleaning the snow and ice from the front walk can be learned by modeling, but for the more inhibitory moral commands, modeling does not seem to be a natural method. It is possible to imagine arranging circumstances in some artificial way, such that modeling *could* teach children not to be adulterous, or aggressive. However, if our civilization had to depend solely on modeling it is conceivable that things might be even more chaotic than they are today.

It is also possible to use positive reinforcement to teach inhibition of forbidden behavior; but again, reinforcing a child twenty-four hours a day while he is *not* stealing seems a rather inefficient method and not very specific. Following the excellent exposition of Gordon Trasler (1972) I would suggest that the avoidance of transgression (that is, lawful behavior) demanded by the moral commandments is probably in the main learned via contingent negative reinforcements (punishments) applied by society, family, and peers. I would guess that the critical morality-training forces in childhood are (1) the punishment of antisocial responses by family, society, and friends and (2) the child's individual capacity to learn to inhibit antisocial responses.

Let us take a specific example. How do children learn to inhibit aggressive impulses? Frequently when child A is aggressive to child B, child A is punished by a peer or perhaps his mother. After a sufficient quantity or quality of puniushment, just the thought of the aggression should be enough to produce a bit of anticipatory fear in child A. If this fear response is large enough, the raised arm will drop and the aggressive response will be successfully inhibited.

Our story suggests that what happens in this child after he has successfully inhibited such an antisocial response is critical for his learning of civilized behavior. Let us consider the situation again in more detail. (1) Child A contemplates aggressive action. (2) Because of previous punishment he suffers fear. (3) He inhibits the aggressive response. What happens to his anticipatory fear? (4) It will begin to dissipate, to be reduced. We know that fear-reduction is the most powerful, naturally occurring reinforcement that psychologists have discovered. So the reduction of fear (which immediately follows the inhibition of the aggression) can act as a reinforcement for this inhibition and will result in the learning of the inhibition of aggression. The fear-reduction-reinforcement increases the probability that the inhibition of the aggression will occur in the future. After many such experiences, the normal child will learn to inhibit aggressive impulses. Each time such an impulse arises and is inhibited, the inhibition will be strengthened by reinforcement.

What does a child need in order to learn effectively to be civilized (in the context of this approach)?

1. A censuring agent (typically family)
2. An adequate fear response
3. The ability to learn the fear response in anticipation of an asocial act
4. Fast dissipation of fear to quickly reinforce the inhibitory response

Now we wish to concentrate on point 4. The speed and size of a reinforcement determine its effectiveness. An effective reinforcement is one which is delivered immediately after the relevant response. In terms of this discussion, the faster the reduction of fear, the faster the delivery of the reinforcement. The fear response is, to a large extent, controlled by the autonomic nervous system. We can estimate the activity of the ANS by means of peripheral indicants such as heart rate, blood pressure, and skin conductance. The measure of most relevance will peripherally reflect the rate or speed at which the ANS recovers from periods of imbalance.

If child A has an ANS that characteristically recovers very quickly from fear, then he will receive a quick and large reinforcement and learn inhibition quickly. If he has an ANS that recovers very slowly, he will receive a slow, small reinforcement and learn to inhibit the aggression very slowly, if at all. This orientation would predict that (holding constant critical extra-individual variables such as social status, crime training, and poverty level) those who commit antisocial acts will be characterized by diminished autonomic responsiveness and slow autonomic recovery. The slower the recovery, the more serious and repetitive the antisocial behavior predicted.

I have already indicated the ability of the autonomic variables to predict later antisocial behavior. Recall the British study by Wadsworth, the Hare study in the maximum security prison, and our own research in Denmark. I can also mention that in nine other studies with different methods, different definitions of antisocial behavior, and in different nations, the antisocial individuals are characterized by sluggish autonomic behavior—diminished responsiveness and slow recovery as would be predicted by this theory.

What is the precise relevance of these statements for the primary prevention of antisocial behavior? I believe that these statements encourage the hypothesis that predelinquents have distinguishing characteristics that could be used to select them for intervention research well before they become serious criminals. We have always been able to specify variables which would preselect the delinquent, for example, social class. But not all male members of the lower classes become delinquent. By combining the social-familial variables with the individual variables, we should improve our selection procedures.

The selection variables and theory should help us in choosing intervention techniques.

References

Bell, B., Mednick, S.A., Gottesman, I.I., and Sergeant, J. "Electrodermal parameters in young normal male twins." In S.A. Mednick and K.O. Christiansen (eds.), *Biosocial Bases of Criminal Behavior*. New York: Gardner Press, 1977.

Borgstrom, C.A. "Eine serie von Kriminellen Zwillingen." *Archiv fur Rassenbiologie*, 1939.

Carlsson, G. "Crime and behavioral epidemiology: Concepts and applications to Swedish data." In S.A. Mednick and K.O. Christiansen (eds.), *Biosocial Bases of Criminal Behavior*. New York: Gardner Press, 1977.

Christiansen, K.O. "A preliminary study of criminality among twins." In S.A. Mednick and K.O. Christiansen (eds.), *Biosocial Bases of Criminal Behavior*. New York: Gardner Press, 1977a.

———. "A review of studies of criminality among twins." In S.A. Mednick and K.O. Christiansen (eds.), *Biosocial Bases of Criminal Behavior*. New York: Gardner Press, 1977b.

Crowe, R. "An adoptive study of psychopathy: preliminary results from arrest records and psychiatric hospital records." In R. Fieve, D. Rosenthal, and H. Brill (eds.), *Genetic Research in Psychiatry*. Baltimore: Johns Hopkins University Press, 1975.

Dalgaard, O.S., and Kringlen, E. "A Norwegian twin study of criminality." *British Journal of Criminology* 1977, 16:213-232.

Farrington, D.P. "Longitudinal research on crime and delinquency." In N. Morris and M. Tonry (eds.), *Crime and Justice 1978: An Annual Review of Criminal Justice Research*, Chicago: University of Chicago Press, 1979.

Godwin, J. *Murder USA: The Ways We Kill Each Other*. New York: Ballatine Books, 1978.

Hutchings, B., and Mednick, S.A. "Criminality in adoptees and their adoptive and biological parents: a pilot study." In S.A. Mednick and K.O. Christiansen (eds.), *Biosocial Bases of Criminal Behavior*. New York: Gardner Press, 1977.

Kety, S.S., Rosenthal, D., Wender, P.H., and Schulsinger, F. "The types and prevalence of mental illness in the biological and adoptive families of adopted schizophrenics." In D. Rosenthal and S.S. Kety (eds.), *The Transmission of Schizophrenia*. Oxford: Pergamon, 1968.

Krantz, H. *Lebensschicksale kriminellen Zwillinge*. Berlin: Julius Springer, 1936.

Lange, J. *Verbrechen als Schiskal*. Leipzig: Georg Thieme, 1929. English ed., London: Unwin Brothers, 1931.

Legras, A.M. *Psychese en Criminalitet bij Twellingen*. Utrecht: kemink en Zoon N.B., 1932. A summary in German can be found in "Psychosen und Kriminalität bei Zwillingen." *Zeitschrift für die gesamte Neurologie und Psychiatrie*, 1933, 198-228.

Loeb, L., and Mednick, S.A. "Asocial behavior and electrodermal response patterns." In S.A. Mednick and K.O. Christiansen (eds.), *Biosocial Bases of Criminal Behavior*. New York: Gardner Press, 1977, pp. 245-254.

Lykken, D.T. A Study of anxiety in the sociopathic personality. *Journal of Abnormal and Social Psychology*, 1957, 55:6-10.

Mednick, S.A. "Electrodermal recovery and psychopathology." In S.A. Mednick, F. Schulsinger, J. Higgins, and B. Bell (eds.), *Genetics, Environment and Psychopathology*. Oxford: North-Holland, 1974.

Mednick, S.A. and Hutchings, B. "Some considerations in the interpretation of the Danish adoption studies." In S.A. Mednick and K.O. Christiansen (eds.), *Biosocial Bases of Criminal Behavior*. New York: Gardner Press, 1977.

Mednick, S.A., Schulsinger, F., and Venables, P. "Risk research and primary prevention of mental illness." *International Journal of Mental Health*, 1979, 7(3)(4):150-164.

Rosanoff, A.J., Handy, L.M., and Rosanoff, F.A. "Criminality and delinquency in twins." *Journal of Criminal Law and Criminology*, 1934, 24:923-934.

Schulsinger, F. "Psychopathy: heredity and environment." In S.A. Mednick and K.O. Christiansen (eds.), *Biosocial bases of Criminal Behavior*. New York: Gardner Press, 1977.

Siddle, D.A.T. "Electrodermal activity and psychopathy." In S.A. Mednick and K.O. Christiansen (eds.), *Biosocial Bases of Criminal Behavior*. New York: Gardner Press, 1977.

Slater, E. The incidence of mental disorder. *Annals of Eugenics*, 1953, 6:172.

Stumpfl, F. *Die Ursprunge des Verberchens. Dargestellt am Lebenslauf von Zwillingen*. Leipzig: Georg Thieme, 1936.

Trasler, G. "Criminal behavior." In H.J. Eysenck (ed.), *Handbook of Abornmal Psychology*. London: Putnam, 1972.

Yoshimasu, S. "The criminological significance of the family in the light of the studies of criminal twins." *Acta Criminologiae et Medicinae Legalis Japanica*, 1961, vol. 27.

14 Delinquency in Developing and Developed Societies

Theodore N. Ferdinand

The difference between developing and developed societies is rapidly becoming a central problem in sociology. The value systems of traditional and modernizing societies (Inkeles and Smith 1974; Hagen 1962), the political and economic structures that emerge during colonial rule in developing societies (Hoogvelt 1976: part two), and the impact of world systems of trade on developing societies (Wallerstein 1974) have all inspired major scholarly efforts in the recent past. This growing concern with the developing world is not, however, an entirely recent phenomenon.

Sociologists have long been interested in the differences between folk and urban societies; between mechanical and organic solidarity; or between *Gemeinschaft* and *Gesellschaft*. But the difference lies in the fact that the current interest in developing and developed societies focuses on their changing structures and organization, that is, on the process of becoming developed.

Earlier sociological interest had focused on the differences between traditional and urban society and had conceived of the two as relatively static, distinct versions of social organization. Furthermore, early sociologists tended to see the two as basically independent phenomena occurring naturally without interference from one another, whereas today developing and developed societies are regarded as parts of an overarching system embracing most nations—developed as well as developing—of the world.

This concern has also influenced crinologists (Clinard and Abbott 1972), but thus far it has not inspired a thoroughgoing treatment of the criminologic differences between developing and developed societies.

This essay seeks to draw attention to the more theoretic aspects of this question by proposing an explanation of the differences in delinquent behavior found among developing and developed societies. I shall proceed by examining, first, the sociocultural nature of developing societies and a distinctive type of delinquency that frequently appears in such societies. Second, I shall describe the nature of developed societies by appealing to the insights of Daniel Bell and others, and I shall pinpoint a prominent pattern of delinquency in developed societies. On this basis some connections between the social structures of developing and developed societies and their delinquency problems will be identified and some suggestions for coping with them will be offered.

Through comparative endeavors such as this not only will we gain increasing insight into the crime problems of different kinds of societies, but we will help to correct a major deficiency in American criminology: its narrow focusing on criminality among only a limited number of societies—usually advanced and usually Western.

The Developing Society

Developing societies have received considerable attention in one guise or another both from classical thinkers and modern theorists. Henry Maine (1917: ch. 5, 9) drew a sharp distinction between societies based on status and contract. Similarly, Durkheim (1933: ch. 3) contrasted the mechanical solidarity of primitive society with the differentiated organic solidarity of more advanced societies, and Howard Becker (1956: ch. 12, 13) pointed to much the same distinction when he compared sacred and secular societies. Perhaps the most perceptive treatment of this question, however, was that offered by Toennies (1957) in his analytic discussion of *Gemeinschaft* and *Gesellschaft*.

Clearly, all these theorists were contrasting a developing society in which commercialism and an urban social organization were dominant with an underdeveloped society in which communalism and a type of tribal organization were dominant. But their theorizing was drawn largely from Western experience, and for this reason is deficient in certain respects for the analysis of developing societies today (Portes 1976). For one thing, the development of Western societies was largely an orthogenic process unguided by any external model, and for another it took place in the context of an undeveloped world so that Western development was not conditioned or channeled by other more advanced economic or political systems. Since developing societies today are both guided and constrained by more advanced societies, the classical theories of Maine at al. cannot be applied without taking into account the crucial diffferences.

But developing societies today share generally two characteristics with the model of developing societies implicit in classical theory. In both, urban-based commercialism is the dominant form of social organization, and in both this pattern contrasts sharply with the village-based communalism of the hinterland. Thus, the fundamental problem facing developing societies today (as well as the developing Western world of the eighteenth and nineteenth centuries) is the necessity of absorbing a constant stream of migrants from the folk-oriented hinterland and acculturating them to the commercial patterns of the city.

Where the language and cultural level of the migrants permit an easy assimilation to urban social patterns, as in nineteenth century Japan, the process can often be accomplished with a minimum of strain. But where the hinterland has remained isolated from the urban cultural patterns of the major cities, as in parts of Mexico or India, acculturation of rural migrants is often more difficult, and where urban society emerges only sporadically in a pervasive folk culture, as in black Africa, the cities are nearly overwhelmed by the crush of migrants, and the social and political problems they engender are often beyond the capacity of local government to resolve. Thus, the ease with which developing societies modernize depends in part upon the degree of social and cultural compatibility between their urban centers and the hinterlands they serve (Hunter 1969: ch. 1, 9). Where compatibility is high, the developing society emerges with relatively little social disruption or dislocation. But where compatibility is minimal, modernization often proceeds only with great difficulty.

There are many reasons why social and cultural compatibility between urban centers and their hinterlands might be slight. In some cases, as with much of Africa and India, the cultural contrast between tribal villages in the hinterland and urban centers are so great that they have remained for lengthy periods essentially two distinct cultures: the former subordinate and slowly declining in relation to the latter. But because the tribal villages remain a significant social and political force in such societies, the process of assimilation is neither rapid nor simple. In other cases, as with the Amish in North America, the peasants of Sicily, or the criminal tribes of India, traditional communities effectively resist acculturation to the advancing urban culture with the result that they remain for extended periods as cultural islands in a developing urban society. And in still other cases, as with the Eskimos and Indians of North America, isolated, tribal communities are simply overwhelmed by an encroaching urban civilization with the result that their traditions weaken and their social structure disintegrates. The settlements may persist, but more as caricatures of urban society than as islands of traditional culture.

All of these represent variations on the general theme of the developing society, and each of them presents a distinct pattern of delinquency in accordance with its specific structural and cultural features. But since it would be impossible to consider them all here, we shall concentrate primarily on the more general case of the emerging urban center and its delinquent patterns in a developing society.

Delinquency in Developing Societies

Developing societies are nourished by a market economy, and their patterns of crime and delinquency reflect this fact. Through the selective processes of the labor market, social classes emerge and an unskilled class with a subsistence standard of living is differentiated from the rest. For obvious reasons many of the migrants from the hinterland fall into this class and are reduced to a hand-to-mouth existence. Their social and cultural life in the city is often closely defined by the culture of their villages, but the pressures of urban living force upon many families a distinctive structural adaptation.

The father tends to play a limited role in such families, spending most of his time outside the home with other adult males; the mother, her unmarried female relatives, and her older female children spend most of their time at home governing the younger children; and the older boys in the family spend much of their time on the street with other boys in similar circumstances. Thus, three groups with distinctive cultures emerge in the slums where one stood before: an adult male culture in which the members have limited family responsibilities, an adult female culture which centers on child rearing, and a young male culture which centers on street life.

Oscar Lewis (1959, 1961) has described this pattern as the culture of poverty, and he regards it as a stable adjustment to marginal city life.[1] Other scholars (Gans 1969; Leacock 1971) have questioned the stability of the culture of poverty, but they have not challenged the accuracy of his description.

The emergence of two distinct street cultures means among other things that social links between these groups, that is, adult men and young males, and the larger community are somewhat weakened and, therefore, that deviance of several kinds including crime become somewhat more likely. The delinquency that develops among the young males often assumes a distinctive form. The older boys typically have weak family ties in the city (Weinberg 1964; Oloruntimehin 1973; Ferracutti et al. 1975), and without binding obligations, such boys often find companionship with other youths in the streets. Gangs of rootless boys, therefore, appear within nearly every neighborhood in the migrant quarter. These cliques arise on the basis of friendship patterns and rarely surpass ten or fifteen boys in all. Crime in a common pastime in such gangs, but it is primarily utilitarian in that it focuses upon material goods that are readily used by boys (DeFleur 1970:81-85, 118-122, 141-140).[2]

The appearance of street gangs and cliques in such slums reflects more the absence of significant responsibilities for young people than overt social pressures molding them into juvenile groups (Thrasher 1963:65-67). The cliques and gangs develop to organize the behavior of a group—juveniles—that otherwise would have no meaningful position in the community. Young people, particularly young males, have very little to contribute to their families by remaining at home, and they have great difficulty in finding regular employment. The street offers them an "occupation" which can fill their lives until something more substantial comes along. We see, then, how a new status emerges in a developing society before there is a role for its incumbants to play, and how juvenile cliques and gangs develop to offer them a role.

In contrast to more primitive societies, the structure of developing urban societies provides no smooth transition between childhood and adulthood, particularly among the lower economic strata. And adolescence emerges principally as a response to this problem, but it is an empty status with few institutionalized forms. Children from the middle and upper economic strata tend to be occupied with their academic and familial duties and are carefully segregated from the street culture of the adolescent gangs. Thus, adolescence in developing societies tends to be largely a lower-class problem, and initially, at least, is dealt with through the courts and the police (Kett 1977:150-151).

The generality of this pattern is striking. During the eighteenth and nineteenth centuries both London and Paris developed substantial slums in which something resembling the culture of poverty took firm root. Crime, delinquency, and public disorders were commonplace, and contemporary observers (Rude 1971; Chevalier 1973) spoke ominously of the "dangerous classes" which lived in such areas. Similarly, American cities during the nineteenth century developed large slum areas in which gangs of young men and boys committed a wide variety of crimes (Brace 1872; Asbury 1939). Criminological studies of developing societies today reveal approximately the same conditions. Clinard and Abbott (1973: ch. 5), for example, report a close association between criminality and slums in developing societies. Many of the major cities of South America, Asia, and Africa are dominated by impoverished migrant areas in which the family has dissolved into several simpler structures, and crime and delinquency abound. Indeed, according to Clinard and Abbott (1973: 134-135), more than one-third of the people in the following cities live in slums: Recife, Mexico City, Lima, Caracas, Manila, Calcutta, and Karachi. Clinard and Abbott (1973: 140-142) further report that in Kampala, Uganda, slum dwellers commit more crimes of all types in proportion to their numbers than residents of other areas of the city. The changing structure of the family and community in such areas together with their marginal economic and social position seem to be the main factors behind their high crime rates (Clinard and Abbott 1973:139-187).

The Developed Society

Although the developed society presents a surprisingly consistent picture wherever it has appeared (Sweden, the Netherlands, Great Britain, Japan, and West Germany), sociological theorists have not yet agreed on its salient dimensions.[3] Daniel Bell (1973: ch. 3) sees it as dominated by rationalistic institutions governed, if not by scientists and other members of the intelligensia, at least by political leaders who depend heavily on such people for advice. Similarly, Zbigniew Brzezinski (1970:9) regards modern technology and electronics as the key characteristics of developed societies, and Ralf Dahrendorf (1959: ch. 7, 8) sees the modern world as dominated by bureaucratic structures.

For all their variety, however, these theorists are unanimous regarding the difference between advanced societies today and urban society of the nineteenth century. They are in agreement that since World War II we have moved through a threshold from the industrial, bourgeois, urban society of the pre-World War I era to something that is quite different. Daniel Bell (1973:36-40) labels it postindustrial but others have described it as postbourgois, postcapitalist, and even as postcivilized. They agree that the developed world of today differs fundamentally from that of the late nineteenth and early twentieth centuries, but they cannot agree on what it is that distinguishes today's developed society from earlier versions of urban civilization.

Let me propose, however, that the distinguishing feature of developed societies today is the overwhelming importance of bureaucratic organizations. Virtually every function that is important in such societies is performed by large-scale organizations, and for better or worse this fact has overarching significance for the values and mores of such societies, for the quality of life its citizens enjoy, and for the ways in which they are organized and governed.

Although developing societies are often organized around a market economy, the developed society has no basic dependence upon the eccentricities of the market (Galbraith 1971: ch. 17). The rise and fall of wages, prices, and credit obey a higher dicta—that of national or at least organizational policy defined not simply in terms of economic criteria (Bates 1974). In short, the market is harnessed in developed societies to serve the ends of society, and it is manipulated to achieve that purpose.

Many other basic functions have also been adjusted to national purposes, for example, education. The specific ends of education are nearly infinite, but overall the purpose of education is to permit the citizens to fulfill themselves while contributing effectively to the development of their society. Education is not regarded as a privilege reserved only for the gifted or the favored. A developed society cannot function effectively if only a thin stratum possesses the skills to serve effectively in highly sophisticated posts. Hence, in developed societies virtually everyone is encouraged to receive at least a secondary education.

Many developed societies have had a large measure of success in eliminating chronic unemployment, a rootless lower class, and the culture of poverty so prominent in developing societies. Nations like Sweden, the Netherlands, West Germany, and Great Britain have largely absorbed the improverished migrants that dominated their great cities in the nineteenth century, and the crimes endemic in that class have shrunk to very low levels, in comparison with their levels before World War I. Similarly, the financial burden associated with most of life's problems—health, education, unemployment—has largely been eased by welfare programs (Janowitz 1976: ch. 3) of the 1950s and 1960s. For all their bureaucratic efficiency, however, developed societies still face many serious problems, and since our basic concern here is with delinquency, let us consider just how it is affected by the pervasive rationalization and bureaucratization of society.

Delinquency in Developed Societies

An asolescent culture has emerged in Western societies in which the pleasures of adolescence freed from the burdensome responsibilities of adulthood are narcissitically championed. Those youths in the forefront of this movement endorse a cluster of attitudes that are highly distinctive (Mays 1961; Keniston 1968; Roszak 1969; Fiedler 1965; Kett 1977:269-272). First, there is a determined rejection of the conventions surrounding the expression of feelings and emotions. Open displays of affection and methods of achieving and prolonging ecstacy are widely cultivated, whereas a traditional, cautious discipline of the feelings and emotions is strongly condemned. For many young people, one's emotions have become almost a symbol of one's liberation and definitely not something to control or suppress. Second, many adolescents frankly reject the burden of conventional careers, parenthood, and family responsibilities. They seem reluctant to quit the pleasures of adolescence, and they reject the competitiveness and careerism of their more conventional peers. Finally, there is an increasing tendency among some adolescents to challenge directly adult authority—whether in the home, school, or community, especially where it is arbitrary, unimaginative, and punitive. These values in their essence encourage a commitment to freedom and self-indulgence that contrasts sharply with the dominant values of adult culture which encourage personal discipline and a long-run perspective.[4]

The relationship between the ethos of adolescent society and delinquency in developed societies is far from simple, but the congruence between the two is certainly suggestive. Before World War I delinquency in the Western world was not unlike that found today in developing societies. It included primarily youths from families that had recently migrated to the urban center with few resources to negotiate the turbulent challenges of the city. These youngsters and their families were often outsiders eager to embrace the values of urban society. They were anxious to enter the mainstream but were denied admission because of their lack of skills and sophistication.

The adolsecents who were well established and properly educated were assured of stable careers and had little to do with the gangs that formed the training ground of street adolescents.

The delinquent that is typical of developed societies, on the other hand, is deeply committed to the values of adolescent society. He adopts its language, dress, and musical fads, and he carefully arranges his life style in terms of its standards. He may or may not be firmly integrated in other groups—his family or social groups in the community—and he may or may not be involved in school and other conventional activities. But the key fact is that he is not an alienated youngster who has been unable to find a satisfactory position for himself in modern society. He has found a rich, satisfying, and meaningful niche as an adolescent with other adolescents, and the behaviors these relationships inspire do not express his alienation and the isolation, but rather his consciousness of his status as an adolescent in an adult society. His behavior is a celebration of his membership in adolescent society and must be viewed in this context. From the standpoint of adults, his behavior may appear irrational, utilitarian, or malicious, but for him it is an expression of his status as an adolescent.

The crystallization of these values among adolescents has sponsored a number of novel, even bizarre, gangs or groups in different societies. For example, the hippies and yippies in America bear a certain resemblance to the *provos* of Holland, and the motorcycle gangs of America's highways parallel the *raggare* of Stockholm. There are national variations on the overall pattern, but many of these gangs present a consistent set of characteristics.

First, since group solidarity is an important value among adolescents, they adopt a variety of distinctive mannerisms (language, dress, facial expressions, walking posture), all of which identify their specific group membership. Second, since girls today are exposed through secondary education to the pressures of adolescent society every bit as much as boys, they are much more prominent in its activities, including delinquency, than was formerly the case. Third, since there are typically many different kinds of adolescent groups with many different values and goals, rivalry between these groups is inevitable and group conflicts regarding relative status will be common. Fourth, since the values and goals of adolescent groups often conflict with those of important adult groups in the community, their autonomy through adult groups and values will be vigorously expressed both behaviorally and symbolically. Fifth, they will display very little interest in moving beyond the adolescent society into adulthood, marriage, and a legitimate full-time job. Sixth, since delinquents, like other adolescents, have an accute awareness of self as well as the status differences between their group, other adolescent groups, and adult society, their self-esteem will be closely related to the mode of their participation in adolescent society. Those who belong to key cliques and gangs will enjoy higher status and higher self-esteem among their peers than those who do not. And, seventh, since the activities of these groups are often symbolic of their solidarity, their actions when resulting in crime will often express a bizarre or extreme quality that is rare in the delinquent behavior of individual, anomic adolescents.

In support of this analysis, several keen observers in western Europe have noted remarkable shifts in delinquency since World War II. One of the most interesting accounts is that by T.R. Fyvel (1964) of the Teddy boys of London. In the early 1950s a group of South London working-class boys adopted the dress of upper-class young people and began to use it as the symbol not merely of their group but of their philosophy of life. Since the style they affected was Edwardian, they were called "Teddy boys" or simply "Teds."

Their philosophy was not particularly complicated: it focused upon girls, hanging around as a group, and excitement. But according to Fyvel (1964: ch. 4, 5), it also included a new theme: a defiant assertion of the validity of their views and their willingness to attack savagely any who regarded either their dress or ideas as inappropriate or illegitimate. They were adolescents establishing a new cultural pattern, and their bizarre Edwardian uniform stood as a challenge, a chip on their collective shoulders, to outsiders. Anyone who accepted their challenge could expect a sound thrashing or worse for their trouble. The Teddy boys were not concerted, systematic delinquents for the most part, although they engaged in their share of sexual adventures, petty thefts, violent assaults, and rowdiness. Their delinquency was only incidental to their basic purpose: proclaiming their version of adolescent society as an independent and noteworthy aspect of modern society. Collectively they were as good as anyone else, and they were willing to fight to prove it.

The Teddy boys came from a narrow slice of the London social structure (Fyvel 1964:119-132, 191-196). They were working-class boys who had left school at fifteen, obtained temporary employment, and were bent upon enjoying life before the dull routines of family and job closed in. The certainties of adulthood to them seemed threatening and restricting—and their youth presented an opportunity for self-indulgence and freedom which they intended to enjoy.

Jackson Toby (1967) came to much the same conclusion regarding Swedish youth. The *raggare* of Stockholm included gangs of adolescents and young adults, many of whom own cars and flock to downtown Stockholm nightly to race and have a good time. The opportunity for carefree fun is seized enthusiastically by Swedish youth, and the result is large groups of unruly youths who delight in each other's company and who defy the rest of society to interfere with their free and spirited life. As in

London the gangs are not systematically delinquent, but in their defiance of the larger society they indulge in all manner of sexual adventures, drugs, and alcohol, and from time to time provoke fights with other youths.

Paul Friday (1970: ch. 6, 7) undertook a controlled study of Swedish delinquents in Stockholm in the late 1960s and found that although they did not see poor performance in school as preventing their success as adults, they definitely did feel blocked from economic success. Moreover, when their sense of being prevented from achieving success as an adult is coupled with frequent association with other delinquents, the two together intensify sharply the seriousness of their crimes (Friday 1970:258-266). It would appear that Friday has uncovered among the youth of Stockholm much the same pattern that was described by Fyvel in London. Those young people, whose adult careers are unlikely to be rewarding or satisfying, seem to exact compensation in the form of delinquency and irresponsible behavior, and when this sense of hopelessness is coupled with frequent association with delinquents, a delinquent outcome is virtually sealed.

The appearance of these distinctive groups in both Sweden and Great Britain was accompanied by remarkable increases in arrests among young people. In Sweden between 1946 and 1955 arrests of juveniles of fifteen to seventeen years rose by 38 percent, and arrests of young adults of eighteen to twenty years shot up by 57 percent (Toby 1967). Similarly, in England and Wales arrests of juveniles fourteen to sixteen years increased by 98 percent between 1946 and 1965, and arrests of young adults of seventeen to twenty-one years skyrocketed by 137 percent during the same period (McClintock and Avison 1968: table 6.9). Although the emergence of the adolescent society seems to have stimulated arrests among the younger stratum, it has had its greatest impact on the young adult, the stratum that is physically and sexually mature but not firmly established in adult society. The juvenile is still living at home and materially dependent upon his parents; he is physically smaller and less sexually active than the young adult, and all in all less eligible for membership in adolescent society. His delinquency accordingly increased more slowly than the older members of his generation.

In Holland youth groups closely resembling those found in England and Sweden have also made their appearance since World War II. Throngs of ill-kept young people, *provos*, congregate in the central plazas of major Dutch cities and idle away their time smoking marijuana, drinking beer, and trading fantastic stories with one another. They are not so much delinquent as they are repelled by the conventional routines of bougeois society and intent upon creating a less controlled and less organized style for themselves.

According to Buikhuisen (1966-67:1-19), a Dutch criminologist who has studied them, they engage in theft and sexual offenses, but their main inter-

est is not criminality so much as immunity from the responsibilities and pro-
hibitions of conventional society. Their repudiation of bourgeois society is
expressed in their behavior as well as their values: they periodically create
disturbances at public ceremonies and engage in various kinds of spon-
taneous vandalism against cars and public facilities. By looking into their
backgrounds, Buikhuisen was able to establish that in comparison with
other delinquents the *provos* were on relatively good terms with their
parents, but that they abhorred formal school, had little ambition to improve themselves, and most enjoyed superficial relations with other young
people in conspicuous places. They were mostly sixteen to eighteen years old
and from lower socioeconomic social strata. They congregated to provide
an alternative for one another—a youth subculture with values suited to
young people who reject both conventional adolescent roles and the need to
prepare themselves for adulthood. Their kinship with their English and
Swedish counterparts is clear.

The social foundations of these extraordinary increases in youth crime
clearly are to be found in the bureaucratic structure of developed societies.
Both Fyvel (1964: ch. 15, 16) and Toby (1967) attributed them to the spread
of affluence, the commercial manipulation of teenagers, and the revolution
of rising expectations—all symptoms of a developed society, perhaps, but
not fundamental dimensions of its structure.

As developed societies emerged in Western Europe and North America,
not only was the basic structure of society altered, but the life chances of all
its citizens were profoundly affected. Instead of many small firms and
organizations interacting via the impersonal mechanism of the marketplace,
most important functions in society were assumed by large-scale organizations bureaucratically organized and hierarchically coordinated not simply
by the market but most directly by an overarching governmental authority.
Some developed societies have evolved more rapidly than others, but most
have expanded their control by now over the market mechanism and private
organizations that utilize it so that untrammeled market forces no longer
enjoy free play in setting the pace or direction of economic growth. Not
only have these societies assumed close control over the market, but they
have also devised ways of mobilizing large private organizations behind national goals when necessary. In the United States the giant oil companies,
the drug industry, the auto companies, the steel industry, the financial sector are all closely controlled in one way or another by the federal government, and each from time to time is required to adjust its activities to national policy. The bureaucratization of society makes organization for national purpose much simpler.

The urban society of the nineteenth century, on the other hand, with its
thousands of small firms interacting through a national market presented
no such opportunity. Although it was more chaotic and disorganized than

modern society, it was more fluid and penetrable. The free spirited, unorthodox individual was probably more comfortable in the turmoil and discord of the nineteenth century than in the orderly halls of modern society.

These changes have had a profound impact all through society, but they have affected particularly the young people and their passage into adulthood. In urban society of the nineteenth century, dominated as it was by the market, the middle- or working-class youngster who was broadly adapted to urban culture needed in addition only a rudimentary education in order to become self-sufficient. If he could read, write, and do simple arithmetic, he could enter business as an entrepreneur or enter the labor force as a worker. The techniques of business or of labor were sufficiently simple that it made no great technical demands upon those who wished to begin as recruits (Roberts 1975). True, an advanced education was necessary for those who aspired to religion, law, or medicine, and apprenticeships were necessary for those who hoped to become skilled workers in traditional crafts like carpentry, masonry, or plumbing. But most young people could enter the work force with only a primary education and prosper, if they had other qualities to buoy themselves up. There were many hazards facing the businessman or the laborer in the markets, but an extended education was not required of young people before they might apply for full-time employment.

In modern developed societies, however, virtually all the rewarding careers that carry responsibility are in and through large-scale organizations, which in turn set formidable educational requirements for those who seek administrative positions. A college degree is often the minimum requirement with the result that young people who aspire to important careers today face sixteen or more years of education. The passage into adulthood, mariage, and stable employment, therefore, must be postponed until at least the early twenties, and even more importantly, it requires an exercise of enormous self-discipline among young people who work diligently in school for approximately seventeen years with very little tangible reward for their troubles.

Adults assure them that their diligence will indeed be rewarded, but they can have no concrete evidence of that fact until they have already completed the course, and, of course, for a sizable number, their self-denial and diligence do not pay off. They do not find rewarding and responsible positions in important organizations.

Many realize early in the game that no worthy career awaits them, and many others find school in itself highly disagreeable. For a variety of reasons many young people reject the warning to deny themselves the joys of adolescence so that their adulthood can be filled with a rewarding career and elect instead to make the best of their youth while they still have it. The society has organized them into age grades in the school system, and they have taken the opportunity to fashion an age-graded society of their own with values which reflect their needs and aspirations, not those of their parents or other adults. On the face of it, therefore, the adolescent society is a repudiation of one of the most basic values of middle-class adult society: that an important career is the ultimate fulfillment of the individual, and those young people who are swept up in the adolescent society find themselves alienated to some extent from middle-class culture and adults.

The emergence of an unorthodox youth culture ocurred, first, in postwar England, perhaps because the organization of careers in England was much more orderly and predictable there. At the age of eleven, English children were set on an educational track that led either to a university and higher responsibility or to an early completion of school and an adult career of routine subordination. Moreover, the working class in England has a long tradition of living for leisure time and tolerating work only as a means to an end (Downes 1966:236-237). Dissociation from the work ethic insulates the working class from the disappointment that unfulfilled ambitions would create and protects those who in a relatively static economy cannot expect to improve their economic or social position appreciably from one generation to the next.

English working-class teenagers have confronted the dilemma presented them by the orderly organization of the schools and its denial to them of real opportunity, and they have fashioned a hedonistic, nonutilitarian adolescent movement that at bottom is a realistic adjustment to a basically hopeless situation (Gillis 1974:193-196).

Albert Cohen (1955) was the first to identify the cultural foci of working-class gangs as nonutilitarianism, maliciousness, negativism, versatility, short-run hedonism, and group autonomy, and he correctly saw subcultural working-class delinquency as an attempt to legitimate working-class youngsters and their values in a middle-class world. The relevance of his analysis to delinquency in developed societies is clear, and an English criminologist, David M. Downes (1966:198-208), after comparing Cohen's paradigm with delinquent groups in two sections of London's East End, concluded that his teenagers lacked only malice and negativism to qualify as working-class subcultural delinquents.

For all his perceptiveness in describing today's delinquency, however, Cohen failed to see its roots in broad structural changes in Western society. But another criminologist, Lois B. DeFleur (1970), inadvertently revealed the close relationship between Cohen's pattern of working-class delinquency and developed societies when she sought unsuccessfully to fit Cohen's theory to delinquent gangs in Cordoba, Argentina.

Cordoba was just emerging as an industrial city when DeFleur did her study of its delinquency problem. Until World War II it had been a regional center for a large agricultural hinterland, but following World War II it became a manufacturing city and grew explosively from 386,838 in 1947 to 589,153 in 1960. Many of the migrants to Cordoba were skilled laborers from Italy, Japan, and the Near East, but many were Argentine farm laborers from the hinterland with minimal industrial skills (DeFleur 1970: ch. 3). Cordoba in 1962 was a good example of a city in a rapidly developing society with substantial slums and considerable crime and delinquency. As might be expected, DeFleur (1970:118-129) found little evidence for nonutilitarianism, maliciousness, or negativism, the three most salient behavioral patterns in Cohen's analysis. But she (1970:130-146) did find ample evidence of small, loosely organized bands of juveniles from slum areas in Cordoba who engaged in periodic stealing primarily to augment their meager income from legitimate sources. DeFleur was obviously looking in the wrong place to test Cohen's thesis.

Cohen's analysis was based on his understanding of delinquency as it appeared in American cities, and there is considerable evidence that the adolescent society and its associated delinquency abounds in the larger American cities. But delinquency in America does not conform exactly to the pattern found in western Europe.

In England the disenchantment of working-class adolescents with the middle-class striving ethic was a factor in their delinquency, and in the United States the growing alienation of black, inner-city youngsters from white, middle-class culture has similarly contributed to the spirit of aggressive autonomy that many black teenagers express today. The emergence of large delinquent gangs in American cities with distinctive modes of dress and a pattern of nonutilitarian, malicious, negativistic behavior during the 1950s and 1960s can be viewed as a local variant of the more general adolescent movement noted above.

Conclusions

I have contrasted the patterns of delinquency frequently encountered in developing and developed societies. Deliquency in developing societies is regarded as primarily an outgrowth of the failure of such societies to offer adolescents and young adults who are poorly prepared for urban life socially and economically rewarding roles, as they move beyond the authority of their parental family. In developed societies, however, a new type of delinquency has arisen within the context of a more general adolescent movement that, among other things, repudiates the importance of preparing for adult careers and adult life. In developing societies the adolescents who are drawn into delinquency have often been excluded from full participation in the mainstream of urban life and earnestly seek a fuller role. In developed societies the new delinquents tend to be those who participate fully in the urban culture and particularly in the urban, adolescent culture and have little desire to enter the broader stream of their society. The contrast between these two types of delinquents could hardly be sharper when viewed in this fashion.

Both types are found commonly in most advanced societies.[5] But it is obvious that remedial and preventive measures designed for one type will not be appropriate for the other. The English prewar delinquent who sought ready admission to the industrial work force responded well to the vocational and educational programs of the borstals; whereas today the Teddy boys and their successors in London may well regard such programs as rather transparent efforts to induct them into the dull routines of English working-class adulthood. The oft-noted postwar decline in the effectiveness of the borstals may reflect some such shift in ideology among the youths they serve. And by the same token, perhaps the failure of the war on poverty to have any mesurable effect on delinquency in American cities during the 1960s reflects a similar failure to articulate the appropriate remedial measures to the nature of the youths involved. A youngster who is deeply involved in an adolescent culture that repudiates the value of careerism is not likely to respond to programs which focus almost exclusively upon remedial educational and vocational programs.

Similarly, recent changes in the juvenile court in the United States can be viewed as an attempt to deal more directly with the problems posed by the new delinquent. In its early years the juvenile court was designed to serve as a surrogate parent for disoriented but responsive youth whose main failing was their lack of close familial and communal ties. Since the 1960s, however, the juvenile court in many states has begun to draw a distinction between juveniles who repeatedly commit serious offenses, that is, delinquent offenders, and those who deviate primarily from the conventional role of the adolescent, that is, status offenders. Although there is no solid evidence that serious delinquents are usually gang members, there is some indication that core gang members tend to be much more delinquent than others (Klein 1971:70-92). The institutionalization of delinquency in gangs appears to have intensified the problem, which in turn has prompted the juvenile court in heavily urbanized states to move some distance from the early concept of the court as basically a benevolent guardian of disoriented, rootless youth who need primarily a guiding hand to find their way into a conventional life in adult society.

The emergence of a new type of delinquent in developed societies is certainly not the only factor involved in the failures or changes just noted. But the congruence between the new pattern of delinquency and the shifts in the juvenile justice system indicated above is sufficiently close to warrant careful scrutiny.

Notes

1. Liebow (1967) offers an interesting description of this trifurcation of the black family in Washington, D.C.

2. Thrasher (1963) also describes such gangs in his study of Chicago juveniles during the 1920s.

3. The United States, the Soviet Union, and France, for example, would probably qualify as developed societies in terms of most definitions, but the heterogeneity and complexity of their social structures is so great that their inclusion here would only tend to confuse the basic concept.

4. Naturally, a substantial number of adolescents in developed societies still endorse the values of their parents and follow in only a superficial way the values and urgings of their peers. But the adolescent culture as described here is a significant factor in the lives of enough teenagers to warrant considering it carefully.

5. Kraus (1975) discovered two distinct types of delinquency in Sidney, Australia, that approximated the patterns described here for developing and developed societies. He found also that their social environments closely resembled those postulated here for these two patterns of delinquency.

References

Asbury, Herbert (1939) *The Gangs of New York: An Informal History of the Underworld*. New York: Blue Ribbon Books.

Bates, Frederick L. (1974). "Alternative models for the future of society: from the invisible to the visible hand." *Social Forces* 53 (September):1-11.

Becker, Howard (1956). *Man in Reciprocity*. New York: Praeger.

Bell, Daniel (1973). *The Coming of Post-Industrial Society*. New York: Basic Books.

Brace, Charles Loring (1872). *The Dangerous Classes of New York*. New York: Sheldon.

Brzezinsky, Zbigniew (1970). *Between Two Ages: America's Role in the Technetronic Era*. New York: Viking Press.

Buikhuisen, W. (1966-67). "Research on teenage riots." *Sociologica Neerlandica*, 4 (1):1-19.

Chevalier, Louis (1973). *Laboring Classes and Dangerous Classes in Paris during the First Half of the Nineteenth Century*. F. Jellineh, trans. New York: H. Fertig.

Clinard, Marshall B., and Abbott, Daniel J. (1973). *Crime in Developing Countries* New York: John Wiley and Sons.

Cohen, Albert (1955). *Delinquent Boys*. New York: Free Press.

Dahrendorf, Ralf (1959). *Class and Class Conflict in Industrial Society*. Stanford, Calif.: Stanford University Press.

DeFleur, Lois B. (1970). *Delinquency in Argentina*. Pullman: Washington State University Press.

Downes, David M. (1966). *The Delinquent Solution*. New York: Free Press.

Durkheim, Emile (1933). *The Division of Labor in Society*. G. Simpson, trans. New York: Free Press.

Ferracutti, Franco, Dinitz, Simon, and Acosta de Bienes, Esperanza (1975). *Delinquents and Nondélinquents in the Puerto Rican Slum Culture*. Columbus: Ohio State University Press.

Fiedler, Leslie (1965). "The new mutants." *Partisan Review* 32 (Fall):505-525.

Friday, Paul (1970). Differential opportunity and differential association in Sweden: a study of youth crime. Doctoral dissertation, University of Wisconsin.

Fyvel, T.R. (1964). *Troublemakers: Rebellious Youth in an Afffluent Society*. New York: Schocken Books.

Galbraith, John Kenneth (1971). *The New Industrial State*. 2d ed. Boston: Houghton Mifflin.

Gans, Herbert J. (1969). "Culture and class in the study of poverty: An Approach to anti-poverty research." In Daniel P. Moynihan (ed.), *On Understanding Poverty*. New York: Basic Books.

Gillis, John R. (1974). *Youth and History*. New York: Academic Press.

Hagen, E.E. (1962). *On the Theory of Social Change*. Homewood, Ill.: Dorsey.

Hoogvelt, Ankie M.M. (1976). *The Sociology of Developing Societies*. London: Macmillan.

Hunter, Guy (1969). *Modernizing Peasant Societies*. New York: Oxford University Press.

Inkeles, Alex, and Smith, David H. (1974). *Becoming Modern: Individual Change in Six Developing Countries*. Cambridge: Harvard University Press.

Janowitz, Morris (1976). *Social Control of the Welfare State*. New York: Elsevier.

Keniston, Kenneth (1968). *Young Radicals*. New York: Harcourt, Brace.

Kett, Joseph F. (1977). *Rites of Passage: Adolescence in America 1790 to the Present*. New York: Basic Books.

Klein, Malcolm (1971). *Street Gangs and Street Workers*. Englewood Cliffs, N.J.: Prentice-Hall.

Kraus, J. (1975). "Ecology of juvenile delinquency in metropolitan Sydney." *Journal of Community Psychology* 3:384-395.

Leacock, Eleanor B. (ed.) (1971). *The Culture of Poverty*. New York: Simon and Schuster.

Lewis, Oscar (1959). *Five Families*. New York: Basic Books.

_____ (1961). *The Children of Sanchez*. New York: Random House.

Liebow, Eliot (1967). *Tally's Corner*. Boston: Little, Brown.

McClintock, F.H., and Avison, N. Howard (1968). *Crime in England and Wales*. London: Heinemann.

Maine, Sir Henry (1917). *Ancient Law*. New York: E.P. Dutton.

Mays, John Barron (1961). "Teen-age culture in contemporary Britain and Europe." *Annals* 338 (November):22-32.

Oloruntimehin, Olufunmilayo (1973). "A study of juvenile delinquency in a Nigerian city." *British Journal of Criminology* 13:157-169.

Parsons, Talcott (1966). *Societies: Evolutionary and Comparative Perspectives*. Englewood Cliffs, N.J.: Prentice-Hall.

Portes, Alejandro (1976). "On the sociology of national development: theories and issues." *American Journal of Sociology* 82: (1):55-85.

Roberts, Bryan R. (1975). "Center and periphery in the development process: the case of Peru." In Wayne A. Cornelius and Felicity M. Trueblood (eds.), *Latin American Urban Research*, vol. 5, pp. 77-106. Beverly Hills, Sage.

Roszak, Theodore (1969). *The Making of a Counter Culture*. New York: Doubleday.

Rude, George (1971). *Hanoverian London, 1714-1808*. Berkeley: University of California.

Spender, Stephen (1968). *The Year of the Young Rebels*. New York: Random House.

Thrasher, Frederic M. (1963). *The Gang: A Study of 1,313 Gangs in Chicago*. Abridged ed. Chicago: University of Chicago Press.

Toby, Jackson (1967). *Affluence and Adolescent Crime*. Task Force Report: Juvenile Delinquency and Youth Crime, The President's Commission on Law Enforcement and Administration of Justice. Appendix H. 132-144. Washington, D.C.: U.S. Government Printing Office.

Toennies, Ferdinand (1957). *Community and Society*. C.P. Loomis, trans. New York: Harper and Row.

Wallerstein, Immanuel (1974). *The Modern World System*. New York: Academic Press.

Weinberg, S. Kirson (1964). "Juvenile delinquency in Ghana: A comparative analysis of delinquents and non-delinquents." *Journal of Criminal Law, Criminology and Police Science* 55:471-481.

Political Implications of Juvenile Delinquency: A Comparative Perspective

James F. Short, Jr.

Throughout much of the world, political conflict is an important component of those events which dominate the news.

> Northern Ireland, "constantly invaded," as Elliot and Hickie (1977) note, for nearly two thousand years, yields its periodic toll of the dead and injured.

> Greek and Turkish communities on Cyprus continue hundred of years of political and cultural conflict, often flaring into violence.

> The uneasy peace between Jews and Arabs, internationally and internally, defies lasting solution.

> Military, communal, and other groups of the political right and left vie for control in a variety of countries.

> Politically motivated homicides mark struggles between dissident minorities and extremist political groups and those currently in power in several European countries, even in the course of normal political campaigning.

> Violence explodes in apartheid South Africa, spilling over into heretofore peaceful white areas.

> Elsewhere in Africa political and economic cleavages involve both traditional tribal and colonial lines of division.

> Political kidnapping, homicides, and coups become commonplace in several South American countries.

I am grateful to Washington State University and to the John Simon Guggenheim Memorial and Rockefeller Foundations for generously supporting the travel and study which are reflected in this chapter. The opportunity to share these ideas with colleagues on a variety of occasions has aided in their refinement—a process which continues as of this writing. Special mention should be made of discussions at Denison University, the University of California at Santa Cruz, and the Western Society of Criminology, and with Washington State University colleagues, Irving Tallman and John Boley. I am grateful for all of these. They are not, of course, responsible for my interpretations of their good advice.

Politically motivated bombings and violent confrontations occur in the
United States and Canada, as long-standing grievances become increasingly politicized.

These phenomena are familiar enough in the news of the day, and they
are the subject of hundreds of studies by scholars in a variety of disciplines.
Less familiar to many or taken for granted and regarded as unremarkable
or unimportant by others is the fact that the bulk of the participants in these
conflicts are young people. Though the kidnapping or killing of older
leaders receives more headline attention, it is the young who are most often
killed and who do most of the abducting, killing, and other activities
associated with political terrorism, riots, and politically motivated
predatory activity. And it is the young who commit most of the serious
street crime in this and other countries.

Few places on earth, it seems, escape either political violence or "ordinary" crimes. Research into the nature of relationships between youth involvement in crime and in politics, and with the conditions and processes
which shape these relationships is therefore of both theoretical and practical
importance. The scholarly community has generally regarded politics and
crime as quite distinct phenomena. In the United States especially, the
tendency has been to acknowledge political crime as an aberration or to ignore it as unimportant. A few "new historians" and quantitatively oriented
political scientists, "new criminologists" and a few "old sociologists" have
begun to challenge some of these assumptions, but the challenge has been
sporadic and unsystematic, often more ideological than empirical or
theoretical.

Gangs and Politics in the United States

Whyte (1943) and Thrasher (1927, rev. 1963) before him, and others earlier
still, described the political interests and activities of gangs as essentially
status quo in orientation, with the gang serving, and being served by, the
power, prestige, and economic advantage of entrenched political organizations. Thrasher summarized the nature of these relationships as follows:

> To repay the politician for putting gang members on official pay-rolls, and
> providing subsidies, protection, and immunities from official interference,
> the gang often splits with him the proceeds of its illegitimate activities; con-
> trols for him the votes of its members, hangers-on, and friends, and per-
> forms for him various types of "work" at the polls, such as slugging, in-
> timidation, kidnapping, vandalism (tearing down signs, etc.), ballot-fixing,
> repeating, stealing ballot boxes, miscounting, falsifying returns, etc.
> [Thrasher 1963:331-332]

For a variety of reasons the alliance of youth gangs and politicians weakened—though it certainly did not disappear—during the Depression of the 1930s and the World War which followed it. Following World War II the ethnic composition of cities had changed greatly. In northern cities, especially, the large influx of black citizens with little political power or sophistication contributed to weakened social controls and rising rates of ordinary crime. The predatory and conflict behavior of juvenile gangs became part of the focus of youth and youthfulness that preoccupied public and scholarly attention alike. This in turn was followed, during the Kennedy and Johnson years in the White House, by a resurgence of interest in gangs and politics. The war on poverty channeled private foundation and federal program funds to local communities, to combat poverty and to shore up political constituencies (Piven and Cloward 1971). In a few instances grants and contracts were made directly with gangs. The purposes of these funds, on the part of grantors and grantees alike, doubtless were multiple and motivated by goals both base and idealistic. Their success in program terms was inevitably limited (see Poston 1971; Short 1974, 1976).

A series of papers describe studies of the complex and changing relationships between gangs and politics which my colleagues and I have pursued since the late 1950s (Short 1973, 1974a, b, 1975, 1976; Short and Moland 1976; Short and Boley 1978). Briefly, we began a three-year period of intensive field work with several Chicago gangs in the spring of 1959—a propitious time, politically, since the 1960 conventions and campaigns were more than a year away, while civil rights ferment pursuant to the 1954 Brown decision of the U.S. Supreme Court was well under way. We were interested in the political interests, awareness, and activities of the gangs we studied, but that was not our primary focus. It was characteristic of delinquency theory and research of that period that the subject of politics was rarely mentioned except with reference to the adult community. In that context, institutional and interpersonal relationships between those engaged in conventional and criminal activities were regarded as important to social control of juvenile misbehavior in the community, and to legitimate and illegitimate opportunities for the young (Kobrin 1951; Cloward and Ohlin 1960). But politics as an area of interest and activity of the young was virtually ignored by the theories and little relevant empirical information existed.

Theoretical neglect was not altogether unwarranted. Scholars independently agree that the level of political interest and sophistication of gang members was at a low ebb during the depression, World War II, and immediate postwar years (Miller 1974, 1976; Suttles 1972; Kalberg and Suttles 1974). The 1960s brought a new type of public attention to gangs, however, and helped to create the "super gangs" of that period, culminating in the establishment of YOU (Youth Organization United), an umbrella organization designed to establish a network of youth groups from the street as a means of harnessing the energies of street youth and the funds of private and federal funding agencies. There has been a great deal of mythmaking concerning YOU, its predecessor, the Real Great Society, and a few super gangs (Poston 1971; Fry 1973; Dawley 1973). Little objective, systematic information is available concerning the organization or activities of any of these groups. There have been limited successes and spectacular failures. These have been discussed in numerous publications (in addition to those previously cited, see Spergel 1969). Suffice to say that the myths concerning the skills, motivations, and accomplishments of these super gang organizations distorted both the problems and the potentialities of ghetto youth. Because they did not recognize and compensate for severe limitations in skills necessary to the accomplishment of complex organizational and economic tasks, supporters of the gangs raised unrealistic hopes and expectations. They also failed to provide much needed assistance and supervision. By putting road blocks in the path of legitimate aspirations, those in opposition undercut already slim hopes of success in legitimate enterprises launched by gangs and their supporters (Fry 1973; Sherman 1970; Spergel 1969).

The most objective assessment of these matters is that the great bulk of ghetto youngsters, including gang members, were affected little by the politicization of a few gangs, or by the many enterprises which were begun under their auspices, few of which continue to exist (Miller 1976). Certainly economic success has been quite limited, by any criterion.

Only among the white gang boys that we studied did we find any degree of political interest or activity. They were often in the front lines of civil rights battles, opposing the advance of integration in housing and public facilities; in this following the ideological predilections of their parents (see Lipset 1971). Black gang members—their homes and their turf—were buried deep in the ghetto. Preoccupied within the limited horizons of their street world, the gang boys we studied evidenced no interest in either the civil rights movement of that era or with the presidential campaign which in 1970 was especially intense in Chicago (Short 1976).

The rhetoric of some black and Latino gangs especially, though not exclusively, retains a political flavor, and in prisons the political radicalization of a few gangs has reached a high level. A close observer of one such prison, however, notes that participation in a variety of prison rackets, such as control over desirable jobs, contraband goods, and the like, has achieved ascendancy over political aspirations of gangs who continue to compete and conflict much as they did in the street (Jacobs 1974, 1976).

We have also studied the political—especially the civil rights—interests and activities of the young black men who were members of the gangs we studied more than a decade earlier. Briefly, we found little political activity but strong attitudinal support for traditional civil rights groups and programs such as the NAACP, the Urban League, voter registration, and education, rather than more militant organizations and programs. The super gangs rated poorly among these men, even by some who had belonged to one of the largest and most political super gangs, the Vice Lords (Short and Moland 1976).

Greatly oversimplified, our conclusion is that the relation between youth, delinquency, and politics in the United States, although evidencing a wide spectrum of political activity and philosophy, has been tenuous and parochial, controlled by rather than controlling events in the external environment. In the long view, perhaps a beginning has been made by groups presently most disadvantaged in American society toward political involvement that in the future may be better organized and more efficient and effective (see Horowitz and Schwartz 1974). The future is clouded with many problems, the most important of which may be the political climate within which it is to develop. It is here, I think, that comparative study may contribute most to our understanding.

A Comparative Perspective

In few countries is the relationship between delinquent and political problems of youth perceived either as a problem or a possible solution. In England, a few radical scholars approach the relationship in largely ideological terms, with little systematic empirical inquiry. The apparent closeness of the relationship in Ulster has only rarely been carefully studied. In Israel, where political activity is at least conceptualized as a possible therapeutic or preventative strategy, the nation's most serious political conflicts—between Jews and Arabs, internal as well as external—have been virtually ignored by youth work agencies who concentrate instead on ethnic differences among Jews in that country (Cohn 1976; Cromer 1977).

The remainder of this chapter explores differences and similarities among nations in relations between youth, delinquency, and politics. Generalization concerning similarities is somewhat easier than is the case with respect to differences. The former occur, not surprisingly, at the microsociological level, where cultural differences tend to be submerged by the immediacy of ongoing interaction, and where young people share problems related to growing up—problems of survival in the adult world, of status with age mates, and relations with members of the opposite sex (the familiar "rating and dating" rituals and motivations)—in short, problems of socialization, self-development, and relations with others. On the street, solutions to these problems often assume exploitative forms, as the street becomes an arena for playing out status threats (Short and Strodtbeck 1965;

Short 1974b; Keiser 1969; Jansyn 1966), frequently involving violent and predatory behavior; where dating, for example, becomes a contest of "making out" with little regard for emotional and physical consequences (Short, Strodtbeck, and Cartwright 1962).

There is a certain timeless and universal quality to the patterns of behavior shared by one-sex peer groups and to heterosexual interaction among the young. To be sure, there is also much variation, attributable to cultural and structural factors, as well as to more elusive phenomena such as fads and fashions, which—though extremely important to "the action" at any given time—rise and often fall with little lasting trace on more stable patterns of interaction.

It is primarily at the macrosociological level that explanations of differences in relations between youth, delinquency, and politics are to be found. I will focus on three cultural and structural dimensions which are especially relevant to these relationships. These three dimensions have to do with (1) the nature of political parties and specifically of the relations of youth to these parties; (2) the relation between social class and communal grievances; and (3) the position of societies, and of groups within societies, with respect to modernization.

Political Parties

Although it is perhaps not a fundamental cause of differences in delinquency rates between the United States and other countries, the greater diversity of political parties in many countries is worthy of note. What appears to happen in the relatively democratic nations of western Europe, for example, is that political parties are much more oriented toward and successful in attracting the participation of young people than is the case in the United States, where our two major parties strive for relatively centrist positions out of fear of alienating large blocks of voters. In the United States, the most passionate political identities form not around the major parties, but around issues and occasionally around candidates identified with these issues. In many other countries, however, parties differ sufficiently to encourage the identity and participation of the most passionate advocates. I have been impressed in discussion with young and old alike in several European countries with the intensity of party identity on the basis of issues and ideologies. Political parties in these and other countries focus on youth to a greater extent than in this country. And the nonvoter issue of so much concern in the United States is a nonissue in these countries. England seems closer to the United States in this respect, with both Labor and Conservative parties striving to accommodate extreme positions from right and left within centrist policies, and the Liberals fighting a losing battle to retain a faltering constituency. English gangs tend to be apolitical much as U.S. gangs, though they frequently become involved in conflicts that are part of the larger society, for example, relations with minority groups (Daniel and McGuire 1972).[1]

Implications of this difference for youth, delinquency, and politics doubtless are complex, depending on the degree of legitimacy accorded political institutions, the institutional-coercive balance (in Gurr's, 1972, terminology), the nature and organization of forces contending for political power in any given society (Snyder and Tilly 1972), and the nature of world system relationships of that society (Chirot 1977). In this chapter we can only suggest the relevance of such root causes. On a more simplistic level we suggest only that more of those youth who, in the United States, become identified as delinquents, in other countries with more diversified political parties become politically interested and active.

Hackler's observations (1961) concerning Austria are apposite. Political organizations of labor unions and other voluntary associations in that country involve a wide spectrum of interest and age groups in political activity. Hackler reports that "In Vienna . . . the Boy Scout organizations, and a variety of other youth gangs are clearly divided into socialist and conservative organizations. Even the hiking clubs were organized along political lines" (private communication).

Comparative observation suggest two further points: (1) in many countries political activity occurs along a wide political spectrum, from far right to far left; and (2) university students appear to be more active politically than are nonstudents. Research on youth in a variety of developing and modern countries over many years is consistent on the latter point (Lipset 1971). A French director of criminological research described to me radical left students from North Africa, some of whom are law students, who sometimes resort to violence in enforcing within their own group a political doctrine comprising elements of Marxism, Maoism, and ethnic values. L'Occident, a right wing group of students— many of whom are in law—are organized to fight left wing groups. They often wear white leather or plastic jackets and helmets. Other political symbols include wearing T-shirts featuring a favored politician's likeness. Communes and socialist youth groups also are well organized and often very active in political campaigns and in unsanctioned collective activity, for example, the "revolution" in 1968. All of these groups, my informant suggested, draw off youth who otherwise would be organized in street gangs. Still, he said, there are many street gangs that profess no political ideology and behave very much like our delinquent gangs, only becoming involved in predatory or violent behavior related to politics when convenient upheavals occur—much as U.S. gangs did during the riots of the 1960s.

These observations suggest the importance of political consciousness as an important variable determining types of political and delinquent behavior. Compared to other young people, particularly lower-class young people, university students are more politically aware, informed, and concerned, as well as active. Our black gang members lacked political consciousness, and this, more than any positive sense of the legitimacy of political institutions, appeared to account for their lack of interest in political matters. We must therefore account for the convergence of political activity and delinquency. Surely political consciousness has a good deal to do with this convergence. And, whether conceived as "the deprivation of awareness" (Touraine 1973, cited in Seeman 1975) or in a more social-psychological and multidimensional sense (Seeman 1972), alienation and efficacy are involved. We will not attempt here to resolve ancient and recent debates concerning these elusive but important phenomena. Again, however, comparative observations are relevant. Evidence from the United States, where delinquents played little role in the riots of 1960s (except for taking advantage of targets of opportunity, see Miller 1976), suggests that riot participants were characterized by "a strong sense of personal political competence (i.e., efficacy) combined with a deep distrust of the political system" (Paige 1971:810). These clearly were not our gang delinquents. Other evidence from that stormy decade has long since dispelled the riff-raff theory of riot participation (see Skolnick 1969), that is, the notion that the riots were the product of delinquents, criminals, and other ne'er-do-wells. But how does grievance become transplanted into political efficacy and activity? A variety of answers at different levels of explanation have been given to this question, from political socialization to social movements and organization (Shorter and Tilly 1974). Although we cannot address these explanations in a systematic way, the second of our three structural and cultural dimensions provides important insights that illuminate the conditions under which political criminality becomes widespread.

Convergence of Structurally and Culturally Induced Grievance

We may begin with observations concerning the absence of political violence. Here legitimacy of political institutions appears to be crucial. For example, Schwartz (1972) concludes from her ethnographic study of a village in central Mexico that when the legitimacy of political institutions is not questioned, conflicts within the political system and levels of individual violence are unrelated, and neither leads to political violence. Perhaps legitimacy is the critical variable in Von der Mehden's wide-ranging study *Comparative Political Violence* (1973).

Von der Mehden notes that the coincidence of class and communal grievances occasions high levels of political violence. Broadening this notion only slightly, it may be hypothesized that political violence is higher and more widespread among the populace to the extent that grievances associated with structural cleavages (for example, social class) and communal antagonisms (for example, those associated with value systems related to religion, tribe, or ethnicity) converge.

Von der Mehden's capsule descriptions of political conflict in several societies are sufficient only to illustrate the argument. It is clear that youth have played significant roles in all the conflicts studied. The problem comes in specifying which youth and what roles. The range of our concerns can be seen from the examples of specific instances of political violence discussed by Von der Mehden. They include: Indonesia, 1965-1966; Malaysia, 1969; Cambodia, 1970-1971; Rwanda, 1963-1964; Zanzibar, 1964; Northern Nigeria, 1966; and brief examination of the history of political violence in Burma, Thailand, and Northern Ireland. More recent events in some of these countries enrich the data base for such studies. The relevance of the Von der Mehden materials is suggested by the following: Regarding the violence in Indonesia in 1965-1966, what began as a conflict among military officers spread rapidly throughout east Java, Bali, and the other islands of the Republic. There followed mass and individual executions by villagers, Moslem youth groups, and several noncentral government units. Antagonisms were varied and widespread, related to religion, political ideology, economic grievance related to land use, the position of the Chinese community vis-à-vis native people, and apolitical personal grudges. Vigilante-type action and specific mention of Moslem youth groups are provocative hints but insufficient as data to evaluate the hypothesis systematically.

Similarly, observations concerning the much publicized massacres of minority Ibos in northern Nigeria in 1966 are suggestive, but inconclusive, for example, "In the rural areas (of Rwanda) the populace ran amok—apparently with support from local leaders."

It is instructive, at this point to examine a particular case—Northern Ireland—in view of the previous discussion.

Northern Ireland

A great deal has been written about Northern Ireland, that embattled section of an embattled isle. We are thus in a somewhat better position to evaluate the forces which are there at work.

Elliott and Hickie (1971) note the importance of the historical roots of the troubles in Northern Ireland:

History is very much a part of the present in Northern Ireland: discussions of massacres and battles, political pogroms that took place two or three hundred years ago, are a part of the everyday language of the Ulsterman. When one of the authors was interviewing in Northern Ireland during the fighting in Londonderry, he quite often heard comparisons between fighting of the day before and some other battle whose name he did not recognize, only later to discover that reference was to battles fought two or three hundred years previously. . . . Ever since the Gallic invasions of 1 B.C. Ireland has been constantly invaded, not least because of a tradition of political disunification covering the whole island. [pp. 29-30]

More directly to the point of our discussion:

The conflict was made the more intractable since the hostility and opposition fell along well demarcated social and cultural lines. There was a gulf between the two social structures as well as between cultural beliefs. . . . Although the English language is used by both groups, the Irish language and the illegal tricolour flag is something special to many Catholics. From the religious differences come crucial rules about marital and sexual behavior, and dietary rules. An awareness of Cromwell's massacres at Drogheda and Wexford and of the decisive Protestant victory at the Boyne is socialised into school children and it becomes as much a part of the consciousness of belonging to each faith as being black is for an American Negro. The fact that such aspects of group identity are invisible does not make them any less powerful in determining lines of cooperation and cleavage.

The general point seems clear. Convergence of antagonisms associated with social (class) and cultural (communal) cleavages leads to high levels of and widespread participation in political violence.

The effects of such cleavages on children have rarely been discussed, but in Northern Ireland, the role of youth gangs is often explicit. References are found to "running battles" between police, "Paisleyite supporters and teen-age gangs" (Elliott and Hickie 1971:47) and to "mass enlistments into the UDA or the IRA"; noting further that "the Tartan gangs . . . go well beyond the old youth sections of the IRA and of the Orange League in ferocity" (Jenvey 1972:125). Reports of mob action are common, and while reference to the composition of such collectivities is rare, there can be little doubt that most are young people, primarily working or lower class, and many also are members of street gangs. Jenvey's discussion of "Sons and Haters," published in *New Society* in 1972, focuses on the gangs:

Gangs are nothing new in these districts of inner Belfast. Most of the Tartans would have been members of such gangs anyway. Anti-Catholic slogans and loyalist songs, and on the other side anti-Protestant and nationalist rhymes, have been chanted for years by Belfast youth gangs. The purpose of the chants, however, mainly used to be to rouse support for an attack on a rival gang in neighboring territory, and to boost group loyalty, rather than to pledge support for parents' prejudices.

The name "Tartans," derived from the tartan scarves which were worn by gang members with their blue denim outfits. It was coined first by gangs, ages ranging from twelve to eighteen, in the Protestant working class areas. A new umbrella name did not change the pattern of gang membership or recruitment. Tartans from neighbouring districts (some of only a few streets), continued to be sworn enemies and to fight each other pretty regularly. Sometimes Catholic gangs fought other Catholics; or Protestants other Protestants. But as the sectarian conflict waged by the adults intensified, a redefinition of loyalties in line with the religious divide occurred. Groups of Protestant Tartans began banding together to form a joint assault force against the local Catholics. The attacks were directed mainly at Catholic property—chiefly pubs—though direct confrontation with rival Catholic gangs took place if the latter happen to cross their paths.[2]

Jenvey agrees with Richard Rose as to the importance of intergenerational support on both sides of the conflict. For Jenvey, "one of the major effects of living with the troubles has been to direct the young away from rebellion against the adult world . . . toward conformity with their parents and the local community." Rose notes that widespread opposition to official policies among adults on both sides "has important consequences for maintaining discord from generation to generation."

Insofar as disaffected women have husbands with similar views, their children will be raised in a household in which both parents display attitudes undermining the regime. It is much easier for children to accept such views than would be the case if fathers often advocated extreme political action, while mothers were bemoaning such opinions and their consequences. The permeation of whole families by anti-regime outlooks puts very strong and immediate emotional sanctions behind attitudes of disaffection and defiance. [Rose 1971:331]

A more systematic survey of Ulster youth, by James Russell, finds that approximately two-thirds of the 3,000 school boys studied approved of political violence (Russell 1973). Working-class boys "were more ready to approve of disorders than middle-class boys," especially among Protestants, but escalation of violence is eroding these differences, for among Catholic primary school boys (who were surveyed a year after the secondary school boys) "in the weeks after Bloody Monday, the sons of school teachers and doctors joined the ranks of the more violent" (p. 205). It remains the case, however, that "outside of school, and adult-created youth groups, boys who lead the neighborhood gangs more readily approve of disorder than those on the fringe of such groups and boys who are outsiders" (p. 206).

Observers also note that it is often difficult to know which events in the troubles are politically motivated and which merely criminal. When the

Queen visited Ulster in 1966, "the visit was successful and large crowds turned up to cheer her. There were only two small incidents involving the throwing of a concrete block and a bottle, which the police did not consider political, but merely the work of hooligans" (Elliott and Hickie 1971:47).

Until recently, for the vast majority of young people ideological fervor probably played little role in the class and religious cleavages of Northern Ireland. Few were attracted to active participation on either side. The London Sunday *Times'* Insight Team of reporters could write—in retrospect—of the "death of the IRA" in the early and mid-1960s. Cathal Goulding, an IRA leader of the 1950s who tried unsuccessfully to steer IRA strategy in a more peaceful direction, noted that for those young men who were participating, "the fight had become an end in itself. They were not planning to achieve the freedom of Ireland. They simply wanted to *fight* for it" (Sunday *Times* Insight Team 1972), suggesting that the fighting at this time involved status games similar to those observed in our studies of Chicago gangs.

As the conflict escalated and participation became more widespread, gangs became more involved, as noted above. The transition from street conflict to political conflict was not easy, however, as Jenvey (1972) notes:

> Yet the alliance of old enemies was uneasy. Once back on home ground, the Tartans soon split up into their old groupings within the street gang structure. This could be exasperating for the few politically conscious young people among them. One Tartan complained to me, dispairingly, that his gang persisted in engaging in inter-Tartan territorial disputes, despite the greater struggle being fought around them. The local identity of each Tartan gang remains even now. Boys still refer to themselves as members of the Tartan of their locality, rather than simply as "Tartans."[3]

Compare these observations with Keiser's description of the Vice Lords' reaction to hostile threats from other gangs, and the notoriety achieved by the Blackstone Rangers. When Bull, a Vice Lord who was a member of a Black Nationalist organization, spoke out against a resumption of gang fighting, on the premise that "all the clubs on the West Side should stop fighting among themselves and unite against the Whites," he was sharply challenged by the other boys, one of whom said, "The Cobras may be my "brothers," but if one of them motherfuckers jump on me I'll bust a cap in his ass [shoot him]" (Keiser 1969).

It is not difficult to find parallels between street gang warfare in the United States and the troubles in Ulster. Prior to the present escalation of violence, conflict often assumed forms which might be characterized as a "nonzero sum game," much as most gang conflict was before firearms became commonplace (Short and Strodtbeck 1965; Horowitz and Schwartz 1974). In both, the lack of objective communication between conflicting groups contributes to the violation of tenuous understandings and rules and periodic truces which mark their rivalry (Elliott and Hickie 1971:35). In both, violence often becomes "the least common communicator" (p. 65); indeed the least common denominator of behavior within as well as between groups in conflict. Some of the excesses in both doubtless are due to the fact that the young lack discipline, skill, and sophistication in a variety of ways, and they often are less constrained by rational consideration of the consequences of their actions than are their elders. In the spring of 1976, following several bombings in London, attributed to and claimed by the IRA, a much-respected English scholar was heard to remark that the problem of terrorism would be infinitely more serious were it not for the ineptness of the terrorists who often injure, and sometimes kill, themselves, and leave a trail of clues for authorities to follow.

The Ulster case suggests the limits of the number and diversity of parties notion and the overriding importance of conflicts associated with structural cleavage (social class) and communal grievance. So intense are the latter in Ulster that virtually the entire society is polarized. Beyond individuals structural and cultural levels of political consciousness, efficacy-alienation, and grievance, the conflict assumes an added dimension as a phenomenon of collective behavior. While this may not alter its fundamental nature, it often changes the organizational character of the conflict and contributes a special dynamic to it (see Short 1974a; Shorter and Tilly 1974). In the case of Northern Ireland this has had international as well as internal repercussions. The (largely young) participants in the conflict are now actors on a much larger stage.

Modernization

The third dimension of our theoretical sketch concerns modernization. Our comparative study of youth, delinquency, and politics began with a proposal to study the role of indigenous youth groups in modern industrial societies. Even this broad scope soon proved too limiting, as is clear from the earlier discussion. Both reading and personal contacts revealed that the conflicts in which youth are engaged in many countries often are ancient in origin, and primordial in nature for example, the troubles in Northern Ireland and Jewish-Arab relations in Israel. Furthermore, the research on Chicago gangs suggested parallels between modern and developing, or modernizing, countries.

A great deal has been written in recent years about the rise and the significance of the nation-state and the process of modernization, by which primitive groups are transformed into nation-states (Swanson 1960, 1971; Bendix 1964; Meyer and Nagel 1975). There is much disagreement as to the nature of this transformation—its relationship to existing and emerging world systems, and the extent to which it is characterized by particular stages and sequences of development (see Wallerstein 1974; Chirot 1976; Stokes and Harris 1979). Without attempting to resolve these important questions, it is possible to note parallels between problems and perspectives of delinquent gangs and traditional societies. Specifically, delinquent gangs experience difficulties in "going conservative," that is, in moving toward political activity and respectability, which are similar to those experienced by societies in the course of transition between societal types, today especially in becoming modern. Gang interests and activities—like those of developing societies—tend to be primordial (concerning turf and group identity) rather than with the roles of individual members, or their development in relation to the larger community; with the local neighborhood action rather than civic pride or personal problems of individual emmbers (Short, Strodtbeck, and Cartwright 1962; Rivera and Short 1967a, b). Indeed, the gang as a context for behavior tends to discourage attempts by youth to cope with emerging problems of adulthood, including relationships with individuals and institutions in the larger society. Of equal importance, adults in a variety of institutional contexts tend either to confirm the gang's parochial and predatory identity, or to accept too readily and naively the willingness and ability of gangs to transform themselves into agents of change and community betterment (Poston 1971; Short 1974b, 1976).

The fundamental problem for gangs as well as for traditional societies, is to achieve that "new cultural outlook" which Eisenstadt refers to as "perhaps the most pervasive aspect of modernization. . . ."

> This outlook has been characterized by an emphasis on progress and improvement . . . on individuality as a moral value, and concomitant stress on the dignity of the individual and . . . on efficiency. This has been manifest in the development of some new personality orientations, traits, and characteristics—greater ability to adjust to the broadening societal horizons; some ego-flexibility; widening spheres of interest; growing potential empathy with other people and situations; a growing emphasis on the present as the meaningful temporal dimension of human existence. [Eisenstadt 1966:5]

Similarly, Inkeles (1975) summarizes his work in this area as follows (see also Inkeles and Smith 1974):

> A modern *nation* needs participating citizens, men and women who take an active interest in public affairs and who exercise their rights and perform their duties as members of a community larger than that of the kinship network and the immediate geographical locality. In their turn, modern *institutions* need individuals who can keep to fixed schedules, observe abstract rules, make judgements on the basis of objective evidence, and follow authorities legitimized not by traditional or religious sanctions but by technical competence. The complex production tasks of the industrial

order, which are the basis of modern social systems, also make their demands. Workers must be able to accept both an elaborate division of labor and the need to coordinate their activities with a large number of others in the work force. Rewards based on technical competence and objective standards of performance, on strict hierarchies of authority responsive to the imperatives of machine production, and on the separation of the product and producer, all are part of this milieu, and require particular personal properties of those who are to master its requirements. [pp. 323-324]

It is precisely in these areas of social skills and adjustments that gang boys, as individuals, experience the greatest difficulty in adjusting to the larger society in which they must find jobs and live as citizens (see Short and Strodtbeck 1965; Gordon 1966; Caplan 1973). Especially for the black youngsters we studied, these difficulties were exacerbated by gang membership.[4]

Aside from these analogies between gangs and nations in transition, modernization may have more fundamental significance, both as a subset of structural grievance, and a variable in its own right. Nationhood which brings under central political authority groups differing along communal or tribal lines may exacerbate communal differences by creating structural grievance as political hegemony favors one or more group(s) over another or others. While modernization may (by definition in some treatments of the subject) break down traditional cleavages, it may create or exacerbate other problems, as citizens are cut adrift from traditional values and groups. The African studies of Clinard and Abbot (1973, 1976) and Weinberg (1976), for example, demonstrate that social control of delinquent behavior is related to the breakdown of traditional tribal authority in Uganda and Ghana. They also suggest behavioral correlates of structural and cultural variables similar to those in the American experience. Regretably they do not address the political questions discussed in this chapter.

Answers to the latter questions, we suggest, are to be found in variables and processes previously discussed in this chapter. Modernization—its pace and its relationship to world systems—gives rise to differing degrees of political alienation (in a structural sense) and political efficacy (in a psychological sense) (Boley 1978). It may also result in quite different subcultural and collective patterns of delinquency, as suggested by Ferdinand in chapter 14, this volume. Implications of these differences for delinquency control, as Ferdinand suggests, are profound.

Discussion

The purpose of this chapter has been to explore rather than explain or propose solutions for the relationships examined. We feel obligated, in conclusion to make explicit our assumptions as to the larger significance of the inquiries, particularly with respect to implications for social policy. Fundamentally, the significance of the study lies in the distribution of power and in the balance which is struck between social control and the aspirations and interests of both "haves" and "have-nots" throughout the world. Some will view the problem as one of achieving control over the more objectionable manifestations of juvenile crimes; others in terms of the development of social, economic, and political resources, awareness and activity by those now lacking in this respect. Both types of claims are valid, but the latter, we believe, is the most crucial test for the future.

In the United States there is a certain irony in the fact that current social control efforts, particularly with respect to those types of behavior labeled white-collar crime and organized crime, occur as increased opportunities develop in the areas for minorities so long associated with ordinary, street crime (Ianni 1974). If our theoretical suggestions and review of the evidence in this paper are correct, the needs and aspirations of the world's have-nots will be manifest in political competition and conflict from local to world system levels. If the attempt is made to resolve these problems chiefly by means of coercive control, the likelihood of increased political turmoil and criminality in their varied forms is high indeed.

Notes

1. To the extent that separatist movements in Scotland and Wales develop, involvement of gangs in these parts of Britain are likely to increase. The extreme of such involvement is found in Ulster.

2. Sue Jenvey, "Sons and Haters: Ulster Youth in Conflict," *New Society*, 21 (July 1972):126. This article first appeared in *New Society*, London, the weekly review of the social sciences. Reprinted with permission.

3. Jenvey, *Sons and Haters*. Reprinted with permission.

4. Evidence from other studies suggests that, among white and Chicano gangs (Schwartz and Horowitz 1974), gang experience can be politically advantageous. The record, for American blacks at the bottom of the social and economic ladder, however, is less encouraging. Here, leadership has arisen occasionally from prisons and the streets, but it has more often been snuffed out by internecine strife in those settings, or by opposition of sometimes debatable legitimacy (Sherman 1970; Dawley 1973; Fry 1973; Short 1974b, 1976). Caplan (1973) notes that those skills which commend themselves on the street, "hustling, rapping, signifying, gang leadership, psyching out people, fighting, athletics, and so forth . . . are incompatible with and often antithetical to the conventional skills required on the job market."

References

Bendix, Rinehart (1964). *Nation-Building and Citizenship*. New York: John Wiley and Sons.

Boley, John (1978). Modernization and the political alienation of youth: a comparative analysis of delinquency. M.A. Thesis, Washington State University.

Bremner, Robert H. (1974). *Children and Youth in America*. Cambridge: Harvard University Press.

Caplan, Nathan (1973). "Street skills of many hard-to-employ youths may hinder success in job training programs." *Newsletter*, Institute for Social Research, University of Michigan, 19(1):5-7.

Cloward, R.A. and Ohlin, L.E. (1960). *Delinquency and Opportunity: A Theory of Delinquent Gangs*. New York: Free Press of Glencoe.

Cohn, Yona (1976). Delinquency prevention—a system approach. Unpublished manuscript.

Cromer, Gerald (1977). The Israeli Black Panthers: a case study of the politicization of juvenile delinquents. Unpublished manuscript.

Daniel, Susie, and McGuire, Pete (eds.) (1972). *The Paint House: Words from an East End Gang*. Middlesex: Penguin Books.

Dawley, David (1973). *A Nation of Lords*. Garden City, N.Y.: Anchor Press.

Eisenstadt, S.N. (1966). *Modernization: Protest and Change*. Englewood Cliffs, N.J.: Prentice-Hall.

Elliott, R.S.P., and Hickie, John (1971). *Ulster: A Case Study in Conflict Theory*. London: Longman.

Ferdinand, Theodore N. (1980). "Delinquency in developing and developed societies." In David Shichor and Delos H. Kelly, *Critical Issues in Juvenile Delinquency*. Lexington, Mass.: Lexington Books, D.C. Heath.

Field, Alexander (1972). Education Reform and Manufacturing Development, Massachusetts 1937 to 1965. Unpublished doctoral dissertation, University of California, Berkeley.

Fry, John R. (1973). *Locked-Out Americans*. New York: Harper and Row.

Gordon, Robert A. (1966). "Social level, disability, and gang interaction." American Journal of Sociology 73 (July):42-62.

Gurr, Ted Robert (1972). "Sources of rebellion in Western societies." Chapter 10 in James F. Short, Jr. and Marvin E. Wolfgang (eds.), *Collective Violence*. Chicago: Aldine-Atherton.

Gurr, Ted Robert, with Grabosky, Peter N., Hula, Richard C., Masotti, Louis A., Pierce, David, Person, Lief, and Sperlings, Sven, *Rogues, Rebels, and Reformers: A Political History of Urban Crime and Conflict*. Beverly Hills: Sage.

Hackler, James (1961). "The integration of a lower class culture: some implications of a rigid class structure." *Sociological Quarterly* 2:203-13.

Holt, John (1973). *Escape from Childhood.* New York: Simon and Schuster.

Horowitz, Ruth, and Schwartz, Gary A. (1974). "Honor, normative ambiguity and gang violence." *American Sociological Review* 39 (April:238-251).

Ianni, Francis A.J. (1974). *Black Mafia: Ethnic Succession in Organized Crime.* New York: Simon and Schuster.

Inkeles, Alex, and Smith, David H. (1974). *Becoming Modern: Individual Change in Six Developing Countries.* Cambridge: Harvard University Press.

Jacobs, James B. (1974). "Street gangs behind bars." *Social Problems* 21 (Winter):395-409.

———— (1977). *Statesville.* Chicago: University of Chicago Press.

Jansyn, L.R. (1966). "Solidarity and delinquency in a street corner group." *American Sociological Review* 31 (October):600-614.

Jenvey, Sue (1972). "Sons and haters: Ulster youth in conflict." *New Society* 20 (July):125-127.

Kalberg, Stephen, and Suttles, Gerald D. (1974). Gangs, the police and politicians in Chicago during 1964-1970. Paper prepared for the E.W. Burgess Memorial Symposium, University of Chicago.

Keiser, R. Lincoln (1969). *The Vice Lords: Warriors of the Streets.* New York: Holt, Rinehart, and Winston.

Kobrin, Solomon (1951). "The conflict of values in delinquency areas." *American Sociological Review* 16 (October):657-662.

Lipset, S.M. (1971). "Youth and politics." In Robert K. Merton and Robert Nisbet (eds.), *Contemporary Social Problems.* New York: Harcourt Brace Javonovich.

Meyer, John W., and Nagel, Joane P. (1975). The changing status of childhood. Paper prepared for presentation at the annual meetings of the Society for the Study of Social Problems, San Francisco, August.

Miller, Walter B. (1974). "American youth gangs: past and present." In Abraham S. Blumberg (ed.), *Current Issues in Criminology.* New York: Alfred A. Knopf.

———— (1976). "Youth gangs in the urban crisis era." In James F. Short, Jr. (ed.), *Delinquency, Crime, and Society.* Chicago: University of Chicago Press.

National Commission on Civil Disorders (1968). *Report.* Washington, D.C.: U.S. Government Printing Office.

Piven, F.F., and Cloward, R.A. (1971). *Regulating the Poor.* New York: Pantheon Books.

Poston, R.W. (1971). *The Gang and the Establishment*. New York: Harper and Row.

Rivera, Ramon J. and Short, James F., Jr. (1967a). "Occupational goals: a comparative analysis." In Malcolm W. Klein (ed.), *Juvenile Gangs in Context*, pp. 70-90. Englewood Cliffs, N.J.: Prentice-Hall.

_____ (1967b). "Significant adults, caretakers and structures of opportunity," *Journal of Research in Crime and Delinquency* 4 (January):76-97.

Rose, Richard (1971). *Governing without Consensus: An Irish Perspective*. London: Faber and Faber.

Russell, James (1973). "Violence and the Ulster schoolboy." *New Society* 26 (July):204-206.

Schwartz, Lola Romanucci (1972). "Conflict without violence and violence without conflict in a Mexican Mestizo village." In James F. Short, Jr., and Marvin E. Wolfgang (eds.), *Collective Violence*, ch. 11. Chicago: Aldine-Atherton.

Seeman, Melvin (1972). "Alienation and engagement." In A. Campbell and P.E. Converse (eds.), *The Human Meaning of Social Change*, ch. 12. New York: Russell Sage.

_____ (1975). "Alienation studies." In A. Inkeles, J. Coleman, and N. Smelser (eds.), *Annual Review of Sociology*, 1:91-123.

Sherman, Lawrence (1970). Youth Workers, Police, and the Gangs: Chicago, 1956-1970. Master's thesis, University of Chicago.

Short, James F., Jr. (1973). "Gangs and politics: images and realities." In Mary Jeannette Hageman (ed.), *The Negley K. Teeters Symposium on Crime in America*, pp. 42-50. Oneonta, N.Y.: Hartwick College.

_____ (1974a). "Collective behavior, crime, and delinquency." In Daniel Glaser (ed.), *Handbook of Criminology*. New York: Rand McNally College Publishing Co.

_____ (1974b). "Youth, gangs, and society: micro- and macrosociological processes." *Sociological Quarterly* 15 (Winter):3-19.

_____ (1975). "Gangs, violence and politics." In Duncan Chappell and John Monahan (eds.), *Violence and Criminal Justice*, pp. 101-112. Lexington, Mass.: Lexington Books, D.C. Heath.

_____ (1976). "Gangs, politics, and the social order." In James F. Short, Jr. (ed.), *Delinquency, Crime, and Society*. Chicago: University of Chicago Press.

Short, James F., Jr., and Boley, John (1978). Youth, delinquency, and politics: a comparative perspective. Paper prepared for meetings of the International Sociological Association, Uppsala, Sweden, August.

Short, James F., Jr., and Strodtbeck, Fred L. (1965). *Group Process and Gang Delinquency*. Chicago: University of Chicago Press.

Short, James F., Jr., and Moland, John, Jr. (1976). "Politics and youth gangs: a follow-up study." *Sociological Quarterly* 17 (Spring):162-179.

Short, James F., Jr., Strodtbeck, F.L., and Cartwright, D.S. (1962). "A strategy for utilizing research dilemmas." *Sociological Inquiry* 32 (Spring): 185-202.

Shorter, Edward, and Tilly, Charles (1974). *Strikes in France, 1830-1968.* Cambridge: Cambridge University Press.

Skolnick, Jr. (1969). *The Politics of Protest: Violent Aspects of Protest and Confrontation.* Staff report to National Commission on the Causes and Prevention of Violence (Staff Report 3). Washington, D.C.: U.S. Government Printing Office.

Snyder, David and Tilly, Charles (1972). "Hardship and collective violence in France, 1830 to 1960." *American Sociological Review* 37 (October):520-532.

Spergel, Irving (1969). Politics, policies and the youth gang. University of Chicago, School of Social Service Administration (mimeographed).

Stokes, Randall and Harris, Anthony (1979). "South African development and the paradox of racial particularism: toward a theory of modernization from the center." *Economic Development and Cultural Change.*

Sunday Times Insight Team (1972). Ulster. Middlesex: Penquin Books.

Suttles, Gerald (1972). Recent social movements and the politicization of juvenile corner groups in Chicago. Lecture given at the CUNY Graduate Center (unpublished).

Swanson, Guy E. (1960). *The Birth of the Gods.* Ann Arbor: University of Michigan Press.

_____ (1971). "An organizational analysis of collectivities." *American Sociological Review* 36 (August).

Thrasher, Frederick M. (1927). *The Gang.* Rev. 1963. Chicago: University of Chicago Press.

Touraine, A. (1973). *Production de la Societe.* Paris: Editions du Seiul.

von der Mehden, Fred R. (1973). *Comparative Political Violence.* Englewood Cliffs, N.J.: Prentice-Hall.

Wallerstein, Immanuel (1974). *The Modern World System.* New York: Academic Press.

Whyte, W.F. (1943). *Street Corner Society.* Chicago: University of Chicago Press.

16 Some Issues of Social Policy in the Field of Juvenile Delinquency

David Shichor

Introduction

Social scientists have begun to show an increasing interest in the relationships between their specific fields of study and the formation of social policies and their implementation.

A major issue that emerges when we try to study these issues is connected with the definition of social policy. As Freeman and Sherwood (1970) point out, there is not one simple definition of this concept. They distinguish at least four different definitions of social policy: (1) a philosophical concept or principle that leads members of organizations and political entities to search for solutions of their collective problems; (2) a product of the conclusions reached by those who are concerned with the betterment of societal conditions; (3) a process by which stability is maintained in society and at the same time a continuous attempt to improve conditions; (4) a framework for action, a well-defined policy, that is available and possible to implement (Freeman and Sherwood 1970:2-3).

Dror (1971) claims that social policy is really concerned with the control of society and its individual members. Indeed, social policy concerning crime and juvenile delinquency is closely involved with social control. This chapter deals with some of the issues involved in policymaking and its implementation in the field of juvenile delinquency.

The Role of the Social Scientist in Policymaking

The role of the social scientist in policymaking has been analyzed quite extensively. Social policymaking is basically a political activity. Traditionally the goals are set by politicians; social scientists, if they are called upon, try to advise them on the basis of research and relevant knowledge, or by designing and conducting research which is connected with the contemplated policy (Littrell and Sjoberg 1976:5).

This does not mean that the advice and recommendations suggested by social scientists are necessarily accepted. In reviewing the work of Caplan et al. (1975) which deals with the utilization of social science knowledge in social policy decision, Davis and Selasin (1978:111) point out that:

85 percent of the national-level policy makers interviewed believed that social science knowledge can contribute to the improvement of government policies, but noted that most policy users call on the information to serve as a check on the validity of preexisting beliefs. Further, policymakers like to use information found in newspapers, allowing a feeling that their awareness does not lag behind others.

Wilson (1978:82-83) voices an even more pessimistic view about the same subject when he states that "only rarely have I witnessed serious governmental attention being given to serious social research . . .I have only rarely observed serious social science being presented to government agencies."

Weiss (1977:5) sounds similar concerns in regard to planning in health policies. Although these statements might reflect the general situation in policymaking, there are known instances in which the input of social scientists was important in the setting of certain social policies, for instance, in the case of school desegration and busing or the introduction of determinant sentencing in several states. Pelz (1978) sounds more optimistic in making his assessment, claiming that if "utilization of information" taken in a wider perspective, that is, acceptance of social science perspective, or "conceptual use (change in understanding or thinking), and symbolic use (legitimating an existing policy)" (Pelz 1978:357) then the influence of social science knowledge on social policy is much more extensive than is generally supposed.

It seems to be the case that when policymakers take into consideration the recommendations of social scientists, they are selective in choosing the material, and this selectivity is largely influenced by their political aims and views.

Social Policy and Juvenile Delinquency

Juvenile delinquency is considered to be a major social problem in most of the modern industrial societies and in many of the developing nations as well. This phenomenon is frequently in the news media, causes a great deal of public concern particularly in large urban areas, and occupies the minds of policymakers and the personnel of agencies which deal with the juvenile population. In terms of social policy the major objectives in this field are the prevention and reduction of juvenile delinquency.

Glaser (1972:28), in dealing with the crime problem, points out that there are two contrasting policy strategies available in trying to reduce crime. One concerns itself mainly with individual offenders, the other with altering the conditions responsible for crime rates. Generally, governmental policymakers tend to concentrate on programs directed toward the treatment of individual law violators rather than on programs directed toward affecting basic changes in social conditions and social arrangements which are conducive to delinquent involvement (Schur 1969). Accordingly, social policies in the field of juvenile delinquency can be divided into two main types. The first is mainly concerned with preventive strategies, is usually directed toward a large group of youngsters, and tries to intervene before delinquent involvements occur. The second includes efforts which are concerned with the treatment and rehabilitation of individuals and which are usually implemented after the delinquent involvement. There are many political issues and controversies involved concerning the actual policymaking in the field of juvenile delinquency and its analysis. The review of these issues in this chapter will refer mainly to Western industrial societies.

In very general terms there are three major political approaches concerning criminal and juvenile justice policies (1) the radical, (2) the liberal mainstream, and (3) the conservative.

The Liberal Mainstream Approach

The liberal approach is probably the most influential and widespread approach in Western industrial societies concerning juvenile delinquency. Liberal mainsteam criminology is not a unified school of thought which can be easily defined or characterized. It is rather connected with some ways of thought and actions which arc tagged by others as liberal. It covers a wide spectrum of approaches to social policy regarding juvenile delinquency; however, some common grounds are discernible. Generally, "the social order or societal structure is still seen as relatively viable, with little in the way of any suggestion, that American society is headed on any course toward total dissolution" (Gibbons and Garabedian 1974:51).

The liberal approach to crime and delinquency dates back to the classical school of criminology that developed at the end of the eighteenth century as a direct outcome of the period of enlightenment (Radzinowicz 1966). Although the proponents of this approach were fighting for human rights and equality before the law, it suggested mainly the retributive and deterrent reactions to lawbreakers. However, the neoclassical school, which arose after the French Revolution and embraced the basic premises of the classical doctrine, recognized that certain groups of people, among them the juveniles, cannot be considered fully rational, and therefore full individual responsibility cannot be attributed to them. This was one of the avenues which opened the possibility for the legislation of juvenile law and establishment of separate procedures. In addition, some other factors came into play in the development of liberal social policy toward juvenile delinquents. Doig points out that the historical development can be viewed or interpreted from two different vantage points: the liberal and the conservative. The former perspective sees the development of juvenile law and juvenile justice system "as shaped by reformers who sought to help young people develop into emotionally and intellectually competent, productive adults" (1975:140). These principles influenced also the treatment and rehabilitation approach toward juveniles who did not commit serious crimes. This development was described somewhat more vividly by Platt (1969) as the outgrowth of the child-saving movement. The general attitude in the public was also influenced by the ideas of this movement during the nineteenth and the early twentieth century:

> The great majority of Americans, judges included, believed that universal education was a social panacea; that children, especially children of the poor, had few legal rights; that impoverished parents lacked moral character and were incapable of providing healthy conditions for child rearing; and that anything which the government could do to instill their children with proper values was for the better. [Schlossman 1977:17]

At the very same period the concept of parens patriae has developed from the English poor laws. New York law used the Latin phrase "in loco parentis" to express "the power of the state to control the child once it had obtained custody rather than a state interest which is over and above the interest of a parent" (Rendleman 1974:84). This liberal trend contributed to the establishment of the juvenile court at the very end of the last century, an institution which carried on the spirit of protective ideology.

This protective approach, coupled with the acceptance of some of the basic premises of the positivistic school of Lombroso and his followers, finally incorporated also the psychological and psychiatric approaches of explanation and treatment of crime and delinquency. These developments focused the interest on the individual who breaks the law and were largely deterministic. Criminals and delinquents were seen as people who are not accountable for their actions and whose behavior can be changed only through therapy and treatment (Taylor, Walton, and Young 1973:37). Individual therapy and treatment became the major methods of handling juvenile delinquency. Consequently, social policy during a large part of the twentieth century concentrated on the establishment of suitable facilities, mainly juvenile treatment institutions where individual therapy could be administered.

With the development of some more sophisticated social psychological explanations of delinquency, like Sutherland's "differential association" theory, and with the increasing empirical evidence that the large bulk of juvenile delinquency is committed in group situations, group-oriented social psychological treatment practices were devised and introduced. This trend brought in also the community-based residential and semiresidential treatment centers (Provo, Highfields, Silverlake, and so on). Since the late 1950s some new perspectives have influenced this liberal school, particularly with the development of the labeling theory (Lemert 1951; Becker 1963; Erikson 1962; Schur 1971; Goffman 1963). Since then there has been a considerable trend of shifting from studying offenders and their characteristics, to the study of how laws are legislated, how people become defined as offenders, and the ways they are dealt with by the juvenile justice system. These changes have expanded greatly the range of problems addressed by social scientists and influenced many liberal criminologists to be more critical of the social system and to question many of the established practices employed to deal with juvenile delinquency and delinquents. On the social policy level it led to a reevaluation of many of the existing programs (Kessebaum 1974).

In the last few years some liberal criminologists suggest that juveniles should be left alone wherever possible (Schur 1973); or if intervention deems to be necessary they should be dealt with in their community, except in the most dangerous cases (President's Commission 1967; Ward 1972).[1] According to this approach, since the various programs aimed at curbing juvenile delinquency or correcting delinquents do not seem to work, the best strategy is simply not to invoke them, especially since sometimes they can even make things worse (Empey 1980). The most often suggested policies by this trend are deinstitutionalization, diversion, and due process.

The liberal trend, which became the mainstream approach in dealing with the problems of juvenile delinquency in Western industrialized societies, has come under fire from two opposing points of view—the radical and the conservative approaches.

Radical Criminology

Radical criminologists claim that the real causes of crime and juvenile delinquency are rooted deeply in the existing social system.[2] In capitalist society, the means of production are owned by a small minority, the ruling class, which exploits a large segment of the population who work for them. This system also develops an exteme egoism which weakens the fiber of society and erodes the feeling of solidarity (Bonger 1969:40-47). The capitalist system "produces deviance" also by creating surplus population "which must be neutralized or controlled if production relations and conditions for increased accumulation are to remain unimpaired" (Spitzer 1975:643). A large part of this population is comprised of youth.[3] Thus, large-scale juvenile delinquency is inherent in the capitalist social order.

Radical criminologists are extremely critical of the liberal mainstream criminologists. One of their major claims is that mainstream criminologists do not try to change the social conditions leading to lawbreaking. Many radicals view liberal social scientists as co-opted by the establishment. These professionals are seen as serving the ruling class by doing research to facilitate government policies and providing advice to implement them. They also provide respectability for the official policies, including definition of crime and its control. This is seen as the "prostitution of science." Mainstream social scientists do their work under the liberal myth of "value-free" science (Gouldner 1963). The liberal position is summed up by Gouldner (1970:59) succinctly: "Accept the system, work within it, but also try to maintain some distance from it."[4]

The liberal stand is considered by the radicals to be a conservative one, because it supports the status quo. These criminologists, by refraining from taking any firm stance, serve the ruling class (Schwendinger and Schwendinger 1975).

According to this critique social scientists tend to provide only a "social engineering" model of change at the best.

> Courses of action are suggested by the policy scientists in terms of available technical information and according to the needs of the existing arrangements of the society. In other words, policy science rationalizes capitalist society. The practice that is offered, by and for the professional elite, is that of technical control. [Quinney 1977:161]

Some others label policies supported by social scientists to better social conditions in capitalist society "correctionalism," a counterproductive effort since it strengthens the existing oppressive system rather than effecting real change (Taylor, Walton, and Young 1975). In this respect, all social scientists involved in one way or other in the formulation of social policies can be viewed as conservatives supporting the status quo.

In a similar vein, Krisberg (1975:18) states:

> Piecemeal reform efforts, when applied to social issues such as crime, racism, poverty, or mental illness, support the myth that progress and improvement can occur without major restructuring of the social order . . . The standards of practicality are always taken from those who rule and who wish to preserve their status quo.

In terms of action programs the approach of radical criminology is to negate any efforts aimed at correcting individual behavior problems[5] and to concentrate on policies which would bring to a total change of the capitalist socio-economic system. "Only with the collapse of capitalist society and the creation of a new society, based on socialist principles, will there be a solution to the crime problem" (Quinney 1973:16).

Therefore, the actual course of action suggested by radical criminologists is the involvement in political activism. That is the Marxist concept of "praxis" a revolutionary action necessary for the transformation of society through the growing class awareness of the proletariat (Giddens 1971:60).

As one of the outcomes of the inherent contradictions of capitalist society many working-class people possess a false consciousness since they are led not to understand their true interest (Israel 1971:94). This explains at least partially that lower-class law violators tend to victimize other lower-class people.

On the public policy level of handling juvenile delinquency, radical criminologists tend to advocate increased "local control, decentralization, community control, a new populism, and citizen power" (Miller 1974:23). This is in line with the claim that in a truly socialist society formal law will be replaced with custom, and the communities will handle social control (Quinney 1977:191-192).

Conservative Approach

The conservative approach suggests the return to the retributive principle of justice (Van den Haag 1975; Wilks and Martinson 1976; Wilson 1975). According to this approach, determinate sentencing should prevail based upon the seriousness of the offense and prior delinquent behavior, social and psychological factors would not be considered as important. The main aim of this approach is incapacitation rather than rehabilitation (Empey 1979).

Historically, Doig (1975:141-142) traces the origins of the conservative approach to the nineteenth century atmosphere which led to the development of the juvenile justice system. At that time according to him, this approach emphasized the "control and resocialization" aspects of juvenile justice rather than the "helping" aspect. The major motives of this approach were:

1. An interest (on the part of police and other community officials) in removing idle youths from the street, where they might cause trouble or commit crimes.
2. A desire (especially among upper-class leaders) for ways to remove the child from the home (particularly immigrant homes), in order to educate and socialize the young to accept "American" values.
3. A demand (by businessmen) that young people be taught the discipline and minimal skills necessary to permit the expanding factory system to absorb them and operate efficiently.
4. A need (on the part of some women in the "child-saving" movement) to find acceptable social and professional roles in an industrializing urbanizing society.
5. A concern that young people be given the tools and education needed to earn a living within the existing economic and social structure.

Doig points out that the evolution of juvenile justice system was affected by both the reformers whose main concern was "helping the young" and by those whose main purpose was to "control and resocialize" the youth. With time a third important factor came into the picture, namely, the natural inclination of organizations and agencies to increase, maintain, and perpetuate their power and influence. This later factor has been given added significance by recent findings and claims that rehabilitation does not work and we do not know how to change people. Senator Edward Kennedy, the incoming chairman of the Senate Judiciary Committee, in November 1978 made the statement at the annual conference of the International Association of Chiefs of Police: "There has been a notorious lack of rehabilitation and an equally notorious increase in arbitrariness and injustice," and later, "We know now that the ability of such courts to rehabilitate the violent juvenile or predict future criminal behavior must be viewed with increasing suspicion." (Los Angeles Times 1978:27). This idea clearly) supports the conservative claim for incapacitation.

The conservative demand not to handle juveniles too leniently and not to let them out only with a "slap on their wrist," coupled with some liberal demands for due process in the juvenile court, led to changes in legal proceedings which resemble more and more regular criminal procedures and got away from the old protective and rehabilitative policies.

Miller (1974:21) enumerated several of the "crusading issues" of the conservative trend: (1) concern over excessive leniency toward lawbreakers; (2) a strong claim that there is too much concern for the welfare and the rights of offenders over those of their victims, the general public, and law enforcement officers; (3) a conviction that there is a constant "erosion of discipline and of respect for constituted authority"; (4) a deep concern with the actual cost of crime borne by law-abiding citizens; (5) a pessimistic view that there is an excessive and growing permissiveness in all spheres of life in modern societies including the attitudes and behavior toward the law.

The underlying assumptions behind this set of "crusading issues" are the following:

1. The individual is directly responsible for his own behavior.
2. A central requirement of a healthy and well-functioning society is a strong moral order which is explicit, well defined, and widely adhered to.
3. Of paramount importance is the major arenas of one's customary activity—particularly those locations where the conduct of family life occurs.
4. Adherence to the legitimate directives of constituted authority is a primary means for achieving the goals of morality, correct individual behavior, security, and other valued life conditions.
5. A major device for ordering human relations in a large and heterogeneous society is that of maintaining distinctions among major

categories of persons on the basis of differences in age, sex, and so on, with differences in religion, national background, race, and social position of particular importance. [Miller 1974:22]

Critical Issues in the Various Policy Orientations

The major objective of the radical orientation, as mentioned, is the abolition of the capitalist social system and the building of a socialist society. Therefore, more or less detailed and immediate social policies concerning juvenile delinquency are seldom suggested. There is an "emphasis on decentralization, community control of police, reduced use of imprisonment, repeal of victimless crime legislation, stengthened civil liberties, reduction in administrative discretion" (Greenberg 1978).

The radical aims and attempts do not seem to be much different from some of the liberal suggestions. To a degree they can be even viewed as "correctionalism" since their implementation might rather strengthen than weaken the prevailing social structure. There is also a wide-scale neglect of the fact that in those societies that so far have espoused the socialist ideology and are basically totalitarian in nature, there are still serious problems of juvenile delinquency, and their social control policies are not necessarily more humane than in capitalist societies, in fact often times they are more punishment oriented (Shichor 1978). While among radical social scientists there is "a despair over the present" in regard to bettering the capitalist system, they strongly believe "in the far reaching perfectibility of social institutions (and human beings)" (Hollander 1973:151). However, those who believe that revolution will change all evil are in a way "as optimistic as 'liberal' theorists who conclude that the system can and will endure if it is only reformed" (Killian 1971:281).

The liberal orientation toward reducing and controlling juvenile delinquency have suggested measures that are directed toward individual offenders rather than implementation of serious changes in the prevailing social arrangements. It was also mentioned that in the last two decades many of the liberal criminologists advocated community treatment, diversion, decriminalization of certain offenses, deinstitutionalization of delinquents, and simply nonintervention. These policies also were questioned lately, since the amount and extent of delinquency has not declined, and some evaluation studies indicated little or no serious positive results of these programs. Some researchers, for instance, found that certain diversion programs, instead of reducing the number of juveniles who are getting processed by the social control system, handled juveniles who would have been sent home but now were placed into formal programs (see, for example, Berg and Shichor 1979). This phenomenon was coined the "widening of the net" by some professionals.

Some legal scholars claim that often these programs, instead of helping youngsters in trouble, violate their civil rights (Nejelski 1976). Similarly, other liberal policies were also criticized.

Attempts to decriminalize certain offenses and to deinstitutionalize some of the adult and juvenile offenders were seen by conservatives as indications of "coddling" of criminals and delinquents. Radicals, on the other hand, regard these attempts as fulfilling only social control functions. They point out that these attempts might have been the result of the overcrowding of facilities and budgetary reasons more than liberal ideologies (Young 1975; Scull 1977). Residential treatment centers also have not been entirely successful in their treatment efforts, although at least their cost was greatly reduced (Empey and Lubeck 1971; Lerman 1973).

Schur (1973:127) summarized some of these results in the following:

> it is not merely the absence of favorable results that has unmasked the euphemisms in this area. A recognition of the probability of distinctly harmful results also has been growing . . . Thus, while many delinquency policies and programs are motivated by the well-intended conviction that they are in the "best interests" of the children involved, their objective effects show the contrary . . . there is now widespread recognition that the legal processing of juveniles, whatever it is called and however it is described, is in fact significantly primitive and potentially stigmatizing.

Thus, the basic question seems to remain what measures can be suggested, if any, to prevent or reduce juvenile delinquency, assuming that a revolution changing the current capitalist social system will not occur.

Some Middle-of-the-Road Suggestions

There are certain policy approaches to delinquency prevention which, although not advocating the full-scale change of the prevailing social system, claim that basic changes are necessary if a meaningful reduction in juvenile delinquency is to be effected.

Empey, following a similar line to the one suggested by Burns and Stern (1967), claims that the primary goal of a social policy aimed at delinquency prevention and reduction should be "to develop a legitimate identity among young people and a belief in the importance of conforming to social rules" (Empey 1978:591). In this approach the basic assumption is that "it is the denial of access to the type of institutional experiences that are the sources of conformity in adult life that lies at the root of much adolescent alienation and rebellion" (Polk and Kobrin 1972:4).

This approach negates the claims of the labeling theorists whereby the offender gets involved in lawbreaking because of the adverse effects of negative societal reaction to deviance from norms and the subsequent stigmatization of these people.[6]

Three major issues are involved in establishing a more responsible role for juveniles in American society. First, an effort should be made to develop a stake in conformity for the juveniles (Toby 1957). This means "a sense of competence, a sense of usefulness, a sense of belonging, and a sense that they have the power to affect their own destinies through conventional means" (Polk and Kobrin 1972:5). Second, a legitimate identity and a stake in conformity can be achieved through the provision of "socially acceptable, responsible and personally gratifying roles. Such roles have the effect of creating a firm attachment to the aims, values, and norms of basic institutions and of reducing the probability of criminal involvement" (Empey 1978:592). And finally:

> Since social roles are a function of institutional design and process, any strategy of delinquency prevention must address the present state of institutional instability and change. Means must be sought by which roles for children are more clearly defined by which they are reinforced by significant others, and by which they expand the range of opportunities and responsibilities open to young people. [Empey 1978:592]

These principles show a similarity to the concept of "social bond" comprised of "attachment," "commitment," "involvement," and "belief." Hirschi (1969) suggests that the breaking of these components to a serious degree leads to delinquent behavior; conversely, their reinforcement can prevent delinquent involvement.

Thus, this approach claims that "the invention of the adolescent" (Musgrove 1965), that is, the exclusion of juveniles from serious social roles and the attribution of a marginal status to them between childhood and adulthood, leads to delinquent behavior. Greenberg (1977), writing in the Marxist tradition, suggests similarly that juvenile delinquency is related to the fact that juveniles are excluded from entry into the labor force.

While this thesis seems to deal with a major problem, the basic questions remain: (1) What are the possibilities for the wide-scale increase of the juveniles' stake in conformity? (2) What are the best policies to do so?

Empey (1978:593-598) suggests concentration on programs of child care, schooling, linking school and work, and job creation. These seem to be among the traditional areas of concern and activities and so far did not result in any serious breakthrough.

Similarly, Krisberg and Austin (1978) suggest a possible avenue to the prevention of juvenile delinquency which although it does not imply a complete societal change would lead to certain middle-range changes. They recommend the community-controlled approach to delinquency since that "emphasizes placing power and resources at the disposal of those people closest to the needs and problems of youth" (Krisberg and Austin 1978:573). This approach is considered to be a part of a general effort to im- prove the quality of life for all people in the community, since "separation of delinquency prevention from attention to human needs creates a false distinction" (Krisberg and Austin 1978:574). This approach, again, would focus on the same components on which many other prevention programs do: employment programs, educational programs involving community members, and so forth.

These authors claim that there are two broad strategies of delinquency prevention: (1) assumes that delinquency is committed mainly by lower- class juveniles and therefore in terms of social policy, the major thrust should be the improvement of their life conditions and increasing their op- portunities for achievement in the context of the existing social structure; (2) assumes that delinquency is an outcome of the prevailing capitalist value system, and the social system has to be reformed in order to prevent or reduce delinquent involvement.[7]

In general terms the first approach seems to reflect mainstream liberal criminological thinking, while the second one could be seen as representing radical perspectives.[8]

The authors suggest that policymakers adopt a critical perspective and identify the inherent contradictions of capitalist society which carry in them the conditions conducive for delinquent behavior. They characterize the core of this perspective as "to encourage people to become aware of their society, to evaluate its fairness and humanity, and to seek more liberating social arrangements" (Krisberg and Austin 1978:577). This statement is hardly different from the liberal stance on the ideological level. Krisberg and Austin admit that the suggested critical perspective does not offer answers per se, except in an indirect way. The problem is that when we deal with the issue of social policy this may not be enough.

Conclusion

The review of social policies in the field of juvenile delinquency indicates the problems involved in suggested viable policies and ways to implement them. As seen, social policy suggestions offered by social scientists are strongly connected with their political persuasions. Whereas mainstream liberal social scientists try to devise and implement programs taking current social arrangements as more or less given, many of the radical criminologists claim that the efforts should be directed toward changing the capitalist social system which breeds the sources of juvenile delinquency. At the same time, conservative criminologists demand that policymakers discontinue liberal prevention and treatment programs claiming that they do not alleviate the delinquency situation, and that they are "coddling" young criminals and leaving the public largely unprotected. Delinquents "are the products of the leniency of the law—of the privilege granted them—as much as of anything else" (Van den Haag 1975:249). Their major suggestion is to attempt to change the situation by aiming at incapacitating the dangerous offenders. The logical outcome of these approaches is that mainly the liberal cirminologists are those who are suggesting elaborated measures directed to the immediate situation. Their approach is claimed to be a pragmatic one. Radzinowicz (1966) openly endorses the pragmatic position as realistic, yet pragmatism is often attacked particularly by the radicals (see, for example, Cohen 1974), since it is a compromise with a current situation and does not work for change.

The most viable course of action in my opinion seems to be the middle-range one, which means trying to alleviate the problem of delinquency in Western industrial societies while making certain structural changes (for example, changing the status of juveniles and increasing the function of the community in dealing with delinquents) without radically changing the social system, on the one hand, or without locking up for a long period of time increasingly large numbers of juveniles, on the other. The reason for this suggestion is that many of the social changes occurring in societies which espoused radical perspectives (USSR, Cuba, China) so far did not lead to the abolition of formal repressive social control, but often increased it and made it even more arbitrary (Shichor 1978). On the other hand, conservative perspectives on crime control may lead also to more repression and arbitrariness under the slogans of "law and order" and "protection of society."

In this connection Schur's words seem to be worth remembering:

> a totally problemless society doesn't exist. Societies, virtually by definition, exhibit behavioral norms and violation of these norms . . . it is by the violation and the social reactions to them that members of the society maintain an adequate sense of what the norms are. [1973:7-8]

So it seems to be that what is true in many other fields is true also regarding delinquency policies as well, namely, we have to thrive for a social situation in which delinquency is completely prevented with the clear knowledge that this situation is beyond reach, and at the same time hoping that we can substantially reduce its extent. Even this qualified goal can only be achieved if social policies will address themselves to wider issues which would lead to changes in the prevailing social arrangements, even if not to complete social revolution.

Notes

1. Dinitz and Conrad (1980) in their extensive research reported in this book found that the really dangerous cases constitute only about 2 percent of the juveniles.

2. This argument is similar to that of Durkheim (1958:65) who states, "bound up with the fundamental conditions of all social life, and by that very fact it is useful, because these conditions, of which it is a part, are themselves indispensable to the normal evolution of morality and law."

3. Youth unemployment is much higher than the national average particularly among minorities in large urban areas.

4. Shichor (1978) points out that the question of co-optation might be a delicate one for some of the radical criminologists. The fact that their works are published widely or that some of them are involved in contract research with government agencies might be an indication of their successful socialization into the capitalist system. In addition they may be seen as serving the establishment by speaking for political dissidents and helping to let some of the frustration out and being used as evidence of the "openness" of the system.

5. It is interesting to note that in societies which embraced the Marxist ideology like the Soviet Union, Cuba, and China—social control efforts are often centered on individual correction (sending political dissidents to psychiatric hospitals and so forth).

6. Labeling theory was lately criticized on theoretical grounds; for example, Wellford (1975) and also several empirical studies failed to confirm some of the major claims of this approach regarding juvenile delinquents (Foster and Dinitz 1972; Giordano 1975).

7. This argument is similar to the radical criticism, (Platt 1969).

8. Krisberg and Austin (1978) do not make a reference to the conservative way of thought which was mentioned earlier in the chapter.

References

Becker, Howard S. (1963). *The Outsiders*. Glencoe: Ill. Free Press.

Berg, Dennis, and Shichor, David (1979). "Methodological and theoretical issues in juvenile diversion." In Delos H. Kelly (ed.), *Deviant Behavior*. New York: St. Martin's Press.

Bonger, Willem (1969). *Criminality and Economic Conditions*. Abridged ed. Bloomington: Indiana University Press.

Burns, Virginia M., and Stern, Leonard W. (1967). "The Prevention of juvenile delinquency." In *Task Force Report: Juvenile Delinquency and Youth Crime*. Washington, D.C.: U.S. Government Printing Office.

Caplan, N., Morrison, A., and Stambaugh, R.J. (1975). *The Use of Social Science Knowledge in Policy Decisions at the National Level.* Ann Arbor: University of Michigan, Institute for Social Research.

Cohen, Stanley (1974). "Criminology and the Sociology of Deviance in Britain." In Paul Rock and Mary McIntosh (eds.), *Deviance and Social Control.* London: Tavistock.

Davis, Howard R., and Salasin, Susan E. (1978). "Strengthening the Contribution of Social R&D to Policy Making." In Lawrence E. Lynn, Jr., (ed.), *Knowledge and Policy: The Uncertain Connection.* Washington, D.C.: National Academy of Sciences.

Dinitz, Simon, and Conrad, Joseph P. (1980). "The Dangerous Two Percent." In David Shichor and Delos H. Kelly (eds.), *Critical Issues in Juvenile Delinquency.* Lexington, Mass.: Lexington Books, D.C. Heath.

Doig, Jameson W. (1975). " 'For the Salvation of Children': The Search for Juvenile Justice in the United States." In John A. Gardiner and Michael A. Mulkey (eds.), *Crime and Criminal Justice.* Lexington, Mass.: Lexington Books, D.C. Heath.

Dror, Yehezkel (1971). *Public Policymaking Reexamined.* Scranton: Chandler.

Durkheim, Emile (1958). *The Rules of Sociological Method.* 8th ed. Glencoe: Free Press.

Empey, LaMar T. (1978). *American Delinquency: Its Meaning and Construction.* Homewood, Ill.: Dorsey.

_____ (1980). "Revolution and counterrevolution: current trends in juvenile justice." In David Shichor and Delos H. Kelly, *Critical Issues in Juvenile Delinquency.* Lexington, Mass.: Lexington Books, D.C. Heath.

Erickson, Kai T. (1962). "Notes on the sociology of deviance." *Social Problems* 6:307-314.

Foster, Jack, and Dinitz, Simon (1972). "Perceptions of Stigma Following Public Intervention for Delinquent Behavior." *Social Problems* 30 (Fall):202-209.

Freeman, Howard E., and Sherwood, Clarence C. (1970). *Social Research and Social Policy.* Englewood Cliffs, N.J.: Prentice-Hall.

Gibbons, Don C., and Garabedian, Peter (1974). "Conservative, liberal and radical criminology: some trends and observations." In Charles E. Reasons, *The Criminologist: Crime and the Criminal.* Pacific Palisades: Goodyear.

Giddens, Anthony (1971). *Capitalism and Modern Social Theory: An Analysis of the Writings of Marx, Durkheim and Max Weber.* London: Cambridge University Press.

Giordano, Peggy C. (1976). "The sense of injustice? An analysis of juveniles' reactions to the justice system." *Criminology* 14 (1):93-112.

Glaser, Daniel (1972). *Adult Crime and Social Policy*. Englewood Cliffs, N.J.: Prentice-Hall.

Goffman, Erving (1963). *Stigma*. Englewood Cliffs, N.J.: Prentice-Hall.

Gouldner, Alvin W. (1962). "Anti minotaur: the myth of value-free sociology." *Social Problems* (2).

———— (1970). *The Coming Crisis of Western Sociology*. New York: Basic Books.

Greenberg, F. David (1977). "Delinquency and the age structure of society," *Contemporary Crises* 1 (2):189-223.

———— (1978). Personal communication.

Hirschi, Travis (1969). *Causes of Delinquency*. Berkeley and Los Angeles: University of California Press.

Hollander, Paul (1973). "Sociology, selective determinism, and the rise of expectations." *American Sociologist* 8 (November):147-153.

Israel, Joachim (1971). *Alienation: From Marx to Modern Sociology*. Boston: Allyn and Bacon.

Kessebaum, Gene (1974). *Delinquency and Social Policy*. Englewood Cliffs, N.J.: Prentice-Hall.

Kennedy, Edward M. (1978). Speech at the Annual Conference of the International Association of Chiefs of Police, New York. Quoted in *Los Angeles Times* November 17, 1978, sec. II. 7.

Killian, Lewis M. (1971). "Optimism and pessimism in sociological analysis." *The American Sociologist* 6 (4):281-286.

Krisberg, Barry (1975). *Crime and Privilege: Toward a New Criminology*. Englewood Cliffs, N.J.: Prentice-Hall.

Krisberg, Barry, and Austin, James (1978). *The Children of Ishmael: Critical Perspectives on Juvenile Justice*. Palo Alto: Mayfield.

Lerman, Paul (1975). *Community Treatment and Social Control*. Chicago: University of Chicago Press.

Lemert, Edwin M. (1951). *Social Pathology*. New York: McGraw-Hill.

Lincoln, Suzanne **Bugas** (1976). "Juvenile Referral and Recidivism." In Robert M. Carter and Malcolm W. Klein (eds.), *Back on the Street*. Englewood Cliffs, N.J.: Prentice-Hall.

Littrell, W. Boyd, and Sjoberg, Gideon (eds.), (1976). *Current Issues in Social Policy*. Beverly Hills: Sage.

Miller, Walter B. (1974). "Ideology and criminal justice policy: some current issues." In Charles E. Reasons (ed.), *The Criminologist: Crime and the Criminal*. Pacific Palisades: Goodyear.

Musgrove, F. (1965). *Youth and the Social Order*. Bloomington: Indiana University Press.

Nejelski, Paul (1976). "Diversion: unleashing the hound of heaven?" In Margaret K. Rosenheim (ed.), *Pursuing Justice for the Child*. Chicago: University of Chicago Press.

Pelz, Donald C. (1978). "Some expanded perspectives on use of social science in public policy." In J. Milton Yinger and Stephen J. Cutler (eds.), *Major Social Issues*. New York: Free Press.

Platt, Anthony M. (1969). *The Childsavers: The Invention of Delinquency*. Chicago: University of Chicago Press.

Polk, Kenneth and Kobrin, Solomon (1972). *Delinquency Prevention through Youth Development*. Washington, D.C.: U.S. Government Printing Office.

Quinney, Richard (1977). *Class, State, and Crime*. New York: David McKay.

Radzinowicz, Leon (1966). *Ideology and Crime*. New York: Columbia University Press.

Rendleman, Douglas R. (1974). "Parens patriae: from chancery to the juvenile court." In Frederic L. Faust and Paul J. Brantingham (eds.), *Juvenile Justice Philosophy*, pp. 72-119. St. Paul: West Publishing Co.

Schlossman, Steven L. (1977). *Love and the American Delinquent*. Chicago: University of Chicago Press.

Schur, Edwin M. (1969). *Our Criminal Society: The Social and Legal Sources of Crime*. Englewood Cliffs, N.J.: Prentice-Hall.

_____ (1973). *Radical Non-Intervention*. Englewood Cliffs, N.J.: Prentice-Hall.

Schwendinger, Herman, and Schwendinger, Julia (1977). "Social class and the definition of crime." *Crime and Justice* 6 (Spring-Summer):4-13.

Scull, Andrew T. (1977). *Decarceration: Community Treatment and the Deviant—a Radical View*. Englewood Cliffs, N.J.: Prentice-Hall.

Shichor, David (1978). The new criminology: some critical issues. Paper presented at the Annual Meeting of the Society for the Study of Social Problems, San Francisco.

Spitzer, Steven (1975). "Toward a Marxian theory of deviance." *Social Problems* 22 (June):638-651.

Taylor, Ian, Walton, Paul, and Young, Jock (1973). *The New Criminology*. London: Routledge and Kegan Paul.

_____ (1975). *Critical Criminology*. London: Routledge and Kegan Paul.

Toby, Jackson (1957). "Social disorganization and a stake in conformity." *Journal of Criminal Law, Criminology and Police Science* 48 (May-June):12-17.

Van den Haag, Ernest (1975). *Punishing Criminals*. New York: Basic Books.

Ward, David A. (1972). "Evaluative research for corrections." In Lloyd E. Ohlin, *Prisoners in America*. Englewood Cliffs, N.J.: Prentice-Hall.

Weiss, Carol H. (ed.) (1977). *Using Social Research in Public Policy Making*. Lexington, Mass.: Lexington Books, D.C. Heath.

Wellford, Charles (1975). "Labelling theory and criminology: an assessment." *Social Problems* 2 (February):332-345.

Wilks, Judith, and Martinson, Robert (1976). "Is the treatment of criminal offenders really necessary?" *Federal Probation*, 40 (March):3-8.

Wilson, James Q. (1975). *Thinking about Crime*. New York: Basic Books.

———. (1978). "Social science and public policy." In Lawrence E. Lynn, Jr. (ed.), *Knowledge and Policy: The Uncertain Connection*. Washington, D.C.: National Academy of Sciences.

Young, Jock (1975). "Working-class criminology." In Ian Taylor, Paul Walton, and Jock Young (eds.), *Critical Criminology*. London: Routledge and Kegan Paul.

Index

About the Contributors

Christine Alder received the B.A. in philosophy from LaTrobe University, Victoria, Australia. She is currently a research assistant with the Marion County Youth Study and a graduate student in sociology at the University of Oregon. Her dissertation research is on female delinquency, and she has also worked with research projects on rape. Ms. Alder's major areas of interest are criminology and delinquency and the sociology of women. She has coauthored papers on the parole system and on juvenile delinquency.

Gordon Bazemore is a doctoral student in sociology at the University of Oregon. He is currently education coordinator at the Institute of Policy Analysis in Eugene, where he is participating in a Law Enforcement Assistance Administration-funded evaluation of juvenile-justice restitution programs. Mr. Bazemore's research experience includes the Marion County Youth Study and other criminal-justice evaluation projects. His teaching and research interests include delinquency and criminology, youth studies, and intervention research, and he has coauthored papers on education, rural delinquency, and the parole system.

John P. Conrad is senior project director at the American Justice Institute. Prior to this appointment, he was senior fellow at the Center on Crime and Justice of the Academy for Contemporary Problems and codirector of the Academy's Dangerous Offender Project. He received the B.A. in political science from the University of California and the M.A. in social service administration from the University of Chicago. Before joining the Academy, Mr. Conrad was chief of the Center of Crime Prevention and Rehabilitation of the Law Enforcement Assistance Administration and a consultant to the National Advisory Commission on Criminal Justice Standards and Goals.

Simon Dinitz, is professor of sociology at Ohio State University and senior fellow at the Center on Crime and Justice of the Academy for Contemporary Problems. He is also codirector of the Academy's Dangerous Offender Project. He received the bachelor's degree from Vanderbilt University and the master's and doctoral degrees from the University of Wisconsin. Dr. Dinitz is coauthor of thirteen books and numerous articles and reports, and in 1967 he received the American Psychiatric Association's Hofheimer Prize for *Schizophrenics in the Community: An Experiment in the Prevent of Hospitalization.*

Delbert S. Elliott is director of the Behavioral Research Institute and professor of sociology at the University of Colorado. He received the B.A. from Pomona College and the M.A. and Ph.D. from the University of Washington. Dr. Elliott is the senior author of *Delinquency and Dropout*, and coauthor of *The Social Psychology of Runaways*. He has contributed numerous articles to professional journals and books and is a member of the American Sociological Association, the Society for the Study of Social Problems, and the American Society of Criminology.

LaMar T. Empey, professor of sociology at the University of Southern California, was formerly chairman of the Sociology Department and director of the Youth Studies Center there. He has been a member of several research review panels; has served as a consultant to major national commissions on crime and violence; and has published widely in the fields of delinquency and crime. Among his published works are *American Delinquency: Its Meaning and Construction; The Future of Childhood and Juvenile Justice; Juvenile Justice: The Progressive Legacy and Current Reforms; The Silverlake Experiment* (with Steven Lubeck); *The Provo Experiment* (with Maynard Erickson); and *Explaining Delinquency* (with Steven Lubeck).

Maynard L. Erickson is professor of sociology at the University of Arizona. He is a graduate of Washington State University, and his areas of specialization include juvenile delinquency, criminology, social control, evaluation research, juvenile justice policy, methodology, and statistics. He has published widely in juvenile delinquency, deterrence research, criminology, and juvenile justice policy.

Theodore N. Ferdinand received the Ph.D. from the University of Michigan in 1961 and has taught since then at Northeastern University and Northern Illinois University. He has been professor of sociology at the latter institution since 1970. His principal publications include *Juvenile Delinquency* (with Ruth Shonle Cavan); *Juvenile Delinquency: Little Brother Grows Up;* and *Typologies of Delinquency*. He has also published articles in several journals, including *American Journal of Sociology, Social Problems, American Sociologist, American Science,* and *British Journal of Criminology.*

Rose Giallombardo is a graduate of the University of Connecticut and received the M.A. and Ph.D. from Northwestern University. A sociologist with an international reputation for her work on women's prisons, Dr. Giallombardo is the author of the classic studies *Society of Women: A Study of a Women's Prison* and *The Social World of Imprisoned Girls*. Her other books include *Juvenile Delinquency* and *Contemporary Social Issues*. She was formerly a research associate in sociology and associate professor at the University of Chicago and has taught at Northwestern University Dental School and New York University. At present she is engaged in research on the problems of adjudicated delinquent girls within the institutional setting.

Don C. Gibbons is professor of sociology and urban studies at Portland State University. He received the B.A., M.A., and Ph.D. in sociology from the University of Washington. He formerly taught at San Francisco State University and the University of British Columbia. Professor Gibbons is the author of *Delinquent Behavior; Society, Crime, and Criminal Careers; Changing the Lawbreaker*; and *The Criminological Enterprise*. He is also coauthor of *Becoming Delinquent, The Study of Deviance*, and *Criminal Justice Planning* and has published widely in sociology and criminal justice journals.

Jack P. Gibbs received the Ph.D. in sociology from the University of Oregon in 1957. He is presently professor of sociology at Vanderbilt University. He has been affiliated with the University of Texas, Washington State University, and the University of Arizona. Dr. Gibb's teaching and research interests include deviance, social control, the sociology of law, human ecology, and the methodology of theory construction. His most recent book was *Crime, Punishment, and Deterrence*.

Frank R. Hellum, formerly project director of the National Evaluation of Deinstitutionalization of Status Offender Programs at the Social Science Research Institute, University of Southern California, is now a senior research associate with the National Council on Crime and Delinquency in San Francisco. His background includes both teaching and research in the sociology of crime and delinquency.

John W.C. Johnstone is professor of sociology at the University of Illinois. Since receiving the Ph.D. at the University of Chicago in 1961, he has worked as senior study director at the National Opinion Research Center and as survey coordinator for the Canadian Royal Commission on Bilingualism and Biculturalism. He is author of *Volunteers for Learning* (1965), *Young People's Images of Canadian Society* (1969), *The New People* (1976), and numerous articles on mass communications, youth, and juvenile delinquency. The research on which the chapter in this volume is based was conducted when he was a visiting scholar at the Institute for Juvenile Research, Chicago. Currently, he is conducting research on the effects of social environments on adolescent development.

Malcolm W. Klein received the B.A. from Reed College and the M.A. and Ph.D. in social psychology from Boston University. After several years of teaching and research in medical sociology at Boston University, he moved to Los Angeles in 1960 to conduct educational research at the John Tracy Clinic. From 1962 to 1968 he directed applied and basic research projects dealing with juvenile gangs. From 1969 on, Dr. Klein's research has centered around comprehensive criminal justice planning. Since 1968, he has been a member of the sociology faculty at the University of Southern California. Dr. Klein is the author or editor of *Juvenile Gangs in Context* (1967), *Street Gangs and Street Workers* (1971), *Back on the Streets: The Diversion of Juvenile Offenders* (with Robert M. Carter, 1975), and *The Juvenile Justice System* (1976).

Solomon Kobrin is a senior research associate at the Social Science Research Institute of the University of Southern California and emeritus professor of sociology. Prior to coming to the University of Southern California, Professor Kobrin was for many years a staff member of the Institute for Juvenile Research in Chicago, actively engaged in research on juvenile delinquency. Most recently he was coprincipal investigator (with Malcolm W. Klein) of an evaluation study of a Law Enforcement Assistance Administration-sponsored national program to foster the deinstitutionalization of status offenders.

Sarnoff A. Mednick received the Ph.D. in psychology from Northwestern University in 1954 and the M.D. from the University of Copenhagen in 1976. He is currently research professor and professor of psychology at the Social Science Research Institute of the University of Southern California. His research has emphasized the primary prevention of human mental and social illnesses. As director of the Psykologisk Institut in Copenhagen, he has initiated longitudinal studies of children at risk for antisocial behavior and mental illness. He is also a consultant in mental health for the European Regional Office of the World Health Organization.

Walter B. Miller is a research fellow at the Center for Criminal Justice of the Harvard Law School and director of the National Survey of Collective Youth Crime. Trained as an anthropologist, he has devoted most of his professional career to problems of crime, delinquency, and low-income populations. He has taught at Harvard, Brandeis, Boston University, and other colleges, and was the first Robert A. Pinkerton Visiting Professor of Criminal Justice at the State University of New York at Albany. He has served as consultant or advisor to several agencies and programs, including the President's Committee on Juvenile Delinquency and Youth Crime, the Manpower Advisory Committee of the U.S. Department of Labor, and the

National Conference on Poverty of the American Academy of Arts and Sciences. One of his numerous publications, "Lower Class Subculture and Gang Delinquency," was designated by a comprehensive literature survey as the single most frequently cited article in the criminological literature and was rated as the second best article published in this field.

John W. Peterson is a Ph.D. candidate in the Sociology Department at the University of Southern California. As a participant in the evaluation study of the Law Enforcement Assistance Administration National Status Offender Program, he has been responsible for conducting major portions of the data analysis task.

Kenneth Polk is a professor of sociology at the University of Oregon. In addition, he has taught at Boston College, La Trobe University (Melbourne), University of Mexico, and Bradford College (England). He has participated in many research investigations in crime and delinquency, including the Marion County Youth Study.

James F. Short, Jr., is professor of sociology and director of the Social Research Center at Washington State University, where he was also dean of the graduate school from 1964 to 1968. He currently serves as secretary of the American Sociological Association. He has also served as the at-large member of the Council of the American Sociological Association and is editor of the *American Sociological Review.* He received the M.A. and Ph.D. from the University of Chicago. Dr. Short has authored or edited ten books, including *Suicide and Homicide* (with A.F. Henry, 1954); *Group Process and Gang Delinquency* (with F.L. Strodtbeck, 1965); and *Delinquency, Crime, and Society* (1974). His current research activities include evaluation of the impact of the Seattle and Denver Income Maintenance Experiments on Crime and Juvenile Delinquency; organizational crime; and the political implications of juvenile delinquency.

Katherine S. Teilmann received the Ph.D. in sociology in 1976 from the University of Southern California, where she is a research assistant professor at the Social Science Research Institute. Her research and publications have centered on the juvenile justice system's handling of juvenile offenders ranging from status offenders to felons. Dr. Teilmann is currently principal investigator of a project to assess the impact of a new juvenile justice law that was implemented in California in 1977.

About the Editors

David Shichor received the B.A. from Hebrew University, the M.A. from California State University, Los Angeles, and the Ph.D. from the University of Southern California. Currently, he is associate professor of sociology at California State College, San Bernardino. He has published articles and chapters in books in the fields of criminology, juvenile delinquency, corrections, and victimology.

Delos H. Kelly is an associate professor of sociology at California State University, Los Angeles. He is also the founder and editor of *California Sociologist*, a professional journal for sociologists and social workers. Professor Kelly received the Ph.D. from the University of Oregon in 1970. Upon completion of his doctorate, he served as a research associate for that University's Marion County Youth Study and then taught at SUNY College at Geneseo for five years. Dr. Kelly has published more than thirty articles in various professional journals. His most recent publications include *Deviant Behavior: Readings in the Sociology of Deviance*; *Delinquent Behavior: Interactional and Motivational Aspects*; *How the School Manufactures "Misfits"*; and *The Organizational Creation of Social Deviants: An Examination of the Educational Processing of Students*. Another book, *Criminal Behavior: Readings in Criminology*, is forthcoming.